iological Weapons:
imiting the Threat

BCSIA Studies in International Security
Published by The MIT Press

Sean M. Lynn-Jones and Steven E. Miller, series editors
Karen Motley, executive editor
Belfer Center for Science and International Affairs (BCSIA)
John F. Kennedy School of Government, Harvard University

Allison, Graham T., Owen R. Coté, Jr., Richard A. Falkenrath, and Steven E. Miller, *Avoiding Nuclear Anarchy: Containing the Threat of Loose Russian Nuclear Weapons and Fissile Material* (1996)

Allison, Graham T., and Kalypso Nicolaïdis, eds., *The Greek Paradox: Promise vs. Performance* (1996)

Arbatov, Alexei, Abram Chayes, Antonia Handler Chayes, and Lara Olson, eds., *Managing Conflict in the Former Soviet Union: Russian and American Perspectives* (1997)

Blackwill, Robert D., and Michael Stürmer, eds., *Allies Divided: Transatlantic Policies for the Greater Middle East* (1997)

Brown, Michael E., ed., *The International Dimensions of Internal Conflict* (1996)

Brown, Michael E., and Šumit Ganguly, eds., *Government Policies and Ethnic Relations in Asia and the Pacific* (1997)

Elman, Miriam Fendius, ed., *Paths to Peace: Is Democracy the Answer?* (1997)

Falkenrath, Richard A., *Shaping Europe's Military Order: The Origins and Consequences of the CFE Treaty* (1994)

Falkenrath, Richard A., Robert D. Newman, and Bradley A. Thayer, *America's Achilles' Heel: Nuclear, Biological, and Chemical Terrorism and Covert Attack* (1998)

Feldman, Shai, *Nuclear Weapons and Arms Control in the Middle East* (1996)

Forsberg, Randall, ed., *The Arms Production Dilemma: Contraction and Restraint in the World Combat Aircraft Industry* (1994)

Hagerty, Devin T., *The Consequences of Nuclear Proliferation: Lessons from South Asia* (1998)

Heymann, Philip B., *Terrorism and America: A Commonsense Strategy for a Democratic Society* (1998)

Kokoshin, Andrei A., *Soviet Strategic Thought, 1917–91* (1998)

Lederberg, Joshua, *Biological Weapons: Limiting the Threat* (1999)

Shields, John M., and William C. Potter, eds., *Dismantling the Cold War: U.S. and NIS Perspectives on the Nunn-Lugar Cooperative Threat Reduction Program* (1997)

Biological Weapons: Limiting the Threat

Editor
Joshua Lederberg

BCSIA Studies in International Security

The MIT Press
Cambridge, Massachusetts
London, England

Second printing, 1999

© 1999 by the Belfer Center for Science and International Affairs
John F. Kennedy School of Government
Harvard University
Cambridge, Massachusetts 02138
(617) 495-1400

Library of Congress Cataloging-in-Publication Data

Biological weapons : limiting the threat / edited by Joshua S. Lederberg.
p.   cm.—(BCSIA studies in international security)
Includes bibliographical references and index.
ISBN 0-262-12216-2 (hardcover : alk. paper).—ISBN 0-262-62128-2 (pbk.: alk. paper)
1. Biological weapons. 2. Biological warfare. 3. Biological arms control.
4. United States—Military policy. I. Lederberg, Joshua. II. Series.
UG447.8.B566   1999
327.1'745—dc21   98-52950
                                                                                                                              CIP

Cover photo: Transmission electron micrograph showing Venezuelan equine encephalitis (VEE) virions budding from cytoplasmic membrane of Vero cells. Photo by Tom Geisbert. This photo was previously published in the *Journal of the American Medical Association,* vol. 278, no. 5 (August 6, 1997), p. 439.

10 9 8 7 6 5 4 3 2
Printed in the United States of America

Contents

Acknowledgments

The current volume originated in a *JAMA* (*Journal of the American Medical Association*) theme issue on biological warfare, which appeared in August 1997 and was edited by Annette Flanagin and myself. Although directed preeminently to the medical community, it embraced a broad range of historical and policy-directed analysis as well, a perspective that warrants wider access than a serial item in a medical library. We are most grateful to the publishers and editors of *JAMA*, not to mention the contributing authors, for their cooperation in assembling and updating this volume. Thanks are also due to a number of authors who responded to our original invitation to participate, but who for one (usually incidental) reason or another are not represented in the final volume. That Secretary of Defense William Cohen took time from his extraordinarily busy schedule to submit his foreword deserves our special gratitude. I would also like to express my thanks to Professor Graham Allison for encouraging this project under the auspices of the Belfer Center for Science and International Affairs (BCSIA) at Harvard University's John F. Kennedy School of Government. BCSIA Series Editor Sean Lynn-Jones and Executive Editor Karen Motley have been remarkably patient and accommodating. During the time that she was Associate Director of the Harvard Sussex Program on Chemical and Biological Warfare Armament and Arms Limitation at BCSIA, Marie Isabelle Chevrier generously provided invaluable help and advice on several chapters in this volume. Scott Schless, Deputy Director of Counterproliferation Policy in the Office of the Secretary of Defense, was of particular assistance. To all others who participated in the creation of this volume, I also offer my thanks.

—*Joshua Lederberg*

Foreword

William S. Cohen

This volume assembled by Dr. Joshua Lederberg addresses one of the most important challenges to U.S. and global security—the threat posed by biological weapons. In virtually every corner of the globe, the United States and its allies face a growing threat from the proliferation of nuclear, biological, and chemical (NBC) weapons and their delivery systems. In addition to indigenous weapons development programs, NBC weapons, delivery systems, and technology may be "for sale" to the highest bidder.

In Northeast Asia, North Korea's extensive NBC weapons program threatens Japan, South Korea, and U.S. forces and interests in the region. In North Africa and the Middle East, rogue states—Libya, Syria, Iran, and Iraq—are poised to use all means at their disposal to threaten U.S. and allied interests in the region and beyond. Many of these countries have ties to terrorists, religious zealots, or organized crime groups who are also seeking to use these weapons.

The explosive growth in global trade and wide availability of key biological-related technologies and know-how have made it easier for even less developed states to acquire or develop biological weapons capabilities. Past constraints on the actions of regional powers imposed by the bipolar order have fallen away. Our experience in Desert Storm demonstrated that proliferation will occur despite our strongest preventive efforts. Rogue nations can succeed in developing extensive biological capabilities without our knowledge; and U.S. and coalition forces face significant limitations in current military capabilities for dealing with a biological weapons–armed adversary. With advanced technology and an interdependent world with porous borders, the ability to unleash mass sickness, death, and destruction today has reached a far greater order of magnitude.

Our American military superiority presents a paradox. Because our potential adversaries know they cannot win in a conventional war with the United States, they are more likely to try unconventional or asymmetrical methods such as biological or chemical weapons. In addition to being used on the battlefield, biological weapons also may be used as tools of terrorism against allies and even the American people. A lone terrorist could hold a city's population hostage with the threat of a biological weapon and unravel the very fabric of our culture—our sense of being safe within our borders.

With scientific advances over the last fifty years, the technology to produce these weapons has become more commonplace. It is not outside the realm of possibility to produce a lethal biological agent with only a minimum of technological know-how. As the new millennium approaches, the United States faces a heightened prospect that regional aggressors, third-rate armies, terrorist cells, and even religious cults will wield disproportionate power by using—or threatening to use—biological weapons against our troops in the field or our citizens at home.

The most glaring example of terrorist use of NBC weapons to date was the 1995 release of the nerve agent sarin in the Tokyo subway system by the Aum Shinrikyo cult. This attack crossed what had previously been a psychological boundary. The Aum Shinrikyo incident illustrates the potential threat posed by terrorist groups when they have access to materials to assemble chemical and biological weapons, have members knowledgeable about such technologies, and possess sufficient financial resources to procure the necessary materials.

Virtually all the equipment, technology, and materials needed for biological agent production are dual use—both as a help to mankind and as a potential scourge. Very little differentiates a facility producing vaccines or antibiotics from one that produces lethal pathogens or toxins. Therefore, any facility being used for the good of mankind could also be used to produce these lethal agents, and could be disguised as a legitimate business. For example, known biological agents such as anthrax, botulinum toxin, plague, and tularemia are used for legitimate clinical research to find ways to treat the resulting infections or produce vaccines against them. This type of work could easily be channeled into weapon research efforts without any real indications that covert biological warfare work is under way.

DoD Response

Since December 1993 the Department of Defense (DoD) has had a Counterproliferation Initiative (CPI) to address the threats posed by NBC weapons. The CPI supports our national counterproliferation policy, first by contributing to U.S. government efforts to prevent the acquisition of NBC weapons or to reverse it when it has occurred. If prevention fails, we must have the capabilities needed to deter the use of NBC weapons and to defend against their use. And finally, we want to ensure that our forces are equipped and trained to prevail in future conflicts wherever we may face NBC threats—recognizing that our nuclear deterrent will always be a factor but should not be the only response option.

Prevention

The primary objective of U.S. policy is to prevent countries from acquiring NBC weapons and their delivery systems or to roll back these programs when proliferation has occurred. To accomplish this objective, we utilize diplomacy, and the Defense Department contributes to U.S. prevention efforts by supporting the State Department in negotiating and implementing various arms control regimes, such as the Chemical Weapons Convention and the Biological Weapons Convention.

However, history has shown that we cannot expect to prevent proliferation in all cases and at all times. The goal of the Defense Department's Counterproliferation Initiative is to deter and prevent the use of NBC weapons, in part by ensuring that U.S. and coalition forces are trained, equipped, and prepared to fight and win in a chemical- or biological-contaminated environment.

Deterrence

In deterring the threat, we depend both on a strong conventional military force and a smaller—but still powerful—nuclear force. We have, in fact, a broad spectrum of conventional and nuclear force options available with which to deliver a devastating and overwhelming response to NBC use against us. There is another aspect of deterrence that is often overlooked, however. If our forces are equipped, trained, and prepared to deal with the effects of chemical or biological weapons use against them, that defensive capability takes on a deterrent effect of its own. Such preparation and readiness can devalue the effects of chemical and biological weapons, and thus decrease the likelihood of their use against U.S. and coalition forces. Thus, effective counterforce capabilities and active and passive defenses take away the tactical advantages that an adversary might otherwise perceive it could gain by employing such weapons.

Detection and Defense

To ensure that U.S. forces can cope with chemical and biological weapons threats, I directed an increase in funding for counterproliferation programs by approximately $1 billion over the next five years. These resources will go directly toward improving our forces' capability to detect and defeat biological and chemical weapons, and protect themselves on the battlefield should these weapons be used.

Early detection and warning is the key to avoiding chemical/biological contamination. As a result, DoD is concentrating biological and chemical defense research, development, and acquisition efforts on providing its warfighters real-time capabilities to detect, identify, locate, and warn against all such threats below threshold effects levels. Current emphasis is on multi-agent sensors for biological agent detection and stand-off/remote early warning detection of both chemical and biological agents.

Notably, the Defense Department is introducing improved, lighter weight, individual protective equipment that will enhance our forces' ability to continue operations in a contaminated environment. During Desert Storm, we did not have any sophisticated biological weapons detection equipment. Today the Army has fielded the Biological Integrated Detection System (BIDS) which can detect the presence of and identify biological agents in less than 45 minutes. The Navy has deployed the Interim Biological Agent Detector (IBAD) on its ships. In addition, the Army is developing a new generation BIDS which will detect and identify more threat agents in less time and intends to field the improved version starting in 1999. We are also developing a Joint Biological Point Detection System that will be fielded by all of the services during the 2001–2003 time frame.

Critical elements of medical biological defense include the ability to rapidly identify an agent and to provide prophylactic and/or therapeutic protection from the agent. Often the most effective countermeasure is pre-deployment active immunization. The Defense Department is establishing policies, responsibilities, and procedures for stockpiling biological agent vaccines and determining when and which personnel should be immunized. We have also identified which biological agents constitute critical threats, and are determining the amount of vaccine that should be stocked for each. We awarded a prime systems contract in November 1997 to pursue advanced development of biological defense products, to obtain Food and Drug Administration (FDA) licenses, and to produce vaccines using our U.S. pharmaceutical industrial base. We currently have R&D efforts under way to develop vaccines against all validated threat agents.

These efforts, driven by the FDA licensing requirements, will extend well into the next decade.

Anthrax Vaccination Policy

U.S. forces face a clear danger from possible exposure to biological weapons around the world. Anthrax is one of the most lethal biological agents we could face. Once symptoms occur—within 24–72 hours after exposure—death is almost a certainty. Therefore, we have a moral obligation to protect our forces by providing them immunity against this lethal BW agent. In December 1997, I made the decision to vaccinate all U.S. forces to protect against anthrax. Initial vaccinations will be given to service members assigned to, deploying to, or alerted for assignment to the Persian Gulf and Korea. The plan to vaccinate the total force, both active and reserve, will take seven to eight years to complete.

DoD Role in Responding to Domestic NBC Threats

We have a rapidly growing program to deal with the possibility of terrorist or foreign state use of biological and chemical weapons within the United States. The Defense Department is prepared to play a significant role in supporting other government agencies, such as the FBI for crisis management and the Federal Emergency Management Agency (FEMA) for consequence management.

Significant DoD assets, including active forces, National Guard, and other reserve components could be integrated into a coordinated federal response at the onset of a domestic NBC incident. The Defense Department is also implementing the Domestic Terrorism Preparedness Program to train and exercise local first-responders, including firemen, law enforcement officials, and medical personnel. Two parallel efforts are ongoing: first, training responders in the nation's largest 120 cities (we have completed training in the first 31 cities as of September 1998 and anticipate the program will be completed by the end of 2001); and second, developing training modules and establishing mechanisms to provide federal expertise to every community in the nation, using mass media formats, such as the Internet, video, and CD-ROM.

Conclusion

The proliferation of weapons of mass destruction and the capability to produce them are serious threats to U.S. security. There is no single, simple counter to these weapons; no "silver bullet" exists. Instead, an integrated counterproliferation strategy is required, with each component building upon the strength of the others. The strategy must include efforts to prevent countries from acquiring NBC weapons, roll back these programs where proliferation has occurred, deter the use of NBC weapons, and ultimately detect and defend against such use should it occur.

In the past several years, the DoD has devoted much attention and shifted significant resources to dealing with threats posed by chemical and biological weapons. We have made major progress in a short time. The essays in this book present many perspectives and insights that will stimulate further thinking about how to respond to this threat.

Part I
Introducing and Framing the Issues

Chapter 1

Introduction

Joshua Lederberg

The transcendence of biological warfare (BW)—over medicine and public health, private criminal acts, terrorism, interstate warfare, and international law directed at the elimination of BW—makes this one of the most intricate topics of discourse, poses very difficult security problems, and opens some novel challenges in the ethical domain. (See Table 1.1.) That same transcendence confounds efforts to organize governmental and intergovernmental measures of control: health authorities will need to negotiate with the military, with law enforcement, and with environmental managers. And all will have to cope with how to enhance security without imposing intolerable stresses on personal liberties and on freedom of travel and of commerce.

Prior to the August 1997 BW theme issue from which this volume developed, the topic of BW had last been covered systematically by the *Journal of the American Medical Association* (*JAMA*) as part of a discourse on weapons of mass destruction in August 1989.[1] We recall that 1989 marked the bicentennials of the U.S. presidency and of the French Revolution. By year's end, perhaps not by pure coincidence, 1989 also marked

This chapter was adapted from Joshua Lederberg, "Infectious Disease and Biological Weapons: Prophylaxis and Mitigation," *Journal of the American Medical Association* (*JAMA*), Vol. 278, No. 5 (August 6, 1997), pp. 435–436. © 1997 American Medical Association.

1. Jane M. Orient, "Chemical and Biological Warfare: Should Defenses Be Researched and Deployed?" *Journal of the American Medical Association* (*JAMA*), Vol. 262, No. 5 (August 4, 1989), pp. 644–648; Victor W. Sidel, "Weapons of Mass Destruction: The Greatest Threat to Public Health," *JAMA*, Vol. 262, No. 5 (August 4, 1989), pp. 680–682; and David L. Huxsoll, Cheryl D. Parrott, and William C. Patrick III, "Medicine in Defense against Biological Warfare," *JAMA*, Vol. 262, No. 5 (August 4, 1989), pp. 677–679.

Table 1.1. Germs as Arms: Basic Issues.

BW (biological warfare) versus CW (chemical warfare): living germs versus chemicals; germs might self-amplify and spread; germs are biologically unstable and could mutate to higher virulence

Underlying science is unalterably dual-use: licit defensive exploration targeted against natural disease

Production is dual-use up to point of weaponization

Facilities moderate scale; few external signatures easily concealed or masked by licit programs

Weapons are potent, but unfamiliar and unreliable in military context

Tactical defense is easy: physical barriers (masks, suits)

Latent period up to 36 hours: disease may be treatable; hence need to focus on civil health preparedness

Hardly understood until now, these are "strategic" weapons. At the same time, they are accessible to small powers or groups and seen as answer to a superpower confident about the "revolution in military affairs"

Capabilities can scarcely be denied; remedial and intelligence focus on intentions needed

---

the collapse of the Soviet empire, and with that the end of the Cold War. The Biological Weapons Convention (BWC) had been in place since 1972; nevertheless, compliance with that convention on the part of great states, notably Russia, was the centerpiece anxiety in 1989. U.S. national policy was likewise concentrated on the defense of troops in tactical combat settings.

Medical interests, notably symbolized by the World Health Organization's pleas, had played a significant role in the diplomatic priority given to the BWC, and then to concern for its enforcement.[2] Since 1989, the Persian Gulf War, the escalation of terrorism, and a recrudescence of many infections have added new dimensions to concerns for the malicious incitement of disease. Iraq was proven to have developed and militarized a repertoire of BW agents, notably anthrax spores.[3] Terrorists achieved new levels of violence in New York, Oklahoma City, and Tokyo and operated on ever more incomprehensible and unpredictable rationales. Having deployed chemical weapons in Tokyo and dabbled in BW, terrorists would soon be attempting to deploy BW on an increasing scale. It is not difficult to find recipes for home-brew botulinum toxin on the World Wide Web; terrorists justify this with the proposition that every citizen should have the parity of power with government. Meanwhile, the growth of biotechnology has great promise for new modes of diag-

---

2. World Health Organization (WHO), *Health Aspects of Chemical and Biological Weapons* (Geneva: WHO, 1970).

3. See the chapter by Raymond A. Zilinskas in this volume.

nosis and therapy, but if left unchecked, advances in this field will allow for even more troublesome microbiological agents of destruction.

This volume touches on a set of timely concerns that unite national security and public health, concerns that cry out for the well-articulated convergence of the human community worldwide. Various chapters in this book discuss the historical,[4] diplomatic,[5] and legal[6] background; modalities of diagnosis and management;[7] and case studies of small-scale BW attacks that have already been perpetrated, though amateurish in design and ending with limited malefaction.[8]

While BW is widely regarded as the absolute perversion of medical science, the problems of invoking humanitarian regulation of means of warfare are well understood.[9] Resort to warfare is tied to the use of any means necessary for the survival of the state, including organized violence. It is mainly the peacetime behavior of states that can be regulated by international law, and this has evolved toward greater coherence and impact in an interdependent global economy. Even in the thrall of violent combat, states will also be deterred when there is a firm international resolve: Iraq did not, after all, use its massive stockpiles of anthrax in the Gulf War.[10]

The twentieth century has seen the exercise of massive violence on an immense scale, even without major resort to BW. What distinguishes BW is the understanding that its habitual practice would be ruinous to personal security and civil order, perhaps more grievously than any other weapon likely to get into the hands of disgruntled individuals or rogue states. One *sine qua non* for the elimination of BW is its utter delegitimation; in the language of the Geneva Protocol of 1925, it must remain "justly condemned by the general opinion of the civilized world."[11]

As a matter of international law, any debate has already been settled

---

4. See the chapter by George W. Christopher et al. in this volume.

5. See the chapters by Robert P. Kadlec, Allan P. Zelicoff, and Ann M. Vrtis, and Richard Danzig and Pamela B. Berkowsky in this volume.

6. See the chapter by James R. Ferguson in this volume.

7. See the chapters by David R. Franz et al., and Harry C. Holloway et al. in this volume.

8. See the chapters by Thomas J. Török et al., and Shellie A. Kolavic et al. in this volume.

9. Hedley Bull, *The Control of the Arms Race* (New York: Praeger for the Institute for Strategic Studies, 1961); and Joshua Lederberg, "The Control of Chemical and Biological Weapons," *Stanford Journal of International Studies*, Vol. 7 (1972), pp. 22–44.

10. See the chapter by Raymond A. Zilinskas in this volume.

11. Protocol for the Prohibition of the Use in War of Asphyxiating, Poisonous or Other Gases, and of Bacteriological Methods of Warfare (Geneva Protocol), 1925.

by the wide adoption of the 1972 BWC: the abnegation of biological weapons is approaching the status of a norm of international behavior, going beyond a mere contract for mutual compliance. When an international consensus can be achieved and sustained, as happened after Iraq's invasion of Kuwait, severe sanctions can be imposed by the international community. The task is to build that moral consensus and give it sustainability and priority over more transient aspects of perceived national interest, like commercial advantage or access to resources.[12] We are happily less burdened by the choosing of sides in the Cold War and the strange bedfellows engendered by that process. There is much to answer for in the nonchalance exhibited by most of the world when Iraq used chemical weapons in its wars against Iran and on its own Kurd dissidents.[13]

Writing fifty years ago, Vannevar Bush remarked, in puzzling why BW had not been deployed at the height of World War II: "Without a shadow of a doubt there is something in man's make-up that causes him to hesitate when at the point of bringing war to his enemy by poisoning him or his cattle and crops or spreading disease. Even Hitler drew back from this. Whether it is because of some old taboo ingrained into the fiber of the race. . . . The human race shrinks and draws back when the subject is broached. It always has, and it probably always will."[14] Bush could not offer these as reliable reassurances, and he surely played a large role in instituting and maintaining what became the U.S. offensive BW development program. This program started during World War II, and escalated in the Cold War competition with the Soviet Union until 1969, with President Nixon's unilateral abnegation. In due course this was followed by the successful negotiation of the BWC of 1972, and its coming into force internationally in 1975.

Scrupulous adherence to the BWC on the U.S. side, coming to the bar with clean hands, is of course an absolute prerequisite to the moral platform of BW prohibition. There is no more powerful instrument for that credibility than self-inspection. In free societies, that responsibility will largely devolve on well-informed scientific and medical professionals. That community also has deep-seated ties with peers even in some

---

12. Leonard A. Cole, *The Eleventh Plague: The Politics of Biological and Chemical Warfare* (New York: W.H. Freeman, 1996).

13. H. Kadivar and S.C. Adams, "Treatment of Chemical and Biological Warfare Injuries: Insights Derived from the 1984 Iraqi Attack on Majnoon Island," *Military Medicine*, Vol. 156 (1991), pp. 171–177.

14. Vannevar Bush, *Modern Arms and Free Men* (New York: Simon and Schuster, 1949), pp. 142, 146.

authoritarian states, bonds that should be cultivated to develop common ground even against obstacles of parochial interest.

Unlike nuclear weapons, the capability for BW is unlikely to be reliably contained by any degree of legal prohibition and formal verification. The facilities required for producing and dispensing BW agents are modest, easily concealable, and almost indistinguishable from licit production of pharmaceuticals and vaccines. The same holds for the underlying technical knowledge, which is part and parcel of medical research and education. The potential for grave enhancement of virulence and the intractability of pathogens for BW use go hand in hand with the advances of biotechnology for human life enhancement.[15] Verification still plays a role as part of a lawful process of investigation and indictment of malefactors. But the key to consolidation of the law on BW is its rigorous enforcement, and this will require a consensus even among U.S. friends and allies that has yet to be achieved—partly out of the expectation that the United States will always bear the onus as enforcer of last resort. Moral conviction and discreet technical education about the implications of leaving BW unchecked then go hand in hand.

As for the smaller and more marginal states, the United States should anticipate some ambivalence about forgoing weapons that might mitigate the overwhelming military power of a super-state. To enlist their unreserved cooperation in denying the use of BW, the United States should be far more proactive in mobilizing its health technology to stamp out rampant infectious disease globally.[16] Tuberculosis remains the earth's prime killer, and malaria, with hundreds of millions of infected people, the greatest drain on human vitality. It is scandalous that these coexist with a technology that will soon have plotted the entire human genome. Lacking robust technical solutions to the malevolent use of BW, the United States has little to call upon besides this common moral ground to prevent attack.

If despite deterrence, law, and moral suasion, the means of attack cannot be forsworn, the obligation remains to be prepared to blunt them. Physicians and local health services, along with police and firefighter first-responders, are in the front lines to deal with health emergencies. This same apparatus is needed to deal with natural disease outbreaks: recall Legionella, Influenza A-H5N1, and *Escherichia coli* O157:H7 of recent

---

15.   A.P. Pomerantsev, N.A. Staritsin, Y.V. Mockov, and L.I. Marinin, "Expression of Cereolysine Ab Genes in Bacillus Anthracis Vaccine Strain Ensures Protection against Experimental Hemolytic Anthrax Infection," *Vaccine,* Vol. 15 (1997), pp. 1846–1850.

16.   Joshua Lederberg, "Infection Emergent," *JAMA,* Vol. 275, No. 3 (January 17, 1996), pp. 243–245.

vintage. The local responders also need to be trained in exercises entailing support from the Public Health Service and, if need be, military personnel. While BW attacks may be widely dispersed, they are amenable to medical intervention far more than trauma from explosives or chemicals, provided diagnosis is timely and resources can be mobilized. In many cases, there may be little or no advance warning. Vigilance in understanding the fate of victims near the dose-epicenter might provide an alert for the much larger cohorts likely to receive smaller doses and exhibit longer incubation times—a window of opportunity for treatment.

Several chapters in this volume point to recent progress, and a long way still to go, in the coordination of resources among a host of U.S. governmental agencies: federal, state, and local.[17] Recent press reports also speak to a rising tide of attention by responsible officials.[18] In view of the rapid dispersal of people via jet aircraft and the globalization of commerce, including foodstuffs, that coordination needs to be extended to a global venue. This scarcely exists at all at the present time, although the WHO has energetic programs to deal with influenza and HIV, and could be the nucleus of more extensive disease surveillance. With the growing recognition that BW is a strategic weapon, directed most effectively at large urban populations, cooperative public health measures might well reach the agenda of U.S. security alliances like NATO. Military force protection against BW and chemical warfare (CW) is fairly advanced; with the dissemination of vaccines, antidotes, and masks, these weapons are not likely to confer great tactical advantage to the perpetrator. Civil populations, near actual and potential theaters of combat or clandestine attack—and that no longer excludes the U.S. homeland—deserve comparable protection, if only to reduce the temptations for the aggressors and soften the dilemmas and collateral harm of retaliation.

---

17. See the chapters by Holloway et al. and Jonathan B. Tucker in this volume.

18. Judith Miller and William J. Broad, "Clinton Expected to Back Plan to Deter Terrorist Attack," *New York Times*, April 26, 1998, p. 1.

Chapter 2

Why Should We Be Concerned About Biological Warfare?

Richard Danzig and Pamela B. Berkowsky

There is a widespread tendency to think about defense against biological warfare as unnecessary, as someone else's responsibility, or as simply too difficult. Unfortunately, however, the dangers posed by biological weapons did not disappear when the United States began to dismantle unilaterally its own offensive program in 1969. The dangers did not vanish with the signing of the Biological Weapons Convention of 1972, and they did not dissipate with the end of the Cold War or the threat of nuclear retaliation against Iraq during the Persian Gulf conflict. Only by planning and investing in the right training and defensive measures can we diminish the likelihood that biological weapons will be used and reduce the risks, disruption, and casualties in the event that such weapons are used.[1] Fortunately, significant improvements can be made in our defensive posture at relatively modest levels of investment, and both the Department of Defense and the medical community can play substantial roles in this regard.

Biological weapons are unfortunately characterized by low visibility, high potency, substantial accessibility, and relatively easy delivery. The basic facts are well known: a millionth of a gram of anthrax constitutes a

---

This chapter was adapted from Richard Danzig and Pamela B. Berkowsky, "Why Should We Be Concerned About Biological Warfare?" *Journal of the American Medical Association (JAMA)*, Vol. 278, No. 5 (August 6, 1997), pp. 431–432.

This commentary was written when both authors worked for the Office of the Undersecretary of the Navy, U.S. Department of the Navy, Washington, D.C.

---

1. Richard Danzig, "Biological Warfare: A Nation at Risk—A Time to Act," *INSS Strategic Forum 58* (Washington, D.C.: National Defense University, Institute for National Strategic Studies), January 1996.

lethal inhalation dose. A kilogram, depending on meteorological conditions and means of delivery, has the potential to kill hundreds of thousands of people in a metropolitan area. These small quantities make the concealment, transportation, and dissemination of biological agents relatively easy. Many of these agents—bacteria, viruses, and toxins—occur naturally in the environment. Moreover, many are used for wholly legitimate medical purposes, such as the development of antibiotics and vaccines, and much of the technology required to produce and "weaponize" them is available for civilian or military use. Unlike nuclear weapons, missiles or other advanced systems are not required for the delivery of biological weapons. Since aerosolization is the predominant method of dissemination, extraordinarily low-technology methods, including agricultural crop dusters, backpack sprayers, and even purse-size perfume atomizers will suffice. Small groups of people with modest finances and basic training in biology and engineering can develop an effective biological weapons capability. Recipes for making biological weapons are even available on the Internet.

These unique characteristics make both military and civilian society vulnerable to biological weapons. It is true that their delayed effects and vulnerability to weather make these weapons ill-suited to military purposes, such as seizing territory. But biological weapons can effectively impede the mobilization and massing of troops that would be required to sustain our role in a conventional conflict. Most disturbingly, they can be used to threaten civilian populations and create mass panic. Used this way, biological weapons can achieve military goals by undercutting the civilian support necessary for military operations or by holding civilians hostage to prevent military operations.

Why Have Biological Weapons Been Low on Our Agenda?

If biological weapons are so potent and so cheap, if the technology is readily available, and if so many of our adversaries have biological warfare capabilities, then why has this issue been so low on our national security agenda?

There are three principal reasons. First, because defense against a biological attack is both unfamiliar and difficult, there is a natural tendency to put it aside in favor of problems that are more comfortable. This is abetted by a second factor: the belief that because biological weapons have never been used, they therefore never will be. And this is in turn buttressed by a sense that a regime can be deterred from using biological weaponry if we make it clear that this would invite nuclear retaliation.

These modes of thought are dangerously inappropriate. If we address deterrence first, many argue that Saddam Hussein's unwillingness to unleash Iraq's biological arsenal, in the face of not-so-subtle threats of nuclear retaliation, validates the primacy of our deterrent. However, nations are not the only potential users of biological weapons. If one of the most likely scenarios entails their use by non-state actors, small groups, or even individuals, a nuclear deterrent may be ineffective. Of course, terrorists can often be associated with state sponsors, but the quantum of proof we would require before responding to such a perceived linkage with a nuclear attack would be awfully high. Consider, for example, the forensic difficulty in assigning responsibility for the tragic attack against Pan Am Flight 103 that exploded over Lockerbie, Scotland, in 1988. In the event of a biological contingency, it is especially easy to mask the nature and source of an attack and even to obscure whether it is a natural occurrence. In such circumstances, can we credibly rely on a threat of assured nuclear retaliation? Depending on the agent used, if those exposed just got sick but did not die, what would constitute a proportional response?

The assumption that biological weapons will not be used in the future because they have not been used in the past is based on an error of fact. History is replete with examples in which biological weapons have been used, including the following: in the Middle Ages, infected cadavers were catapulted over the walls of European cities and castles under siege; in the French and Indian Wars, the British supplied Indians with smallpox-infected blankets; during World War II, Japanese Unit 731 experimented with biological weapons on prisoners of war in Manchuria, resulting in more than 1,000 deaths.[2]

There are also abundant examples that bring the threat much closer to home. In 1995, two members of a Minnesota militia group were convicted of possession of ricin, which they had produced themselves for use in retaliation against local government officials.[3] In 1996, an Ohio man with connections to an extremist group was able to obtain bubonic plague cultures through the postal service.[4] It has even come to light that Aum Shinrikyo, the Japanese cult organization responsible for the sarin attacks on the Tokyo subway system, was working on anthrax and botulism as

2. See the chapter by George W. Christopher et al. in this volume.

3. Karl Vick, "Plea Bargain Rejected in Bubonic Plague Case," *Washington Post*, April 3, 1996, p. A8; and Tom Morganthau, "A Shadow over the Olympics," *Newsweek*, May 6, 1996, p. 34.

4. Vick, "Plea Bargain Rejected in Bubonic Plague Case."

weapons.[5] The group's biological capability, its production and testing and laboratory infrastructure, and its experimental delivery systems existed for years while escaping detection by Western intelligence.

While it is often said that familiarity breeds contempt, no national security establishment can let unfamiliarity breed neglect. Biology is unfamiliar terrain. As Alan Beyerchen has pointed out, the history of the absorption of technology into the war-fighting capabilities of the Department of Defense suggests a reason for this blind spot.[6] World War I brought chemists and war-fighters together; World War II brought physicists into the fold; and the Cold War represented an era of the primacy of the computing, telecommunications, and electronics communities in the defense arena. What little connection the U.S. government maintained with the biological community dissipated when, in 1969, we forswore any offensive biological and toxin weapon capability. But our forbearance does not imply that of others. The UN inspections of Iraq after the Persian Gulf conflict should be a wake-up call in this regard.[7] Along with the information of a high-level defector who had responsibility for Iraq's unconventional weapons program, these inspections revealed a large-scale biological production and "weaponization" effort that had gone substantially undetected by the West.

What Should We Do About the Threat of Biological Warfare?

The Department of Defense has embarked on a challenging program to enhance its capabilities to defend against biological warfare. The program includes, among other things, the development and fielding of state-of-the-art biodetectors; the creation and designation of selected military units with expertise in medical prophylaxis, hazard mitigation, and decontamination; investments in vaccine and antibiotic research, development, and stockpiling; refinement and acquisition of masks and improvements in air filtration systems to preclude infection via inhalation; improved intelligence collection and analysis; enhanced training; and the development of doctrine regarding how to preempt and, when necessary, respond to a biological attack.

5.   K.B. Olson, "Biological Weapons and the Terror in Japan," *Terrorism*, Vol. 1 (August 1997), p. 1.

6.   Alan Beyerchen, "From Radio to Radar: Interwar Military Adaptation to Technological Change in Germany, the United Kingdom, and the United States," in Williamson Murray and Allan R. Millett, eds., *Military Innovation in the Interwar Period* (Cambridge: Cambridge University Press, 1996), pp. 265–299.

7.   See the chapter by Raymond A. Zilinskas in this volume.

An additional critical element of this program, however, is the need for an enhanced relationship between the military and those agencies charged with protecting the civilian population of the United States. In that regard, biological weapons necessarily alter our strategic thinking about national security and the nature of warfare. Wars may not always be fought on set-piece traditional battlefields, and it is time to throw away the anachronistic notion that the military's only role is to defend the United States against threats on foreign soil.

In the event of a domestic incident of biological weapons use, no matter who the perpetrator is, it is unlikely that the response would be left to local law enforcement and health officials or even to the Federal Bureau of Investigation, the Federal Emergency Management Agency, or the U.S. Public Health Service. The military would undoubtedly be called on because of its resources, capabilities, and expertise. At the same time, if a biological incident were to occur in a military context, the Department of Defense would look to and need the help of such civilian agencies as the Centers for Disease Control and Prevention (CDC).

Although achieving it is one of our greatest challenges, an enhanced cooperation between military and civilian institutions is also likely to pay big dividends. In some respects, the Atlanta Olympics bombing was a good case in point, and the multi-agency partnerships that spanned federal, state, and local jurisdictions will serve as a model for future response.[8] Not only were the Olympics a model of cooperation, but they also marked a milestone for our response capabilities. In the immediate aftermath of the Centennial Park pipe-bomb explosion, bomb fragments were analyzed by Department of Defense assets—set up at a temporary laboratory at the CDC headquarters—to detect the presence of chemical or biological agents; none was found. This marked the first time that a domestic explosive had been routinely screened for those agents.

To facilitate and enhance this civil-military cooperation, Congress recently enacted the Defense Against Weapons of Mass Destruction Act of 1996, which seeks to enhance our domestic preparedness in several fundamental ways, including the following: by strengthening the federal government's ability to prevent and respond to terrorist incidents involving weapons of mass destruction; by enabling the Department of Defense and other federal supports to state and local prevention and response efforts; and by improving the capabilities of state and local emergency responders themselves. More than one hundred cities in the United States

---

8. Jonathan B. Tucker, "National Health and Medical Services Response to Incidents of Chemical and Biological Terrorism," *Journal of the American Medical Association*, Vol. 278, No. 5 (August 6, 1997), pp. 362–368.

have already been designated under the provisions of this legislation; their fire, police, rescue, and hospital emergency department personnel will receive training and equipment in an ambitious program conducted by the Department of Defense that began in the summer of 1997.[9]

From another vantage point, the good news wrapped inside the particular problems posed by biological weapons is that in this arena, public health is the best form of civil defense. Our everyday domestic investments to detect and diagnose disease can and should be strengthened because of our national security trends. Biological weapons are not respectful of traditional boundaries of geography, bureaucracy, or conceptual compartmentalization. In that fact lies our challenge, our opportunity, and our call to action.

---

9. Nicholas Horrock, "The New Terror Fear: Biological Weapons: Detecting an Attack Is Just the First Problem," *U.S. News & World Report*, May 12, 1997, p. 36.

Part II
Background and History

Chapter 3

Biological Warfare: A Historical Perspective

George W. Christopher, Theodore J. Cieslak, Julie A. Pavlin, and Edward M. Eitzen, Jr.

Humans, regrettably, have used available technologies for destructive as well as for beneficial purposes throughout history. Modern attempts to weaponize biological toxins such as botulinum and ricin were anticipated by the use of curare and amphibian-derived toxins as arrow poisons by aboriginal people using neolithic technology. The terms "toxic" and "toxin" are derived from the ancient Greek *toxikon pharmakon* (arrow poison); *toxon* designated either "bow" or "arrow."[1] While the deliberate use of microorganisms and toxins to harm others has been attempted for centuries, the study of the history of biological warfare (BW) is confounded by several factors. These factors include difficulties confirming allegations of biological attack, the lack of reliable microbiologic and epidemiologic data regarding alleged or attempted biological attacks, the use of allegations of biological attack for propaganda, and the secrecy surrounding biological weapons programs. However, a review of historical sources demonstrates that interest in developing biological weapons has persisted throughout history, and is likely to continue into the future.

This chapter was adapted from George W. Christopher et al., "Biological Warfare: A Historical Perspective," *Journal of the American Medical Association (JAMA)*, Vol. 278, No. 5 (August 6, 1997), pp. 412–417.

The opinions expressed in this chapter are those of the authors and do not reflect the positions or policies of the Department of the Air Force, the Department of the Army, the Department of Defense, or the U.S. government. This chapter is dedicated to the late Jay P. Sanford, M.D., in appreciation for his invaluable contributions to the fields of infectious diseases, military medicine, and medical education.

---

1. Philip B. Gove, ed., *Webster's Third New International Dictionary of the English Language, Unabridged* (Springfield, Mass.: Merriam-Webster, 1981), p. 2419.

Early Attempts at Biological Weapons Use

Recognition of the potential impact of infectious diseases on armies resulted in the crude use of fomites—filth, cadavers, animal carcasses, and contagion—as weapons. These have been used to contaminate wells, reservoirs, and other water sources of armies and civilian populations under attack since antiquity, through the Napoleonic era, and into the twentieth century. The use of fomites directly against humans has continued, as evidenced by the smearing of pungi sticks with excrement by the Viet Cong.[2]

One of the earliest recorded attempts of using fomites against a population illustrates the complex epidemiologic issues raised by biological warfare. During the siege of Kaffa (now Feodossia, Ukraine) in 1346, the attacking Tatar force experienced an epidemic of plague. They attempted to convert their misfortune into an opportunity by catapulting the cadavers of their deceased into the city to initiate a plague epidemic. An outbreak of plague was followed by the retreat of defending forces and the conquest of the city. Ships carrying plague-infected refugees (and possibly rats) sailed to Constantinople, Genoa, Venice, and other Mediterranean ports, and are thought to have contributed to the second plague pandemic.[3] However, given the complex ecology and epidemiology of plague, it may be an oversimpification to implicate the biological attack as the sole cause of the plague epidemic in Kaffa. Plague may have been imported into Kaffa by a natural cycle involving sylvatic and urban rodents and their fleas,[4] while the population under siege may have been at increased risk of epidemics due to deterioration of sanitation and hygiene. Since fleas that transmit plague leave cadavers to parasitize living hosts, we would suggest that the corpses catapulted over the walls of Kaffa may not have been carrying competent plague vectors.

Smallpox was used as a biological weapon against Native Americans. During the French and Indian War (1754–67), Sir Jeffrey Amherst, commander of British forces in North America, suggested the deliberate use

2. Stockholm International Peace Research Institute (SIPRI), *The Problem of Chemical and Biological Warfare*, Vol. I, *The Rise of CB Weapons* (New York: Humanities Press, 1971), chap. 2, pp. 214–228.

3. Vincent J. Derbes, "De Mussi and the Great Plague of 1348: A Forgotten Episode of Bacteriological War," *Journal of the American Medical Association (JAMA)*, Vol. 196, No. 1 (April 4, 1966), pp. 59–62.

4. Andrew G. Robertson and Laura J. Robertson, "From Asps to Allegations: Biological Warfare in History," *Military Medicine*, Vol. 160, No. 8 (August 1995), pp. 369–373; and Bjorn P. Berdal and Tov Omland, "Biologiske vapen-konvensjoner og historikk," *Tidsskr Nor Laegeforen*, Vol. 110, No. 6 (June 1990), pp. 736–740.

of smallpox to "reduce" Native American tribes hostile to the British. An outbreak of smallpox at Fort Pitt resulted in the generation of fomites and an opportunity to execute Amherst's plan; on June 24, 1763, Captain Ecuyer, one of Amherst's subordinates, gave blankets and a handkerchief from the smallpox hospital to the Native Americans, and recorded in his journal that he hoped it would "have the desired effect." While this adaptation of the Trojan Horse ruse was followed by epidemic smallpox among Native American tribes in the Ohio River valley, other contacts between colonists and Native Americans may have contributed to these epidemics.[5] Smallpox epidemics among immunologically naive tribes of Native Americans following initial contacts with Europeans had been occurring for over two hundred years.[6] In addition, the transmission of smallpox by fomites was inefficient compared to respiratory droplet transmission.[7] Both of these early attempts at biological warfare illustrate the difficulty of differentiating naturally occurring epidemics from alleged or attempted biological attack. This problem has had continued relevance, as naturally occurring endemic diseases have been ascribed to alleged biological attacks for propaganda purposes.

The Era of Modern Microbiology

The formulation of Robert Koch's postulates and the development of modern microbiology during the nineteenth century afforded the capability to isolate and produce stocks of specific pathogens. Substantial evidence suggests that Germany developed an ambitious biological warfare program during World War I, featuring covert operations in neutral trading partners of the Allies to infect livestock and contaminate animal feed to be exported to Allied forces.[8] *Bacillus anthracis* and *Burkholderia (Pseudomonas) mallei*, the etiologic agents of anthrax and glanders, were to be used to infect Romanian sheep to be exported to Russia. Cultures confiscated from the German Legation in Romania in 1916 were identified as *B. anthracis* and *B. mallei* at the Bucharest Institute of Bacteriology and Pathology. Argentinian dray animals intended for export to Allied forces were infected with *B. anthracis* and *B. mallei*, resulting in the deaths of

---

5. SIPRI, *The Rise of CB Weapons*, p. 215.

6. Frank Fenner, Donald A. Henderson, Isao Arita, Zdnek Jezek, and Ivan D. Ladnyi, *Smallpox and its Eradication* (Geneva: World Health Organization [WHO], 1988), pp. 235–240.

7. Ibid., p. 191.

8. Martin Hugh-Jones, "Wickham Steed and German Biological Warfare Research," *Intelligence and National Security*, Vol. 7, No. 4 (October 1992), pp. 379–402.

over two hundred mules. Operations in the United States included attempts to contaminate animal feed and to infect horses intended for export.[9] *B. mallei* was allegedly used by German saboteurs operating in Mesopotamia to inoculate 4,500 mules, and in France to infect horses of the French cavalry.[10]

In response to the horror of chemical warfare during World War I, international diplomatic efforts were directed toward limiting the proliferation and use of weapons of mass destruction. The first diplomatic attempt at limiting biological warfare was the 1925 Geneva Protocol for the Prohibition of the Use in War of Asphyxiating, Poisonous or Other Gases, and of Bacteriological Methods of Warfare. This treaty prohibited the use of biological weapons. However, the treaty did not proscribe basic research, production, or possession of biological weapons,[11] and many countries ratified the Protocol while stipulating a right to use biological or chemical weapons against states that had not ratified or complied with the protocol.[12] There were no provisions for inspection. States parties to the Geneva Protocol that began basic research programs to develop biological weapons following World War I included Belgium, Canada, France, Great Britain, Italy, the Netherlands, Poland, and the Soviet Unon.[13] The United States did not ratify the Geneva Protocol until 1975.

Japan conducted biological weapons research in occupied Manchuria from 1932 until the end of World War II under the direction of Shiro Ishii (1932–42) and Kitano Misaji (1942–45). Unit 731 at Ping Fan was the center of the Japanese biological weapons development program, and featured 150 buildings, five satellite camps, and a staff of over 3,000 scientists and technicians. Additional units were located at Mukden, Changchun, and Nanking. Prisoners were infected with pathogens including *B. anthracis*, *Neisseria meningiditis*, *Shigella* spp., *Vibrio cholerae*, and *Yersinia pestis*. At least 3,000 prisoners died at Ping Fan.[14]

---

9. Jules Witcover, *Sabotage at Black Tom: Imperial Germany's Secret War in America, 1914–1917* (Chapel Hill, N.C.: Algonquin Books, 1989), pp. 93, 126–127, 136–137, 238.

10. Robertson and Robertson, "From Asps to Allegations," p. 371.

11. R.R. Baxter and Thomas Buergenthal, "Legal Aspects of the Geneva Protocol of 1925," in Carnegie Endowment for International Peace, *The Control of Chemical and Biological Weapons* (New York: Carnegie Endowment for International Peace, 1971), p. 2.

12. Ibid., pp. 18–19.

13. Sheldon H. Harris, *Factories of Death* (New York: Routledge, 1994), p. 157.

14. Sheldon Harris, "Japanese Biological Warfare Research on Humans: A Case Study of Microbiology and Ethics," in Raymond A. Zilinskas, ed., *The Microbiologist and Biological Defense Research: Ethics, Politics, and International Security. Annals of the New York Academy of Science*, Vol. 666 (December 31, 1992), pp. 21–52.

Twelve large-scale field trials of biological weapons were conducted against Chinese cities.[15] Attacks featured contaminating water supplies and food items with pure cultures of *B. anthracis, V. cholerae, Shigella* spp., *Salmonella* spp., and *Y. pestis.* Cultures were also tossed directly into homes and sprayed from aircraft.[16] Plague was allegedly developed as a biological weapon by allowing laboratory-bred fleas to feed on plague-infected rats. These potentially infected fleas were then harvested and released from aircraft over Chinese cities. As many as fifteen million fleas were released per attack to initiate epidemics of plague.[17] Dr. P.Z. King, Director General of the Chinese National Health Administration, attributed epidemic plague to these attacks; however, rigorous epidemiologic and bacteriologic data are not available.[18] In addition, the Japanese had not adequately prepared, trained, or equipped their own troops for the hazards of biological weapons; an attack on Changteh in 1941 reportedly led to approximately 10,000 biological casualties and 1,700 deaths among Japanese troops, with most cases due to cholera.[19] Large-scale field trials were terminated in 1942, although basic research continued until the end of the war.[20]

Adolf Hitler reportedly issued orders prohibiting biological weapons development in Germany. However, restrictions were lifted following military reverses in 1943, and a biological weapons research facility was established at Posen. Research was conducted on aircraft spray-tank dissemination of suspensions of *Y. pestis, V. cholerae, R. prowazeki,* and yellow fever virus, and on the possible use of insects against crops and animals. However, results lagged far behind those of other countries, and a German offensive biological weapons threat never materialized. The only reported German tactical use of biological warfare was the pollution of a large reservoir in northwestern Bohemia with sewage in May 1945, and the dropping of Colorado beetles on potato crops in southern England.[21] Ironically, the combination of a vaccine and a serologic test was used as a biological defense against the Nazis. The German army avoided areas

---

15. Ibid., p. 33.

16. Ibid., pp. 32–35; and Peter Williams and David Wallace, *Unit 731: Japan's Secret Biological Warfare in World War II* (New York: Free Press, 1989), chap. 6.

17. Ibid., p. 65.

18. P.Z. King, "Bacterial Warfare," *Chinese Medical Journal,* Vol. 61, No. 3 (July–September 1943), pp. 259–263.

19. Williams and Wallace, *Unit 731,* pp. 69–70.

20. Harris, "Japanese Biological Warfare Research on Humans," pp. 34–35.

21. SIPRI, *The Rise of CB Weapons,* pp. 117, 223.

with epidemic typhus by using the Weil-Felix reaction for diagnosis. Consequently, physicians used formalin-killed *Proteus* OX-19 as a vaccine to induce biologic false-positive tests for typhus in an area of occupied Poland. Residents were protected from deportation to concentration camps.[22]

The Allies developed biological weapons for potential retaliatory use in response to German biological attack. Bomb experiments of weaponized spores of *B. anthracis* were conducted on Gruinard Island near the coast of Scotland, and resulted in heavy contamination. Viable anthrax spores persisted until the island was decontaminated with formaldehyde and sea water during 1986.[23]

The U.S. BW Program

An offensive biological program began in 1942 under the direction of a civilian agency, the War Reserve Service (WRS). The program included a research and development facility at Camp Detrick, Maryland, testing sites in Mississippi and Utah, and a production facility in Terre Haute, Indiana. Experiments were conducted using pathogens including *B. anthracis* and *Brucella suis*. However, the production facility lacked adequate engineering safety measures; tests of the fermentation and storage processes using nonpathogenic *Bacillus subtilis* var. *globigii* as a *B. anthracis* simulant disclosed contamination of the plant and environs. These findings precluded large-scale production of biological weapons during World War II, although 5,000 bombs filled with *B. anthracis* spores were produced at a pilot plant at Camp Detrick.[24] After the war, the production facility was leased and converted to commercial pharmaceutical production. Basic research and development activities were continued at Camp Detrick. Ishii, Kitano, and other Japanese scientists in U.S. custody who had participated in the Unit 731 program were granted immunity from war crimes prosecution on the condition that they would disclose information obtained during their program. Secret debriefings were conducted during the post-war era.[25]

---

22.   E.S. Lazowski and S. Matulewicz, "Serendipitous Discovery of Artificial Weil-Felix Reaction Used in 'Private Immunological War'," *American Society for Microbiology News*, Vol. 43, No. 6 (June 1977), pp. 300–302.

23.   R.J. Manchee and W.D.P. Stewart, "The Decontamination of Gruinard Island," *Chemistry in Britain*, Vol. 24, No. 7 (July 1988), pp. 690–691.

24.   Robert Harris and Jeremy Paxman, *A Higher Form of Killing* (New York: Hill and Wang, 1982), p. 103.

25.   Williams and Wallace, *Unit 731*, chap. 15.

The program was expanded during the Korean War (1950–53). A new production facility incorporating adequate biosafety measures was constructed at Pine Bluff, Arkansas. Technical advances allowed large-scale fermentation, concentration, storage, and weaponization of microorganisms; production was begun in 1954. In addition, a program to develop countermeasures including vaccines, antisera, and therapeutic agents to protect troops from possible biological attack was begun in 1953.

Animal studies were performed at Fort Detrick, at remote desert sites, and on barges in the Pacific Ocean. Human experimentation using military and civilian volunteers was initiated in 1955. Biological munitions were detonated inside a one-million-liter hollow, metallic spherical aerosolization chamber at Fort Detrick known as the "eight ball." Volunteers inside the chamber were exposed to aerosols of *Francisella tularensis*, and *Coxiella burnetii*. These and other challenge studies were done to determine vulnerability to aerosolized pathogens, and the efficacy of vaccines, prophylaxes, and therapies under development. Additional studies were done using simulants. *Aspergillus fumigatus*, *B. subtilis* var. *globigii*, and *Serratia marcescens* were selected for use as simulants; these organisms were thought to be nonpathogenic, and were used to study production and storage techniques, as well as aerosolization methods, the behavior of aerosols over large geographic areas, and the effects of solar irradiation and climatic conditions on the viability of aerosolized organisms. Cities were surreptitiously used as laboratories to test aerosolization and dispersal methods; simulants were released during covert experiments in New York City, San Francisco, and other sites in 1949 to 1968.[26]

Concerns regarding potential public health hazards of simulant studies were raised after an outbreak of nosocomial *S. marcescens* (formerly *Chromobacterium prodigiosum*) urinary tract infections at Stanford University Hospital between September 1950 and February 1951,[27] following covert experiments using *S. marcescens* as a simulant in San Francisco.[28]

---

26. U.S. Congress, Senate Committee on Human Resources, Subcommittee on Health and Scientific Research, *Biological Testing Involving Human Subjects by the Department of Defense, 1977: Hearings before the Subcommittee on Health and Science Research of the United States Senate, March 8 and May 23, 1977*, 95th Cong., 1st sess., 1977 (Washington, D.C.: U.S. Government Printing Office [U.S. GPO], 1977), pp. 1–21; and U.S. Department of the Army, *U.S. Army Activity in the U.S. Biological Warfare Programs*, Vol. II, *Annexes* (Washington, D.C.: U.S. Department of the Army Publication DTIC B193427 L, 1977), appendix IV to annex E.

27. Richard P. Wheat, Anne Zuckerman, and Lowell A. Rantz, "Infection due to Chromobacteria: Report of Eleven Cases," *Archives of Internal Medicine*, Vol. 88, No. 4 (October 1951), pp. 461–466.

28. U.S. Department of the Army, *U.S. Army Activity in the U.S. Biological Warfare Programs*, Vol. II, appendix II to annex E.

The outbreak involved eleven cases, resulting in one transient bacteremia and a fatal case of endocarditis. All patients had undergone urinary tract catheterization, and five had undergone cystoscopy for urologic indications. Exposure to multiple antibiotics was cited as a contributing factor.[29] No similar outbreaks were reported by other San Francisco area hospitals. The outbreak is thought to represent an early example of nosocomial epidemics due to opportunists of low virulence related to antibiotic use, new medical devices, and surgical procedures.[30] In view of the temporal relationship of the outbreak with the simulant studies, the army convened an investigative panel in 1952, including members from the Communicable Disease Center, the National Institutes of Health, the City of New York Health Department, and Ohio State University. The panel did not comment directly on the possible association of the nosocomial outbreak and the simulant studies. The panel recommended continued use of *S. marcescens* in view of its low virulence, but added that a search for better simulants to replace *S. marcescens* should be pursued.[31] However, simulant studies utilizing *S. marcescens* continued until 1968. Public interest in these covert experiments was aroused in 1976 following press releases reporting them, and implying that endocarditis death was a direct result of the simulant testing. It was further implied that sudden increases in the incidence of pneumonia in Calhoun County, Alabama, and Key West, Florida, were related to simulant studies at those locales. As a result of the ensuing public outcry, Senate hearings were held in 1977, and the army was severely criticized for the continued use of *S. marcescens* following awareness of the Stanford outbreak.[32] Nonetheless, several facts cast doubt on an etiological relationship between military use of *S. marcescens* and outbreaks of human disease. The Centers for Disease Control and Prevention (CDC) reported that in one hundred outbreaks of *S. marcescens* infection, none were caused by the 8UK (biotype A6, serotype 08:H3, phage type 678) strain used by the army. Numerous reports during the 1970s postulated a link between the army experiments and cases of *S. marcescens* endocarditis, septic arthritis, and osteomyelitis in California heroin addicts; where strains were available for testing, they were like-

29. Wheat, Zuckerman, and Rantz, *Archives of Internal Medicine*, p. 466.

30. Victor L. Yu, "*Serratia marcescens*. Historical Perspective and Clinical Review," *New England Journal of Medicine*, Vol. 300, No. 16 (April 19, 1979), p. 889.

31. U.S. Department of the Army, *U.S. Army Activity in the U.S. Biological Warfare Programs*, Vol. II, annex F.

32. Stephen Weitzman, in U.S. Congress, Senate Committee on Human Resources, Subcommittee on Health and Scientific Research, *Biological Testing Involving Human Subjects by the Department of Defense, 1977*, pp. 264–266.

wise shown to differ antigenically from the army test strain.[33] A review of the role of *S. marcesens* in the army biological program has been published.[34]

There were 456 cases of occupational infections acquired at Fort Detrick during the offensive biological program, at a rate of less than ten infections per million hours worked. The rate of occupational infection was well within the contemporary standards of the National Safety Council, and below the rates reported from other laboratories. There were three fatalities due to occupationally acquired infection: two cases of anthrax in 1951 and 1958, and a case of viral encephalitis in 1964. The mortality rate was lower than those of other contemporary surveys of laboratory-acquired infections. There were forty-eight occupational infections and no fatalities reported from production and testing sites. The safety program included the development and use of new vaccines as well as engineering safety measures.[35]

By the late 1960s, the United States military had developed a biological arsenal that included numerous bacterial pathogens, toxins, and fungal plant pathogens that could be directed against crops to induce crop failure and famine.[36] (See Table 3.1.) In addition, weapons for covert use utilizing cobra venom, saxitoxin and other toxins were developed for use by the CIA; all records regarding their development and use were destroyed during 1972.[37]

Korean War and Cold War Allegations

The Soviet Union, China, and North Korea accused the United States of using biological warfare against North Korea and China during the Korean War. These accusations were supported by a series of investigations conducted by the International Scientific Commission, a group of scientists, and other organizations. Although these investigations were described as impartial, they were carefully controlled by the North Korean

---

33. J.J. Farmer III, Betty R. Davis, P.A.D. Grimont, and F. Grimont, "Source of American *Serratia*," *Lancet*, Vol. 2 (August 27, 1977), p. 459.

34. Yu, "*Serratia marcescens*," pp. 887–893.

35. U.S. Department of the Army, *U.S. Army Activity in the U.S. Biological Warfare Programs*, Vol. II, annex G.

36. Ibid., annex D.

37. U.S. Congress, Senate Select Committee to Study Governmental Operations with Respect to Intelligence Activities on U.S. Intelligence Agencies and Activities, *Unauthorized Storage of Toxic Agents: Hearings before the U.S. Senate Intelligence Committee, September 16–18, 1975*, 94th Cong., 1st sess., 1975, CIS 76-S961-1.

Table 3.1. Biological Agents Stockpiled by U.S. Military (Destroyed 1971–73).

Lethal Agents[a]
  Bacillus anthracis
  Botulinum toxin
  Francisella tularensis
Incapacitating Agents[a]
  Brucella suis
  Coxiella burnetii
  Staphylococcal enterotoxin B
  Venezuelan equine encephalitis virus
Anticrop Agents[b]
  Rice blast
  Rye stem rust
  Wheat stem rust

NOTES: [a]Weaponized
[b]Stockpiled, but not weaponized

and Chinese governments. The United States admitted to having biological warfare capabilities but denied using biological weapons, and requested impartial investigations. The International Red Cross suggested the formation of a special commission to investigate, and the World Health Organization offered to intervene. Neither China nor North Korea responded to the International Red Cross, and the World Health Organization's offer was rebuffed as a disguised attempt of espionage. Consequently, the United States and fifteen other nations submitted a resolution to the United Nations requesting the formation of a neutral commission to investigate; however, implementation of the resolution was prevented by the Soviet Union. The credibility of the United States was undermined by its failure to ratify the 1925 Geneva Protocol, by knowledge of its offensive biological warfare program, and by its suspected covert collaboration with the Unit 731 scientists.[38] Although unsubstantiated, the accusations of U.S. use of biological weapons attracted wide attention and resulted in a loss of international good will toward the United States. This episode demonstrated the propaganda value of false allegations of biological warfare.[39]

Numerous unsubstantiated allegations were made during the Cold

38. John Ellis van Courtland Moon, "The Korean War Case," in Zilinskas, ed., *The Microbiologist and Biological Defense Research*, pp. 53–83.

39. Mary Rolicka, "New Studies Disputing Allegations of Bacteriological Warfare During the Korean War," *Military Medicine*, Vol. 160, No. 3 (March 1995), pp. 97–100.

War era. These included Soviet accusations of U.S. biological weapons testing against Canadian Eskimos and of a U.S. and Colombian biological attack on Colombian and Bolivian peasants, and a Chinese accusation of U.S. plans to initiate an epidemic of cholera in southeastern China[40] and of the covert release of dengue in Cuba.[41] Similarly, U.S. allegations that Soviet armed forces and their proxies had used trichothecene mycotoxins ("Yellow Rain"), potent inhibitors of DNA and protein synthesis derived from fungi of the genus *Fusarium*, in Laos (1975–81), Kampuchea (1979–81), and Afghanistan (1979–81) are widely regarded as erroneous. The remote locations of the alleged attacks made intelligence investigations extremely difficult. Attacks were never witnessed by Western intelligence operatives, and samples of the aerosols were not recovered. Confounding factors included contradictory testimonies from alleged victims; discrepancies in reported symptoms; low disease rates in the allegedly exposed populations; the recovery of mycotoxin in less than 10 percent of the clinical and environmental samples submitted; the presence of *Fusaria* spp. as environmental commensals; the possible decay of toxin under prevailing environmental conditions; conflicting results of toxin assays from different laboratories; the similarity of alleged yellow rain deposits recovered from environmental surfaces to bee feces in ultrastructural appearance and pollen and mold content; and the natural occurrence of showers of bee feces from swarms of honey bees in the rain forests of southeast Asia.[42]

Disarmament Efforts

During the late 1960s, there was increasing international concern regarding the indiscriminate nature, unpredictability, epidemiologic risks, and lack of epidemiologic control measures for biological weapons, as well as the ineffectiveness of the 1925 Geneva Protocol for preventing biological weapons proliferation. In July 1969, Great Britain submitted a proposal to the Committee on Disarmament of the United Nations, which prohibited the development, production, and stockpiling of biological weapons, and provided for inspections in response to alleged violations. During the following September, the Warsaw Pact nations unexpectedly submitted a

40.   SIPRI, *The Rise of CB Weapons*, pp. 223–227.

41.   Bill Schaap, "U.S. Biological Warfare: The 1981 Cuban Dengue Epidemic," *Covert Action*, No. 17 (Summer 1982), pp. 28–31.

42.   Thomas D. Seeley, Joan W. Nowicke, Matthew Meselson, Jeanne Guillemin, and Pongthep Akratanakkul, "Yellow Rain," *Scientific American*, Vol. 253, No. 3 (March 1985), pp. 128–137.

Table 3.2. Estimates of Casualties Produced by Hypothetical Biological Attack.

Agent	Downwind Reach (km)	Dead	Incapacitated
Rift Valley fever	1	400	35,000
Tick-borne encephalitis	1	9,500	35,000
Typhus	5	19,000	85,000
Brucellosis	10	500	125,000
Q fever	>20	150	125,000
Tularemia	>20	30,000	125,000
Anthrax	>20	95,000	125,000

NOTE: These estimates are based on the following scenario: release of 50 kg of agent by aircraft along a 2 km line upwind of a population center of 500,000.
SOURCE: World Health Organization (WHO), *Health Aspects of Chemical and Biological Weapons* (Geneva: WHO), 1970.

biological disarmament proposal similar to the British proposal, but without provisions for inspections. Two months later, the World Health Organization issued a report regarding the potential consequences of biological warfare. Estimates of the potential casualty figures that could result from biological attacks were staggering.[43] (See Table 3.2.) Subsequently, the 1972 Convention on the Prohibition of the Development, Production, and Stockpiling of Bacteriological (Biological) and Toxin Weapons and on their Destruction was developed. The treaty prohibits the development, possession, and stockpiling of pathogens or toxins in "quantities that have no justification for prophylactic, protective or other peaceful purposes." The treaty also prohibits the development of delivery systems intended to disperse biological agents, and requires states parties to destroy stocks of biological agents, delivery systems, and equipment within nine months of ratifying the treaty. Transferring biological warfare technology or expertise to other countries is also prohibited. Signatories that have not yet ratified the Convention to become states parties are obliged to refrain from activities that would defeat the purpose of the treaty until they explicitly communicate their intention not to ratify. However, there are unresolved controversies regarding the quantities of pathogens required for benevolent research, and the definition of "defensive" research. In addition, the Soviet Union and Warsaw Pact nations continued to consider toxins chemical rather than biological weapons. Allegations of infractions may be lodged with the Security Council, which

43. World Health Organization (WHO), *Health Aspects of Chemical and Biological Weapons* (Geneva: WHO, 1970), pp. 98–99.

may in turn initiate inspections of accused states parties; however, this provision is undermined by the right of Security Council members to veto proposed inspections.

The treaty was ratified in April 1972, and went into effect in March 1975. Signatory nations included over one hundred nations including Iraq, and the members of the Security Council including the United States and the Soviet Union. Review conferences were held in 1981, 1986, 1991, and 1996. Annual reports regarding biological research facilities, scientific conferences held at specified facilities, scientific exchanges, and epidemics are submitted to the United Nations as an additional confidence-building measure.[44]

U.S. President Richard Nixon had already terminated the U.S. offensive biological weapons program by executive order in 1969. The United States adopted a policy never to use biological weapons, including toxins, under any circumstances whatsoever. National Security Decisions 35 and 44, issued during November 1969 (microorganisms) and February 1970 (toxins), mandated the cessation of offensive biological research and production, and the destruction of the biological arsenal. Research efforts were directed exclusively to the development of defensive measures, such as diagnostic tests, vaccines, and therapies for potential biological weapons threats. Stocks of pathogens and the entire biological arsenal were destroyed between May 1971 and February 1973 under the auspices of the U.S. Department of Agriculture, the Department of Health, Education, and Welfare, and the Departments of Natural Resources of Arkansas, Colorado, and Maryland. Small quantities of pathogens were retained at Fort Detrick to test the efficacy of investigational preventive measures and therapies. The CIA was admonished during a 1975 Congressional hearing for illegally retaining samples of toxins after presidential orders mandating their destruction.[45]

While many welcomed the termination of the U.S. offensive BW program for moral and ethical reasons, the decision to terminate it was motivated by pragmatic considerations. Given the available conventional, chemical, and nuclear weapons, biological weapons were not considered essential for national security. The potential effects of biological weapons on military and civilian populations were still conjectural, and for obvious ethical and public health reasons, could not be empirically studied. Biological weapons were considered untried, unpredictable, and potentially

44. Nicholas A. Sims, *The Diplomacy of Biological Disarmament* (New York: Plenum, 1983), pp. 322–335.

45. U.S. Congress, Senate Select Committee, *Unauthorized Storage of Toxic Agents*, pp. 200–203.

hazardous for the users as well for those under attack. Field commanders and troops were unfamiliar with their use. In addition, the United States and allied countries had a strategic interest in outlawing biological weapons programs in order to prevent the proliferation of relatively low-cost weapons of mass destruction. By outlawing relatively inexpensive biological weapons programs, the proliferation of weapons of mass destruction could hopefully be curtailed.[46]

After the termination of the offensive biological program, the U.S. Army Medical Research Institute of Infectious Diseases (USAMRIID) was established in order to continue the development of medical defenses for U.S. military members against potential biological attack. The mission of USAMRIID is to research strategies, products, information, and training programs for medical defense against potential biological weapons. Endemic or epidemic infectious diseases due to highly virulent pathogens requiring high-level containment for laboratory safety are also studied. USAMRIID is an open research institution; no research is classified. The in-house programs are complemented by contract programs with universities and other research institutions.

Developments Following the 1972 Convention

Events in several signatory nations of the 1972 Biological Weapons Convention, including Iraq and the former Soviet Union, have demonstrated activities outlawed by the convention. Unfortunately, these events demonstrate the ineffectiveness of the convention as the sole means for eradicating biological weapons and preventing further proliferation.

Biological weapons were used for covert assassination during the 1970s. Ricin, a lethal toxin derived from castor beans, was weaponized by the KGB and deployed by the Bulgarian secret service. Metallic pellets 1.7 mm in diameter were channeled, filled with ricin, and sealed with wax intended to melt at body temperature. The pellets were discharged from spring-powered weapons disguised as umbrellas. These weapons were used to assassinate Georgi Markov, a Bulgarian defector living in London, and were also employed during an unsuccessful assassination attempt against another defector, Vladimir Kostov, in 1978. Similar weapons may have been used for at least six other assassinations.[47]

---

46. Thomas Dashiell, "A Review of U.S. Biological Warfare Policies," in Brad Roberts, ed., *Biological Weapons: Weapons of the Future?* (Washington, D.C.: Center for Strategic and International Studies, 1993), pp. 4–5.

47. Neil C. Livingstone and Joseph D. Douglass, *CBW: The Poor Man's Atom Bomb*, National Security Paper No. 1 (Cambridge, Mass. and Washington, D.C.: Institute for Foreign Policy Analysis, 1984), p. 17.

An epidemic of anthrax occurred during April 1979 among people who lived or worked within a distance of 4 kilometers in a narrow zone downwind of a Soviet military microbiology facility in Sverdlovsk (now Ekaterinburg, Russia). In addition, livestock died of anthrax along the extended axis of the epidemic zone out to a distance of 50 kilometers.[48] The facility was suspected by Western intelligence of being a biological warfare research facility, and the epidemic was attributed by Western analysts to the accidental airborne release of anthrax spores. The Soviets maintained that the epidemic was due to ingestion of contaminated meat purchased on the black market. Finally, in 1992, Russian President Boris Yeltsin admitted that the facility had been part of an offensive biological weapons program, and that the epidemic had been due to an accidental release of anthrax spores.[49] Air filters had not been activated early on the morning of April 3.[50] Inhalation anthrax was identified at autopsy as the cause of death in victims.[51] At least seventy-seven cases and sixty-six deaths occurred, constituting the largest epidemic of inhalation anthrax in history.[52] The Soviet Union continued an offensive biological warfare program after the 1972 Convention under the aegis of Biopreparat, an organization under the Ministry of Defense.[53] During the 1970s and 1980s, Biopreparat operated at least six research labs and five production facilities, and employed up to 15,000 scientists and technicians. The extensive program of the former Soviet Union is now controlled largely by Russia. Yeltsin stated in 1992 that he would end further offensive biological research and production; however, the degree to which the program has been reduced is not known.[54]

---

48. See the chapter by Matthew Meselson, Jeanne Guillemin, Martin Hugh-Jones, Alexander Langmuir, Ilona Popova, Alexis Shelokov, and Olga Yampolskaya in this volume.

49. R. Jeffrey Smith, "Yeltsin Blames '79 Anthrax on Germ Warfare Efforts," *Washington Post*, June 16, 1992, p. A-1.

50. Vera Rich, "Russia: Anthrax in the Urals," *Lancet*, Vol. 339 (February 15, 1992), pp. 419–420.

51. Faina A. Abramova, Lev M. Grinberg, Olga V. Yamposkaya, and David H. Walker, "Pathology of Inhalation Anthrax in 42 Cases from the Sverdlovsk Outbreak of 1979," *Proceedings of the National Academy of Sciences of the United States of America*, Vol. 90 (March 1993), pp. 2291–2294.

52. See the chapter by Meselson, Guillemin, Hugh-Jones, Langmuir, Popova, Shelokov, and Yampolskaya in this volume.

53. Milton Leitenberg, "The Biological Weapons Program of the Former Soviet Union," *Biologicals*, Vol. 21 (1993), pp. 187–191.

54. Sherman McCall, "A Higher Form of Killing," *Naval Institute Proceedings*, Vol. 121, No. 2 (February 1995), pp. 40–45.

Before the Persian Gulf War, intelligence reports suggested that the Iraqi regime had sponsored an ambitious biological warfare program. Coalition forces prepared for potential biological warfare by training in protective masks and equipment, reviewing decontamination procedures, and immunizing troops against potential biological warfare threats. Approximately 150,000 U.S. troops received an FDA-licensed toxoid vaccine against anthrax, and 8,000 received a botulinum toxoid vaccine approved by the FDA as an investigational new drug (IND). In addition, thirty million 500-milligram oral doses of ciprofloxacin were stockpiled in the theater of operations to provide a one-month course of chemoprophylaxis for the 500,000 U.S. troops in the event that anthrax spores were used as a biological weapon.

Information regarding the Iraqi offensive BW program was obtained after the war during United Nations weapons inspections. Iraqi officials admitted to having had an offensive biological weapons program, which included basic research on *B. anthracis*, rotavirus, camel pox virus, aflatoxin, botulinum toxins, mycotoxins, and an anti-crop agent (wheat cover rust). Research, production, and weaponization facilities were located at Salman Pak, Al Hakam, and other sites, only some of which had been destroyed during the war. Further disclosures were made by the Iraqi regime after the defection of General Hussein Kammal Hassan during August 1995. The Iraqis admitted to preparing biological weapons immediately before the outbreak of hostilities. These included one hundred bombs filled with botulinum toxin, fifty with anthrax spores, and sixteen with aflatoxin; and thirteen Scud missile warheads weaponized with botulinum toxin, ten with anthrax spores, and two with aflatoxin. The Iraqis claim to have produced 19,000 liters of concentrated botulinum toxin (nearly 10,000 liters weaponized), 8,500 liters of concentrated anthrax spores (6,500 liters weaponized), and 2,200 liters of aflatoxin (1,580 liters weaponized). Other prototype biological weapons included spray tanks capable of being mounted on remotely piloted aircraft to deliver aerosols of biological agents.[55] Fortunately, biological weapons were not used during the war. The Iraqi government claims to have destroyed its biological arsenal after the war. Research and production facilities that had escaped destruction during the war were demolished by the United Nations Special Commission on Iraq (UNSCOM) in 1996. The Persian

---

55. United Nations Security Council, *Report of the Secretary General on the Status of the Implementation of the Special Commission's Plan for the Ongoing Monitoring and Verification of Iraq's Compliance with Relevant Parts of Section C of Security Council Resolution 687 (1991)*, Document S/1995/864 (New York: United Nations, 1995), pp. 19–28.

Gulf War and post-war findings have lead to a recent decision by the U.S. military to develop a plan to immunize troops against anthrax.[56]

The biological threat posed by non-state-sponsored terrorists was demonstrated by the intentional contamination of salad bars in Oregon restaurants with *Salmonella typhimurium* by the Rajneeshee cult during late September 1984. This incident resulted in 751 cases of enteritis and 45 hospitalizations. Although the Rajneeshees were suspected, and despite rigorous epidemiologic analyses by the Wasco-Sherman Public Health Department, the Oregon State Health Division, and the CDC,[57] the origin of the epidemic as a deliberate biological attack was not confirmed until a cult member admitted to the attack in 1986.[58] The threat of biological terrorism resurfaced following the Aum Shinrikyo sarin attack on the Tokyo subway system in March 1995. Police raids and investigations of the cult's facilities disclosed evidence of a rudimentary biological weapons program. The cult was allegedly conducting research of *B. anthracis*, *C. botulinum*, and *C. burnetii*; the arsenal seized by police allegedly contained botulinum toxin and drone aircraft equipped with spray tanks.[59] The cult had allegedly launched three unsuccessful biological attacks in Japan using *B. anthracis* and botulinum toxin, and had sent members to the former Zaire in 1992 in order to obtain Ebola virus, possibly for weapons development.[60]

Conclusion

The history of biological warfare is difficult to assess due to a number of confounding factors. These include difficulties in verification of alleged or attempted biological attacks, the use of allegations of biological attacks for propaganda purposes, the paucity of pertinent microbiological or

56. Bradley Graham, "Military Chiefs Back Anthrax Inoculations; Initiative Would Affect All of Nation's Forces," *Washington Post*, October 2, 1996, p. A-1.

57. J. Weaver, U.S. House of Representatives, *The Town That Was Poisoned*. Congressional Record, 99th Cong., 1st sess. (Washington, D.C.: U.S. GPO, February 28, 1985), H901-H905; and Oregon Health Division, "Salmonellosis in the Dalles," *Communicable Disease Summary*, Vol. 33, No. 20 (September 29, 1984), pp. 1–2.

58. See the chapter by Thomas J. Török et al. in this volume; and James Long, "Rajneesh Dies in Indian Commune," *Oregonian*, January 20, 1990, p. A1.

59. R. Jeffrey Smith, "Japanese Cult Had Network of Front Companies, Investigators Say," *Washington Post*, November 1, 1995, p. A-8.

60. David E. Kaplan and Andrew Marshall, *The Cult at the End of the World* (New York: Crown Publishing Group, 1996).

epidemiologic data, and the incidence of naturally occurring endemic or epidemic diseases during hostilities.

Biological warfare has been attempted since antiquity. Early efforts featured the use of fomites directly against opposing troops or their water supplies. Further development of potential biological weapons has paralleled advances in basic and applied microbiology. These technical capabilities have allowed the isolation, mass production, and weaponization of specific pathogens and toxins. According to contemporary reports, Japanese field trials in China were followed by widespread disease. In addition, these attacks may have resulted in significant morbidity and mortality among unprepared Japanese troops. The epidemiologic consequences of these attacks cannot be rigorously determined in retrospect.

Allegations of other biological attacks have been made since World War I. However, most of these have not been confirmed in the absence of compelling microbiologic or epidemiologic data supporting a biological attack. Furthermore, the Rajneeshee incident demonstrated that biological attacks may be easy to conceal despite state-of-the-art microbiology and epidemiologic analysis. These incidents underscore the difficulty of differentiating biological attacks from naturally occurring epidemics or endemic disease, and emphasize the increased risk of epidemics during hostilities due to the deterioration of hygiene, sanitation, and public health infrastructure. The practice of ascribing naturally occurring epidemic or endemic diseases to alleged biological attacks for propaganda purposes demonstrates the perception of psychological vulnerability to the threat of biological warfare.

Confirmed incidents involving biological weapons since World War II include the Sverdlovsk accident, the ricin assassination attempts, the Rajneeshee incident, and the discovery of the Aum Shinrikyo biological weapons effort. The most immediate threat of biological warfare to date was posed by Iraq during the Persian Gulf War. The reasons behind Saddam Hussein's decision not to use his biological arsenal are unknown. The most frequently proposed hypothesis put forth by Western military analysts and intelligence sources has been possible Iraqi concern regarding the risk of provoking massive retaliation. Alternatively, other considerations may have included the possible ineffectiveness of Hussein's biological weapons, and hazards to his own forces due to deficiencies in Iraqi training and equipment.[61]

International agreements to limit biological weapons proliferation have not been completely effective, as evidenced by events in the former

---

61. Lyle Goldstein, "Saddam's Biological Warfare Card," *Washington Post,* October 11, 1996, p. A-24 (letter).

Soviet Union and Iraq, which demonstrated activities prohibited by the Biological Weapons Convention of 1972. Efforts to formulate legally binding measures to verify compliance with the Biological Weapons Convention have been undertaken, but as of the Fourth Review Conference in December 1996, they have not been successful. Disagreements continue regarding the utility of routine inspections at biological research facilities, and the political, economic, commercial, and security consequences of such inspections. The Ad Hoc Group of Government Experts on Verification (VEREX) will continue to negotiate measures to verify compliance and is charged with completing its work as soon as possible, and no later than 2001. A fifth review conference is to be held in 2001.[62]

There is concern in the West regarding the possibility of proliferation or enhancement of state-sponsored offensive programs in countries hostile to the Western democracies, and the possible use of biological weapons by terrorist organizations. Biological defense in the U.S. military has been focused for the past twenty-eight years on the development of countermeasures including detection capabilities, personal protective equipment, vaccines, diagnostics, and therapies to protect U.S. military members.

---

62. United Nations, *Final Document: Fourth Review Conference of the Parties to the Convention on the Prohibition of the Development, Production, and Stockpiling of Bacteriological (Biological) and Toxin Weapons and on their Destruction*, BWC/CONF.IV/9 (Geneva: United Nations, 1996), pp. 14–29; and Chemical and Biological Arms Control Institute, "The Fourth Review Conference of the Biological and Toxin Weapons Convention: Doing No Harm" (unpublished manuscript, Alexandria, Va., February 1997), p. 3.

Chapter 4

Clinical Recognition and Management of Patients Exposed to Biological Warfare Agents

David R. Franz, Peter B. Jahrling, Arthur M. Friedlander, David J. McClain, David L. Hoover, W. Russell Byrne, Julie A. Pavlin, George W. Christopher, and Edward M. Eitzen, Jr.

The breakup of the Soviet Union, the perceived dominance of the United States as a conventional military world power, and the rise of radical groups focused on destroying what they believe to be evil have raised concern regarding the use of biological warfare (BW) against military forces in combat and even as a new tool of terrorists against civilians.

The potential impact of biological weapons is well illustrated by a 1970 World Health Organization (WHO) publication.[1] It is estimated that fifty kilograms of aerosolized *Bacillus anthracis* (anthrax) spores, for example, dispensed by an airplane two kilometers upwind of a population center of 500,000 unprotected people under ideal meteorological conditions would travel more than twenty kilometers and kill or incapacitate up to 220,000 people, nearly half of those in the path of the biological cloud. If *Francisella tularensis* (tularemia) were dispensed, the number of dead or incapacitated would be about 155,000. Thus, if properly used as

This chapter was adapted from David R. Franz, Peter B. Jahrling, et al., "Clinical Recognition and Management of Patients Exposed to Biological Warfare Agents," Journal of the American Medical Association (JAMA), Vol. 278, No. 5 (August 6, 1997), pp. 399–411.

1. World Health Organization (WHO), *Health Aspects of Chemical and Biological Weapons: Report of WHO Group of Consultants* (Geneva: WHO, 1970), pp. 72, 99.

offensive weapons under ideal meteorological conditions, certain biological agents could cause mass casualties.

In addition to their detrimental health effects on the targeted population, the hostile use of BW agents would be likely to impact the health care system significantly. Patients would present in unprecedented numbers, and demands for intensive care might overwhelm medical resources. Special medications or vaccines not generally available in standard pharmaceutical stocks might be required. Health care professionals and laboratory personnel might need added physical protection, and autopsy and interment of remains could present unusual hazards.

The medical response to the threat or use of biological weapons differs depending on whether medical measures are used before exposure or after exposure and whether symptoms are present. If provided before exposure, active immunization or prophylaxis with antibiotics may prevent illness. Active immunization is probably the best modality for future protection of military forces against a wide variety of biological threats. For civilian populations, pre-exposure medical countermeasures would likely not be used. After exposure, but before symptoms arise, active or passive immunization, as well as pretreatment with therapeutic antibiotics or antiviral drugs, may ameliorate disease symptoms. Diagnostic and reference lab capabilities will be necessary to triage individuals potentially exposed and to identify definitively the agent used. After the onset of illness, only diagnosis of the disease, general supportive care, and specific medical treatment are left to health care providers. Effective vaccines, antibiotics, antivirals, and antitoxins exist for several of the most likely BW agents. Additional vaccines and new therapies are under development.

Bacteria, viruses, or toxins (of microbial, plant, or animal origin) may be used as BW agents. Examples of microbial agents and toxins that could be used as BW agents include B. anthracis (anthrax), botulinum toxin, Yersinia pestis (plague), staphylococcal enterotoxin B (SEB), and Venezuelan equine encephalitis (VEE) virus. Despite the very different characteristics of these organisms and toxins, these agents used as weapons share some common characteristics. They can be dispersed in aerosols of particle size approximately 1 to 10 μm, which in certain weather conditions may remain suspended for hours and, if inhaled, can penetrate into distal bronchioles and terminal alveoli of the exposed. The aerosols may be delivered by simple technology, including industrial sprayers with nozzles and energy sources modified to generate the smaller particle size. For many agents, the most efficient delivery form would be dry powder, similar to talcum; however, drying is technically difficult, and wet materials could be used. The aerosol could be delivered in two ways: from a line source, such as an airplane or boat, traveling upwind of the intended target; or from a point source containing the agent, such as a stationary sprayer or missile bomblets, in an area upwind of the target. The meteorological conditions in the target area are very important in the use of BW agents as aerosols, because higher wind speeds and turbulence tend to break up the aerosol cloud. Other possible routes of exposure for BW agents include oral, intentional contamination of food and water, and percutaneous. In general, these other routes of exposure are considered less important than the respiratory route in the context of agent use in BW. However, terrorists may not be constrained by the agent characteristics, the route of exposure required on the biological battlefield, or by the relatively brief list of BW agents listed here.

Diseases produced by the offensive use of biological agents against military forces or civilians could be disabling or lethal. Because biological agents produce a more prolonged period of illness than chemical agents, the impact on the health care infrastructure could be enormous. Person-to-person spread could be important for some agents, and local disease cycles might occur if a competent vector for a bacterium or virus is present in the environment. Table 4.1 presents an overview of several BW threat agents, the disease syndromes resulting from exposure to them, and medical countermeasures available to clinicians.

Anthrax

Anthrax is caused by *B. anthracis*, a gram-positive, sporulating bacillus. The reservoir of *B. anthracis* is the soil; the organism is distributed worldwide.[2] The organism exists in the infected host as the vegetative bacillus and in the environment as a spore. Spores do not form in the infected host unless the body tissues are exposed to air. Anthrax spores can survive adverse environmental conditions and can remain viable for decades. The spore is the stage of the bacterial life cycle that is the usual infective form. Animals contract spores while grazing. Susceptible animals include cattle, sheep, goats, and horses, but other animals may develop infection. Humans contract anthrax via inoculation of minor skin lesions with spores from contact with infected animals, their hides, wool, or other products;

---

2. P.C.B. Turnbull, ed., "Proceedings of the International Workshop on Anthrax," *Salisbury Medical Bulletin*, Supplement Vol. 87 (1996), pp. 1–139; and Philip S. Brachman and Arthur M. Friedlander, "Anthrax," in Stanley A. Plotkin and Edward A. Mortimer, Jr., eds., *Vaccines* (Philadelphia: W.B. Saunders, 1994), pp. 729–739.

Table 4.1. Summary of Biological Warfare Agents.

Agent	Infective Dose (Aerosol)	Incubation Period	Diagnostic Samples (BSL)[a]	Diagnostic Assay	Patient Isolation Precautions
Anthrax	8,000 to 50,000 spores	1–5 d	Blood (BSL-2)	Gram stain Ag-ELISA Serology: ELISA	Standard precautions
Brucellosis	10–100 organisms	5–60 d (occasionally months)	Blood, bone marrow, acute and convalescent sera (BSL-3)	Serology: agglutination Culture	Standard precautions Contact isolation if draining lesions present
Plague	100–500 organisms	2–3 d	Blood, sputum lymph node aspirate (BSL-2/3)	Gram or Wright-Giemsa Stain Ag-ELISA Culture Serology: ELISA, IFA	Pneumonic: droplet precautions until patient treated for 3 d
Q fever	1–10 organisms	10–40 d	Serum (BSL-2/3)	Serology: ELISA, IFA	Standard precautions
Tularemia	10–50 organisms	2–10 d	Blood, sputum serum EM of tissue (BSL-2/3)	Culture Serology: agglutination	Standard precautions

NOTES: Information on diagnostics, medical management, and vaccines is available by contacting Commander, USAMRIID, at 301-619-2833 (phone) or 301-619-4625 (fax). Readers are advised to consult product literature before administering drugs or vaccines. BSL indicates biosafety level; Rx, chemotherapy; Px, chemoprophylaxis; Ag, antigen; ELISA, enzyme-linked immunosorbent assay; IV, intravenously; q, every; IM, intramuscular; qd, each day; bid, twice daily; PO, by mouth; IFA, immunofluorescence assay; IND, Investigational New Drug; SC, subcutaneous; EM, electron microscopy; PCR, polymerase chain reaction; VIG, vaccinia immune globulin; DOD, Department of Defense; VEE, Venezuelan equine encephalitis; EEE, eastern equine encephalitis; WEE, western equine encepha-

Table 4.1. (*Continued*)

Chemotherapy (Rx)	Chemoprophylaxis (Px)	Vaccine Availability	Comments
Ciprofloxacin 400 mg IV q 8–12 h Doxycycline 200 mg IV, then 100 mg IV q 8–12h Penicillin 2 million units IV q 2 h plus streptomycin 30 mg/kg IM qd (or gentamicin)	Ciprofloxacin 500 mg PO bid x 4 wk If unvaccinated begin initial doses of vaccine Doxycycline 100 mg PO bid 4 x wk plus vaccination	Michigan Biological Products Institute vaccine (licensed): 0.5 mL SC at 0, 2, 4 wk and 6, 12, 18 mo, then annual boosters	Vaccine: boost at-risk annually. Alternates for Rx: gentamicin, erythromycin, and chloramphenicol
Doxycycline 200 mg/d PO plus rifampin 600–900 mg/d PO x 6 wk	Doxycycline and rifampin for 3 wk in inadvertently inoculated persons	No vaccine available for human use	Trimethoprim-sulfamethoxazole may be substituted for rifampin; however, relapse rate with this drug may be up to 30 percent
Streptomycin 30 mg/kg IM qd in 2 divided doses x 10 d (or gentamicin) Doxycycline 200 mg IV then 100 mg IV q 12 h x 10–14 d Chloramphenicol 1 g IV q 6 h x 10–14 d	Tetracycline 500 mg PO qid x 7 d Doxycycline 100 mg PO q 12 h x 7 d	Greer inactivated vaccine (licensed): 1.0 mL, then 0.2 mL boost at 1–3 and 3–6 mo	Boost at-risk 12, 18 mo, and yearly. Plague vaccine not protective against aerosol in animal studies. Alternate Rx: Chloramphenicol or trimethoprim-sulfamethoxazole Rx: chloramphenicol for plague meningitis
Tetracycline 500 mg PO q 6 h x 5–7 d Doxycycline 100 mg PO q 12 h x 5–7 d	Tetracycline start 8–12 d postexposure x 5 d Doxycycline start 8–12 d postexposure x 5 d	IND 610-inactivated whole cell vaccine given as a single 0.5 mL, SC	Recommend skin test before vaccination
Streptomycin 30 mg/kg IM qd x 10–14 d Gentamicin 3–5 mg/kg/d x 10–14 d	Doxycycline 100 mg PO q 12 h x 14 d Tetracycline 2 g/d PO x 14 d	Live attenuated vaccine (IND): scarification	Culture difficult and potentially dangerous

Table continued on next page

litis; NA, not available; RVF, Rift Valley fever; KHF, Korean hemorrhagic fever; YF, yellow fever; RT-PCR, reverse transcriptase polymerase chain reaction; Ab, antibody; CCHF, Congo-Crimean hemorrhagic fever; AHF, Argentine hemorrhagic fever; BHF, Bolivian hemorrhagic fever; CDC, Centers for Disease Control and Prevention.

[a] Jonathan Y. Richmond and Robert W. McKinney, *Biosafety in Microbiological and Biomedical Laboratories* (Washington, D.C.: U.S. Department of Health and Human Services [HHS], 1993), HHS Publication CDC 93-8395.

Table 4.1. *(Continued)*

Agent	Infective Dose (Aerosol)	Incubation Period	Diagnostic Samples (BSL) [a]	Diagnostic Assay	Patient Isolation Precautions
Smallpox	Assumed low—10–100 organisms	7–17 d	Pharyngeal swab, scab material (BSL-4)	ELISA, PCR, virus isolation	Airborne precautions
Viral encephalitides	10–100 organisms	VEE, 2–6 d EEE/WEE, 7–14 d	Serum VEE (BSL-3) EEE (BSL-2) WEE (BSL-2)	Viral isolation Serology: ELISA or hemogglutination inhibition	Standard precautions (mosquito control)
Viral hemorrhagic fevers	1–10 organisms	4–21 d	Serum, blood Most viral hemorrhagic fevers (BSL-4) and RVF, KHF, and YF (BSL-3)	Virus isolation Ag-ELISA RT-PCR Serology: Ab-ELISA	Contact precautions Consider additional precautions if massive hemorrhage
Botulinum	0.001 µg/kg (type A)	1–5 d	Nasal swab (possibly) (BSL-2)	Ag-ELISA, mouse neutral	Standard precautions
Staphylococcal enterotoxin b	30 ng/person (incapacitating); 1.7 µg/ person (lethal)	1–6 h	Nasal swab, serum, urine (BSL-2)	Ag-ELISA Serology: Ab-ELISA	Standard precautions

Table 4.1. (*Continued*)

Chemotherapy (Rx)	Chemoprophylaxis (Px)	Vaccine Availability	Comments
Cidofovir (effective in vitro)	Vaccinia immune globulin 0.6 mL/kg IM (within 3 d of exposure; best within 24 h)	Wyeth calf lymph vaccinia vaccine (licensed) DOD cell-culture derived vaccinia vaccine (IND): scarification	Preexposure and post-exposure vaccination recommended if > 3 y since last vaccination
Supportive therapy analgesics anticonvulsants as needed	NA	VEE DOD TC-83 live attenuated vaccine (IND): 0.5 mL SC x 1 dose VEE DOD C-84 (formalin inactivated TC-83) (IND): 0.5 mL SC for up to 3 doses EEE inactivated (IND): 0.5 mL SC at 0 and 28 d WEE inactivated (IND): 0.5 mL SC at 0, 7, and 28 d	TC-83 reactogenic in 20 percent. No seroconversion in 20 percent. Only effective against subtypes 1A, 1B, and 1C. Vaccine used for nonresponders to TC-83 EEE and WEE inactivated vaccines are poorly immunogenic, and multiple immunizations are required
Supportive therapy Ribavirin (CCHF/ arenaviruses) 30 mg/kg IV initial dose 15 mg/kg IV q 6 h x 4 d 7.5 mg/kg IV q 8 h x 6 d Antibody passive for AHF, BHF, Lassa fever, and CCHF	NA	AHF Candid #1 vaccine (x-protection for BHF) (IND) RVF inactivated vaccine (IND)	Aggressive management of secondary infections and hypotension is important
DOD heptavalent antitoxin for Serotypes A-G (IND): equine despeciated 1 vial (10 mL) IV CDC Trivalent equine antitoxin for Serotypes A, B, E (licensed)	NA	DOD pentavalent Toxoid for serotypes A-E (IND): SC at 0, 2, and 12 wk, then yearly boosters	Skin testing for hypersensitivity before equine antitoxin administration Ventilatory assistance
Ventilatory support and supportive care	NA	No vaccine avaliable	Vomiting and diarrhea may occur if toxin is swallowed

from ingesting contaminated meat; from inhaling spores during the processing of wool for textiles; or possibly from the bites of infected flies.[3]

Anthrax spores were weaponized by the United States in the 1950s and 1960s before the U.S. offensive BW program was terminated. Iraq admitted to a United Nations inspection team in August 1991 that it had conducted research on the offensive use of *B. anthracis* before the Persian Gulf War and, in 1995, admitted to "weaponizing" anthrax. Other countries have also been suspected of weaponizing anthrax spores. The deaths of at least sixty-six people after an accidental release of anthrax spores in the former Soviet Union underscore the weapons potential of this agent.[4]

CLINICAL FEATURES

Anthrax has three clinical presentations in humans: cutaneous, gastrointestinal, and inhalational.[5] A biological attack with anthrax spores would most likely occur by aerosol delivery and would result in inhalational anthrax. This illness, known as woolsorter's disease, occurs in the textile and tanning industries among workers handling contaminated wool, hair, and hides.[6] After being inhaled and deposited in the lower respiratory tract, spores are phagocytized by tissue macrophages and transported to hilar and mediastinal lymph nodes. The spores germinate into vegetative bacilli, producing a necrotizing hemorrhagic mediastinitis.[7]

Inhalation anthrax begins with a prodrome featuring fever, malaise, and fatigue. A nonproductive cough and vague chest discomfort may be present. This prodrome may be followed by symptomatic improvement for two to three days or may progress directly to the abrupt onset of severe respiratory distress with dyspnea, stridor, diaphoresis, and cyanosis. Bacteremia, septic shock, metastatic infection (meningitis in approximately half of cases), and death usually follow within twenty-four to

---

3. Brachman and Friedlander, "Anthrax," pp. 729–739.

4. See the chapter by Matthew Meselson et al. in this volume.

5. Brachman and Friedlander, "Anthrax," pp. 729–739; Werner Dutz and Elfriede Kohout, "Anthrax," *Pathology Annual*, Vol. 6 (1971), pp. 209–248; and Arthur M. Friedlander, "Anthrax," in R. Zajtchuk, ed., *Textbook of Military Medicine: Medical Aspects of Chemical and Biological Warfare* (Washington, D.C.: U.S. Department of the Army, Surgeon General, and the Borden Institute, 1997), pp. 467–478.

6. Philip S. Brachman, "Inhalation Anthrax," *Annals of the New York Academy of Science*, Vol. 167 (1980), pp. 83–93.

7. See the chapter by Meselson et al. in this volume; Friedlander, "Anthrax," pp. 467–478; Brachman, "Inhalation Anthrax," pp. 83–93; and Faina A. Abramova, Lev M. Grinberg, Olga V. Yampolskaya, and David H. Walker, "Pathology of Inhalational Anthrax in 42 Cases From the Sverdlovsk Outbreak of 1979," *Proceedings of the National Academy of Science, USA*, Vol. 90 (1993), pp. 2291–2294.

thirty-six hours.[8] Once symptoms of inhalational anthrax appear, treatment is almost invariably ineffective, although there are anecdotal reports of patients surviving after early, aggressive therapy.[9]

DIAGNOSIS AND MANAGEMENT

Physical findings are usually nonspecific. The chest x-ray film is typically without infiltrates but may reveal a widened mediastinum with pleural effusions, which may be hemorrhagic. Meningitis, often hemorrhagic, has been reported in up to 50 percent of cases.[10] *Bacillus anthracis* can be visualized by Wright or Gram stains of peripheral blood and isolated by blood cultures, but often not until late in the disease course. Vegetative bacilli are present during infection and sporulation does not occur *in vivo*. Animal studies of inhalational anthrax demonstrate that bacilli and toxin appear in the blood late on the second day or early on the third day after aerosol challenge. Toxin levels parallel the development of bacteremia. An enzyme-linked immunosorbent assay (ELISA) to detect circulating toxin is available for rapid diagnosis.

Historically, penicillin has been the treatment of choice for inhalational anthrax, with two million units given intravenously every two hours. Some animal studies suggest that addition of streptomycin may have additional benefit. All naturally occurring strains tested to date have been sensitive to erythromycin, chloramphenicol, gentamicin, and ciprofloxacin. In the absence of antibiotic sensitivity data, treatment should be instituted at the earliest signs of disease with intravenous ciprofloxacin (400 mg every 8–12 hours). Supportive therapy for shock, fluid volume deficit, and adequacy of airway may be indicated.

A licensed vaccine, produced by the Michigan Department of Public Health, is an aluminum hydroxide–adsorbed preparation, derived from culture fluid supernatant taken from an attenuated strain.[11] The vaccination series consists of six subcutaneous doses at zero, two, and four weeks, then at six, twelve, and eighteen months, followed by annual boosters. U.S. military forces are now being immunized with this vaccine. Studies in rhesus monkeys indicate it is protective against aerosol challenge. A recombinant vaccine based on protective antigen (PA) is being developed as a potential replacement product for use in the future.

---

8. Friedlander, "Anthrax," pp. 467–478; and Brachman, "Inhalation Anthrax," pp. 83–93.

9. Ibid.

10. Friedlander, "Anthrax," pp. 467–478; and Abramova, Grinberg, Yampolskaya, and Walker, "Pathology of Inhalational Anthrax," pp. 2291–2294.

11. Brachman, "Inhalation Anthrax," pp. 729–739.

If there is information indicating that a BW attack is imminent or may have occurred, prophylaxis of unimmunized individuals with ciprofloxacin (500 mg by mouth twice a day) or doxycycline (100 mg by mouth twice a day) is recommended.[12] The vaccination series should be initiated for unimmunized individuals. Should an anthrax attack be confirmed, chemoprophylaxis should be continued for at least four weeks and until at least three doses of vaccine have been received by all those exposed.

Brucellosis

Brucellae are small, slow-growing, pleomorphic, gram-negative aerobic nontoxigenic, non-spore-forming coccobacilli. Although the six species of Brucella are closely related,[13] they each characteristically infect different animal hosts, in which they usually cause infertility or abortion. Of the four species that are pathogenic for humans, *Brucella melitensis* usually infects goats, *Brucella suis* infects swine, *Brucella abortus* infects cattle, and *Brucella canis* infects dogs. A pattern of disease severity in humans is as follows: *B. melitensis* > *B. suis* > *B. abortus* > *B. canis*. Most human infections occur by contact with infected animal tissues or ingestion of contaminated raw meat or dairy products. Person-to-person transmission typically does not occur. The bacteria are highly infectious by aerosol and commonly cause infections in laboratory workers.[14] Brucellae are susceptible to commonly used disinfectants and heat but may survive for six weeks in dust and ten weeks in soil or water.

The United States weaponized *B. suis* in the 1940s and 1950s but stopped offensive work on the agent in the 1960s. Other countries have or are suspected to have weaponized brucellae.[15] The organism could be delivered as a slurry in bomblets or, theoretically, as a dry aerosol.

12. Arthur M. Friedlander, Susan L. Welkos, Louise M. Pitt, et al., "Postexposure Prophylaxis Against Experimental Inhalation Anthrax," *Journal of Infectious Diseases*, Vol. 167 (1993), pp. 1239–1243.

13. F. Grimont, J.M. Verger, P. Cornells, et al., "Molecular Typing of *Brucella* with Cloned DNA Probes," *Research in Microbiology*, Vol. 143 (1992), pp. 55–65.

14. Jaime E. Ollé-Goig and Jaume Canela-Soler, "An Outbreak of *Brucella melitensis* Infection by Airborne Transmission Among Laboratory Workers," *American Journal of Public Health*, Vol. 77 (1987), pp. 335–338.

15. David R. Franz, Cheryl D. Parrott, and Ernest T. Takafuji, "The U.S. Biological Warfare and Biological Defense Programs," in Zajtchuk, *Textbook of Military Medicine*, pp. 425–436.

CLINICAL FEATURES

Brucellae are facultative intracellular macrophage parasites, and localize in organs (especially the lung, spleen, liver, central nervous system, bone marrow, and synovium) with large numbers of macrophages.[16] Disease manifestations reflect this distribution. Symptoms and signs are similar in patients with presumed oral, aerosol, or percutaneous infection. Patients usually have fever, chills, and malaise.[17] Respiratory symptoms (cough, pleuritic chest pain) may occur in 20 percent of patients but do not usually denote pneumonia. Sacroiliitis, large joint infections, and vertebral osteomyelitis are the most common osteoarticular manifestations.[18] Genitourinary infections and hepatitis may also occur.[19] Endocarditis and central nervous system infections are rare, but account for nearly all fatalities, which occur in less than 5 percent of untreated patients.[20] Systemic symptoms may last for weeks or months. Even without antibiotics, most patients recover within a year, but relapses are common.[21] Hematological abnormalities, including anemia, neutropenia, and thrombocytopenia, may be present.[22]

16. Abdul Rahman, M. Mousa, Kamal M. Elhag, Mustapha Khogali, and T.N. Sugathan, "Brucellosis in Kuwait," *Transactions of the Royal Society for Tropical Medicine and Hygiene*, Vol. 81 (1987), pp. 1019–1021.

17. Edward J. Young, "An Overview of Human Brucellosis," *Clinical Infections and Diseases*, Vol. 21 (1995), pp. 283–289; and Abdul Rahman, M. Mousa, Kamal M. Elhag, Mustapha Khogali, and Amin A. Marafie, "The Nature of Human Brucellosis in Kuwait: Study of 379 Cases," *Review of Infectious Diseases*, Vol. 10 (1988), pp. 211–217.

18. Eduardo Gotuzzo, Graciela S. Alarcon, Tomas S. Bocanegra, et al., "Articular Involvement in Human Brucellosis," *Seminars in Arthritis and Rheumatism*, Vol. 12 (1982), pp. 245–255; Abdul Rahman, R. Mousa, Saeed A. Muhtaseb, Daood S. Almudallal, Safia M. Khodeir, and Amin A. Marafie, "Osteoarticular Complications of Brucellosis," *Review of Infectious Diseases*, Vol. 9 (1987), pp. 531–543; and Javier Ariza, F. Gudiol, J. Valverde, et al., "Brucellar Spondylitis," *Review of Infectious Diseases*, Vol. 7 (1983), pp. 656–664.

19. A.I.A. Ibrahim, S.D. Shetty, M. Saad, and N.E. Bilal, "Genito-Urinary Complications of Brucellosis," *British Journal of Urology*, Vol. 61 (1983), pp. 294–298.

20. Thomas M. Peery and Lester F. Belter, "Brucellosis and Heart Disease," *American Journal of Pathology*, Vol. 36 (1960), pp. 673–697.

21. A.C. Evans, "Comments on the Early History of Human Brucellosis," in C.H. Larson and M.H. Soule, eds., *Brucellosis* (Baltimore: Waverly, 1950), pp. 1–8.

22. Emilio Crosby, Lucia Llosa, Q.M. Miro, Carlos Carillo, and Eduardo Gotuzzo, "Hematologic Changes in Brucellosis," *Journal of Infectious Diseases*, Vol. 150 (1984), pp. 419–424.

DIAGNOSIS AND MANAGEMENT

Symptoms and signs of brucellosis are nonspecific. A serum tube agglutination test is the usual diagnostic method.[23] Cultures of blood, bone marrow, and focal sites of infection may be positive.[24] The organism grows slowly, but adequately, in conventional blood culture bottles. Cultures must be kept for at least six weeks with periodic blind subculturing onto enriched agar plates. A special biphasic culture technique, the Castaneda bottle, may facilitate Brucella isolation if available.[25]

Patients should be treated with combinations of antibiotics, as treatment with single agents leads to poor response or relapse. A combination of 200 mg per day of doxycycline orally and 600 to 900 mg per day of rifampin orally for six weeks is usually the treatment of choice.[26] Trimethoprimsulfamethoxazole may be substituted for rifampin. For bone and joint infections, endocarditis, and central nervous system disease, streptomycin or another aminoglycoside should be included, and therapy should be prolonged. Treatment of endocarditis may require valve replacement.[27] There is no approved Brucella vaccine for humans.

Plague

Yersinia pestis, the etiologic agent of plague, is a gram-negative bacillus of the family Enterobacteriaceae that is maintained in numerous and diverse rodent reservoirs.[28] Plague is transmitted via flea vectors from rodents to

23. Edward J. Young, "Serologic Diagnosis of Human Brucellosis: Analysis of 214 Cases by Agglutination Tests and Review of the Literature," *Review of Infectious Diseases*, Vol. 13 (1991), pp. 359–372.

24. Eduardo Gotuzzo, Carlos Carillo, Jorge Guerra, and Lucia Llosa, "An Evaluation of Diagnostic Methods for Brucellosis," *Journal of Infectious Diseases*, Vol. 153 (1986), pp. 122–125.

25. Nelson P. Moyer and Larry A. Holcomb, "Brucella," in Patrick R. Murray, Ellen J. Baron, Michael A. Pfaller, Fred C. Tenover, and Robert F. Yolken, eds., *Manual of Clinical Microbiology*, 6th ed. (Washington, D.C.: American Society for Microbiology [ASM], 1995), pp. 549–555.

26. G.A. Luzzi, R. Brindle, P.N. Sockett, J. Solera, P. Klenerman, and D.A. Wartell, "Brucellosis," *Transactions of the Royal Society for Tropical Medicine and Hygiene*, Vol. 87 (1993), pp. 138–141; and Joint FAO/WHO Export Committee on Brucellosis, *WHO Technical Report Series*, Vol. 740 (1986), pp. 1–132.

27. Raymond Chan and Robyn P. Hardiman, "Endocarditis Caused by *Brucella melitensis*," *Medical Journal of Australia*, Vol. 158 (1993), pp. 631–632.

28. Thomas Butler, *Plague and Other* Yersinia *Infections* (New York: Plenum, 1983); and Thomas W. McGovern and Arthur M. Friedlander, "Plague," in Zajtchuk, *Textbook of Military Medicine*, pp. 479–502.

humans and by respiratory droplets from animals to humans or from humans to humans.[29]

During World War II, Japan used plague as a biological weapon against China. The United States studied *Y. pestis* as a potential BW agent in the 1950s before the offensive BW program was terminated, and other countries have been suspected of weaponizing plague.

CLINICAL FEATURES

The clinical presentations of plague are bubonic, septicemic, and pneumonic disease.[30] The most likely clinical presentation after a BW attack would be primary pneumonic plague.[31] After an incubation period of two to three days, patients present with pneumonia featuring the acute and often fulminant onset of malaise, high fever, chills, headache, myalgia, cough with production of a bloody sputum, and clinical sepsis. The chest x-ray film reveals a patchy or consolidated bronchopneumonia. Pneumonic plague progresses rapidly, resulting in dyspnea, stridor, and cyanosis. The terminal course may feature respiratory failure, shock, and ecchymoses.

DIAGNOSIS AND MANAGEMENT

A presumptive diagnosis can be made by identifying a gram-negative coccobacillus and safety-pin bipolar staining organisms in gram-stained or Wright-Giemsa stained smears from peripheral blood, lymph node needle aspirate, sputum, or other clinical specimens. Immunofluorescence staining for the capsule is diagnostic. The diagnosis can be confirmed by culturing the organism from blood, sputum, and bubo aspirates. The organism grows slowly at standard incubation temperatures and may be misidentified by automated systems because of delayed biochemical reactions. Most strains of *Y. pestis* produce F1 capsule antigen *in vivo*, which can be detected in serum samples by immunoassay. A four-fold rise in antibody titer is also diagnostic.

Streptomycin sulfate, tetracycline, chloramphenicol, and gentamicin

---

29. Butler, *Plague and Other* Yersinia *Infections;* and McGovern and Friedlander, "Plague," pp. 479–502; R.D. Perry and J.D. Fetherson, "*Yersinia pestis,*" *Clinical Microbiology Reviews,* Vol. 10 (1997), pp. 35–66; and P. Russell, S.M. Eley, D.L. Bell, R.J. Manchee, and R.W. Titball, "Doxycycline or Ciprofloxacin Prophylaxis and Therapy Against *Yersinia pestis* Infection in Mice," *Journal of Antimicrobial Chemotherapy,* Vol. 37 (1996), pp. 769–774.

30. Butler, *Plague and Other* Yersinia *Infections;* McGovern and Friedlander, "Plague," pp. 479–502; and Perry and Fetherson, "*Yersinia pestis,*" pp. 35–66.

31. Butler, *Plague and Other* Yersinia *Infections;* and McGovern and Friedlander, "Plague," pp. 479–502

sulfate are effective therapies for bubonic plague, especially if begun within twenty-four hours of the onset of symptoms.[32] Plague pneumonia is almost always fatal if treatment is not initiated within twenty-four hours of the onset of symptoms. Streptomycin is given intramuscularly in a dose of 30 mg/kg per day in two divided doses for ten days. Gentamicin may be substituted for streptomycin. Chloramphenicol given intravenously is indicated for treating plague meningitis and in cases of circulatory compromise. Intravenous doxycycline (200 mg initially, followed by 100 mg every twelve hours) for ten to fourteen days is also effective. Results obtained from animal models suggest that quinolones may be effective for treating plague, but they have not been evaluated in humans.[33] Supportive therapy includes intravenous crystalloids and hemodynamic monitoring.

A licensed, killed whole-cell vaccine is available for use in those considered to be at risk of exposure.[34] While epidemiologic evidence supports the efficacy of the current vaccine against bubonic plague, its efficacy against aerosolized Y. pestis is believed to be poor.[35] A candidate vaccine based on recombinant Y. pestis capsule (F1) and V antigens has proven to be effective in protecting animals experimentally exposed to Y. pestis aerosols, and is undergoing further development.

Q Fever

Q fever, a febrile, zoonotic disease with a worldwide distribution, typically results from exposure to domestic livestock animals (mainly sheep, cattle, and goats). The infection is caused by Coxiella burnetii, an obligate intracellular rickettsia-like organism of low virulence but remarkable infectivity.[36]

Coxiella burnetii produces a spore-like form that may cause infection after indirect exposure to infected animals or animal products, which can

---

32. McGovern and Friedlander, "Plague," pp. 479–502.

33. Russell, Eley, Bell, Manchee, and Titball, "Doxycycline and Ciprofloxacin Against Y. Pestis," pp. 769–774.

34. Dan C. Cavanaugh, Francis C. Cadigan, James E. Williams, and John D. Marshall, "General Medicine and Infectious Diseases," in Andre J. Ognibene and O'Neill Barrett, eds., Internal Medicine in Viet Nam (Washington, D.C.: Office of the Surgeon General and Center of Military History, 1982).

35. Dan C. Cavanaugh, Bennett L. Ellsberg, Craig H. Llewellyn, et al., "Plague Immunization," Journal of Infectious Diseases, Vol. 129 (1974), pp. S37-S40.

36. William D. Tigertt and A.S. Benenson, "Studies of Q Fever in Man," Transactions of the Association of American Physicians, Vol. 69 (1956), pp. 98–104.

occur in individuals who live or work in the vicinity of infected animals.[37] In addition, the ability of this spore-like form to withstand heating and drying and to survive on inanimate surfaces allows the organism to persist in the environment for weeks or months after an infected animal has vacated an area and for dissemination by wind with induction of infection at sites miles distant from a source.[38]

Individuals are at risk for acquisition of Q fever, both in the United States and abroad.[39] Q fever is currently recognized as a potential BW agent, with a degree of infectivity and casualty production rivaling that of anthrax.[40] *Coxiella burnetii* was studied as a BW agent before the U.S. BW program ended.[41]

CLINICAL FEATURES

There is no single syndrome characteristic for acute Q fever, and the infection may be manifested by asymptomatic seroconversion in up to 50 percent of infections.[42] The onset of Q fever may be abrupt or insidious, with fever, chills, and headache being the most common symptoms. Diaphoresis, malaise, fatigue, anorexia, and weight loss are also common. Myalgia is a frequent complaint, while arthralgia is less common. Cough

---

37. T.J. Marrie, D. Langille, V. Papukna, and L. Yates, "Truckin' Pneumonia: An Outbreak of Q Fever in a Truck Repair Plant," *Epidemiology and Infections,* Vol. 102 (1989), pp. 119–127; M.M. Salmon, B. Howells, E.J.G. Glencross, et al., "Q Fever in an Urban Area," *Lancet,* Vol. 1 (1982), pp. 1002–1004; and D.L. Smith, J.G. Ayres, I. Blair, et al., "A Large Q Fever Outbreak in the West Midlands: Clinical Aspects," *Respiratory Medicine,* Vol. 87 (1993), pp. 509–516.

38. Smith, Ayres, Blair, et al., "Q Fever Outbreak in the West Midlands," pp. 509–516.

39. A.J. Spicer, "Military Significance of Q Fever: A Review," *Journal of the Royal Society of Medicine,* Vol. 71 (1978), pp. 762–767; and Mark A. Ferrante and Matthew J. Dolan, "Q Fever Meningoencephalitis in a Soldier Returning from the Persian Gulf War," *Clinical Infectious Diseases,* Vol. 16 (1993), pp. 489–496.

40. WHO, *Health Aspects of Chemical and Biological Weapons,* pp. 72, 99.

41. *U.S. Army Activity on the U.S. Biological Warfare Programs,* Vol. II, February 1977, Unclassified Document, L-3, 4, 5, 6.

42. Marrie, Langille, Papukna, and Yates, "Truckin' Pneumonia," pp. 119–127; Salmon, Howells, Glencross, et al., "Q Fever in an Urban Area," pp. 1002–1004; Smith, Ayres, Blair, et al., "Q Fever Outbreak in the West Midlands," pp. 509–516; Spicer, "Military Significance of Q Fever," pp. 762–767; Ferrante and Dolan, "Q Fever Meningoencephalitis in a Soldier," pp. 489–496; *U.S. Army Activity on the U.S. Biological Warfare Programs,* L-3, 4, 5, 6; Didier Raoult and Thomas J. Marrie, "State-of-the-Art Clinical Lecture: Q Fever," *Clinical Infectious Diseases,* Vol. 20 (1995), pp. 489–496; E.H. Derrick, "The Course of Infection with *Coxiella burnetii,*" *Medical Journal of Australia,* Vol. 1 (1973), pp. 1051–1057; and Georges Dupuis, Jacques Petite, Oliver Péter, and Michel Vouilloz, "An Important Outbreak of Human Q Fever in a Swiss Alpine Valley," *International Journal of Epidemiology,* Vol. 16 (1987), pp. 282–287.

tends to appear somewhat late in the illness and may not be a prominent complaint. Chest pain occurs in a minority of patients and may be pleuritic or a vague substernal discomfort. Although nonspecific evanescent skin eruptions have been reported, there is no characteristic rash. Temperature tends to fluctuate, with peaks of 39.4°C to 40.6°C, and approximately 25 percent of the cases are biphasic. In two-thirds of patients with acute disease, the febrile period lasts thirteen days or fewer.[43] Neurological symptoms are not uncommon and have been observed in up to 23 percent of acute cases.[44]

Rales are the most common physical finding; evidence of pleural effusion (including friction rub) and consolidation may also be noted. Although hepatomegaly, splenomegaly, and jaundice have all been reported, they are relatively unusual in acute infection. Reports of abnormalities on chest radiographs vary with locale, but can be identified in 50 percent to 60 percent of symptomatic patients and may persist for several months.[45] An abnormal chest radiograph may be seen in the absence of pulmonary symptoms, while a normal chest radiograph may be observed in a patient with pulmonary symptoms.[46]

Laboratory abnormalities associated with acute Q fever usually involve liver function tests, and patients may present with a clinical and laboratory picture consistent with acute hepatitis. Two-fold and three-fold elevations of aspartate aminotransferase or alanine aminotransferase are observed in 50 percent to 75 percent of patients, while elevations of the alkaline phosphatase and or total bilirubin are observed in only 10 percent to 15 percent.[47] The white blood cell count is usually normal; mild anemia or thrombocytopenia may also be observed.

The case-fatality rate of acute Q fever is low, even without treatment, and chronic disease, usually manifested by endocarditis, probably develops in less than 1 percent of acute infections.[48] Malaise and fatigue lasting for months after acute infection have been reported in up to 32 percent of patients.[49]

---

43. Derrick, "Infection with *Coxiella burnetii*," pp. 1051–1057.

44. Dupuis, Petite, Péter, and Vouilloz, "Q Fever in a Swiss Alpine Valley," pp. 282–287.

45. Smith, Ayres, Blair, et al., "Q Fever Outbreak in the West Midlands," pp. 509–516.

46. Ibid., pp. 509–516.

47. Ibid.

48. Ibid; and Philippe B. Brouqui, Hervé T. Dupont, Michel Drancourt, et al., "Chronic Q Fever," *Archives of Internal Medicine*, Vol. 153 (1993), pp. 643–648.

49. Smith, Ayres, Blair, et al., "Q Fever Outbreak in the West Midlands," pp. 509–516.

DIAGNOSIS AND MANAGEMENT

Diagnosis of Q fever is usually accomplished by serological testing; the most common methods are antibody detection by indirect fluorescent antibody (IFA) or ELISA. Significant antibody titers are not consistently identifiable until two to three weeks into the illness. Convalescent antibody titers, two to three months after onset of illness, typically demonstrate a four-fold increase.[50] After acute infection, significantly elevated antibody titers may persist for years.[51] Chronic infection almost always induces significant antibody titers.[52]

Treatment of acute Q fever shortens the course of the disease and prevents disease when administered during the incubation period.[53] Tetracyclines remain the mainstay of therapy for acute disease. Macrolide antibiotics, such as erythromycin and azithromycin, are also effective. Quinolones, chloramphenicol, and trimethoprim sulfamethoxazole have also been used to treat Q fever, but clinical experience with these antibiotics is limited.

Although an effective vaccine (Q-Vax) is licensed in Australia, all Q fever vaccines used in the United States are investigational.[54] Individuals already immune to Q fever frequently develop severe local reactions at the site of vaccine injection.[55] These reactions can be avoided by prior screening with an intradermal skin test to detect presensitized or immune individuals.[56] Research efforts are underway to develop a Q fever vaccine

50. Iyorlumun I. Uhaa, Daniel B. Fishbein, James G. Olson, Cornelia C. Rives, David M. Waag, and Jim C. Williams, "Evaluation of Specificity of Indirect Enzyme-Linked Immunosorbent Assay for Diagnosis of Human Q Fever," *Journal of Clinical Microbiology*, Vol. 32 (1994), pp. 1560–1565; and David M. Waag, Jeff Chulay, T. Marrie, Marilyn England, and Jim Williams, "Validation of an Enzyme Immunoassay for Serodiagnosis of Acute Q Fever," *European Journal of Clinical Microbiology and Infectious Diseases*, Vol. 14 (1995), pp. 421–427.

51. Didier Raoult, "Treatment of Q Fever," *Antimicrobial Agents and Chemotherapy*, Vol. 37 (1993), pp. 1733–1736.

52. Brouqui, Dupont, Drancourt, et al., "Chronic Q Fever," pp. 643–648.

53. Raoult, "Treatment of Q Fever," pp. 1733–1736.

54. B.P. Martalon, R.A. Ormsbee, and M. Kyrkor, "Vaccine Prophylaxis of Abattoir-Associated Q Fever," *Epidemiology and Infection*, Vol. 104 (1990), pp. 275–287; and James R. Acklund, David A. Worswick, and Barrie P. Marmion, "Vaccine Prophylaxis of Q Fever," *Medical Journal of Australia*, Vol. 160 (1994), pp. 704–708.

55. A.S. Benenson, "Q Fever Vaccine," in J.E. Smadel, ed., *Symposium on Q Fever by the Committee on Rickettsial Diseases* (Washington, D.C.: Armed Forces Epidemiology Board, 1959), pp. 47–60; and J. Frederick Bell, David B. Lackman, Armon Meis, and W.J. Hadlow, "Recurrent Reaction at Site of Q Fever Vaccination in a Sensitized Person," *Military Medicine*, Vol. 129 (1964), pp. 591–595.

56. David B. Lackman, E. John Bell, J. Frederick Bell, and Edgar G. Pickens, "Intra-

that is safe to administer without a prior skin test. The residue of *C. burnetti* organisms following a chloroform-methanol extraction (CMR vaccine) has been tested for safety in human, non-immune volunteers and is presently being tested for safety in Q fever–immune volunteers where sensitization may be a problem.[57]

Tularemia

Francisella tularensis, the etiologic agent of tularemia, is a small, nonmotile, aerobic, facultative intracellular gram-negative coccobacillus. Tularemia (also known as rabbit fever and deer fly fever) is a zoonotic disease, and humans acquire the disease under natural conditions through inoculation of skin or mucous membranes with blood or tissue fluids of infected animals or bites of infected deer flies, mosquitoes, or ticks. Although less common, inhaling contaminated dusts or ingesting contaminated foods or water may also produce clinical disease.[58] Respiratory exposure by aerosol would cause typhoidal tularemia, which often has a pneumonic component. The organism can remain viable for weeks in water, soil, carcasses, and hides, and for years in frozen rabbit meat.[59]

Francisella tularensis was weaponized by the United States in the 1950s and 1960s before the U.S. offensive BW program was terminated, and other countries may have weaponized this agent for delivery by aerosol.

CLINICAL FEATURES
Tularemia may appear in two forms in humans depending on the route of inoculation: ulceroglandular or typhoidal. As few as ten to fifty organisms will cause disease if inhaled or injected intradermally. The most common ulceroglandular form is usually acquired through inoculation of the skin or mucous membranes with blood or tissue fluids of infected animals. The typhoidal form, which occurs mainly after inhalation of infectious aerosols, accounts for 15 percent to 25 percent of naturally occurring cases. Typhoidal or septicemic tularemia manifests as fever,

---

dermal Sensitivity Testing in Man With a Purified Vaccine for Q Fever," *American Journal of Public Health,* Vol. 52 (1962), pp. 87–93.

57. L.F. Fries, D.M. Waag, and J.C. Williams, "Safety and Immunogenicity in Human Volunteers of a Chloroform-Methanol Residue Vaccine for Q Fever," *Infection and Immunity,* Vol. 61 (1993), pp. 1251–1258.

58. Martin E. Evans and Arthur M. Friedlander, "Tularemia," in Zajtchuk, *Textbook of Military Medicine,* pp. 503–512; and Martin E. Evans, David W. Gregory, William Schaffner, and Zell A. McGee, "Tularemia," *Medicine,* Vol. 64 (1985), pp. 251–269.

59. Evans, Gregory, Schaffner, and McGee, "Tularemia," pp. 251–269.

prostration, and weight loss, but without adenopathy.[60] Respiratory symptoms of substernal discomfort and a nonproductive cough may also be present in some cases. Radiological evidence of pneumonia, with associated pleural effusion in some cases, may be present in all forms of tularemia, but is most common with typhoidal disease. The case-fatality rate with all forms of untreated typhoidal disease is approximately 35 percent.[61]

DIAGNOSIS AND MANAGEMENT

Diagnosis can be established by isolating the organism from blood, sputum, skin, or mucous membrane lesions, but it is difficult due to unusual growth requirements and overgrowth of commensal bacteria. Diagnosis of primary typhoidal tularemia is also difficult because signs and symptoms are nonspecific and frequently there is no suggestive exposure history. The diagnosis can best be established retrospectively by serologic testing.[62]

Streptomycin (30 mg/kg per day intramuscularly in two divided doses for 10–14 days) is the treatment of choice.[63] Gentamicin (3–5 mg/kg per day parenterally for 10–14 days) also is effective.[64] Tetracycline and chloramphenicol are effective as well but are associated with significant relapse rates.[65] Although laboratory-related infections with this organism are common, human-to-human spread is unusual and respiratory isolation is not required. A live attenuated tularemia vaccine is available as an Investigational New Drug (IND).[66]

60. Ibid.; Fred R. McCrumb, Jr., "Aerosol Infection of Man With *Pasteurella tularensis*," *Bacteriology Review*, Vol. 25 (1961), pp. 262–267; and Raymond P. Miller and Joseph H. Bates, "Pleuropulmonary tularemia," *American Review of Respiratory Diseases*, Vol. 99 (1969), pp. 31–41.

61. Evans and Friedlander, "Tularemia," pp. 503–512, 251–269.

62. Benenson, "Symposium on Q Fever," pp. 47–60; and Bell, Lackman, Meis, and Hadlow, "Recurrent Reaction at Site of Q Fever Vaccination," pp. 591–595.

63. R.L. Penn, "*Francisella tularensis* (Tularemia)," in G.A. Mandell, J.E. Bennett, and R. Dolen, ed., *Principles and Practices of Infectious Diseases* (New York: Churchill Livingstone, 1995), pp. 2060–2078.

64. Miller and Bates, "Pleuropulmonary tularemia," pp. 31–41; and William D. Sawyer, Harry G. Dangerfield, Al Hogge, and Dan Crozier, "Antibiotic Prophylaxis and Therapy of Airborne Tularemia," *Bacteriology Review*, Vol. 30 (1966), pp. 542–548.

65. Sawyer, Dangerfield, Hogge, and Crozier, "Antibiotic Prophylaxis and Therapy of Airborne Tularemia," pp. 542–548.

66. Donald S. Burke, "Immunization Against Tularemia," *Journal of Infectious Diseases*, Vol. 135 (1977), pp. 55–60.

Smallpox

After the last natural case of variola in Somalia in 1977, smallpox was declared eradicated in 1980 by the WHO.[67] Natural smallpox outbreaks were contained by rapid vaccination of contacts of the index cases, facilitated by the ease of vaccinia administration. There is no animal reservoir for variola; however, monkeys are susceptible to infection.[68] Although a laboratory accident prompted the consolidation of variola virus stocks into two WHO-approved repositories in the United States and Russia, the extent of clandestine stockpiles remains a matter of contention and concern.[69]

The aerosol infectivity, relatively high mortality, and stability of variola make it (and potentially monkeypox virus) a potential threat in BW and terrorism scenarios.[70] Although some have argued that smallpox would have limited potential as a biological weapon,[71] the discontinuation of routine vaccination has rendered civilian and military populations more susceptible to a disease that is infectious by aerosol and infamous for its devastating morbidity and mortality. In 1970, the WHO expressed concerns that smallpox "can easily be produced in large quantities in the laboratory and freeze-dried and its virulence thus preserved for months or years."[72] The theoretical potential that genetic recombination could produce a modified animal poxvirus with enhanced virulence for humans has raised the specter that other poxviruses besides smallpox might constitute serious BW or reemergent public health problems. Mass vaccination of civilian populations is now complicated by the increasing number of immunocompromised patients (e.g., those with human immunodeficiency virus infection, organ transplant, and chemotherapy).

---

67. I. Arita, "Virological Evidence for the Success of the Smallpox Eradication Programme," *Nature*, Vol. 279 (1979), pp. 293–298; and Frank Fenner, D.A. Henderson, I. Arita, Z. Jezek, and I.D. Ladnyi, *Smallpox and Its Eradication* (Geneva: WHO, 1988), p. 1341.

68. E.S. Horgan and M. Ali Haseeb, "Cross Immunity Experiments in Monkey Between Variola, Alastrim, and Vaccinia," *Journal of Hygiene*, Vol. 39 (1939), pp. 615–637.

69. *Report of the Investigation Into the Cause of the 1978 Birmingham Smallpox Occurrence* (London: Her Majesty's Stationery Office, 1980).

70. WHO, *Health Aspects of Chemical and Biological Weapons*, pp. 69–70; and G.J. Harper, "Airborne Microorganisms," *Journal of Hygiene*, Vol. 59 (1961), pp. 479–486.

71. Fenner, Henderson, Arita, Jezek, and Ladnyi, *Smallpox and Its Eradication*, p. 1341.

72. WHO, *Health Aspects of Chemical and Biological Weapons*, pp. 69–70.

CLINICAL FEATURES

After aerosol exposure, variola travels from the upper or lower respiratory tract to regional lymph nodes, where it replicates and gives rise to viremia followed soon thereafter by rash. During the prodrome before onset of pox lesions, variola virus can be recovered from the blood. The abrupt onset of clinical manifestations is marked by systemic toxicity with prominent malaise, fever, rigors, vomiting, headache, and backache; 15 percent of patients develop delirium. Approximately 10 percent of light-skinned patients exhibit an erythematous rash during this phase. Two to three days later, an enanthem appears concomitantly with a discrete rash about the face, hands, and forearms. The mucous membrane lesions shed infectious oropharyngeal secretions in the first few days of the eruptive illness.[73] These respiratory secretions are the most important but not the sole means of virus transmission to contacts. After eruptions on the lower extremities, the rash spreads centrally to the trunk over the next week. Lesions quickly progress from macules to papules and eventually to pustular vesicles. Lesions are more abundant on the extremities and face, and this centrifugal distribution is an important diagnostic feature. In distinct contrast to varicella, lesions on various segments of the body remain generally synchronous in their stage of development. In the second week after onset, the pustules form scabs that leave depressed depigmented scars on healing. Although variola titers in the throat, conjunctiva, and urine diminish with time,[74] virus can readily be recovered from scabs throughout convalescence.[75] Therefore, patients should be isolated and considered infectious until all scabs separate.

During this past century, the prototypical variola major disease caused mortality of 3 percent and 30 percent in the vaccinated and unvaccinated, respectively.[76] Other clinical forms associated with variola major, flat-type and hemorrhagic-type smallpox, were notable for severe mortality. A naturally occurring relative of variola, monkeypox, occurs in Africa and is clinically indistinguishable from smallpox except for a notable enlargement of cervical and inguinal lymph nodes. Secondary

73. A.W. Downie, L. St. Vincent, G. Meiklejohn, et al., "Studies on the Virus Content of Mouth Washings in the Acute Phase of Smallpox," *Bulletin of the WHO*, Vol. 25 (1961), pp. 49–53.

74. J.K. Sarkar, A.C. Mitra, M.K. Mukherjee, S.K. De, and D.G. Mazumdar, "Virus Excretion in Smallpox," *Bulletin of the WHO*, Vol. 48 (1973), pp. 517–522.

75. A.C. Mitra, J.K. Sarkar, and M.K. Mukherjee, "Virus Content of Smallpox Scabs," *Bulletin of the WHO*, Vol. 51 (1974), pp. 106–107.

76. Fenner, Henderson, Arita, Jezek, and Ladnyi, *Smallpox and Its Eradication*, p. 591.

bacterial pneumonia is associated with greater than 50 percent mortality.[77] Concern has been raised whether monkeypox could be weaponized like variola. Although previous evidence suggested that monkeypox had limited potential for person-to-person transmission,[78] recent reports indicate greater potential for sustained inter-human transmission,[79] perhaps owing to declining vaccinia immunity of the population.

DIAGNOSIS AND MANAGEMENT

Given the eradication of endemic smallpox, it requires an astute clinician to distinguish the *forme fruste* of this disease from other vesicular exanthems, such as chickenpox, erythema multiforme with bullae, or allergic contact dermatitis. Many exposed persons may shed virus from the oropharynx without ever manifesting disease. Some close contacts may harbor virus in their throats without developing disease and hence may serve as a means of secondary transmission.[80] Rapid and definitive diagnostic measures are urgently needed to provide effective quarantine and countermeasures to avert panic, anticipated to be a major consequence of smallpox virus release.

The appearance of characteristic virions on electron microscopy or Guarnieri bodies under light microscopy[81] is useful but does not discriminate variola from vaccinia, monkeypox, or cowpox. The traditional method of isolating virus on chorioallantoic membrane is antiquated. Polymerase chain reaction diagnostic techniques promise more accurate and less cumbersome methods of discriminating between variola and other orthopoxviruses.[82]

Clinicians must be prepared to recognize a vesicular exanthem and to initiate appropriate diagnostic confirmation and countermeasures. Any confirmed case of smallpox should be considered an international emer-

---

77. Zdenek Jezek, *Human Monkeypox* (Basel: S. Karger, 1988).

78. Zdenek Jezek and Frank Fenner, "Human Monkeypox," *Virology Monographs*, Vol. 17 (1988), pp. 93–95.

79. "Human Monkeypox—Kasai Oriental, Zaire," *Morbidity and Mortality Weekly Reports*, Vol. 46 (1997), pp. 304–307.

80. Sarkar, Mitra, Mukherjee, De, and Mazumdar, "Virus Excretion in Smallpox," pp. 523–527.

81. Shiro Kato, Michiaki Takahashi, Susumu Kameyama, and Juntaro Kamehora, "A Study on the Morphological and Cyto-Immunological Relationship Between the Inclusions of Variola, Cowpox, Rabbitpox, Vaccinia (Variola Origin) and Vaccinia IHD and Consideration of the Term 'Guarneri Body'," *Biken Journal*, Vol. 2 (1959), pp. 353–363.

82. Sofi M. Ibrahim, James J. Esposito, Peter B. Jahrling, and Richard S. Lofts, "The Potential of 5 Nuclease PCR for Detecting a Single-Base Polymorphism in Orthopoxviruses," *Molecular Cellular Probes*, Vol. 11 (1997), pp. 143–147.

gency with immediate report made to public health authorities. Strict quarantine with respiratory isolation should be applied for seventeen days to all persons in direct contact with the index case, especially the unvaccinated. Immediate vaccination should be undertaken for all persons exposed to either weaponized variola virus or a clinical case of smallpox. Nosocomial transmission of variola generally requires close person-to-person proximity, but there is a potential for airborne spread.[83] Patients with smallpox are infectious from the time of onset of their eruptive exanthem, most commonly from days three to six after onset of fever. Infectivity is markedly enhanced if the patient manifests a cough. Indirect transmission via contaminated bedding or other fomites is infrequent.[84]

Although the antiviral drug methisazone was licensed for the prophylaxis of susceptible contacts of smallpox in the 1960s,[85] its efficacy was controversial; gastrointestinal intolerance limited its use, and it is no longer available. To seek alternate therapeutic strategies, USAMRIID has evaluated a selection of newly developed antiviral drugs for efficacy against vaccinia, monkeypox, camelpox, cowpox, and smallpox (variola major and alastrim minor) viruses using a plaque reduction assay. The drugs were selected to target separately six different functions involved in poxvirus replication, including DNA polymerase activity. Five compounds had significant antiviral activity against variola virus and other poxviruses. From this screen, cidofovir emerged as the most broadly active, and has been evaluated further. Cidofovir (HPMPC, Vistide™) is a drug approved for the treatment of CMV in AIDS patients, and was the best of the DNA polymerase inhibitors tested against orthopoxvi-

---

83. G. Meiklejohn, C.H. Kempe, A.W. Downie, T.O. Berge, L. St. Vincent, and A.R. Rao, "Air Sampling to Recover Variola Virus in the Environment of a Smallpox Hospital," *Bulletin of the WHO*, Vol. 25 (1961), pp. 63–67; A.W. Downie, M. Meiklejohn, L. St. Vincent, A.R. Rao, B.V. Sundaro Babu, and C.H. Kempe, "The Recovery of Smallpox From Patients and Their Environment in a Smallpox Hospital," *Bulletin of the WHO*, Vol. 33 (1965), pp. 615–622; and P.F. Wehrle, J. Posch, K.H. Richter, et al., "An Airborne Outbreak of Smallpox in a German Hospital and Its Significance With Respect to Other Recent Outbreaks in Europe," *Bulletin of the WHO*, Vol. 43 (1970), pp. 669–679.

84. F.O. MacCallum and J.R. McDonald, "Survival of Variola Virus in Raw Cotton," *Bulletin of the WHO*, Vol. 16 (1957), pp. 247–254.

85. D.J. Bauer, Leone St. Vincent, C.H. Kempe, and A.W. Downie, "Prophylactic Treatment of Smallpox Contacts With N-Methylisatin-Thiosemicarbasone (Compound 33T57, Marboran)," *Lancet*, Vol. 2 (1963), pp. 494–496; and A.R. Rao, G.D.W. McKendrick, L. Velayudhan, and Kumari Kamalakshi, "Assessment of an Isothiazole Thiosemicarbazone in the Prophylaxis of Contacts of Variola Major," *Lancet*, Vol. 1 (1966), pp. 1072–1074.

ruses including vaccinia, monkeypox, camelpox, cowpox, and smallpox *in vitro.*

Cidofovir was further evaluated in an animal model of aerosolized orthopoxvirus infection using cynomolgus monkeys challenged with monkeypox virus by a fine particle aerosol. Treatment initiated on the day of infection provided complete protection from clinical and laboratory signs of disease, while placebo-treated monkeys developed classical poxvirus lesions and pulmonary distress, and death due to bronchopneumonia. When treatment initiation was delayed twenty-four hours, there were only mild signs of disease and no deaths in cidofovir-treated primates. There may be an opportunity to test cidofovir in the Democratic Republic of Congo, where endemic monkeypox virus activity in human populations may be continuing.

Of the commercial vaccines used during the WHO smallpox eradication campaign, only calf lymph vaccine (Dryvax, Wyeth-Ayerst) is still available in the United States. A replacement vaccine prepared in cell culture by the Department of Defense using more modern production techniques has been evaluated in human volunteers and is currently an IND product.[86] During the WHO smallpox eradication campaign,[87] vaccination with a verified clinical "take" within the past three years was considered solid immunity to smallpox. With longer intervals between vaccination and subsequent variola exposure, protection is reduced. Given the potential for breakthrough against partial immunity after high-dose aerosol exposure, routine revaccination of all potentially exposed individuals would seem prudent in a BW scenario. If vaccination is accomplished within a few days after exposure, protection is also possible,[88] approaching complete protection in those who have had their primary vaccination previously.[89] Both the Wyeth (Dryvax) and replacement vaccines have been demonstrated to protect monkeys against an aerosol exposure to monkeypox virus at an inhaled dose of 10,000 to 30,000 infectious units, a realistic simulation of a BW attack. Efforts are being

---

86.   David J. McClain, Shannon Harrison, Curtis L. Yeager, John Cruz, Francis A. Ennis, Paul Gibbs, Michael S. Wright, Peter L. Summers, James D. Arthur, and Jess A. Graham, "Immunological Responses to Vaccinia Vaccines Administered by Different Parenteral Routes," *Journal of Infectious Diseases,* Vol. 175 (1997), pp. 756–763.

87.   Fenner, Henderson, Arita, Jezek, and Ladnyi, *Smallpox and Its Eradication,* pp. 311–313.

88.   M.F. Dixon, "Smallpox Vaccination," *British Medical Journal,* Vol. 2, No. 708 (May 30, 1970), p. 539.

89.   D.A. Henderson, "Smallpox," in Kenneth Fuller Maxcy, Milton J. Rosenau, and P.E. Sartwell, eds., *Preventive Medicine and Public Health,* 10th ed. (New York: Appleton Century Crofts, 1973), pp. 104–116.

made to accelerate production of this replacement vaccine and add it to the national stockpile of countermeasures against terrorist threat agents.

Viral Encephalitides

Venezuelan, eastern, and western equine encephalitis viruses (VEE, EEE, and WEE, respectively) are members of the *Alphavirus* genus of the family Togaviridae. Several characteristics of the equine encephalitis viruses lend themselves to weaponization.[90] Although naturally transmitted by mosquitoes, the encephalitic alphaviruses are also highly infectious by aerosol.[91] These viruses can be produced in large amounts in inexpensive and unsophisticated systems, and are relatively stable during storage and manipulation. Readily available strains may produce incapacitating or lethal infection. The alphaviruses are also amenable to genetic manipulation by modern recombinant DNA technology. This capability may be used to develop safer and more effective vaccines.[92]

VEE has eleven distinct subtypes: IA, IB, and IC subtypes are pathogenic for horses and have the capacity for explosive epizootics with epidemic human disease. The enzootic strains (subtypes ID, IE, IF, II, III, IV, V, and VI) are not virulent for equines but have transmission cycles involving rodents and *Culex* mosquitoes of the genus *Melanoconion*.[93] Both EEE and WEE viruses are classified into two distinct geographic complexes.

The epidemiology of the equine encephalitides in humans is closely tied to the ecology of these viruses in naturally occurring endemic foci.[94] Evidence of widespread human VEE infections outside known endemic areas, in the absence of mosquito vectors or equine disease, should be

90. David L. Huxsoll, William C. Patrick, and Cheryl D. Parrott, "Veterinary Services in Biological Disasters," *Journal of the American Veterinary Medicine Association*, Vol. 190 (1987), pp. 714–722.

91. Jonathan Y. Richmond and Robert W. McKinney, *Biosafety in Microbiological and Biomedical Laboratories* (Washington, D.C.: U.S. Department of Health and Human Services [HHS], 1993), HHS Publication CDC 93–8395.

92. Nancy L. Davis, Nathaniel Powell, Gary F. Greenwald, et al., "Attenuating Mutations in the E2 Glycoprotein Gene of Venezuelan Equine Encephalitis Virus," *Virology*, Vol. 183 (1991), pp. 20–31.

93. N. Karabatsos, *International Catalogue of Arboviruses Including Certain Other Viruses of Vertebrates*, 3rd ed. (San Antonio: American Society for Tropical Medicine and Hygiene, 1985).

94. Karl M. Johnson and David H. Martin, "Venezuelan Equine Encephalitis," *Advances in Veterinary Science*, Vol. 18 (1974), p. 79.

viewed with suspicion and could indicate an unnatural release of virus into the environment.

CLINICAL FEATURES

The three equine encephalitis virus complexes within the *Alphavirus* genus are recognized for their potential for neuroinvasion and encephalitis in humans, sometimes in epidemic proportions. However, the majority of infections caused by these viruses are manifested as systemic, viral febrile syndromes consisting of fever, headache, and myalgia. Therefore, in a potential BW scenario, alphaviruses should be considered in the differential diagnosis whenever epidemic febrile illness occurs, especially with progression to neurological disease. Sick or dying equines in the vicinity of an epidemic febrile disease should also suggest the possibility of large-scale alphavirus exposure. These alphaviruses vary markedly in their neurological sequelae. Depending on the virus producing it, the general syndrome of alphavirus encephalitis presents with a varying combination of fever, headache, confusion, obtundation, dysphasia, seizures, paresis, ataxia, myoclonus, and cranial nerve palsies.

An important characteristic of VEE as a biological warfare weapon is that essentially all human infections are symptomatic.[95] Both epizootic and enzootic VEE strains cause similar disease syndromes. Patients develop a prostrating syndrome of chills, high fever (38°C to 40.5°C), headache, and malaise. Photophobia, sore throat, myalgia, and vomiting also are common symptoms. However, only a small percentage of VEE infections progress to neurological involvement (0.5 percent to 4 percent).[96] For those who survive encephalitic involvement of VEE, neurological recovery is usually complete.[97]

Clinical presentation of EEE and WEE infection is similar. Adults typically exhibit a febrile prodrome for up to eleven days before the onset of neurological disease.[98] Symptoms usually begin with malaise, head-

---

95. Peter T. Franck and Karl M. Johnson, "An Outbreak of Venezuelan Equine Encephalitis in Man in the Panama Canal Zone," *American Journal of Tropical Medicine and Hygiene*, Vol. 19 (1970), pp. 860–863.

96. David H. Martin, Gerald A. Eddy, Daniel W. Sudia, William C. Reeves, V.F. Newhouse, and Karl M. Johnson, "An Epidemiological Study of Venezuelan Equine Encephalomyelitis in Costa Rica," *American Journal of Epidemiology*, Vol. 95 (1972), pp. 565–578.

97. Carlos A. Leon, Raon Jaramillo, Soffy Martinez, et al., "Sequelae of Venezuelan Equine Encephalitis in Humans: A Four-Year Follow-up," *International Journal of Epidemiology*, Vol. 4 (1975), pp. 131–140.

98. Kenneth L. Hart, David Keen, and Edward A. Belle, "An Outbreak of Eastern Equine Encephalomyelitis in Jamaica, West Indies, November–December 1962: I. De-

ache, and fever, followed by nausea and vomiting. Viremia is detectable during this febrile prodrome.[99] Over the next few days, the symptoms intensify as somnolence or delirium may progress into coma. The magnitude of morbidity and mortality from aerosol exposure is unknown.

For all three equine encephalitis viruses, patients demonstrate leukopenia early during the course of their febrile illness, followed later by a leukocytosis. Elevated serum aspartate aminotransferase levels are common in VEE infections.

For those patients with central nervous system involvement, a lymphocytic pleocytosis with a cell count of up to $500 \times 10^6/L$ will be observed in the cerebrospinal fluid (CSF). Patients with EEE commonly have an elevated opening pressure after lumbar puncture, and in children especially, the CSF pleocytosis may reach a cell count of $2 \times 10^6/L$.[100]

Of the arboviral encephalitides, EEE is the most severe. High mortality rates and severe neurological sequelae are seen among patients with EEE infection.[101] Case-fatality rates are estimated at 50 percent to 75 percent, but asymptomatic infections and milder clinical illness are certainly underreported.[102] Up to 30 percent of survivors are left with neurological sequelae, such as seizures, spastic paralysis, and cranial neuropathies. Like VEE, WEE is less virulent for adult humans than it is for equines and children, with lower rates of fatalities and neurological sequelae.[103] As with EEE, infants and the elderly with WEE are especially susceptible to severe clinical illness and neurological sequelae, with case-fatality rates of about 10 percent. Some patients are left with permanent residua of motor weakness, cognitive deficits, or a seizure disorder, with children having a higher incidence of neurological sequelae in inverse proportion to their age.

scription of Human Cases," *American Journal of Tropical Medicine and Hygiene*, Vol. 13 (1964), pp. 331–334.

99. Delphine H. Clark, "Two Non-Fatal Human Infections With the Virus of Eastern Encephalitis," *American Journal of Tropical Medicine and Hygiene*, Vol. 10 (1961), pp. 67–70.

100. Robert L. Deresiewicz, Scott J. Thaler, Liangge L. Hsu, and Amir A. Zamani, "Clinical and Neuroradiographic Manifestations of Eastern Equine Encephalitis," *New England Journal of Medicine*, Vol. 336 (1997), pp. 1867–1874.

101. Roy F. Feemster, "Equine Encephalitis in Massachusetts," *New England Journal of Medicine*, Vol. 257 (1957), pp. 701–704.

102. Martin M. Goldfield, James N. Welsh, and Bernard F. Taylor, "The 1959 Outbreak of Eastern Encephalitis in New Jersey," *American Journal of Epidemiology*, Vol. 87 (1968), pp. 32–38.

103. R.O. Hayes, "Eastern and Western Encephalitis," in George W. Beran, ed., *Handbook Series in Zoonoses: Viral Zoonoses, I* (Boca Raton: CRC Press, 1981), pp. 29–57.

DIAGNOSIS AND MANAGEMENT

Specific diagnosis of alphavirus encephalitis can be accomplished by virus isolation or serologic testing.[104] During the first few days of nonspecific febrile illness, virus may be recovered from a patient's serum.[105] Isolates of VEE and WEE virus also have been recovered from throat washes of acutely ill patients. Although viremia is rarely detectable by the time patients present with encephalitic symptoms,[106] hemagglutination-inhibiting, ELISA, or plaque-reduction neutralization antibodies are generally present by the second week of illness.[107] In acute phase serum samples, IgM antibodies are present.[108] Identifying the VEE subtype of an isolate involved can be accomplished by cross-neutralization tests or nucleotide sequence analysis. Four-fold titer rises in convalescent serum samples or isolation of virus are considered diagnostic, but because of serological cross reactions with other alphaviruses, neutralization tests are preferred. Virus may occasionally be isolated from CSF in encephalitis cases and is frequently recovered from postmortem brain tissue of infected patients.

No specific therapy exists for the alphavirus encephalitides, and hence treatment is aimed at management of specific symptoms (e.g., anticonvulsant medication or protection of the airway). A special problem occasionally seen among patients infected by WEE virus is an extremely high fever, which may require aggressive antihyperthermia measures. Experience with both humans[109] and animals indicate that treatment with virus-neutralizing antisera fails to halt progression of disease if brain infection is firmly established. Defense against alphavirus infection, beyond respiratory protection with a high-efficiency particle filter, depends on immunization. Although the requisites for protection against paren-

104. A.L. Rossi Briceño, "Rural Epidemic Encephalitis in Venezuela Caused by a Group A Arbovirus (VEE)," in Joseph L. Melnick, ed., *Progress in Medical Virology, IX* (Basel: S. Karger AG, 1967), pp. 176–203.

105. A.L. Rossi Briceño, "The Frequency of VEE Virus in the Pharyngeal Material of Clinical Cases of Encephalitis," *Gacetta Medicina Caracas*, Vol. 72 (1964), pp. 5–22.

106. Alan R. Hinman, John E. McGowan, and Brian E. Henderson, "Venezuelan Equine Encephalomyelitis," *American Journal of Epidemiology*, Vol. 93 (1971), pp. 130–136.

107. Charles H. Calisher and N. Karabatsos, "Arbovirus Serogroups: Definition and Geographic Distribution," in Thomas P. Monath, ed., *The Arboviruses: Epidemiology and Ecology, I* (Boca Raton: CRC Press, 1988), pp. 19–57.

108. Charles H. Calisher, Ahmed O. El-Kaffawi, Mohammed I. Al-Deen et al., "Complex Specific Immunoglobulin M Antibody Patterns in Humans Infected With Alphaviruses," *Journal of Clinical Microbiology*, Vol. 23 (1986), pp. 155–159.

109. Herman Gold and Bettylee Hampil, "Equine Encephalomyelitis in a Laboratory Technician With Recovery," *Annals of Internal Medicine*, Vol. 16 (1942), pp. 556–569.

teral infection with equine encephalitis viruses are well described,[110] the requirements for protection against infectious aerosols as would be encountered in a BW scenario are certainly more stringent. Although immunity to the homologous serotype after VEE infection is probably lifelong, cross-immunity to heterologous serotypes is weak or nonexistent, and adequate immunization may require polyvalent vaccines. A live attenuated vaccine for VEE (TC-83) has largely eliminated homologous VEE strain infections among at-risk laboratory personnel.[111] However, the TC-83 vaccine is reactogenic, as more than 20 percent of vaccine recipients experience fever, malaise, and headache after vaccination, with half of these severe enough to warrant bed rest for one to two days. Investigational formalin-inactivated vaccines for humans exist for VEE, WEE, and EEE but require multiple injections and are poorly immunogenic. In view of these shortcomings, live attenuated, genetically engineered vaccines have been developed by site-directed mutagenesis of various alphaviruses and show excellent promise with regards to safety and immunogenicity.[112]

Viral Hemorrhagic Fevers

The viral hemorrhagic fever (VHF) syndrome is a useful clinical concept that describes the disease processes associated with infection by a variety of RNA viruses. Viral hemorrhagic fever syndrome is an acute febrile illness characterized by malaise, prostration, generalized signs of vascular permeability, and abnormalities of circulatory regulation. Life-threatening loss of blood volume is rare, although bleeding manifestations often occur as a result of damage to the vascular endothelium. Despite their diverse taxonomy, the VHF agents are all RNA viruses and are typically transmitted to humans by contact with infected animal reservoirs or arthropod vectors whose distributions determine in part the geographic ranges of

110. Ann R. Hunt and John T. Roerhrig, "Biochemical and Biological Characteristics of Epitopes on the E1 Glycoprotein of Western Equine Encephalitis Virus," *Virology*, Vol. 142 (1985), pp. 334–336; and James H. Mathews and John T. Roerhrig, "Determination of the Protective Epitopes on the Glycoproteins of Venezuelan Equine Encephalomyelitis Virus by Passive Transfer of Monoclonal Antibodies," *Journal of Immunology*, Vol. 129 (1982), pp. 2763–2767.

111. Robert W. McKinney, Trygve O. Berge, William D. Sawyer, William D. Tigertt, and Dan Crozier, "Use of an Attenuated Strain of Venezuelan Equine Encephalomyelitis Virus for Immunization in Man," *American Journal of Tropical Medicine and Hygiene*, Vol. 12 (1963), pp. 597–603.

112. Davis, Powell, Greenwald et al., "Attenuating Mutations in the E2 Glycoprotein Gene of Venezuelan Encephalitis Virus," pp. 20–31.

these diseases. Recent changes in human demographics have increased human exposures to these viruses. In addition to natural disease potential, many of the VHF agents are potential BW threats as well. These viruses are highly infectious by aerosol; are associated with high morbidity and, in some cases, high mortality; and may replicate sufficiently well in cell culture to permit weaponization.

Viruses from the Arenaviridae, Bunyaviridae, Filoviridae, and Flaviviridae families are associated with VHF. The Arenaviridae includes the viruses of Lassa fever (Lassa virus),[113] and Argentine, Bolivian, Venezuelan, and Brazilian hemorrhagic fevers (Junin,[114] Machupo,[115] Guanarito,[116] and Sabia[117] viruses, respectively). Among the Bunyaviridae, the significant human pathogens include Rift Valley fever (RVF) virus, which is the causative agent of a major disease in Africa frequently associated with unusual increases in mosquito populations.[118] Congo-Crimean hemorrhagic fever (CCHF) virus is carried by ticks and has been associated with sporadic, yet particularly severe, VHF in Europe, Africa, and Asia.[119] It has frequently been associated with small, hospital-centered outbreaks. Hantaviruses, unlike other Bunyaviridae, are not transmitted by infected arthropods; rather, they infect humans by contact with infected rodents and their excreta. Hantaviruses are significant infectious disease threats to both military and civilian populations.[120] How-

113. Joseph B. McCormick, Patricia A. Webb, John W. Krebs, Karl M. Johnson, and Ethleen A. Smith, "A Prospective Study of Epidemiology and Ecology of Lassa Fever," *Journal of Infectious Diseases*, Vol. 155 (1987), pp. 437–444.

114. Julio Maiztegui, M. Feuillade, and A. Briggilera, "Progressive Extension of the Endemic Area and Changing Incidence of Argentine Hemorrhagic Fever," *Medical Microbiology and Immunology*, Vol. 175 (1986), pp. 149–152.

115. Karl M. Johnson, N.H. Wiebenga, Robert B. Mackenzie, et al., "Virus Isolations From Human Cases of Hemorrhagic Fever in Bolivia," *Proceedings of the Society of Experimental Medicine*, Vol. 155 (1965), pp. 113–118.

116. Rosalba Salas, Nuris De Manzione, Robert B. Tesh, et al., "Venezuelan Haemorrhagic Fever," *Lancet*, Vol. 338 (1991), pp. 1033–1036.

117. Terezinha L.M. Coimbra, Elza S. Nassar, Marcelo N. Buratini, et al., "New Arenavirus Isolated in Brazil," *Lancet*, Vol. 343 (1994), pp. 391–392.

118. Bernard C. Easterday, "Rift Valley Fever," *Advances in Veterinary Science*, Vol. 10 (1965), pp. 65–127.

119. P.J. van Eden, S.F. van Eden, J.R. Joubert, J.B. King, B.W. van de Wal, and W.L. Mitchell, "A Nosocomial Outbreak of Crimean Congo Hemorrhagic Fever at Tygerberg Hospital," *South African Medical Journal*, Vol. 68 (1985), pp. 718–721.

120. H.W. Lee, "Hemorrhagic Fever With Renal Syndrome in Korea," *Review of Infectious Diseases*, Vol. 11 (1989), pp. S864–S876; and Jay C. Butler and Clarence J.

ever, hantaviruses replicate poorly in cell culture and are not considered to be significant BW threats; thus, they are not discussed further here.

Another VHF group with biological warfare potential is the Filoviridae, which includes the agents of Ebola hemorrhagic fever and Marburg disease. Filoviruses have gained notoriety through their association with explosive, although limited, outbreaks. The original Marburg virus outbreak in 1967 was associated with thirty-one cases and nine deaths.[121] Ebola was first recognized in association with two explosive outbreaks that occurred almost simultaneously in 1976. The original outbreaks of Ebola in Zaire[122] and Sudan[123] in 1976 were associated with mortality rates of 92 percent and 53 percent, respectively. In both cases, transmission was exacerbated through reuse of unsterilized needles and syringes and nosocomial contacts.

The flavivirus yellow fever is another VHF virus.[124] Despite its high aerosol infectivity, widespread use and availability of licensed vaccines limit the concern regarding its potential as a BW threat.

CLINICAL FEATURES

The dominant clinical features of VHF are usually a consequence of microvascular damage and changes in vascular permeability.[125] Common presenting complaints are fever, myalgia, and prostration. Initial clinical examination may reveal only conjunctival injection, mild hypotension, flushing, and petechial hemorrhages. Full-blown VHF typically evolves to shock and generalized mucous membrane hemorrhage and often is accompanied by evidence of neurological, hematopoietic, or pulmonary involvement. Hepatic involvement is common, but clinical jaundice is a

---

Peters, "Hantaviruses and Hantavirus Pulmonary Syndrome," *Clinical Journal of Infectious Diseases*, Vol. 19 (1994), pp. 387–395.

121. C.A. Martini and R. Siegert, eds., *Marburg Virus Disease* (New York: Springer-Verlag, 1971).

122. WHO Study Team, "Ebola Haemorrhagic Fever in Zaire, 1976," *Bulletin of the WHO*, Vol. 56 (1978), pp. 271–293.

123. WHO International Study Team, "Ebola Haemorrhagic Fever in Sudan, 1976," *Bulletin of the WHO*, Vol. 56 (1978), pp. 247–270.

124. Thomas P. Monath, "Yellow Fever: Epidemics and Search in the Last Forty Years and Prospects for the Future," *American Journal of Tropical Medicine and Hygiene*, Vol. 45 (1991), pp. 1–43.

125. Clarence J. Peters, Edward D. Johnson, and Kelly T. McKee, "Filoviruses and Management of Viral Hemorrhagic Fever," in Robert B. Belshe, ed., *Textbook of Human Virology*, 2nd ed. (St. Louis: Mosby Year Book, 1991), pp. 699–712.

regular event only with yellow fever. Renal failure is proportional to cardiovascular compromise.[126]

Although all VHF cases share common features, certain clinical characteristics predominate and serve to distinguish among the causative agents. For example, hemorrhagic manifestations are not pronounced for Lassa fever patients, and neurological complications are infrequent. For the South American arenaviruses (Junin and Machupo), neurological and hemorrhagic manifestations are much more prominent. For RVF, hemorrhagic fever is seen in only a small proportion of the cases, as this virus is primarily hepatotropic. Unlike other VHFs, retinitis is a frequently reported component of RVF disease.[127] In contrast, hemorrhagic manifestations are predominant with CCHF infection, which causes a profound disseminated intravascular coagulation (DIC). Marburg and Ebola viruses produce prominent maculopapular rashes, and DIC is a major factor in their pathogenesis.

DIAGNOSIS AND MANAGEMENT

Viral hemorrhagic fever should be suspected in any patient presenting with a severe febrile illness and evidence of vascular involvement who has traveled to an area where the virus is known to occur or when a BW threat is suspected.

Definitive diagnosis in an individual case requires specific virologic diagnosis.[128] Most patients will present with viremia that can be detected by antigen-capture ELISA or reverse transcriptase polymerase chain reaction (RT-PCR). Likewise, early IgM antibody responses to these agents can be detected by ELISA, often during the acute illness. Definitive virus isolation takes longer and requires specialized analysis in a biocontainment laboratory (BSL 3 or BSL 4). When the identity of the VHF agent is totally unknown, isolation in cell culture and direct visualization by electron microscopy followed by immunological identification by immunohistological techniques is often successful. Immunohistological techniques are also useful for retrospective diagnosis of formalin-fixed tissues.

Patients with VHF generally benefit from rapid, nontraumatic hospitalization to prevent unnecessary damage to the fragile capillary bed. Secondary infections are common and should be sought and treated aggressively. Intravenous lines, catheters, and other invasive techniques should be avoided unless clearly indicated in management. The manage-

---

126. Ibid.

127. Ibid.

128. Peter B. Jahrling, "Filoviruses and Arenaviruses," in Murray, Baron, Pfaller, Tenover, and Yolken, *Manual of Clinical Microbiology*, 6th ed., pp. 1068–1081.

ment of bleeding is controversial. In the absence of definitive evidence, it is recommended that mild bleeding manifestations not be treated at all.[129] More severe hemorrhage indicates a need for appropriate replacement therapy. When definite laboratory evidence of DIC develops, heparin therapy should be used if appropriate laboratory control is available.

Management of hypotension and shock is difficult. Patients often are modestly dehydrated, and there are covert losses of intravascular volume through hemorrhage and increased vascular permeability. Nevertheless, these patients often respond poorly to fluid infusions and readily develop pulmonary edema. The diffuse nature of the vascular process may lead to a requirement for support of several organ systems.

Ribavirin, a non-immunosuppressive nucleoside analogue with broad antiviral properties,[130] is of proven value for some of the VHF agents. Ribavirin has been shown to reduce mortality from Lassa fever in high-risk patients[131] and presumably decreases morbidity in all Lassa patients. Treatment is most effective if begun within seven days of onset. In Argentina, ribavirin has been shown to reduce virologic parameters of Junin infection and is now used routinely as an adjunct to immune plasma.[132] Small studies of ribavirin in treatment of Bolivian hemorrhagic fever (BHF) and CCHF have been promising, as have preclinical studies for RVF.[133] Conversely, preclinical studies predict ribavirin will be ineffective against both the filoviruses and the flaviviruses. No other antiviral compounds are currently available for these infections, although for Ebola virus, there are some promising leads. Ebola viral replication is inhibited *in vitro* by a series of nucleoside analogue inhibitors of s-adenosylhomocysteine hydrolase (SAH), an important target for drug development. Treatment of Ebola-infected mice with the lead SAH compound prevents

---

129.   Peters, Johnson, and McKee, "Filoviruses and Management of Viral Hemorrhagic Fever," pp. 699–712.

130.   Peter G. Canonico, Meier Kende, and Bruno J. Luscri, et al., "In-vivo Activity of Antivirals Against Exotic RNA Viral Infections," *Journal of Antimicrobial Chemotherapy*, Vol. 14, Supplement (1984), pp. 27–41.

131.   James B. McCormick, L.J. King, Patricia A. Webb, et al., "Lassa Fever: Effective Therapy With Ribavirin," *New England Journal of Medicine*, Vol. 314 (1986), pp. 20–26; John W. Huggins, "Prospects for Treatment of Viral Hemorrhagic Fevers With Ribavirin, A Broad-Spectrum Antiviral Drug," *Review of Infectious Diseases*, Vol. 11 (1989), pp. S750–S761; and Centers for Disease Control (CDC), "Management of Patients With Suspected Viral Hemorrhagic Fever," *Morbidity and Mortality Weekly Report*, Vol. 37, Supplement (1988), pp. 1–16.

132.   Delia Enria and Julio I. Maiztegui, "Antiviral Treatment of Argentine Hemorrhagic Fever," *Antiviral Research*, Vol. 23 (1994), pp. 23–31.

133.   Huggins, "Prospects for Treatment With Ribavirin," pp. S750–S761.

illness and death, when initiated within several days of infection;[134] experimental studies with primates are in progress.

Argentine hemorrhagic fever (AHF) responds to therapy with two or more units of convalescent plasma containing adequate amounts of neutralizing antibody, provided that treatment is initiated within eight days of onset.[135] Antibody therapy is also beneficial for treating BHF. Efficacy of immune plasma in treatment of Lassa fever[136] and CCHF[137] is limited by low neutralizing antibody titers and the consequent need for careful donor selection. Equine immune globulin against Ebola virus has been proposed for treating this infection, but data obtained from experimentally infected monkeys do not support this recommendation.[138]

A licensed and highly efficacious vaccine for yellow fever is widely available. For AHF, a live attenuated Junin vaccine strain is available as an IND. This vaccine may also provide some cross-protection against BHF. Two IND vaccines for RVF were developed by researchers in the U.S. Army Medical Research and Materiel Command (MRMC): an inactivated vaccine that requires three boosters has been in use for over thirty years;[139] and a live attenuated RVF strain (MP-12) was produced at USAMRIID and has satisfactorily passed phase 2 efficacy testing.[140]

There are no candidate vaccines available for the filoviruses that are yet approved for human use as IND products. However, several promis-

---

134. John Huggins, Zhen-Xi Zhang, and Mike Bray, "Antiviral Drug Therapy of Filovirus Infections: S-adenosylhomocysteine Hydrolase Inhibitors Inhibit Ebola Virus in Vitro and in a Lethal Mouse Model," *Journal of Infectious Diseases,* Supplement (1998).

135. Delia Enria, Nestor Fernandez, Ana J. Briggiler, et al., "Importance of Neutralizing Antibodies in Treatment of Argentine Haemorrhagic Fever With Immune Plasma," *Lancet,* Vol. 4 (1984), pp. 255–256.

136. Peter B. Jahrling, J.D. Frame, Joan B. Rhoderick, and M.H. Monson, "Endemic Lassa Fever in Liberia," *Transactions of the Royal Society for Tropical Medicine and Hygiene,* Vol. 79 (1985), pp. 380–384.

137. A.J. Sheperd, R. Swanepoel, and P.A. Leman, "Antibody Response in Crimean Congo Hemorrhagic Fever," *Review of Infectious Diseases,* Vol. 11 (1989), pp. S801-S806.

138. Peter B. Jahrling, Joan Geisbert, James Swearingen, et al., "Passive Immunization of Ebola Virus-Infected Cynomulgus Monkeys With Immunoglobulin From Hyperimmune Horses," *Archives of Virology,* Supplement 11 (1996), pp. 135–140.

139. Raymond Randall, C.J. Gibbs, C.G. Aulisio, L.N. Binn, and V.R. Harrison, "The Development of a Formalin-Killed Rift Valley Fever Virus Vaccine for Use in Man," *Journal of Immunology,* Vol. 89 (1962), pp. 660–670.

140. G.F. Meadors III, P.H. Gibbs, and C.J. Peters, "Evaluation of a New Rift Valley Fever Vaccine: Safety and Immunogenicity Trials," *Vaccine,* Vol. 4 (1986), pp. 179–184.

ing vaccine strategies are being pursued with success in animal models, including baculovirus recombinant viral proteins and expression of structural protein genes by either naked DNA immunization or suitable presentation vectors, including vaccinia[141] and alphavirus replicons.[142] For Marburg virus, the alphavirus replicon has successfully protected monkeys against challenge, and is the most promising candidate filovirus vaccine to date.

Botulinum Toxins

Botulinum toxins are proteins of approximately 150,000 molecular weight and are produced by the anaerobic bacterium *Clostridium botulinum*. There are seven distinct but related neurotoxins, A through G, produced by different strains of the clostridial bacillus. All seven types act by a similar mechanism and induce similar effects when inhaled or ingested. Botulinum toxins have caused numerous cases of botulism when improperly prepared or canned foods are ingested. Many deaths have occurred after such incidents. It is feasible to deliver botulinum toxins as a biological weapon, and several countries have weaponized or are suspected to have weaponized one or more of this group of toxins.[143] Iraq admitted to a UN inspection team in August 1991 that it had performed research on the offensive use of botulinum toxins before the Persian Gulf War. Additional information given in 1995 revealed that Iraq had not only researched but had filled and deployed over one hundred munitions containing botulinum toxin. Although an aerosol attack is by far the most likely scenario for the use of botulinum toxins, the agent could theoretically be used to sabotage food supplies.

---

141. K.J. Gilligan, J.B. Geisbert, P.B. Jahrling, and K. Anderson, "Assessment of Protective Immunity Conferred by Recombinant Vaccinia Viruses to Guinea Pigs Challenged with Ebola Virus," in F. Brown, D. Burton, P. Doherty, J. Mekalanos, and E. Norrby, eds., *Vaccines 97* (Cold Spring Harbor, N.Y.: Cold Spring Harbor Press, 1997), pp. 87–92.

142. P. Pushko, M. Parker, J. Geisbert, D. Negley, A. Schmaljohn, P.B. Jahrling, A. Sanchez, and J.F. Smith, "Packaged RNA Replicon of Venezuelan Equine Encephalitis Virus (VEE) as a Vaccine Vector: Immunogenicity and Protection Studies with Ebola NP and GP Genes," in Brown, Burton, Doherty, Mekalanos, and Norrby, *Vaccines 97*, pp. 253–258.

143. R.C. Cochrane, "Biological Warfare Research in the United States," in *History of the Chemical Warfare Service in World War II*, Vol. II (Frederick, Md.: Historical Section, Plans, Training and Intelligence Division, U.S. Department of the Army, 1947).

CLINICAL FEATURES

Botulinum toxins are the most toxic compounds known, with an estimated toxic dose (serotype A) of only 0.001 pg/kg of body weight.[144] Botulinum toxin is 15,000 times more toxic than the nerve agent VX and 100,000 times more toxic than sarin.

Botulinum toxins act by binding to the presynaptic nerve terminal at the neuromuscular junction and at cholinergic autonomic sites.[145] The toxins then act to prevent the release of acetylcholine presynaptically, and thus block neurotransmission. This interruption of neurotransmission causes both bulbar palsies and the skeletal muscle weakness seen in clinical botulism.

The onset of signs of inhalation botulism is dose dependent and may vary from between twenty-four to thirty-six hours to several days after exposure.[146] Bulbar palsies are prominent early, with ocular symptoms, such as blurred vision due to mydriasis, diplopia, ptosis, and photophobia, in addition to other bulbar signs such as dysarthria, dysphonia, and dysphagia. Skeletal muscle paralysis follows, manifested as a symmetrical, descending, and progressive weakness which may culminate abruptly in respiratory failure. Progression from onset of symptoms to respiratory failure has occurred in as few as twenty-four hours in cases of foodborne botulism.

Physical examination usually reveals an alert and oriented patient without fever. Postural hypotension may be present. Mucous membranes may be dry and crusted, and the patient may complain of dry mouth or even sore throat. Gag reflex may be absent. Pupils may be dilated and even fixed. Ptosis and extraocular muscle palsies are commonly observed. Variable degrees of skeletal muscle weakness occur, depending on progression of intoxication in an individual patient. Deep tendon reflexes may be present or absent. With severe respiratory muscle paralysis, the patient may become cyanotic or exhibit narcosis from carbon dioxide retention.

---

144. D.M. Gill, "Bacterial Toxins: A Table of Lethal Amounts," *Microbiology Review* (March 1982), pp. 86–94.

145. Lance L. Simpson, "Peripheral Actions of the Botulinum Toxins," in Lance L. Simpson, ed., *Botulinum Neurotoxins and Tetanus Toxin* (New York: Academic Press, 1989), pp. 153–178.

146. David R. Franz, Louise M. Pitt, M.A. Clayton, Martha A. Hanes, and Kenneth J. Rose, "Efficacy of Prophylactic and Therapeutic Administration of Antitoxin for Inhalation Botulism," in Bibhuti R. Das Gupta, ed., *Botulinum and Tetanus Neurotoxins and Biomedical Aspects* (New York: Plenum, 1993), pp. 473–475; and John L. Middlebrook, "Contributions of the U.S. Army to Botulinum Toxin Research," in ibid., pp. 515–519.

DIAGNOSIS AND MANAGEMENT

The occurrence of an epidemic of cases of a descending and progressive bulbar and skeletal paralysis in afebrile patients typical of classical botulism points to the diagnosis of botulinum intoxication. Individual cases might be confused clinically with other neuromuscular disorders such as Guillain-Barre syndrome, myasthenia gravis, or tick paralysis. The edrophonium (or Tensilon) test may be transiently positive in botulism, so it may not distinguish botulinum intoxication from myasthenia.

Laboratory tests are generally of limited value in the diagnosis of botulism. Studies suggest that inhaled toxin is usually not identifiable in serum or stool, whereas it is with foodborne botulism.[147] Survivors do not usually develop an antibody response due to the subimmunogenic amount of toxin necessary to produce clinical symptoms. Toxin may be present on nasal mucous membranes and detectable by ELISA for twenty-four hours after inhalation.

Respiratory failure secondary to paralysis of respiratory muscles is the most serious complication and, generally, the cause of death. With tracheostomy or endotracheal intubation and ventilatory assistance, fatalities should be less than 5 percent.[148] Intensive and prolonged nursing care may be required for recovery, which may take several weeks or even months.

Animal experiments show that after aerosol exposure, botulinum antitoxin can be very effective, precluding all signs of intoxication if given before the onset of clinical signs.[149] Administration of antitoxin is reasonable if disease has not progressed to a stable state. A trivalent equine antitoxin is available from the CDC for cases of foodborne botulism. Adverse effects of this antitoxin include the risks of anaphylaxis and serum sickness. A "despeciated" [F(ab')2] equine heptavalent antitoxin (against types A through G) has been prepared by the U.S. Army. This product is under IND status. Its efficacy in humans is not yet known.[150] Use of either antitoxin requires skin testing for horse serum sensitivity before administration.

Immunized laboratory animals are fully protected from lethal inha-

147.   Abram S. Benenson, *Control of Communicable Diseases in Man*, 15th ed. (Washington, D.C.: American Public Health Association, 1990), pp. 61–66.

148.   M.M. Salmon, B. Howells, E.J.G. Glencross, et al. "Q Fever in an Endemic Area," *Lancet* (1982), pp. 1002–1004.

149.   Franz, Pitt, Clayton, Hanes, and Rose, "Efficacy of Prophylactic and Therapeutic Administration of Antitoxin," pp. 473–476.

150.   Ibid.

lation challenges with serotype A toxin.[151] A pentavalent toxoid of *C. botulinum* toxin types A through E is available under IND status.[152] Recombinant botulinum neurotoxin (rBoNT) fragments are being produced and studied for use as vaccine candidates which will protect against intoxication from botulinum neurotoxins. Non-toxic recombinant fragments composed of the carboxyl terminal (Hc) portion of botulinum heavy chains from several serotypes have been shown to be effective antigens at eliciting protective immunity against active botulinum toxin.

Staphylococcal Enterotoxin B

Staphylococcus aureus produces a number of exotoxins, one of which is SEB. The toxins are referred to as exotoxins because they are excreted from the organism; however, they normally exert their effects on the gastrointestinal tract and therefore are called enterotoxins. SEB is one of the heat-stable pyrogenic toxins that commonly cause food poisoning in humans after the toxin is produced in improperly handled foodstuffs and subsequently ingested. Because of its extreme toxicity as an incapacitant, inhalation exposure to this toxin could render a high percentage of exposed personnel clinically ill, requiring medical care beginning a few hours after exposure. SEB is relatively stable in aerosols. It causes symptoms when inhaled at very low doses in humans; an inhaled dose perhaps one-hundred- to one-thousand-fold lower than the estimated lethal dose would be sufficient to incapacitate individuals so exposed. Even though SEB is not generally thought of as a highly lethal agent, it can kill, and may incapacitate humans many miles downwind from the release point of a weapon. This toxin could also be used, theoretically, in a Special Forces or terrorist mode to sabotage food or small volume water supplies.

CLINICAL FEATURES

Inhaled SEB can induce extensive pathophysiological changes, including widespread systemic damage and even septic shock. Many of the effects of this family of toxins are mediated by interactions with the host's own immune system. The mechanisms of toxicity are complex, but are related to the toxin binding directly to the major histocompatibility complex and subsequent stimulation of the proliferation of large numbers of T cells.[153]

151. J.E. Brown, written communication, July 1997.

152. Middlebrook, "Contributions of the U.S. Army to Botulinum Toxin Research," pp. 515–519.

153. John D. Fraser, "High-Affinity Binding of Staphylococcal Enterotoxins A and B to HLA-DR," *Nature*, Vol. 339 (1989), pp. 221–223; Joseph A. Mollick, Richard G. Cook,

Because these exotoxins are extremely potent activators of T cells, they are commonly referred to as bacterial superantigens. These superantigens stimulate the production and secretion of various cytokines from immune system cells.[154] Released cytokines are thought to mediate most of the toxic effects of SEB.

Inhalation exposure is projected to cause primarily clinical illness and incapacitation; however, intoxications can be lethal. Intoxication with SEB begins three to twelve hours after inhalation of the toxin. Those exposed may experience the sudden onset of fever, headache, chills, myalgia, and a nonproductive cough. More severe cases may develop dyspnea and retrosternal chest pain. Nausea, vomiting, and diarrhea will also occur in many patients due to inadvertently swallowed toxin, and fluid losses can be marked. The fever may last up to five days and range from 39.4°C to 41.1°C, with variable degrees of chills and prostration. The cough may persist up to four weeks, and patients may not return to normal function for two weeks.

Physical examination of patients with SEB intoxication is often unremarkable. Conjunctival injection may be present, and postural hypotension may develop due to fluid losses. Chest examination is unremarkable except in the unusual case where pulmonary edema develops. The chest x-ray film is also generally normal, but in severe cases, increased interstitial markings, atelectasis, and possibly overt pulmonary edema or an adult respiratory distress syndrome may develop.

DIAGNOSIS AND MANAGEMENT

As is the case with botulinum toxins, intoxication caused by SEB inhalation is a clinical and epidemiologic diagnosis. Because the symptoms of SEB intoxication may be similar to the symptoms triggered by several respiratory pathogens such as influenza, adenovirus, and mycoplasma, the diagnosis may be unclear initially. All of these might present with fever, nonproductive cough, myalgia, and headache. An SEB attack would cause patients to present in large numbers over a very short period of time, probably within twenty-four hours, in contrast with naturally occurring pneumonias or influenza with patients presenting over a more prolonged interval. Staphylococcal food poisoning cases would not pre-

and Robert R. Rich, "Class II MHC Molecules Are Specific Receptors for Staphylococcal Enterotoxin A," *Science,* Vol. 244 (1989), pp. 817–820; and John Kappler, Brian Kotzin, Lynne Herron et al., "Vß-specific Stimulation of Human T Cells by Staphylococcal Toxins," *Science,* Vol. 244 (1989), pp. 811–813.

154. Bradley G. Stiles, Sina Bavari, Theresa Krakauer, and Robert G. Ulrich, "Toxicity of Staphylococcal Enterotoxins Potentiated by Lipopolysaccharide," *Infection and Immunity,* Vol. 61 (1993), pp. 5333–5338.

sent with pulmonary symptoms. Intoxication with SEB tends to progress rapidly to a fairly stable clinical state, whereas pulmonary anthrax, tularemia pneumonia, or pneumonic plague would all progress if left untreated. Tularemia and plague, as well as Q fever, would be associated with infiltrates on chest radiographs, unlike SEB. Nerve agent intoxication would cause fasciculations and copious secretions, and sulfur mustard would cause skin lesions in addition to pulmonary findings. The dyspnea resulting from botulinum intoxication is associated with obvious signs of muscular paralysis, bulbar palsies, lack of fever, and a dry pulmonary tree due to cholinergic blockade. Respiratory difficulties occur late with botulism; in contrast, they occur early with SEB inhalation.

Laboratory findings are not very helpful in the diagnosis of SEB intoxication. A nonspecific neutrophilic leukocytosis and an elevated erythrocyte sedimentation rate may be seen twelve to twenty-four hours after exposure, but these abnormalities are present in many illnesses. Toxin is very difficult to detect in the serum by the time symptoms occur. Data from animal studies show that SEB in the serum is transient; however, SEB or its antigenic metabolites accumulate in the urine and can be detected for several hours postexposure.[155] Therefore, urine samples also should be obtained and tested. Because most patients will develop a significant antibody response to the toxin, acute and convalescent serum that may be helpful retrospectively in the diagnosis should be drawn. ELISA may identify the toxin in nasal swabs taken within twenty-four hours after aerosol exposure.

Currently, therapy is limited to supportive care. Close attention to oxygenation and hydration is important, and in severe cases with pulmonary edema, ventilation with positive end-expiratory pressure and diuretics might be necessary. The value of steroids is controversial. Most patients would be expected to recover after the initial acute phase of their illness, and most would generally return to normal function in one to two weeks.

Although there is currently no human vaccine for immunization against SEB intoxication, several vaccine candidates are in development. Preliminary animal studies have been encouraging and vaccine candidates for both SEB and staphylococcal enterotoxin A, a related toxin, are nearing safety and immunogenicity testing in humans.[156] Experimentally,

---

155. C.T. Liu, USAMRIID, unpublished data, February 1995.

156. Sina Bavari, Mark A. Olson, and Robert G. Ulrich, "Engineered Bacterial Superantigen Vaccines," in F. Brown, E. Norrby, D. Burton, and K. Mekalanos, eds., *Vaccines 96* (Cold Spring Harbor, N.Y.: Cold Spring Harbor Press, 1996), pp. 135–141.

passive immunotherapy can reduce mortality in animal models, but only when given within four to eight hours after inhaling SEB.[157]

The Epidemiology of a BW or Terrorist Attack

Although the likelihood of a biological attack is unknown, and significant defensive preparations are under way, many believe the United States is vulnerable. This is especially true of civilian populations, who often do not have protective equipment or vaccines made available to them. The unfortunate fact remains that humans are often the most sensitive, or the only, detectors of a biological attack.[158] Without knowledge of the attack, an increased number of patients presenting with signs and symptoms caused by the disseminated disease agent are the most likely first indicator that a BW attack has occurred.

A sound epidemiologic investigation of a disease outbreak, whether natural or artificial, will assist medical personnel in identifying the pathogen, as well as instituting the appropriate medical interventions. The CDC realized this as early as 1951, when the Epidemic Intelligence Service was created to train epidemiologists in the event that a BW attack should take place against the United States during the Cold War.[159] Documenting who is affected, possible routes of exposure, signs and symptoms of disease, and the rapid identification of the causative agents will greatly increase the ability to plan an appropriate medical and public health response. Good epidemiologic information will allow the appropriate follow-up of those potentially exposed, as well as help determine public information guidelines and responses to the media.

Many, if not most, diseases caused by weaponized biological agents present with nonspecific signs and symptoms that could be misinterpreted as a natural outbreak. The disease pattern that develops is an important factor in differentiating between a natural event and a terrorist or warfare attack. In most naturally occurring epidemics, there is a gradual rise in disease incidence, as people are progressively exposed to an increasing number of patients, vectors, or fomites that spread the patho-

---

157. Robert G. Ulrich, S. Sidells, Thomas J. Taylor, Catherine Wilhelmsen, and David R. Franz, "Staphylococcal Enterotoxin B and Related Pyrogenic Toxins," in Zajtchuk, *Textbook of Military Medicine*, pp. 621–630.

158. Department of the Army, the Navy, and the Air Force, *NATO Handbook on the Medical Aspects of NBC Defensive Operations* (Washington, D.C.: Departments of the Army, Navy, and Air Force, February 1996).

159. Ibid.

gen. In contrast, those exposed to a BW attack would all come in contact with the agent at approximately the same time. Even taking into account varying incubation periods based on exposure dose and physiological differences, a compressed epidemic curve with a peak in a matter of days, or even hours, would occur. Most point source exposures will present in this fashion, including food-borne outbreaks, which may be natural or possibly intentionally induced. Therefore, further information should be obtained to help establish whether an outbreak is caused by an attack with a BW agent.

The general steps for epidemiologic assessment of any disease can be applied to a BW or terrorist attack.[160] First, public health authorities and health care personnel should formulate a case definition to determine the number of actual cases and verify the epidemic, and from that determine the approximate attack rate. Is the disease rate greater than the background rate of disease that normally occurs? The potential exists for hysteria to be confused with actual disease; therefore, objective criteria should be used to document the number of people affected. Once a case definition has been determined, the epidemic can be described with respect to the timing, place, and other characteristics of those who are ill. The investigation obviously needs to be done expeditiously, but even rudimentary information can be of assistance in determining the source and potential consequences of an outbreak.

The unintended release of anthrax spores from a military compound in the former Soviet Union in 1979 demonstrated some of the epidemiologic indicators of an unnatural epidemic. The location of casualties followed a distinctive downwind pattern from the release site, animals in the same area were affected, and an unusual presentation of the disease, respiratory instead of cutaneous, occurred.[161] Other possible clues of a BW or terrorist attack include high disease rates among exposed individuals; more respiratory cases of disease if the agent is disseminated via aerosol; occurrence of a disease that is unusual in a given geographic area; a naturally vector-borne disease occurring in an area that lacks the appropriate vectors for normal transmission; more than one epidemic occurring at the same time; higher morbidity and mortality than normally expected for a disease; lower attack rates in personnel protected from exposure (such as those inside a building); and suspicious activity or

160. Ibid.; and Theodore C. Eickoff, "Airborne Disease," *American Journal of Epidemiology*, Vol. 144 (1996), pp. S39–S46.

161. Jerold Last, Robert Wallace, Elizabeth Barrett-Connor, eds., *Public Health and Preventive Medicine*, 13th ed. (East Norwalk: Appleton & Lunge, 1992).

discovery of a potential delivery system such as a spray device.[162] If an attack with biological agents is suspected, the proper authorities, whether military or civilian, should be notified immediately.

To minimize the effects of a biological terrorist attack, health care professionals and public health authorities must be aware of the threat of biological warfare and terrorism and have an increased index of suspicion that such an attack can occur. They must have some understanding of the classes of agents that have been and can be weaponized and their effects after inhalation. Surveillance of background disease activity should be ongoing, and any unusual changes in disease occurrence or etiology should be promptly followed up with a directed examination of the facts regarding the increased rates. Through close attention to disease patterns, we can become aware of potential problems in time to institute rapid action that can potentially save many lives, and decrease the impacts of disease, regardless of its origin.

---

162. Department of the Army, the Navy, and the Air Force, *NATO Handbook on the Medical Aspects of NBC Defensive Operations*.

Chapter 5

Biological Weapons and U.S. Law

James R. Ferguson

The past decade has witnessed a major shift in the nature and magnitude of the threat posed by biological weapons. For many years, the dangers of such weapons arose solely from the risk of their use in international conflicts. As a result, the class of potential users consisted entirely of a small number of industrialized countries that had developed (or could develop) a biological arsenal for use in warfare.

All this has now changed. In the last ten years, the class of potential users has expanded to include not only a growing number of developing nations, but also a wide range of non-state actors such as terrorist groups, religious cults, and even individuals.[1] Furthermore, many of these new parties now pose a threat of an entirely different kind—the use of biological weapons as agents of terror, rather than as instruments of war.[2]

The emergence of this threat has carried far-reaching implications for U.S. policy. Where the U.S. government once focused exclusively on preventing other countries from acquiring biological weapons, it now

---

This chapter was adapted from James R. Ferguson, "Biological Weapons and U.S. Law," *Journal of the American Medical Association (JAMA)*, Vol. 278, No. 5 (August 6, 1997), pp. 357–360. © 1997 American Medical Association.

---

1. Richard K. Betts, "The New Threat of Mass Destruction," *Foreign Affairs*, Vol. 77 (January/February 1998), pp. 26–29; Brad Roberts, "New Challenges and New Policy Priorities for the 1990s," in Brad Roberts, ed., *Biological Weapons: Weapons of the Future?* (Washington, D.C.: Center for Strategic and International Studies, 1993), pp. 74–78; John F. Sopko, "The Changing Proliferation Threat," *Foreign Policy*, No. 105 (Winter 1996–97), pp. 6–16; and *Global Proliferation of Weapons of Mass Destruction and Domestic Terrorism: Hearings Before the Senate Committee on Governmental Affairs*, 104th Cong., 1st sess., 1995.

2. Roberts, "New Challenges," pp. 77–78; Sopko, "The Changing Proliferation Threat," pp. 6–16; and Senate Hearings on Global Weapons Proliferation.

focuses increasingly on the use of such weapons by terrorists and other non-state actors. Indeed, Congress recently passed three major statutes in an effort to prevent the use of biological weapons by domestic and international terrorists, as well as by foreign nations.[3] In addition, last year Congress established the framework for a comprehensive regulatory regime to control the domestic use of hazardous toxins and infectious agents. Under this regime, the Centers for Disease Control and Prevention (CDC) regulate the transfer and use of more than thirty toxins, bacteria, and viruses posing significant risks to public health and safety.

Curbing the Acquisition of Biological Weapons by Other Nations: The Biological Weapons Control Act

To understand the goals of the recent legislation dealing with biological weapons, it is first necessary to trace the history of U.S. biological weapons policy since 1972.

Until recently, U.S. policy focused almost exclusively on preventing the acquisition and use of biological weapons by other nations. To this end, the U.S. government relied on three major strategies. First, the United States entered into a series of treaties and other international agreements designed to achieve biological disarmament and to prevent the proliferation of biological arms to countries that did not yet possess them. Second, the United States imposed economic and diplomatic sanctions on governments that persisted in their efforts to develop a biological arsenal. Third, the United States created an extensive system of export controls to prevent the transfer to other countries of U.S. goods and technologies that could be used in the development of biological weapons.

These strategies originated in 1972, when the United States and more than seventy other nations entered into an agreement known as the Biological Weapons Convention (BWC). In Article I of the BWC, the signatory nations pledged that their respective governments would refrain from developing, producing, stockpiling, or acquiring any biological or toxin weapon. In addition, in Article IV of the BWC, the nations pledged that their governments would take all necessary steps to prevent the development or retention of biological weapons by any party within their respective jurisdictions.

---

3. These statutes were the Biological Weapons Act of 1989, 18 U.S.C. § 175 et seq., 1989; The Chemical and Biological Weapons Control and Warfare Elimination Act of 1991, Public Law 102–182, December 4, 1991; and Anti-Terrorism and Effective Death Penalty Act of 1996, Public Law 104–132, April 24, 1996.

In the wake of the BWC, the United States initiated an aggressive arms control policy to prevent foreign governments from acquiring biological arms and other weapons of mass destruction. The U.S. effort became increasingly important in the late 1980s, as several medium-sized nations (including regional aggressors such as North Korea, Libya, Syria, Iraq, and Iran) pursued major weapons programs that included chemical and biological arms.[4]

In response to this development, Congress passed the Chemical and Biological Weapons Control Act in 1991.[5] In this act, Congress established an elaborate system of economic sanctions and export controls to curb the proliferation of biological arms. Most notably, Congress created a broad array of economic and diplomatic sanctions to be imposed on any country that used biological weapons in violation of international law.[6] In addition, Congress authorized the imposition of sanctions on foreign companies that knowingly exported any goods or technologies used in the development of biological weapons to countries designated by the president as terrorist states or prohibited nations.[7]

Finally, Congress amended the Export Administration Act of 1979 to prevent U.S. companies and individuals from exporting to certain prohibited countries any goods or technologies that would "directly and substantially assist a foreign government or group" in developing or delivering a biological weapon.[8] By virtue of this amendment, any domestic company or individual who knowingly exported to a prohibited country materials used for biological weapons was subject to civil and criminal penalties, including imprisonment of up to ten years.

The Biological Weapons Control Act represented a congressional attempt to further the BWC's goal of curbing the transfer of biological weapons to foreign nations. But for many years after the BWC, the United States had no parallel policy governing the use of biological weapons by groups within its own borders—a parallel policy that had been required by Article IV of the BWC. In fact, until recently, the nation did not have

---

4. Roberts, "New Challenges," p. 74; Sopko, "The Changing Proliferation Threat," pp. 6–16; Senate Hearings on Global Weapons Proliferation; Leonard A. Cole, "The Specter of Biological Weapons," *Scientific American* (December 1996), pp. 60, 62; and Office of Technology Assessment (OTA), *Proliferation of Weapons of Mass Destruction: Assessing the Risks* (Washington, D.C.: OTA, 1995).

5. The Chemical and Biological Weapons Control and Warfare Act of 1991.

6. Sanctions Against Use of Chemical or Biological Weapons, 22 U.S.C. § 5605.

7. Sanctions Against Certain Foreign Persons, 22 U.S.C. § T2798.

8. Export Administration Act of 1979, 50 U.S.C. §§ 2401–20 (1979).

a single law prohibiting the acquisition or use of biological weapons by domestic groups, or regulating the domestic sale or transfer of pathogens and toxins.

The need for such legislation became clear in the years following the end of the Cold War. During this period, the United States was confronted for the first time by a serious threat of biological attack on its own soil—a threat that arose not so much from foreign nations as from subnational groups interested in using biological weapons as instruments of terror.[9] These groups included both international terrorists (such as Aum Shinrikyo) and domestic extremists (such as anti-government groups and right wing militias).[10]

To address the threat, Congress passed the Biological Weapons Act of 1989[11] and the Anti-Terrorism Act of 1996.[12] In these statutes, Congress attempted to reduce the dangers of bioterrorism in three ways. First, the statutes imposed severe criminal penalties on the possession, manufacture, or use of biological weapons. Second, the statutes authorized the federal government to seize any pathogens or other materials used to develop a biological weapon or its delivery system. Third, the statutes created a regulatory system for controlling the use and transfer of hazardous biological agents.

These statutes—and the strategies that underlie them—warrant closer inspection.

Curbing the Domestic Threat of Biological Weapons: The Biological Weapons Act of 1989

Congress passed the Biological Weapons Act of 1989 to implement Article IV of the BWC and to protect the nation against bioterrorist acts.[13] The key provisions of the act define as a federal crime the knowing develop-

---

9. Roberts, "New Challenges," p. 78; Sopko, "The Changing Proliferation Threat," pp. 6–16; Senate Hearings on Global Weapons Proliferation; Office of Technology Assessment, *Technology Against Terrorism: Structuring Security* (Washington, D.C.: OTA, 1992), pp. 39–40; and Office of Technology Assessment, *Technology Against Terrorism: The Federal Effort* (Washington, D.C.: OTA, 1991), pp. 13–22.

10. Sopko, "The Changing Proliferation Threat," pp. 6–16; Senate Hearings on Global Weapons Proliferation; Cole, "The Specter of Biological Weapons," pp. 60–62; and Office of Technology Assessment, *Proliferation of Weapons of Mass Destruction*.

11. Biological Weapons Act of 1989, 18 U.S.C. § 175 *et seq.* (1989).

12. Anti-Terrorism and Effective Death Penalty Act of 1996.

13. Senate Report No. 210, 101st Cong., 1st sess., 1989.

ment, manufacture, transfer, or possession of any "biological agent, toxin or delivery system" for "use as a weapon."[14] The act broadly defines "biological agent" to include any "microorganism, virus or infectious substance" capable of causing deleterious changes in the environment; damaging food, water or equipment supplies; or causing diseases in humans, animals, plants, or other living organisms.[15]

Furthermore, the act imposes heavy criminal penalties on those who knowingly violate its prohibitions. Unlike most other federal criminal statutes (which set forth a maximum period of imprisonment), the act expressly provides that a violator can be imprisoned for any term of years, including life. In addition to its criminal provisions, the act vests the federal government with broad civil and investigative powers to prevent the development, production, or stockpiling of biological weapons. For example, the act authorizes the government to apply for a judicial warrant to seize "any biological agent, toxin or delivery system" that is "of a type or in a quantity" that has no "apparent justification for . . . peaceful purposes."[16] This standard enables the government to intervene almost immediately after learning of a *potential* violation of the criminal provisions of the act. Indeed, to pursue a seizure under this standard, the government does not even have to show that the materials to be seized are intended for "use as a weapon." Rather, the government need only show that it has probable cause to believe that the materials have "no apparent [peaceful] justification."

The Biological Weapons Act also authorizes the government to obtain a civil injunction prohibiting any party from attempting to develop or possess a pathogen, toxin, or delivery system having no apparent peaceful justification.[17] This provision enables the government to move quickly to prevent the development or production of biological arms even when the evidence is insufficient to pursue a criminal prosecution. Indeed, to obtain an injunction, the government need only show by a "preponderance of the evidence" that a party is attempting to possess a biological agent or delivery system having no apparent legitimate purpose.

By enacting these provisions, Congress enabled the federal government to intervene swiftly before a potential biological weapon could be used to cause injury or environmental harm. At the same time, however,

---

14. Biological Weapons Act of 1989, 18 U.S.C. § 175.

15. Biological Weapons Act of 1989, 18 U.S.C. § 178(1).

16. Biological Weapons Act of 1989, 18 U.S.C. § 176(a)(2)(b).

17. Biological Weapons Act of 1989, 18 U.S.C. § 177.

Congress recognized that these provisions, if applied too broadly, could deter scientists and physicians from pursuing legitimate research involving pathogens and toxins—for example, the use of virulent toxins to target cancer cells or the human immunodeficiency virus.[18]

As a result, in the final version of the act, Congress implemented a two-part strategy to ensure that the criminal prohibitions would not interfere with legitimate research. First, Congress expressly provided that a criminal violation cannot occur unless an individual acquires a pathogen, toxin, or delivery system with the specific knowledge that the material is intended "for use as a weapon." Congress further provided that the phrase "for use as a weapon" does not apply to any use of a biological agent for "prophylactic, protective or other peaceful purposes."[19]

By including this language (which applies to all non-hostile uses), Congress incorporated a suggestion repeatedly made by representatives of the biomedical community, i.e., to place the burden of proof on the government to establish that an individual intended to use a specific biological agent to cause harm to others.[20] Accordingly, in any prosecution under the act, the government must prove beyond a reasonable doubt that the individual did not intend to use the material for a "peaceful purpose"—a burden of proof that is nearly impossible to carry whenever a scientist, physician, or researcher has a colorable claim of legitimate purpose.

Curbing the Threat of Bioterrorism: The Anti-Terrorism Act of 1996

In the wake of the Oklahoma City bombing, Congress passed the Anti-Terrorism Act of 1996 to provide the federal government with additional tools in the war against domestic terrorism.[21] In the act, Congress conferred on law enforcement agencies a broad range of new investigative, prosecutorial, and regulatory powers dealing with biological, chemical, and other weapons.

First, Congress expanded the government's powers under the Biological Weapons Act by amending several key provisions of the earlier legislation. For example, Congress broadened the criminal provisions of

18. *The Biological Weapons Anti-Terrorism Act of 1989: Hearing Before the Senate Committee on the Judiciary*, 101st Cong., 1st sess., 1989, p. 6.

19. Biological Weapons Act of 1989, 18 U.S.C. § 176.

20. *The Biological Weapons Anti-Terrorism Act of 1989*, p. 6.

21. Anti-Terrorism and Effective Death Penalty Act of 1996.

the earlier act to reach anyone who "threatens" or "attempts" to develop or use a biological weapon.[22] Congress also broadened the same provisions to apply to anyone who uses recombinant technology or any other biotechnological advance to create new pathogens or more virulent forms of existing pathogens.[23]

The Anti-Terrorism Act also established a new regulatory framework for controlling the use of hazardous biological agents. In particular, Congress directed the CDC to establish a regulatory regime that would identify biological agents posing a threat to public health and regulate the transfer and use of such agents.

To achieve this goal, Congress specified that the CDC should create and maintain a list of biological agents having the "potential to pose a severe threat to public health and safety."[24] Congress further specified that the CDC should select the agents based on several factors, including the effect on human health of exposure to the agent, the contagiousness of the agent, the methods by which the agent is transmitted to humans, and the availability and effectiveness of immunizations and treatments for any resulting illness.

Finally, Congress directed the CDC to establish regulations governing the use and transfer of the restricted agents. Congress specified that the regulations should establish procedures that would protect public safety and "prevent access to such agents for use in domestic or international terrorism."

In these ways, the Anti-Terrorism Act laid the groundwork for a broad regulatory system governing the acquisition, use, and transfer of biological agents posing a threat to public health and safety. It remained for the CDC to translate this broad statutory command into specific rules and regulations.

The CDC Regulatory Framework

On April 15, 1997, the CDC's new regulations governing hazardous biological agents went into effect.[25] In drafting the regulations, the CDC sought to accomplish four major goals: the identification of biological agents that are potentially hazardous to public health; the creation of

---

22. Anti-Terrorism and Effective Death Penalty Act of 1996, § 511(b)(1)-(2).

23. Anti-Terrorism and Effective Death Penalty Act of 1996, § 511(b)(3)(C).

24. Anti-Terrorism and Effective Death Penalty Act of 1996, § 511(d).

25. U.S. Department of Health and Human Services, Centers for Disease Control and

procedures for monitoring the acquisition and transfer of the restricted agents; the establishment of safeguards for the transportation of the restricted agents; and the creation of a system for alerting authorities when an improper attempt is made to acquire a restricted agent.[26]

To achieve these goals, the CDC regulations first identify twenty-four select agents and twelve toxins that pose a significant risk to public health.[27] (See Table 5.1.) The current list includes not only twelve viruses and seven bacteria but also recombinant organisms and any genetic elements from any of the listed agents that produce or encode for a factor associated with a disease.

In addition to identifying hazardous agents, the CDC regulations set forth procedures for identifying all facilities possessing such agents and for ensuring that the facilities have appropriate safeguards.[28] The regulations provide that any university, research institution, private company, or individual that acquires any restricted agent or that wants to acquire any agent must register with the federal government. The regulations further provide that, as part of the registration process, each facility must designate a "responsible facility individual" who will certify that the facility and its laboratory operations meet the appropriate biosafety level requirements for working with the specific agent. To ensure compliance, the regulations authorize the government to inspect the facility to determine if it meets the appropriate biosafety level requirements. If the government approves the laboratory, the facility then receives a specific registration number that indicates the facility is authorized to work with the identified agents at the prescribed biosafety level.[29]

The CDC regulations also establish procedures for tracking the transfer of restricted agents from one facility to another.[30] The regulations require that, prior to such a transfer, the shipping and receiving facilities must each complete an "official transfer form" that identifies the registration numbers of the shipping and receiving facilities, the name of the relevant restricted agent, and the proposed use and amount of the agent. A copy of the form must then be maintained in a central repository that,

---

Prevention, "Additional Requirements for Facilities Transferring or Receiving Select Agents; Final Rule," *Federal Register,* Vol. 61 (October 24, 1996), p. 55190.

26. Ibid., p. 55190.

27. Ibid., pp. 55190–55191.

28. Ibid., p. 55191.

29. Ibid., p. 55191.

30. Ibid., p. 55192.

Table 5.1. The CDC List of Select Agents.

Viruses

  Congo-Crimean hemorrhagic fever virus
  Eastern equine encephalitis virus
  Ebola virus
  Equine Morbillivirus
  Lassa fever virus
  Marburg virus
  Rift Valley fever virus
  South American hemorrhagic fever viruses (Junin, Machupo, Sabia, Flexal, Guanarito)
  Tick-borne encephalitis complex viruses
  Variola major virus (smallpox virus)
  Venezuelan equine encephalitis virus
  Viruses causing hantavirus pulmonary syndrome
  Yellow fever virus

Exemptions: Vaccine strains of viral agents (Junin virus strain candid #1, Rift Valley fever virus strain MP-12, Venezuelan equine encephalitis virus strain TC-83, and Yellow fever virus strain 17-D).

Bacteria

  Bacillus anthracis
  Brucella abortus, B. Melitensis, B. Suis
  Burkholderia (Pseudomonas) *mallei*
  Burkholderia (Pseudomonas) *pseudomallei*
  Clostridium botulinum
  Francisella tularensis
  Yersinia pestis

Exemptions: Vaccine strains as described in Title 9 Code of Federal Regulations (CFR), 78.1.

Rickettsiae

  Coxiella burnetii
  Rickettsia prowazeki
  Rickettsia rickettsi

Fungi

  Coccidioides immitis

Toxins

  Abrin
  Aflatoxins
  Botulinum toxins
  Clostridium perfringens epsilon toxin
  Conotoxins
  Diacetoxyscirpenol
  Ricin
  Saxitoxin
  Shigatoxin
  Staphylococcal enterotoxins
  Tetrodotoxin
  T-2 toxin

Exemptions: Toxins for medical use, inactivated for use as vaccines, or toxin preparations for biomedical research use at an LD_{50} for vertebrates of more than 100 nanograms per kilogram body weight, and national standard toxins required for biologic potency testing as described in 9 CFR Part 113.

while not publicly accessible, is available to both federal and local law enforcement authorities.

The regulations further provide that the "responsible facility official" at the requesting facility must certify that the requesting researcher is officially affiliated with the facility and that the laboratory meets the appropriate biosafety level requirements.[31] Similarly, the regulations require the responsible facility official at the shipping facility to certify that the receiving facility holds a valid registration number indicating an appropriate biosafety level capability.

The regulations next identify certain clinical uses of restricted agents that are exempt from the regulatory scheme.[32] Under these exemptions, a clinical specimen containing a restricted agent is not subject to regulation if the specimen is intended for diagnostic reference, diagnostic verification, or evaluating the proficiency of diagnostic tests. Any other use, however, is subject to regulation, including any research use.

In addition, the CDC regulations exempt any attenuated strains of restricted agents that have been approved for human vaccination purposes by the Food and Drug Administration. The regulations do apply, however, to all other attenuated, avirulent, or less pathogenic strains of the restricted agents.

Finally, the CDC regulations are enforceable by criminal penalties. In particular, an individual who knowingly makes a false statement on any of the forms required for the registration of facilities or for the transfer of restricted agents is subject to a fine or imprisonment of up to five years. In addition, an individual who knowingly violates other provisions of the regulations is subject to a fine of $250,000 and imprisonment of up to one year.

Conclusion

In the last eight years, Congress has developed a comprehensive legal framework to prevent the illegitimate use of toxins and infectious agents. As part of this framework, Congress has defined as a federal crime virtually every step in the process of developing or acquiring a biological agent for use as a weapon. At the same time, Congress has vested federal law enforcement agencies with broad civil and investigative powers to enable the government to intervene before such weapons are used or even developed. Finally, Congress has established a regulatory regime to monitor the location and transfer of hazardous biological agents and to ensure

---

31. Ibid., p. 55192.
32. Ibid., pp. 55193–55194.

that any use of such agents complies with appropriate biosafety requirements.

The effectiveness of such measures must remain a matter of intense speculation. But at least two features of the recent legislation deserve recognition. First, Congress has erected new barriers to the illicit development and acquisition of biological agents by imposing stringent regulatory controls—including criminal penalties—on the transfer and use of such agents. Second, Congress has enhanced the ability of federal law enforcement agencies to intervene before a biological weapon is used or even developed in the United States. In these ways, Congress has reduced the risks of bioterrorism and promoted the public safety in the transfer and use of hazardous biological agents.

Part III
Arms Control and Biological Weapons

Chapter 6

Biological Weapons Control: Prospects and Implications for the Future

Robert P. Kadlec, Allan P. Zelicoff, and Ann M. Vrtis

One hundred and forty signatory nations have ratified the Biological Weapons Convention (BWC). Officially known as the Convention on the Prohibition of the Development, Production and Stockpiling of Bacteriological (Biological) and Toxin Weapons and on Their Destruction, this treaty was opened for signature on April 10, 1972. When it first entered into force, the BWC was unique among existing weapons control treaties. It prohibited an entire class of weapons, yet lacked specific mandatory enforcement measures to ensure compliance by participants. Events in the last several years have acutely raised the awareness of the BWC's limitations and cast doubt about its current effectiveness to slow, stop, or reverse the current trends in biological warfare proliferation. The number of countries known to have or suspected of having biological weapons capability has doubled since the convention went into force in 1975.[1]

Currently, weapons control delegations from many of the signatory nations are negotiating a legally binding protocol to correct the deficien-

This chapter was adapted from Robert P. Kadlec, Allan P. Zelicoff, and Ann M. Vrtis, "Biological Weapons Control: Prospects and Implications for the Future," *Journal of the American Medical Association (JAMA)*, Vol. 278, No. 5 (August 6, 1997), pp. 351–356.

1. J.D. Holum, *Remarks for the Fourth Review Conference of the Biological Weapons Convention* (Geneva: U.S. Arms Control and Disarmament Agency [ACDA], November 26, 1996).

cies of the BWC and reinforce the existing global prohibition against biological warfare. These diplomatic efforts, directed by the BWC Special Conference in September 1994 and described in detail below, reflect growing concerns about biological weapons proliferation. At the UN General Assembly meeting in September 1996, President Clinton announced the United States commitment to completing this draft effort by 1998. However, the pace of negotiations has gone slowly, resulting in the expectation that a draft protocol will be completed by the next Review Conference in 2001.

The events in this decade alone reveal the challenges confronting arms control negotiators. Russia admitted that the former Soviet Union had violated the BWC. The former Soviet Union did so with near impunity because the BWC has no effective mechanisms to investigate concerns about suspicious activities. Iraq, on the other hand, has been subject to multiple intrusive inspections and monitoring by the UN Special Commission (UNSCOM) since the Persian Gulf War. Even with unrestricted access and a broad range of on-site measures, inspectors failed to uncover any unambiguous evidence of illicit biological weapons activity. UNSCOM's inspections occurred after Iraq's violations, so it is not possible to assess their deterrence value. However, there is a lesson that can be learned. UNSCOM's experience in Iraq challenges the conventional wisdom that intrusive inspections can provide convincing proof of violations and resolve suspicions. A detailed analysis of the UNSCOM inspections is provided elsewhere in this book.[2]

The BWC was originally drafted to formalize the obligations between nations. Global domestic legislation to prevent non-state or terrorist biological weapons proliferation has yet to be universally enacted. The recent use of chemical agents by the Aum Shinrikyo cult in Japan and the cult's unsuccessful attempt to disseminate anthrax spores and botulinum toxin in Tokyo raise the specter of biological weapons terrorism by non-state actors. It remains to be seen whether domestic legislation that criminalizes biological weapons development or use can entirely deter domestic biological weapons terrorist events.

Efforts to heighten public and professional awareness about this threat are necessary. Additionally, capabilities must be enhanced to respond to biological weapons incidents. Currently, ongoing efforts to improve domestic and global surveillance of infectious diseases represent part of an initiative that can strengthen the BWC. Effective surveillance and prompt investigation of unusual or suspicious outbreaks of disease

---

2. See the chapter by Raymond A. Zilinskas in this volume.

can potentially deter biological weapons use by identifying intentional or accidental releases of biological weapons agents, albeit imperfectly. These efforts, coupled with further medical education and research to address the threat posed by both biological weapons proliferation and emerging and reemerging diseases, can provide a scientific foundation to develop capabilities to diagnose, treat, and mitigate such occurrences, whatever their cause.

Historical Background

International action to limit or prevent biological weapons development and use began well before World War I. Declarations signed at the 1899 and 1907 Hague International Peace Conferences called for prohibition of the use of poison during war. The use of chlorine and mustard gases during World War I prompted the victorious Allies to formalize these pre-war prohibitions to strengthen the international norm against this type of weapon.[3] The landmark Geneva Protocol of 1925 reaffirmed the prohibition of the use in war of asphyxiating, poisonous, or other gases and extended this ban to the use of bacteriological weapons. This protocol never truly entered into force as an international agreement before World War II, because the United States and Japan never ratified it. Its terms, however, were largely respected and may account for the virtual absence of both chemical warfare and biological weapons during conflicts in the mid-twentieth century. One notable exception, however, was the dispersal of various biological weapons agents by the Japanese during World War II. The Geneva Protocol did not ban possession of chemical warfare or biological weapons, but rather prohibited the use of these materials as weapons of war. The impact of the Geneva Protocol was additionally weakened by the declarations of the United Kingdom, the former Soviet Union, and France. These three countries stated that they would not be bound to this agreement if their enemies or the allies of their enemies used chemical warfare or biological weapons. Thus, the Geneva Protocol became a "no-first-use" agreement with no legally binding restrictions on the research, development, or deployment of either chemical warfare or biological weapons.

World War II found both Axis and Allied nations devoting varying levels of efforts to biological weapons research and development. Notably, Japan's Unit 731 conducted human experimentation using anthrax, chol-

---

3. U.S. ACDA, *Arms Control Disarmament Agreements: Texts and Histories of the Negotiations* (Washington, D.C.: U.S. ACDA, 1996).

era, typhoid, plague, and typhus.[4] Recently published accounts describe Japanese attacks on Chinese villages and cities with biological weapons.[5] Japan, however, was not alone in the pursuit of biological weapons. The United States, in cooperation with Canada and the United Kingdom, developed and produced anthrax bombs to retaliate against possible German or Japanese first use of biological weapons.[6] The U.S. research and development effort was likened to a smaller version of the Manhattan Project, reflecting the high level of scientific expertise brought together to create an offensive biological weapons program.[7] The end of World War II saw the dawn of the nuclear age, yet many of those involved in the U.S. offensive biological weapons effort, including its head, George Merck, foresaw the potential proliferation of this threat as early as 1946.[8]

In the years immediately following World War II, the international community engaged in little, if any, dialogue to limit or prohibit the development or use of biological weapons. On the contrary, the United States continued to expand its offensive program. The U.S. program included the development and limited production of several biological weapons agents and delivery systems. (See Table 6.1.)[9] Only in the late 1960s did President Nixon, shortly after taking office, direct a study of U.S. policy, programs, and operational concepts regarding both chemical and biological weapons. The National Security Council found in this study that biological weapons were not ideal for tactical battlefield use because of the latency between exposure and onset of symptoms and the difficulty of confining biological weapons' effects to a given target area.[10] On November 25, 1969, Nixon announced the results of this review and

---

4. Peter Williams and David Wallace, *Unit 731: Japan's Secret Biological Warfare in World War II* (New York: Free Press, 1989), p. 23; and Sheldon H. Harris, *Factories of Death: Japanese Biological Warfare, 1932–1934, and the American Coverup* (New York: Routledge, 1994), pp. 59, 68.

5. Harris, *Factories of Death.*

6. Leo P. Brophy, Wyndham D. Miles, and Rexmond C. Cochrane, *The Chemical Warfare Service: From Laboratory to Field* (Washington, D.C.: U.S. Army, 1959); John Bryden, *Deadly Allies: Canada's Secret War, 1937–1947* (Toronto: McClelland & Stewart, 1989), p. 256; and *U.S. Army Activity in the U.S. Biological War Programs*, Vol. 1 (Washington, D.C.: U.S. Army, 1977).

7. George W. Merck, E.B. Fred, I.L. Baldwin, and W.B. Sarles, *Implications of Biological Warfare: The U.S. and UN Report Series No. 5* (Washington, D.C.: U.S. Department of State, 1946), pp. 659–671.

8. Ibid.

9. *U.S. Army Activity in the U.S. Biological War Programs.*

10. *National Security Study Memorandum 59* (Washington, D.C.: National Security Council, May 28, 1969), p. 1.

Table 6.1. Biological Warfare Agents Produced by the United States, 1943–69.

Bacillus anthracis
Botulinum toxin
Brucella suis
Pasteurella tularensis
Coxiella burnetii
Venezuelan equine encephalitis
Staphylococcal enterotoxin
Wheat stem rust
Rye stem rust
Rice blast

the unconditional, unilateral renouncement of biological weapons. His executive order directed the U.S. Department of Defense to dispose of all existing stocks of biological agents and weapons. This unilateral prohibition was further extended in February 1970 to include toxin agents—toxic compounds derived from biological sources.[11]

The 1969 U.S. renouncement was subsequently endorsed by Canada, Sweden, and the United Kingdom. This series of unilateral announcements created an international political momentum within the UN Conference of the Committee on Disarmament for negotiating a legally binding treaty to prohibit biological weapons. The UN Conference of the Committee on Disarmament initially envisioned a treaty to ban the acquisition of materials intended for both chemical warfare and biological weapons, but technical differences between these two classes of weapons, as well as political considerations, led to separate negotiations for the chemical warfare and biological weapons problems.

These negotiations resulted in the BWC and the first agreement since World War II that prohibited an entire class of weapons.[12] The fundamental tenet of the BWC is contained in Article I. Specifically, Article I prohibits the development, production, and stockpiling of microbial or other biological agents or toxins of types and quantities that have no justification for prophylactic, protective, and other peaceful purposes; and weapons, equipment, or means of delivery designed to use such agents or toxins for hostile purposes or in armed conflict.[13] This language implicitly prohibits the exploitation of current and all possible future scientific and

11. U.S. ACDA, *Arms Control Disarmament Agreements.*

12. U.S. ACDA, *Fact Sheet: The Biological Weapons Convention* (Washington, D.C.: U.S. ACDA, August 18, 1993).

13. Holum, *Remarks for the Fourth Review Conference.*

technical developments for purposes inconsistent with peaceful use. This intent clause has been the cornerstone and genius of the BWC and remains the foundation for any future biological weapons control protocol. It has also stood the test of time regarding advancements in recombinant DNA, gene sequencing, and protein synthesis that have occurred in the three decades since the inception of the BWC negotiations.

Despite its all-encompassing and enduring prohibitions, the BWC has no implementation or verification provisions. "Effective verification" is an arms control concept in which determination of compliance can be made by using a series of measures such as declarations of activities, visits to facilities, or other information that would yield accurate and unambiguous data about the nature of activities of potential concern. A treaty with "effective verification" would have a high probability of identifying a signatory nation that was in violation of the treaty's prohibitions on one hand, while being able to determine, with equally high probability, whether a signatory nation was in compliance with the treaty on the other. The medical equivalent of this concept would be a diagnostic test (or series of tests) that is simultaneously both highly sensitive and highly specific. Further, given the relatively rare instances of violation, this diagnostic test must possess the even more stringent characteristics of high positive and negative predictive value. It is essentially impossible to separate the dual-use nature of biological processes and equipment used in legitimate and prohibited activities. Translated into Bayesian terms familiar to physicians, no measures or combination of measures, to date, have been found with the requisite sensitivity or specificity that was useful for detecting violations of the BWC.

The BWC does, however, set forth general guidelines to address concerns or allegations about a breach of its obligations. In these circumstances, a BWC member nation that has a concern about another member nation's activities or that has been the target of a biological weapons attack would submit its complaint to the UN Security Council for review and consideration. The UN Security Council would then determine what further action, if any, should be taken. An inherent limitation of this mechanism is the potential for any one of the five permanent members of the Security Council (the United States, the United Kingdom, France, China, or Russia) to veto or obstruct any further investigation or action against the suspected violator. Currently, the BWC also provides that if the Security Council finds that a member nation was indeed endangered by a violation of the BWC, parties to the BWC would be obligated to provide assistance. One other important provision is that BWC member nations are not relieved of the obligations imposed by the Geneva Protocol.

Table 6.2. Biological Weapons Convention (BWC) Confidence-Building Measures.

1. Exchange of data including name, location, scope, and general description of activities on research centers and laboratories that meet very high national or international safety standards established for handling, for permitted purposes, biological materials that pose a high individual and community risk or specialize in permitted biological activities, directly related to the BWC. Signatory nations further agreed to provide annually detailed information on their biological defense research and development programs, including summaries of the objectives and costs of effort performed by contractors and in other facilities.

2. Exchange of information on outbreaks of infectious diseases and similar occurrences caused by biological agents and toxins and on all such events that seem to deviate from the normal pattern concerning type, development, place, or time of occurrence. The information provided on events that deviate from the norm will include, as soon as it is available, data on the type of disease, approximate area affected, and number of cases.

3. Encouragement of publication of results of biological research directly related to the BWC in scientific journals generally available to signatory nations, as well as promotion of use, for permitted purposes, of knowledge gained in this research.

4. Active promotion of contact between scientists in biological research directly related to the BWC, including exchanges and visits for joint research on a mutually agreed basis.

5. Declaration of legislation whether signatory nations have legislation, regulations, or other measures to prohibit the development, production, stockpiling, acquisition, or retention of microbial or other biological agents or toxins, weapons, equipment, and means of delivery within their territory or anywhere under their jurisdiction or control and in relation to the export or import of pathogenic microorganisms and toxins that are dangerous to humans, animals, and plants.

6. Declaration of past activities in offensive and/or defensive biological research and development programs since January 1, 1946.

7. Declaration of vaccine production facilities, both governmental and nongovernmental, within a nation's territory or under its jurisdiction or control anywhere, which are producing vaccine licensed by the signatory nation for the protection of humans.

Since the BWC entered into force in March 1975, Review Conferences have been held every five years since 1981 to review the operation of the Convention to ensure that its purpose and provisions are being met and to take into account new scientific developments. During the first three pentennial review conferences, incremental progress has been made to increase the transparency of biological activities that could be perceived as being of concern. Nations that have ratified the BWC are encouraged to make voluntary annual data exchanges about high-containment facilities, human vaccine production facilities, military biodefense programs, and outbreaks of disease. These voluntary data exchanges were formalized into confidence-building measures after the Second Review Conference (REVCON) in September 1991. (See Table 6.2.) Despite being broadly

Table 6.3. Twenty-one VEREX[a] Measures.

Off-site Measures	On-site Measures
Information monitoring	Exchange visits
Surveillance of publications	International arrangements
Surveillance of legislation	Continuous monitoring
Data on transfers and transfer requests	By instruments
Multilateral information sharing	By personnel
Remote sensing	Inspections
Surveillance by satellite	Interviews
Surveillance by aircraft	Visual inspections
Ground-based surveillance	Identification of key equipment
Data exchange	Auditing
Declarations	Sampling and identification
Notifications	Medical examination
Inspections	
Sampling and identification	
Observation	
Auditing	

[a] Ad Hoc Group of Governmental Experts.

supported at the time, only about half of the signatory nations have ever filed any voluntary confidence-building measure declarations.[14]

The Third Review Conference reaffirmed and extended the confidence-building measures of the Second Review Conference and agreed to create an Ad Hoc Group of Governmental Experts (also known as verification experts or VEREX) whose mandate was to identify, examine, and evaluate from a scientific and technical standpoint potential verification measures with respect to the prohibitions of the BWC. (See Table 6.3.) The VEREX effort produced a consensus report that resulted in several principal conclusions. First, potential verification measures could be useful in varying degrees in enhancing confidence, through increased transparency, that member nations were fulfilling their BWC obligations. Second, reliance could not be placed on any single measure to differentiate conclusively between prohibited and permitted activities and to resolve ambiguities about compliance, though such measures could provide information of varying utility in strengthening the BWC. Third, concern was expressed that the implementation of any measure should ensure that

14. Ibid.

sensitive commercial proprietary information and national security needs were protected.[15]

It is significant to note that the VEREX process did not state that "effective verification" was possible, only that certain measures in combination could help increase transparency and enhance confidence that members of the BWC were fulfilling their obligations. In short, no combination of measures could be found with sufficient certainty or reliability to convince the VEREX participants that it was possible to uncover violations with a high degree of confidence, while at the same time avoiding false accusations. In technical terms, neither high positive nor negative predictive values could be identified during VEREX.

A BWC Special Conference convened in September 1994 and established the Ad Hoc Group (AHG) to consider appropriate VEREX measures and draft proposals for a legally binding protocol to strengthen the BWC. An interim AHG report was submitted to the Fourth Review Conference in November 1996 that resulted in a call by all signatory nations to complete this work as soon as possible before the next review conference in 2001. Among the specific measures being discussed during the AHG negotiations are the following: declarations of military biodefense facilities and human and veterinarian vaccine facilities; investigations of alleged use; investigations of suspicious outbreaks of disease; and on-site visits to address concerns about compliance.

Despite the VEREX report and AHG deliberations, the issue of verification remains unresolved and controversial. While it is the desire of many delegations to craft a verification protocol, the scope of the elements identified so far is neither exhaustive nor comprehensive.

The Proliferation Reality

Despite the apparent progress of diplomatic arms control efforts to improve the effectiveness of the BWC, trends in biological weapons proliferation reinforce the harsh realities of the problem. In 1975, when the convention was signed, only a handful of countries were known to have or suspected of having an offensive biological weapons program. Today, that number has doubled.[16] More disturbing, however, is a series of events and admissions that occurred since the Third BWC Review Conference in 1991.

---

15. *Ad Hoc Group of Governmental Experts to Identify and Examine Potential Verification Measures from a Scientific and Technical Standpoint Report* (Geneva: United Nations, 1993).

16. Holum, *Remarks for the Fourth Review Conference.*

In 1992, Boris Yeltsin admitted that the former Soviet Union had violated the BWC by developing an offensive biological weapons program. That suspicion had existed before the fall of the Soviet Union, but it was only after Yeltsin's admission that the world began to understand the size and scope of the program.[17] Furthermore, the true nature of the 1979 anthrax outbreak in Sverdlovsk was exposed as an accident at a military biological weapons facility that resulted in human and animal cases and fatalities.[18] In addition, unconfirmed published reports from Russian defectors who were formerly involved in the biological weapons program suggest that they were researching and developing new classes of biological weapons agents. These defectors disclosed that they were developing viral hemorrhagic fevers and genetically engineered biological weapons agents. They specifically mentioned creating a strain of *Yersinia pestis* that was resistant to multiple antibiotics and engineered to overcome the protection of available vaccines.[19]

These disclosures raise two ominous points. First, the Soviet Union, one of the three depositories or sponsors of the BWC, pursued an offensive program in spite of established international legal and moral prohibitions. Second, despite bilateral agreements between the U.S. and Russian governments to resolve concerns about the biological weapons capabilities inherited by the Russian government, concerns still persist about the veracity and completeness of Russian assurances and statements.[20]

Western intelligence agencies determined before the start of the Persian Gulf War that Iraq had an offensive biological weapons program. This determination was only confirmed, however, in 1995 after the defection of the late Lieutenant General Hussein Kamel Hassan. While the pre-war public intelligence determination was correct, the intelligence agencies underestimated the size and scope of the Iraqi pro-

---

17. Defense Nuclear Agency (DNA) Biological Weapons Proliferation, *Global Proliferation: Dynamics, Acquisition, Strategies and Response*, Vol. 4 (Alexandria, Va.: DNA, 1994), p. 10.

18. See the chapter by Matthew Meselson, Jeanne Guillemin, Martin Hugh-Jones, Alexander Langmuir, Ilona Popova, Alexis Shelokov, and Olga Yampolskaya in this volume.

19. Bill Gertz, "Defecting Russian Scientist Revealed Biological Arms Effort," *Washington Times*, July 4, 1992, p. A4; and M. Urban, "The Cold War's Deadliest Secret," *Spectator Magazine*, January 23, 1993, pp. 9–10.

20. Holum, *Remarks for the Fourth Review Conference;* and Robert D. Blackwill, *Arms Control and the U.S.-Russian Relationship: Problems, Prospects and Prescriptions* (New York: Council on Foreign Relations, 1996), pp. 65–66.

gram.[21] Iraq admitted that before the onset of the war, it produced, filled, and deployed aerial bombs, 122 mm rockets, aircraft spray tanks, and Scud missile warheads containing botulinum toxin, aflatoxin, and anthrax spores.[22] Iraq had also conducted research into other potential biological weapons agents including *Clostridium perfringens*, rotavirus, echovirus 71, and camelpox viruses. The U.S. Army estimated that if Iraq had used these weapons, there would have been "enormous fatalities," and the U.S. Army's medical treatment system would have been overtaxed.[23]

The experience of UNSCOM in Iraq has important lessons for negotiators seeking to strengthen the BWC. Iraq successfully deceived, denied, and hid information from UNSCOM inspectors concerning its biological weapons program for four years after the Persian Gulf War. Despite comprehensive mandatory declarations, numerous intrusive routine and challenge inspections to eighty biocapable facilities, including breweries, food production plants, pharmaceutical plants, and medical laboratories, UNSCOM found "no incriminating evidence that would identify any of the sites as linked to a proscribed biological weapons program."[24] Yet, based on Kamel Hassan's detailed technical analysis of materials taken from the Al Hakam single-cell protein and biopesticide facility, Iraq developed and maintained a standby biological weapons capability under the constant scrutiny of UN routine and no-notice inspections.[25]

UNSCOM first visited the Al Hakam facility in August 1991. Despite suspicions and constant monitoring, the facility remained operational, producing metric tons of the dry form of the biopesticide *Bacillus thuringiensis*. In December 1994 and June 1995, sampling and analysis of spray driers at that facility showed that the *B. thuringiensis* produced there was in a small (less than 10-μm) particle size. This small size was inconsistent with biopesticide applications but well suited for aerosolized biological weapons purposes.[26] The fermentation process used at this facility also lent itself to rapid conversion from production of *B. thuringiensis* to *Bacillus anthracis*. As a result of this technical analysis and Kamel Hassan's

---

21.   Barbara Starr, "Iraq Reveals a Startling Range of Toxin Agents," *Jane's Defence Weekly*, November 11, 1995, p. 4.

22.   Rolf Ekeus, *Memorandum to the Biological Weapons Convention Fourth Review Conference* (New York: United Nations, November 20, 1996).

23.   U.S. Department of the Army, *Lessons Learned From Operation Desert Shield/Desert Storm* (Washington, D.C.: U.S. Department of the Army, July 19, 1991).

24.   Ekeus, *Memorandum to the Biological Weapons Convention*.

25.   Richard Spertzel, *Sampling and Analysis as a Monitoring Tool* (New York: UN Special Commission, October 3, 1996), p. 7.

26.   Ibid.

information, UNSCOM razed the Al Hakam facility in the summer of 1996.

Despite their achievements, UNSCOM's Chairman Rolf Ekeus cannot report that Iraq has forsaken its past biological weapons capability "until Iraq is able to provide a full accounting of biological weapons produced and destroyed unilaterally."[27] The U.S. intelligence community estimates that Iraq could reconstitute its biological weapons program in a matter of weeks once sanctions are removed.[28] The UNSCOM experience with Iraq raises questions about the effectiveness of various measures, no matter how intrusive, to detect or verify conclusively the existence of prohibited activities.

The recent terrorist actions of the Aum Shinrikyo cult in Japan deserve mention when considering the future of biological weapons proliferation and the potential impact of international arms control. Unlike the biological weapons programs associated with the Soviet and Iraqi governments, the events in Japan point out the risk of chemical warfare and biological weapons terrorism by a terrorist group, other non-state actors like this cult, or even a deranged individual. While it is widely known that the Aum Shinrikyo cult perpetrated a sarin nerve agent attack in the Tokyo subway system, less publicity was given to the biological weapons capabilities they reportedly developed as well.[29] Unconfirmed reports suggest that this cult attempted to produce and disseminate both botulinum toxin and anthrax before they launched the sarin attack.[30]

While existing confidence-building measures include the voluntary declaration of domestic legislation, regulations, and other measures to criminalize or restrict the development, production, or possession of biological weapons, full compliance by all signatory nations has yet to be achieved with either the voluntary declarations or the relevant domestic legislation. Even if all countries party to the BWC do comply, it does not preclude the possibility of some person or group attempting to obtain and use biological weapons. In the United States in the last few years, individuals associated with right wing extremist activities have attempted to procure and produce biological weapons agents such as *Y. pestis* and

27. Ekeus, *Memorandum to the Biological Weapons Convention.*

28. Elaine Sciolino, "Iraqis Could Pose a Threat Soon, CIA Chief Says," *New York Times International,* January 16, 1992, p. A9.

29. David E. Kaplan and Andrew Marshall, *The Cult at the End of the World* (New York: Crown, 1996), p. 55.

30. Ibid.

the toxin ricin.[31] Potential disaster was averted only because alert local and federal authorities recognized the potential risk and interdicted these persons before any possible harm could occur. An international legally binding protocol between nations could be expected to achieve some measure of deterrence of a terrorist biological weapons attack—but not complete deterrence. Requiring nations to comply with mandatory enactment of domestic legislation that criminalizes biological weapons possession or activity would be helpful but not foolproof. Implementing legislation associated with a BWC protocol may limit the access terrorists would have to certain materials such as cultures of pathogenic organisms. It would not, however, necessarily restrict their access to dual-use equipment and supplies. Biological weapons terrorist attacks can only be reasonably deterred or prevented by the constant vigilance and focused efforts of domestic law enforcement agencies.

Is There Any Hope?

These events underscore the inherent limits of any future protocol to effectively restrict biological weapons proliferation. In this context, the BWC protocol currently being negotiated would provide greater transparency of certain but not all biological activities that could be used for offensive biological weapons purposes. It is unlikely that all facilities capable of producing pathogenic organisms in a given country will be subject to declarations or inspections.

Given the sheer number and diversity of possible relevant facilities, the BWC negotiators have already narrowed the likely categories of declarable activities and facilities to biosafety level 4 laboratories, facilities that produce vaccines, and military and biodefense programs. They have already excluded from consideration hospitals, medical laboratories and biosafety level 3 laboratories, academic and research institutions, breweries, and food processing plants. They have yet to determine whether all pharmaceutical manufacturers or biotechnology companies will be declared under a future protocol or whether some arbitrary production threshold will be established, limiting declarations to only certain scale producers.

Another important issue being considered during the current AHG negotiations is the protection of intellectual, commercial proprietary, and national security information. With the potential of detailed declarations

---

31. Michael Janofsky, "Looking for Motives in Plague Case," *New York Times,* May 24, 1995, p. A12; and Tom Morganthau, "A Shadow over the Olympics," *Newsweek,* May 6, 1996, p. 34.

Table 6.4. Possible Criteria for Characterizing Suspicious Outbreaks of Disease.

Disease (or strain) not endemic
Antibiotic resistance patterns
Atypical clinical presentation
Case distribution (geographically and/or temporally inconsistent)
Other inconsistent elements (i.e., the number of cases, mortality and morbidity rates, and
  deviation from disease occurrence baseline)

and possible on-site inspections, safeguards must be incorporated to protect these categories of information.

While the ultimate scope of the future BWC protocol cannot be all encompassing, certain measures under consideration can measurably strengthen the existing treaty. President Clinton outlined two specific measures during his speech to the UN General Assembly in September 1996.[32] First, he advocated a mechanism to rectify the current weaknesses associated with investigations of alleged use. The mechanism he proposed would not be held hostage by a single nation's veto, but would be weighed on the merit of the evidence presented to and deliberated on by all the signatory nations. Second, President Clinton endorsed a measure to investigate unusual or suspicious outbreaks of disease. This concept first surfaced during World War II, when U.S. medical experts believed that an unusual outbreak of disease would probably be the first indication of biological weapons agents use.[33] That assumption remains valid today. An unusual disease outbreak could represent the release of biological weapons agents or the occurrence of an emerging or reemerging disease. In either case, an epidemiologic investigation could differentiate between the two possibilities. Indeed, recent experience in the investigation of hantavirus pulmonary syndrome and Ebola virus outbreaks strongly suggests that the international epidemiology community has developed a useful set of tools for rapidly assessing the source and nature of the spread of novel diseases or disease syndromes. Such investigations cannot always conclusively identify the cause of an outbreak, but they do provide an internationally recognized method to investigate such occurrences. A recent U.S. Department of Defense exercise further reinforced this concept by outlining preliminary criteria for suspicious outbreaks of

32. Office of the President, White House, Speech to the UN General Assembly, September 24, 1996, Washington, D.C., press release.

33. Brophy, Miles, and Cochrane, *The Chemical Warfare Service.*

disease that could provide indications of a possible biological weapons event.[34] (See Table 6.4.)

Not all disease outbreaks would automatically be subject to investigation by a future BWC protocol. As in the situation of alleged biological weapons use, evidence concerning the outbreak would be reviewed and deliberated on by all BWC member nations to determine whether a formal investigation should be conducted. In addition to epidemiologic data, other sources of information such as intelligence could be considered. If the weight of the information presented indicated a reason to be concerned about biological weapons or if the characteristics of the outbreak remained unclear or suspicious, a BWC treaty–related investigation could occur. This type of mechanism and process could significantly limit the possibility of false accusations.

At that time, an impartial UN expert international team would respond to such events and be afforded the necessary access to conduct a thorough epidemiologic investigation. The opportunity to collect data, perform hypothesis generation, and conduct statistical analysis could provide greater insight into these outbreaks. Scientific analysis derived from these investigations could offer a valid foundation for later political consideration. Furthermore, these types of investigations would provide greater transparency of national biological events and could enhance confidence in nations' compliance with the BWC. At a minimum, these investigations would provide further support of international public health efforts to enhance surveillance for infectious disease and efforts to control outbreaks. It would also prompt nations to share information concerning disease occurrences more openly and help establish a global epidemiologic baseline. In the future, biological weapons use or accidents resulting in unusual outbreaks of disease could not easily evade investigation under such a protocol. With this mechanism in place, supported by the weight of the international community, occurrences like the accident at the military biological weapons facility at Sverdlovsk could not easily be denied or obstructed for twelve years.

Any future BWC protocol that would, at a minimum, include investigations of alleged use and suspicious outbreaks could significantly advance the cause of biological arms control. Besides reinforcing the existing global norm against these weapons, investigations could provide an important deterrent against biological weapons development and use. Proliferators would be faced with the real potential of being caught should they have an accident involving these weapons or actually use them.

---

34. BDM Federal Inc., *Unusual Outbreak of Disease Exercise* (Reston, Va.: BDM Federal Inc., August 1996).

Conclusion

Biological warfare, in the view of rogue nations, is another potential weapon of mass destruction with which to threaten or inflict harm on their neighbors or their own citizens. The global diffusion of dual-use biotechnology provides these outlaw regimes with the means to perpetrate such attacks. The cost of this technology is significantly less than that associated with the development of nuclear or even chemical weapons. Despite the lesser cost, biological weapons offer the same potential lethality as a nuclear device.

Physicians are well aware of the impact of infectious disease on society and humankind. The eradication of smallpox, considered by some the perfect biological weapons agent, and the control and prevention of other infectious diseases reflect modern medicine's great intellectual and technical advances. Despite these advances, the legal and moral standard against the intentional use of these organisms has eroded, not improved. The concept of biological weapons runs contrary to the basic precepts of the medical profession.

The ongoing efforts to strengthen the BWC should not be considered curative for the biological weapons proliferation problem. Recent events strongly suggest that any future biological weapons arms control agreement may only be palliative against nations intent on pursuing a biological weapons capability. In terms of the potential effectiveness of arms control to prevent bioterrorism, it is important not to be lulled into a false sense of security. It is vital to reaffirm the global biological weapons prohibition with a strengthened BWC, but it is equally vital for the medical community to prepare for the likelihood of biological weapons use.

The principles of prevention that help clinicians conceptualize strategies against disease are relevant when the medical profession considers the problem of biological weapons proliferation. Primary prevention of biological weapons proliferation requires education, specific protective measures, and environmental modification. For the medical community, further education stressing the recognition of this threat is both timely and necessary. Primary prevention of biological weapons also rests on creating a strong global norm that rejects biological weapons development or use. The medical and scientific communities play an important role in raising the awareness of and reinforcing this norm during international professional exchanges and meetings. Historically, offensive biological weapons development required the support of medical researchers. Each of us in the medical field has a duty to voice our profession's revulsion at this form of warfare. Focusing intense public scrutiny on those who continue to violate the BWC can be effective adjunct therapy.

Secondary prevention implies early detection and prompt treatment of disease. A strengthened BWC can help ensure that biological weapons proliferators who develop or use these weapons will stand a greater likelihood of being exposed and caught. A future protocol that ensures an effective mechanism to permit investigation of occurrences such as suspicious outbreaks of disease or alleged use of biological weapons can simultaneously enhance global security and public health. The medical community plays an integral role in secondary biological weapons prevention because it participates in the network of disease surveillance and reporting that may provide the first indication of biological weapons use. Additionally, the medical community will be at the "tip of the spear" when it comes to the treatment of survivors of biological weapons incidents. Therefore, efforts to improve disease surveillance and to continue research and development of improved diagnostic capabilities, therapeutic agents, and effective response plans capable of mitigating the effects of infectious disease occurrences remain paramount. Such efforts serve two noble purposes: public health and arms control.

Finally, the role of tertiary prevention, which limits the disability from disease, cannot be forgotten. The tools of primary and secondary prevention are imperfect. Thus, as the BWC is prepared to provide assistance to those nations that have been the targets of biological weapons, the medical community must be prepared to deal with the sequelae should the unthinkable happen.

Chapter 7

An Effective Prohibition of Biological Weapons

Graham S. Pearson and
Marie Isabelle Chevrier

In the past year, greater worldwide attention has been paid to the danger of biological weapons (BW)—the use of disease as a weapon of war. This attention reflects the concern over events of the past few years: the Iraqi biological weapons program uncovered by the United Nations Special Commission (UNSCOM) on Iraq; worries that BW proliferation is on the rise; the awareness of widespread vulnerability to biological terrorism; and the enhanced public sensitivity to the dangers of disease. The latter led the Director General of the World Health Organization (WHO) to say in its 1996 report that "we also stand on the brink of a global crisis in infectious diseases. No country is safe from them. No country can any longer afford to ignore their threat."[1] Later that same year, the United States expressed its dismay over BW proliferation at the Fourth Review Conference of the Biological Weapons Convention (BWC): "Overall the United States believes that twice as many countries now have or are actively pursuing offensive biological weapons capabilities as when the Convention went into force."[2]

As the world population continues to increase, new areas of land are occupied. Greater overcrowding results in ever greater demands for both

This chapter was adapted from Graham S. Pearson, "The Complementary Role of Environmental and Security Biological Control Regimes in the 21st Century," *Journal of the American Medical Association (JAMA)*, Vol. 278, No. 5 (August 6, 1997), pp. 369–372. © 1997 American Medical Association.

1.   World Health Organization, *The World Health Report 1996: Fighting Disease, Fostering Development* (Geneva: WHO, 1996).

2.   John D. Holum, Director, U.S. Arms Control and Disarmament Agency (ACDA), Statement, Biological Weapons Convention Fourth Review Conference, November 26, 1996.

plants and animals as sources of food, providing greater opportunities for new or old diseases to spread in humans, animals, or plants with consequential damaging socioeconomic effects to the countries involved. Disease has caused more casualties in all wars than the actual weapons of war,[3] and concerns about new and emerging diseases abound.[4]

With the Geneva Protocol of 1925, which prohibits the use in war of biological (bacteriological) weapons, and the opening for signature in 1972 and entry into force in 1975 of the BWC prohibiting the development, production, acquisition and stockpiling of biological weapons, one might think that there would be minimal security concerns about deliberate disease or biological warfare.[5] This is not the case. It is widely recognized that the BWC lacks any compliance monitoring or verification mechanisms. Because of this weakness in the disarmament treaty, the deliberate use of disease is recognized by some analysts as the major security concern relating to weapons of mass destruction.

In this chapter, we address what is required to achieve an effective prohibition of biological weapons and identify the various necessary and complementary elements within it. We consider the prospects for the Ad Hoc Group negotiations to draft a legally binding protocol to strengthen the BWC, and conclude that an effective prohibition of biological weapons can be achieved. The package of necessary measures will be both efficient and effective as well as balanced to meet the requirements of developing and developed countries alike.

The Increasing Danger from Biological Weapons

Although biological warfare capabilities were developed during and following World War II, the development of nuclear weapons saw the abandonment of biological weapons programs by the United States, the United Kingdom, Canada, and France. Unilateral BW disarmament by these countries led to the negotiation of the BWC. For the first time, a convention had been agreed that totally prohibited a whole class of

---

3. Swedish National Defense Research Establishment, *FOA informerar om: A Briefing Book on Biological Weapons*, 1995.

4. Laurie Garrett, *The Coming Plague: Newly Emerging Diseases in a World Out of Balance* (New York: Farrar, Strauss and Giroux, 1994).

5. League of Nations, Protocol for the Prohibition of the Use in War of Asphyxiating, Poisonous or Other Gases, and of Bacteriological Methods of Warfare, Geneva, June 17, 1925, Treaty Series, Volume XCIV, Nos. 1, 2, 3 and 4, pp. 65, 1929; and United Nations General Assembly, Convention on the Prohibition of the Development, Production and Stockpiling of Bacteriological (Biological) and Toxin Weapons and on their Destruction, Resolution 2826 (XXVI), 2022nd Plenary meeting, December 16, 1971.

weapons. Although the number of states parties has grown over the years from 33 in 1975 to 140 states parties and 18 signatories today, it has become evident that a number of states have sought to retain biological weapons.[6]

Notably, in April 1992, Russian President Boris Yeltsin said that the former Soviet Union had continued an offensive biological weapons program until 1992, although it was a co-depositary of the BWC along with the United Kingdom and the United States. A trilateral process involving Russia, the United Kingdom, and the United States, which was intended to build confidence that the former Soviet Union's offensive program had indeed been terminated in 1992, has stagnated for four years. The 1997 annual report of the U.S. Arms Control and Disarmament Agency to the U.S. Congress reiterates the statements made in reports of the three preceding years. The report states that "previous assessments of Russian compliance have highlighted the dichotomy between what appears to be the commitment from President Yeltsin and other members of the Russian leadership in attempting to resolve BWC issues and the continued involvement of 'old hands' in BWC Protocol negotiations and in what Russia describes as its defensive BW program." The reports go on to say that "some facilities . . . may be maintaining the capability to produce BW agents" and that "with regard to the trilateral process that began in 1992 . . . the progress has not resolved all US concerns."[7] At the Fourth Review Conference of the BWC, the British Foreign Minister stated that "the existence of a massive offensive biological weapons program conducted illegally for years in the Soviet Union has also recently come to light. The United Kingdom, with the United States continues to work with Russia to re-establish confidence following President Yeltsin's admission that this program had existed and the 1992 Joint Statement."[8]

The Gulf War created a real prospect that chemical and biological weapons might be used by Iraq against the coalition forces. The letter from U.S. President Bush to Saddam Hussein of January 5, 1991, made it clear "that the United States will not tolerate the use of chemical or

6. United Nations, Ad Hoc Group of the States Parties to the Convention on the Prohibition of the Development, Production and Stockpiling of Bacteriological (Biological) and Toxin Weapons and on their Destruction, BWC/AD HOC GROUP/INF. 11, September 8, 1997.

7. See ACDA, *Threat Control Through Arms Control*, Annual Reports to Congress, 1994, 1995, 1996, and 1997, generally submitted in July of the following year. For a fuller account of the Russian BW program, see Milton Leitenberg, "Biological Weapons Arms Control," *Contemporary Security Policy*, Vol. 17, No. 1 (April 1996), p. 1.

8. David Davis, MP, Minister of State for Foreign and Commonwealth Affairs, Statement, Biological Weapons Convention Fourth Review Conference, November 26, 1996.

biological weapons . . . The American people would demand the strongest possible response. You and your country will pay a terrible price if you order unconscionable acts of this sort." Following the Gulf War, the cease-fire resolution, UNSCR 687 (1991),[9] established UNSCOM and charged it with overseeing the destruction of Iraq's chemical and biological weapons and means of delivery. Iraq has sought, above all, to hide its biological weapons capability, initially only admitting a biological defense program. Only when faced with evidence of an offensive program in 1995 did Iraq first admit production of biological warfare agents and eventually its weaponization. It has become clear through the efforts of UNSCOM that Iraq had a very significant biological weapons program. Iraq produced agents such as anthrax and botulinum toxin in large quantities, had weaponized these agents, and had filled ballistic missile warheads and aerial bombs that had been deployed with pre-delegated authority for them to be used. Iraq has still not cooperated with UNSCOM in fully declaring its biological weapons program. Moreover, it is alarming that in 1998, apart from the United States and the United Kingdom, other members of the Security Council appeared not to recognize the consequences for international security if the Security Council failed to support UNSCOM in its efforts to uncover fully and destroy Iraq's biological weapons program.

The terrorist threat is also real. Aum Shinrikyo, the Japanese sect which carried out the sarin nerve gas attack on the Tokyo subway system on March 20, 1995, had also been seeking biological weapons. Indeed, on more than one occasion, the group tried to disseminate biological agents in Tokyo.[10]

The increasing dangers of biological warfare, whether by states or by terrorist groups, has drawn top level attention to this problem. The G-8 Heads of State and Government, at their meeting in June 1996 in Lyon, France, stated in their Declaration on Terrorism that "special attention

---

9. United Nations Security Council Resolution 687 established detailed measures for a cease-fire, including deployment of the United Nations Observer Unit; arrangements for demarcating the Iraq-Kuwait border; the removal or destruction of Iraqi weapons of mass destruction and measures to prevent their reconstitution, under the supervision of a Special Commission and the Director General of the IAEA; and creation of a compensation fund to cover direct loss and damage resulting from Iraq's invasion of Kuwait. S/RES/687 (1991), April 3, 1991.

10. U.S. Senate Permanent Sub-Committee on Investigations (Minority Staff), Hearings on Global Proliferation of Weapons of Mass Destruction: A Case Study on Aum Shinrikyo, Staff Statement, October 31, 1995; and David E. Kaplan and Andrew Marshall, *The Cult at the End of the World: The Incredible Story of Aum* (London: Hutchinson, 1996).

should be paid to the threat of utilization of nuclear, biological and chemical materials, as well as toxic substances, for terrorist purposes."[11] Subsequently, the vulnerability of developed countries to such biological terrorism has been recognized and action has been taken by several of them to address preparedness if such incidents should occur. In May 1998, President Clinton said that "we will undertake a concerted effort to prevent the spread and use of biological weapons, and to protect our people in the event these terrible weapons are ever unleashed by a rogue state, a terrorist group or an international criminal organization," and that "we must pursue the fight against biological weapons on many fronts. We must strengthen the international Biological Weapons Convention with a strong system of inspections to detect and prevent cheating. This is a major priority. It was part of my State of the Union address earlier this year, and we are working with other nations and our industries to make it happen."[12]

Current Shortcomings

Why is there such concern about biological weapons in the 1990s when they were totally prohibited in the 1970s? The answer to this lies in the shortcomings of the international instruments: the Geneva Protocol of 1925 and the BWC of 1975. First, while the Geneva Protocol prohibited the use of biological weapons, several states entered reservations that the protocol would no longer apply if they were attacked by such weapons— thereby essentially making it a first-use prohibition. Although many of these states have in recent years removed their reservations, some still remain. Uncertainty about the prohibition of use at the Fourth Review Conference of the BWC in late 1996 caused Iran to propose a formal amendment to include the word "use" in the title and to amend Article I to include the use of biological weapons.[13] The Final Declaration of the

---

11.   United Nations, Letter, dated July 5, 1996, from the Permanent Representative of France to the United Nations addressed to the Secretary-General, A/51/208, S/1996/543, July 12, 1996.

12.   Office of the Press Secretary, Remarks by the President at the U.S. Naval Academy Commencement, The White House, May 22, 1998.

13.   Ambassador Sirous Nasseri, Ambassador and Permanent Representative of the Islamic Republic of Iran to the United Nations Office in Geneva, Statement, Biological Weapons Convention Fourth Review Conference, November 26, 1996; and United Nations, Fourth Review Conference of the Parties to the Convention on the Prohibition of the Development, Production and Stockpiling of Bacteriological (Biological) and Toxin Weapons and on their Destruction, BWC/CONF.IV/CRP. 1, November 25, 1996 also BWC/CONF. IV/COW/WP. 2, November 28, 1996.

conference, however, made it clear that any use would be a violation of the BWC.[14]

Second, the BWC lacked any provisions for the monitoring or verification of compliance—a common feature of other treaties negotiated during the Cold War. It is a severe indictment of the effectiveness of this convention when some twenty years after entry into force one of the co-depositaries stated at a review conference that twice as many countries now have or are seeking biological weapons as when the convention first entered into force. Furthermore, the BWC is not universal—there are currently some 140 states parties and 18 signatories. Israel is among the countries that have not signed the convention, and Egypt and Syria are signatories which have yet to ratify the convention.

The shortcoming of the BWC in respect to compliance was recognized by the states parties at the Second Review Conference in 1986, when they agreed on four politically binding confidence-building measures (CBMs).[15] These were strengthened and extended at the Third Review Conference in 1991.[16] However, after ten years just over half of the states parties have made as much as a single annual declaration, and only about eleven have made the required annual declaration.[17] Moreover, there has been much variation in the quantity and quality of the information declared. The requirement to participate in the CBM information exchange is politically, not legally, binding and hence is not regarded as mandatory by some states.

Finally, when the other weapons of mass destruction—nuclear and chemical weapons—are considered, the shortcomings of the BWC are thrown into sharp relief. Comparisons of the effects of biological, chemi-

---

14. United Nations, Fourth Review Conference of the Parties to the Convention on the Prohibition of the Development, Production and Stockpiling of Bacteriological (Biological) and Toxin Weapons and on their Destruction, BWC/CONF.IV/9, November 25–December 6, 1996, Geneva.

15. United Nations, Second Review Conference of the Parties to the Convention on the Prohibition of the Development, Production and Stockpiling of Bacteriological (Biological) and Toxin Weapons and on their Destruction, BWC/CONF.II/13, September 8–26, 1986, Geneva.

16. United Nations, Third Review Conference of the Parties to the Convention on the Prohibition of the Development, Production and Stockpiling of Bacteriological (Biological) and Toxin Weapons and on their Destruction, BWC/CONF.III/233, September 9–27, 1991, Geneva.

17. Iris Hunger, "Article V—Confidence Building Measures," in Graham S. Pearson and Malcolm R. Dando, eds., *Strengthening the Biological Weapons Convention: Key Points for the Fourth Review Conference* (Geneva: Quaker United Nations Office, September 1996).

cal, and nuclear weapons have long been made.[18] All demonstrate that the effects from a biological warfare attack are much greater than those from a chemical warfare attack, and can also be as great as if not greater than those resulting from a nuclear attack. The costs associated with a biological weapons program are much less than those for a nuclear weapons program, and are being reduced further by the advances in microbiology and biotechnology. Consequently, biological weapons are sometimes referred to as the poor man's atomic bomb. With the indefinite extension of the Nuclear Non-Proliferation Treaty (NPT) in 1995, the opening for signature of the Comprehensive Test Ban Treaty (CTBT) in 1996, and the entry into force on April 29, 1997, of the Chemical Weapons Convention (CWC), with its intrusive verification regime, it is evident that there is now an urgent need to strengthen the regime for the third class of weapons of mass destruction, the BWC, especially when there has been no lessening of international concern about the proliferation of biological weapons.

As Aum Shinrikyo demonstrated, chemical or biological materials may become attractive to sub-state actors, splinter groups, or terrorists; this dimension of BW must also be addressed. Reports following the 1995 attack made it clear that the Aum Shinrikyo sect had started by working on developing biological weapons. BW had been their weapon of choice. It has been reported that they had been working on botulinum toxin and anthrax and had devices that might be used to disseminate such agents, and that they had attempted on more than one occasion to use biological agents—fortunately without success. In 1992, the sect also sent a team to the former Zaire to assist in the treatment of Ebola victims, with the true aim of finding a sample of Ebola virus to take back to Japan for culturing purposes.[19]

While the threats from both terrorists and hostile nations are on the rise, the nature of the two threats is different. Terrorist groups are likely

---

18. United Nations, Chemical and Bacteriological (Biological) Weapons and the Effects of Their Possible Use, Report of the Secretary-General, A/7575/Rev.1, S/9292/Rev. 1, New York, 1969; U.S. Congress, Office of Technology Assessment (OTA), Proliferation of Weapons of Mass Destruction: Assessing the Risks, OTA-ISC-559, S/N 052-003-01335-5, dated August 5, 1993; U.S. Congress, OTA, Background Paper, Technologies Underlying Weapons of Mass Destruction, OTA-BP-ISC-115, S/N 052-003-01361-4, dated December 1993; and the chapter by Karl Lowe, Graham Pearson, and Victor Utgoff in this volume.

19. U.S. Senate Permanent Sub-Committee on Investigations (Minority Staff), Hearings on Global Proliferation of Weapons of Mass Destruction: A Case Study on Aum Shinrikyo, Staff Statement, October 31, 1995; and Kaplan and Marshall, The Cult at the End of the World.

to acquire biological weapons only if they intend to use them. Such groups create havoc and terror by taking action rather than by making threats. Terrorists, for example, are not likely to succeed in compelling governments to release prisoners merely by threatening to use biological weapons, unless they have first demonstrated that they are capable of following through with their threat. Terrorists with a score to settle against governments or institutions could turn to biological weapons as an instrument of revenge. Either way, their utility for terrorists comes mainly from use.

Nations, on the other hand, may stand to gain much more from acquiring biological weapons while circumscribing their actual use. A country's leadership may believe that acquiring biological weapons will deter a nuclear weapons attack or prevent annihilation by an opponent with overwhelming military superiority. A reckless dictator might believe he could ensure his own survival if he acquired biological weapons but reserved their use for those situations that could directly threaten his rule.

While the two threats differ, there is no mistaking their connection. If countries possess biological weapons, they can become more available to terrorists through theft, state sponsorship of the terrorists, or recruitment of knowledgeable personnel to the terrorist cause. Moreover, proliferation of biological weapons in many countries could serve to erode the stigma presently attached to their possession and ultimately lead to groups considering their use legitimate in terrorist campaigns. Winning the battle against state acquisition of biological weapons will not guarantee success in preventing terrorists from using them. But losing the battle against state acquisition will almost certainly guarantee that we fail to deter terrorist acquisition and use.

Actions to Strengthen the Prohibition Regime

In the Third Review Conference in 1991, international action to strengthen the BWC began through the establishment of an Ad Hoc Group of Governmental Experts (VEREX) with the mandate to examine potential verification measures from a scientific and technical viewpoint.[20] VEREX met four times, twice in 1992 and twice in 1993. In 1994, the final report of VEREX was considered by a Special Conference which mandated another Ad Hoc Group (AHG) to consider possible measures for a legally

20. United Nations, Ad Hoc Group of Governmental Experts to Identify and Examine Potential Verification Measures from a Scientific and Technical Standpoint, Report BWC/CONF.III/VEREX/9, Geneva 1993.

binding instrument to strengthen the BWC.[21] This AHG commenced work in early 1995, and finished its twelfth session in October 1998. In September 1996, the AHG agreed to intensify its negotiations, and in July 1997, it made a successful transition to the negotiation of a rolling text of a protocol to strengthen the BWC.

All the essential elements for the protocol are now in the rolling text: mandatory declarations, non-challenge visits (both focused and random), and compliance concern investigations, together with measures to strengthen the implementation of Article X (cooperation for peaceful purposes) and other articles of the BWC. Although some parts of the rolling text are in square brackets indicating alternatives, the essential contents of a protocol to strengthen the BWC are already present.

The individual measures being considered by the negotiators together create an integrated regime in which individual measures complement one another, resulting in a stronger and more effective whole.[22] The central and essential elements to the future protocol are measures that in combination will provide the BWC with a compliance monitoring mechanism that will detect and deter cheaters and will build confidence over time in compliance with the convention. These elements in isolation, however, will not suffice. In its final declaration the special conference stated that "the Conference, determined to strengthen the effectiveness and *improve the implementation of the Convention* and recognizing that effective verification could reinforce the Convention, decides to establish an Ad Hoc Group." It went on to say that "the objective of this Ad Hoc Group shall be to *consider appropriate measures, including possible verification measures*, and draft proposals to strengthen the Convention, to be included, as appropriate, in a legally binding instrument."[23] The aim of the AHG is to strengthen both the effectiveness and the implementation of the convention.

Consequently, measures are also needed to ensure the full implemen-

---

21. United Nations, Special Conference of the States Parties to the Convention on the Prohibition of the Development, Production and Stockpiling of Bacteriological (Biological) and Toxin Weapons and on their Destruction, Final Report, BWC/SPCONF/1, September 19–30, 1994, Geneva.

22. Graham S. Pearson, "The Strengthened BTWC Protocol: An Integrated Regime," University of Bradford Briefing Paper No. 10, July 1998. Available on the web at http://www.brad.ac.uk/acad/sbtwc.

23. United Nations, Special Conference of the States Parties to the Convention on the Prohibition of the Development, Production and Stockpiling of Bacteriological (Biological) and Toxin Weapons and on their Destruction, Final Report, BWC/SPCONF/1, September 19–30, 1994, Geneva. Emphases added.

tation of Article X (cooperation for peaceful purposes) as specifically required in the mandate for the Ad Hoc Group. Other measures to improve the implementation of Article IV (national implementation measures) and Article III (non-transfer for prohibited purposes) are also necessary. Such measures, if crafted appropriately, will also strengthen the effectiveness of the convention.

In addition, strengthening the BWC should not be considered in isolation. The technologies at the heart of the BWC—microbiology and biotechnology—are central to wealth and well-being in the twenty-first century, and are the subject of numerous national, regional, and international initiatives.[24] Measures for the protocol to strengthen the BWC need to be designed to complement and build on those activities already being implemented in other fora that share common objectives. The goal in many of these other fora is to protect human health and environmental safety, while that of the strengthened BWC is to ensure that human, animal, and plant diseases are not used as weapons of war to cause harm.

In considering the measures needed for an effective regime to strengthen the convention, it is important to strike the right balance in identifying those activities and facilities of most relevance to the convention, while avoiding the potential for information overload. A similar philosophy applies to the most relevant agents rather than all possible agents. The regime has to be designed to be efficient and effective, recognizing that the prohibition in the convention is all embracing and covers all possible facilities and all possible agents. The various elements of the integrated regime for the strengthened BWC will complement one another and enhance overall effectiveness. There are at least two main functions of the protocol: to strengthen confidence in compliance and to address concerns in a timely way.

BUILDING CONFIDENCE IN COMPLIANCE

Several elements of the protocol will contribute to confidence building. Public information, whether from the media, the Internet, official communications, or from academic and other publications, provides a baseline of understanding within the BWC organization about the standing of a particular country in respect to its perceived compliance with the BWC. States parties need to provide public information to inform the scientific community about the convention. At the Fourth Review Conference in

24. See, for example, "Article X: Some Building Blocks," University of Bradford Briefing Paper No. 6, March 1998; "Article X: Further Building Blocks," University of Bradford Briefing Paper No. 7, March 1998; and "Article X: Pharmaceutical Building Blocks," University of Bradford Briefing Paper No. 8, July 1998. These are available on the web at http://www.brad.ac.uk/acad/sbtwc.

November 1996, the Final Declaration on Article I made an appeal through the states parties to their scientific communities "to lend their support only to activities that have justification for prophylactic, protective and other peaceful purposes, and refrain from undertaking or supporting activities which are in breach of the obligations deriving from the provisions of the convention."[25] Furthermore, there are benefits to be gained from involving the scientific community in contributing to the implementation of the convention. Greater involvement of the scientific community will create more transparency in biological activities and make it more difficult for states to hide illegal programs successfully. Public information is augmented by the information provided by states parties in the declarations made under the confidence-building measures agreed at the Second Review Conference in 1986 and extended at the Third Review Conference in 1991; under the protocol to strengthen the BWC, additional CBMs may be agreed that could require either the mandatory or voluntary provision of information. Thus far, the Ad Hoc Group has paid little attention to CBMs, as it has rightly focused on the central mandatory compliance measures to strengthen the convention. A future BWC organization should remind states parties of the need to provide CBM declarations, aid them in doing so when necessary, and collate and analyze the information contained therein.

Information from the WHO, the FAO, and the Office International des Epizooties (OIE) will be important to the future BWC organization. By analyzing information from these and other sources such as CBMs, the organization will build expertise and understanding over time of the pattern of natural outbreaks of disease within states parties. Only with this expertise will the BWC organization be able to evaluate reliably disease outbreaks that appear to be unusual. The BWC organization will need to establish close links with WHO, FAO, and OIE so that maximum benefit is derived from the analyses carried out by them. Because it is not in their organizational mandates, these other organizations will not be able to point out outbreaks that might be caused by a BWC noncompliant event.

Information from the Organization for the Prohibition of Chemical Weapons (OPCW) will also be important to the BWC organization. The CWC also covers the prohibition of toxins and there is likely to be an overlap between the two conventions in this respect. Because of the links

---

25. United Nations, Fourth Review Conference of the States Parties to the Convention on the Prohibition of the Development, Production and Stockpiling of Bacteriological (Biological) and Toxin Weapons and on their Destruction, Geneva, November 25–December 6, 1996, BWC/CONF. IV/9, Geneva 1996.

between chemical and biological weapons, the two conventions will have more in common with one another than with any other international treaty or convention. By exchanging information on their experience in implementing similar provisions in the two conventions, both organizations can benefit from the best practices and avoid common difficulties. Traditionally, states which have sought chemical weapons have often gone on to seek biological weapons. Consequently, close liaison between the two organizations will help to ensure that there is an effective prohibition to all chemical and biological weapons. However, the organizations must ensure that appropriate provisions are made for the handling of confidential information in order to maximize the benefits to both. The draft protocol already contains language that in both Articles VII and IX refers to the BWC organization concluding "agreements and arrangements with relevant organizations" such as the OPCW.

Declarations made by states parties will complement the information from other sources. Multilateral information-sharing is included among the possible CBMs for the protocol. Significantly, these declarations are likely to be not only about activities and facilities relevant to compliance with the convention but also about measures taken by states parties to implement Articles III (non-transfer), IV (national implementation), and X (peaceful cooperation) of the convention. Together these will provide the organization with an appreciation of the approaches being taken by the state party to implement the convention. The quality of these declarations will be indicative of the importance ascribed by that country to compliance with the BWC and the protocol.

Confidence in these declarations and all other information available to the BWC organization will be significantly augmented by visits carried out by the BWC organization. Random visits to declared sites will ensure that declarations are accurate. Clarification visits will address ambiguities, uncertainties, anomalies, or omissions in declarations. And voluntary visits will help state parties in their compilation of individual and national declarations. Table 7.1 shows how different sources of information reinforce each other and cumulatively build confidence.

ADDRESSING CONCERNS ABOUT COMPLIANCE

The second key function of the protocol will be to provide a mechanism through which inconsistencies, anomalies, and concerns can be addressed in a timely fashion. Compliance questions that are left unaddressed for a period of time are likely to grow and take on greater importance. The protocol will enable a graduated response to concerns through consultation and clarification, which may take place directly between the states

Table 7.1. Building Confidence in Compliance.

Visits
↑
Declarations
↑
OPCW information
↑
WHO, FAO, OIE information
↑
Confidence-building measures
↑
Public information

parties concerned, with the assistance of the Director-General of the BWC organization, or by requesting the Executive Council to obtain clarification. The protocol also contains provisions for the Technical Secretariat to seek clarification from any state party of any ambiguity, uncertainty, anomaly, or omission. Should such consultation and clarification not resolve the issue, then a clarification visit may take place. Should a clarification visit not satisfactorily resolve the concern, it will then be open for states parties to lodge a request for an investigation. This progression is shown schematically in Table 7.2. The extent to which such clarification visits can be initiated by the BWC organization or by a request of a state party is not finalized in the current text; neither is the question of whether such clarification visits should be initiated after appropriate review by the Executive Council.

Building confidence and addressing compliance concerns are closely connected. The accumulation of information over time about activities and facilities within a state party will build confidence within the BWC organization that it has accurate data on that state party. Building confidence in compliance will depend on the consistency of the information being accumulated, the quality of the declarations by the state party, the way in which visits to that state party by the BWC organization have been received, and the response by the state party to any queries—whether about when declarations will arrive or any substantive aspect of a declaration.

AN INTEGRATED REGIME

The different elements of an effective regime are interrelated and together will have a considerable combined effect that will create confidence in compliance with the convention; ensure that uncertainties, anomalies, and

Table 7.2. Addressing Compliance Concerns.

Investigations
↑
Clarification visits
↑
Consultation, clarification
↑
Information from states parties

concerns are swiftly investigated; and improve the implementation of the convention.

Such an integrated regime should achieve the required consensus support from all the states parties engaged in the work of the Ad Hoc Group because it will contain the necessary balance to meet the aims and objectives of both the developed and the developing world. Developed and developing countries alike share a common desire to see the elimination of the use of deliberate disease to attack humans, animals, and plants and a strengthening of global, regional, and national counters to natural outbreaks of disease. The regime against biological weapons will be strengthened effectively so that states considering acquisition of biological weapons will judge that this is not worthwhile. Access for peaceful purposes to materials and equipment in a transparent manner will be promoted so that states parties can benefit from the burgeoning advances in biotechnology. The regime should be crafted so that existing regulation of the biotechnology industry is taken into account and valuable commercial proprietary information is protected. Additionally, states parties need assistance to build the necessary infrastructure to implement the protocol and achieve additional benefits for public health, environmental safety, and increased trade.

Measures can be devised that will both achieve the effective implementation of Article X of the convention and contribute directly to enhancing transparency and building confidence, thus strengthening the effectiveness of the convention. Although the final creation of the integrated regime has yet to occur, it does appear that the additional burden for developing and developed countries will be modest, while tangible benefits for security, public health, environmental safety, and trade will ensue. The biotechnology industry is already highly regulated in many countries; measures that seek to harmonize such regulations will contribute both to the promotion of trade and to the confidence that dual purpose materials and facilities are only being used for permitted peaceful purposes.

Prospects for the Ad Hoc Group

The delegations to the AHG are addressing how to achieve a balanced regime—one that has clear benefits for all states parties without requiring the imposition of a disproportionate burden upon states or upon those within states who will be required to provide declarations and receive visits. Although there has been much concern about commercial proprietary information, it is becoming clear from the ongoing negotiations that the likely BWC protocol will have safeguards that are at least as strong as the Chemical Weapons Convention, which entered into force in 1997 and will not require such information to be provided in declarations. As the precise nature of the regime is elaborated in detail, it is probable that the concerns of industry will be satisfactorily addressed.

In 1998, political momentum for the successful completion of the negotiations has been accumulating. In his State of the Union address in January, President Clinton called for strengthening the BWC with "a new international system to detect and deter cheating."[26] He also spoke strongly of his desire to achieve a successful completion of the negotiations at the Second Summit of the Americas in Santiago, Chile, in April.[27] In May, President Clinton announced a major U.S. initiative to counter attacks using BW and emphasized the need to strengthen the BWC with "a strong system of inspections to detect and prevent cheating . . . [as a] major priority" in his commencement address at the U.S. Naval Academy.[28]

Other countries have demonstrated their support for the BWC protocol as well. In March 1998, the European Union issued a Common Position that commits the fifteen Member States to "actively promote decisive progress in the work of the Ad Hoc Group."[29] Fourteen European states outside the EU joined the Member States in this commitment. In May, the Foreign Ministers of the G8 committed their countries to action on "the intensification and successful conclusion of the negotiation on measures,

---

26. The White House, Office of the Press Secretary, Washington, D.C., Fact Sheet, The Biological Weapons Convention, January 27, 1998.

27. The White House, Press Briefing by National Security Adviser Sandy Berger, April 18, 1998, Santiago, Chile.

28. The White House, Office of the Press Secretary, "Remarks By The President At The U.S. Naval Academy Commencement," Annapolis, Md., May 22, 1998.

29. United Nations, "Working Paper Submitted by the United Kingdom of Great Britain and Northern Ireland on Behalf of the European Union," BWC/AD HOC GROUP/WP.272, March 9, 1998.

including those for effective deterrence and verification to strengthen" the BWC.[30] In June, the British Foreign Minister addressed the AHG negotiations, urging "an early and successful conclusion" to the negotiations.[31] In March, Australia called for "the convening of a high level meeting to inject into the negotiations the necessary political commitment for urgent action."[32] At a meeting on September 23, ministers from thirty countries and representatives from twenty-seven more called for "redoubled efforts . . . to complete the Protocol . . . at the earliest possible date."[33]

The Non-Aligned Movement (NAM) and other countries said in March that they would "contribute fully to the work of the Ad Hoc Group to promote consensus on key issues."[34] The NAM reiterated its support of the negotiations at a meeting of its Foreign Ministers in May.[35] The Durban NAM Summit, on September 2–3, urged "the conclusion of the negotiations . . . as soon as possible."[36]

China and the United States issued a Joint Presidential Statement in June, supporting "efforts to strengthen the effectiveness of the Convention, including the establishment of a practical and effective compliance mechanism."[37] Russia and the United States issued a Joint Statement in September, urging "further intensification and successful conclusion of [BWC Protocol] negotiations."[38]

---

30. G8 Foreign Minister Meeting, Conclusions, London, May 9, 1998. Available on http://birmingham.g8summit.gov.uk/docs.

31. Foreign and Commonwealth Office, "Time to Accept the Realities of the Control of Biological Weapons," Address by Mr. Tony Lloyd, Minister of the State at the Foreign and Commonwealth Office, 11th Ad Hoc Group Session, Geneva, June 22, 1998.

32. Australian Permanent Mission, "Address by the Permanent Representative to the Conference of Disarmament, His Excellency Mr. John B. Campbell to the BW Ad Hoc Group," Geneva, March 9, 1998.

33. Informal Ministerial Meeting on the Negotiation Towards Conclusion of the Protocol to Strengthen the Biological Weapons Convention, September 23, 1998.

34. Mission Permanente de Colombia, "Statement by the Non-Aligned Movement and Other Countries," Geneva, March 23, 1998.

35. Ministerial Meeting of the Coordinating Bureau of the Non-Aligned Movement, Cartagena de Indias, Colombia, May 19–20, 1998.

36. The Final Document of the XIIth Summit of the Non-Aligned Movement, September 2–3, 1998, Durban, South Africa. http://www.nam.gov.za/finaldocument. html, paragraph 128.

37. Sino-U.S. Presidential Joint Statement on the Protocol to the Biological Weapons Convention, Beijing, China, June 27, 1998.

38. The White House, Office of the Press Secretary, "Joint Statement On A Protocol To The Convention On The Prohibition Of Biological Weapons," September 2, 1998.

These events demonstrate the serious international commitment to the negotiations and the worldwide political will needed to complete them.

Achieving an Effective Prohibition

The community of nations recognized that biological weapons pose a threat to the very existence of mankind when they stated in the Preamble to the 1972 BWC: "Determined, for the sake of all mankind, to exclude completely the possibility of bacteriological (biological) agents and toxins being used as weapons." The threat is even more serious today. Moreover, biological weapons could disproportionately affect the most vulnerable in our world, the young and weak. Consequently, the need to counter disease—whether natural or deliberate—has gained greater importance as the twentieth century draws to a close. What do we need to do to achieve an effective prohibition of biological weapons in the twenty-first century? A number of different activities and actors need to be addressed.

As the majority of states are party to the BWC, this situation is considered first. We need to ensure that states parties who do not possess biological weapons do not acquire them. Second, we need to persuade states parties who have started to acquire such weapons to abandon them and not to develop them further. Third, we need to ensure that states parties that possess biological weapons destroy them. Fourth, we need to prevent the use of biological weapons by states parties that retain biological weapons. Fifth, non–states parties need to be encouraged to become states parties to the BWC and its protocol. Finally, actions need to be taken to counter the acquisition or use of biological weapons by sub-state actors, terrorist groups, or individuals.

A variety of different elements needs to be harnessed to achieve a global all-embracing prohibition of biological weapons. Table 7.3 shows the objectives, targets, and elements directed at states parties to the BWC while Table 7.4 shows the objectives, targets, and elements directed at states that are not parties to the BWC, or sub-state actors.

Conclusion

In considering how to achieve an effective prohibition of biological weapons, it is instructive to look back over the developments in both security and environmental controls. Security controls have developed gradually since the signing of the Geneva Protocol in 1925, with increased attention being given to both biological arms and export controls since the Gulf

Table 7.3. Objectives, Targets, and Elements for States Parties.

Objective	Target	Element

Prevent acquisition	States parties that do not possess BW	1. Strong comprehensive international prohibition and national penal legislation
		2. Effective BWC protocol to monitor and verify compliance and to provide benefits to compliant states
		  • Declarations
		  • Non-challenge visits to declared facilities
		  • Article III regime to demonstrate transfers for peaceful purposes
		3. International individual criminal liability

Prevent further development and encourage abandonment	States parties with rudimentary BW or BW R & D only	1. Strong comprehensive international prohibition and national penal legislation
		2. Effective BWC protocol to monitor and verify compliance and to provide benefits to compliant states
		  • Declarations
		  • Non-challenge visits to declared facilities
		  • Clarification visits to declared facilities
		  • Facility investigations
		  • Field (testing) investigations
		  • Article III regime to demonstrate transfers for peaceful purposes
		3. Export controls
		4. International individual criminal liability

Detect and destroy	States parties that possess BW	1. Strong comprehensive international prohibition and national penal legislation
		2. Effective BWC protocol to monitor and verify compliance and to provide benefits to compliant states
		• Declarations
		• Non-challenge visits to declared facilities
		• Clarification visits to declared facilities
		• Facility investigations
		• Field (testing) investigations
		• Article III regime to demonstrate transfers for peaceful purposes
		3. Export controls
		4. International individual criminal liability
Prevent use	States parties that retain BW	1. Strong comprehensive international prohibition and national penal legislation
		2. Determined international response to threat/use
		3. Effective BWC protocol to monitor and verify compliance and to provide benefits to compliant states
		• Declarations
		• Non-challenge visits to declared facilities
		• Clarification visits to declared facilities
		• Facility investigations
		• Field (testing) investigations
		• Article III regime to demonstrate transfers for peaceful purposes
		4. Export controls
		5. International individual criminal liability

Table 7.4. Objectives, Targets, and Elements for Non–States Parties and Sub-State Actors.

Objective	Target	Element
Prevent acquisition and use	Non–states parties	1. UN Secretary-General investigations of alleged use
		2. Determined international response to threat/use
		3. Incentives for non–states parties to accede to the BWC and its protocol
		• Article X benefits for states parties
		• Trade barriers (as in CWC) for non–state parties
		4. Export controls
		5. International individual criminal liability
Prevent acquisition and use	Sub-state actors/ terrorist groups/ individuals	1. Strong comprehensive national penal legislation
		2. Determined national response to threat/use
		3. National controls on handling and use of agents—Regular inspections of facilities
		4. National regulations on transfer of agents
		5. International individual criminal liability

War of 1990–91. Environmental controls started later than security controls, but have received greater attention and made faster progress over the last six years. Security and environmental (including public health) considerations are both important. They share a common aim of ensuring transparency in the use and transfer of biological materials and thereby building confidence and trust between states that such materials are not being misused.

In order to negotiate a legally binding instrument to strengthen the convention, the ongoing AHG of the BWC is considering existing and enhanced transparency and confidence-building measures, compliance measures, and measures to ensure effective and full implementation of peaceful uses of microbiology. The objective of the negotiations is to devise an integrated protocol incorporating a balance of measures that will be efficient and effective in strengthening the convention. It is already clear that attention will be given to measures to strengthen the undertaking in the BWC not to transfer to any recipient whatsoever, directly or indirectly, and not in any way to assist, encourage, or induce any state, group of states, or international organizations to produce or acquire biological weapons while not impeding the undertaking to promote the peaceful uses of microbiology and biotechnology.

At the Fourth Review Conference there appeared to be a readiness to accept that states parties are required by their obligation under Article III of the BWC to implement a system of monitoring and control of transfers of materials and equipment relevant to the BWC. The non-aligned states called for a multilateral system agreed between the states parties of the convention. The basic ingredients for such a monitoring and control system already exist in the form of requirements arising from Agenda 21 for adequate and transparent safety and trans-border procedures, the draft biosafety protocol, the agreed export-import mechanism for notification of exports to Iraq, and the measures for the legally binding instrument for the BWC. Those working on the BWC protocol need to work together with those working on the biosafety protocol to put together and tailor a transparent system using these existing elements to meet the requirements of the BWC as well as those of the environment. Such a system will be to the mutual advantage of all the states concerned, as cooperative action to minimize the risks from deliberate and natural disease will aid the security and prosperity of the world community.

Furthermore, the essential elements of the protocol to strengthen the BWC—mandatory declarations, non-challenge visits (both random and focused), investigations (both field and facility), and measures to strengthen the implementation of Articles III (non-transfer), IV (national implementation), VII (assistance), and X (peaceful cooperation)—are vital to achieve an effective prohibition regime. This regime must contain a balance of measures that benefits all states parties, both developed and developing, so that there will be universality of adherence to both the BWC and its protocol. Only with this balance will all states identify clear long-term benefits and advantages resulting from the BWC protocol regime.

The draft protocol has language to achieve this effective prohibition of biological weapons. The benefits are clear and far outweigh the burden of compliance with the strengthened regime. The political will to achieve this enhanced regime is indeed worldwide, embracing all regional groups. The Ad Hoc Group needs to continue its work and to accelerate it further in order to achieve the goal of totally eliminating and prohibiting biological weapons before the twenty-first century.

Part IV
Iraq's Biological Weapons Program

Chapter 8

Iraq's Biological Warfare Program: The Past as Future?

Raymond A. Zilinskas

The United Nations Special Commission (UNSCOM) and the International Atomic Energy Agency (IAEA) have investigated Iraq's weapons of mass destruction programs since April 1991. During 1995 and 1996, UNSCOM analysts were able to clarify most aspects of Iraq's biological warfare program. This chapter, which draws on information available in open sources[1] and my experience as a member of the UNSCOM investigation, assesses the military impact that biological weapons might have had if employed during the Persian Gulf War, analyzes the potential of a resurgent Iraqi biological warfare program, and discusses the implica-

This chapter was adapted from Raymond A. Zilinskas, "Iraq's Biological Weapons: The Past as Future?" *Journal of the American Medical Association (JAMA)*, Vol. 278, No. 5 (August 6, 1997), pp. 418–424. © 1997 American Medical Association.

1. *Report of the Secretary-General on the Status of the Implementation of the Special Commission's Plan for the Ongoing Monitoring and Verification of Iraq's Compliance with the Relevant Parts of Section C of Security Council Resolution 687 (1991),* UN Document S/1995/864, October 11, 1995; *Tenth Report of the Executive Chairman of the Special Commission Established by the Secretary-General Pursuant to Paragraph 9(b)(i) of Security Council Resolution 687 (1991), and Paragraph 3 of Resolution 699 (1991) on the Activities of the Special Commission,* UN Document S/1995/1038, December 17, 1995; *Report of the Secretary-General on the Activities of the Special Commission Established by the Secretary-General Pursuant to Paragraph 9(b)(i) of Resolution 687 (1991),* UN Document S/1996/848, October 11, 1996; Republic of Iraq, National Monitoring Directorate, *The Iraqi Implementation of SCR's 687 (1991) Section (C), 715 (1991) and 1051 (1996). Report Covering the Period 11 April to 11 October 1996; Report of the Secretary-General on the Activities of the Special Commission Established by the Secretary-General Pursuant to Paragraph 9(b)(i) of Resolution 687 (1991),* UN Document S/1997/301, April 11, 1997; and *Report of the Secretary General on the Activities of the Special Commission Established by the Secretary-General Pursuant to Paragraph 9(b)(i) of Resolution 687 (1991),* UN Document S/1997/774, October 6, 1997.

tions of such a program for regional stability and international arms control.

Before beginning with the substantive part of this chapter, it is important for the reader to be aware that a biological weapon is more than simply a pathogenic microorganism or toxin.[2] In actuality, it is a system composed of four major components—payload (the biological agent), munition (a container that keeps the payload intact and virulent during delivery), delivery system (missile, artillery shell, aircraft, etc.), and dispersal mechanism (an explosive force or spray device to dispense the agent to the target population). This report includes an analysis of each component of Iraq's biological weapons individually and of their functioning in unison as a system.

Iraq's Biological Warfare Program

After initial explorations in the late 1970s, Iraq's biological warfare program commenced in earnest in 1985. By the time Operation Desert Storm ended with a cease-fire in April 1991, Iraqi scientists had investigated the biological warfare potential of five bacterial strains, one fungal strain, five types of viruses, and four toxins. In addition, two bacterial species, *Bacillus subtilis* and *Bacillus thuringiensis*, were developed for use as simulants (i.e., non-pathogens used for testing purposes).

Two pathogenic bacterial species were studied—*Bacillus anthracis* (the cause of the disease anthrax) and *Clostridium perfringens* (the cause of gas gangrene). Research on *B. anthracis* was initiated in 1985 at Muthanna State Establishment, the principal Iraqi chemical weapons facility, but was transferred in 1987 to Salman Pak, just south of Baghdad, which became the center for biological warfare research and development. Some strains of *B. anthracis* were imported from culture collections in France and the United States; others were local isolates. At Salman Pak, four strains were characterized, their media and storage requirements were established, and their pathogenicity evaluated in animal models. Research findings were applied at the Al Hakam Single-Cell Protein Production Plant, Iraq's major development and production facility for biological warfare agents, to begin mass production of *B. anthracis* in 1989. Eventually, approximately 8,000 liters of solution, with a *B. anthracis* spore and cell count of 10^9 per milliliter, were produced. Of this, 6,000 liters were used to fill weapons; the remainder was stored at Al Hakam.

2. Raymond A. Zilinskas, "Terrorism and Biological Weapons: Inevitable Alliance?" *Perspectives in Biology and Medicine*, Vol. 34, No. 1 (Autumn 1990), pp. 44–72.

A reference strain of *C. perfringens* was imported from the United States in 1985. In 1988, experimental work using mice commenced in order to determine the infectivity of *C. perfringens* spores, the ability of spores to initiate disease, and their degree of virulence. During 1990, 340 liters of solution containing *C. perfringens* were produced at Al Hakam. The Iraqis claim, however, that no attempt was made to develop this agent for weapons use.

One fungal strain with crop-destroying potential, wheat cover smut, was evaluated for use as a weapon. Research carried out at Salman Pak in 1985 demonstrated that wheat cover smut spores sprayed over immature wheat plants would be lethal to the crop. In 1988, young wheat plants growing in large fields near the town of Mosul were infected with this agent; the infected wheat subsequently was harvested and moved to Fudaliyah for storage. The Iraqis claim that no attempt was made to recover fungus from the harvest and that the infected crop was destroyed in 1990. The investigation of wheat smut implies that Iraqi leaders knew that biological weapons were more than anti-personnel weapons; they could also be employed against crops as part of economic warfare.

Beginning in early 1990, scientists at the Foot and Mouth Disease Center at Al Manal investigated five types of viruses for their potential utility as biological weapons. Two viruses, Congo-Crimean hemorrhagic virus and Yellow Fever virus, were found to be unsuitable since they required vectors for dispersal. The remainder, enterovirus 17, human rotavirus, and camelpox virus, were researched further, and a large egg incubator was obtained to mass-produce the viruses. Reportedly only certain growth characteristics of the viruses were elucidated before the program was terminated in 1990. Enterovirus 17 and human rotavirus may have been investigated for use as incapacitating biological warfare agents (both cause gastrointestinal disorders), while camelpox might have been considered an "ethnic" weapon (i.e., persons reared where no camels exist might prove especially susceptible to this zoonotic disease).

Substantial attention was given to weaponizing aflatoxin, botulinum toxin, ricin, and tricothecenes. (Many types of aflatoxin, botulinum, and tricothecene toxins are known to exist; however, since the Iraqis manufactured crude solutions containing undefined mixtures of toxin types, these toxins are referred to in the singular in this chapter.) Iraqi research of organisms that produce aflatoxin, including *Aspergillus flavus* and *Aspergillus parasiticus*, led to the development of methods for growing aflatoxin-producing fungi on wet rice. Individual types of aflatoxin were identified, and some aflatoxin-containing solutions were tested in animal models. Production of aflatoxin began in 1989 at Salman Pak, where approximately 2,200 liters of solution were eventually manufactured. An unknown quantity of this cache was used to fill weapons; the remainder was stored.

Using a *Clostridium botulinum* strain imported from the United States, the Iraqis produced 20,000 liters of solution containing botulinum toxin of unknown strength and types at Al Hakam and Al Manal during 1989 and 1990. Of this, 12,000 liters were used in field-testing or to fill warheads; unused toxin-containing solution was stored at Al Hakam.

The castor bean plant (*Ricinus communis*), grown widely in Iraq, naturally produces ricin. During 1989, approximately 10 liters of concentrated ricin solution were manufactured at Salman Pak. While some was tested in animal models and some used as payload in artillery shells, the fate of most is unknown. Ricin might have been researched because it is plentiful and known to be effective for assassination.[3]

In 1990, Iraqi scientists investigated the ability of two fungal species, *Fusarium oxysporium* and *Fusarium granarium*, to produce tricothecene mycotoxins. Fungi were grown on damp, supplemented rice; the toxins they produced were extracted by organic solvents and dried in a rotary evaporator. The Iraqis claim to have produced 20 milliliters of tricothecene-containing solution, some of which was tested in animal models. The fate of the remainder is unknown. Tricothecenes may have been investigated because some can penetrate skin and because of their alleged history as components of "yellow rain." (During the late 1970s, the U.S. State Department alleged that the Vietnamese, abetted by the Soviet Union, had used toxin weapons against the Hmong and other native peoples of the Indochina peninsula.[4] Supposedly the main constituents of the dispersed agent, named yellow rain because of its appearance, were tricothecenes.)

The microbial and toxin agents produced at Al Hakam, Al Manal, and Salman Pak usually were transported to the Muthanna State Establishment, where they were used as payloads in various types of munitions. The Muthanna State Establishment was well suited for this function, since it was Iraq's main filling facility for chemical weapons.

Iraq's chemical arsenal included 250-pound (LD-250) and 400-pound (R-400) bombs of Spanish design. Based on successful chemical warfare, some of these bombs were adapted to hold 60 and 85 liters of biological

---

3. John Emsley and David Pallister, "Bulgarian Brolly Baffles Germ Warfare Boffins," *New Scientist*, Vol. 80 (October 12, 1978), p. 92.

4. U.S. Department of State, *Chemical Warfare in Southeast Asia and Afghanistan. Report to the Congress from Secretary of State Alexander M. Haig, Jr., March 22, 1982 (Special Report No. 98)* (Washington, D.C.: U.S. Department of State, 1982).

solution, respectively. Further, bombs designated to carry biological or toxin agents received special treatment. Most significantly, walls of the chambers containing the payload were coated with an inert epoxy paint to protect the biological agents from the toxic effects of contact with metal. Testing determined that the R-400 was the more suitable munition for biological warfare. In 1990, 200 R-400 biological bombs were produced; of these, 100 were filled with botulinum toxin, 50 with anthrax, and 7 with aflatoxin. These biologically armed bombs were deployed at two sites before Operation Desert Storm took place, ready for immediate use.

A few 155 mm caliber artillery shells were filled with ricin for field-testing. Reportedly, tests did not go well, and no further attempts were made by the Iraqis to develop artillery shells for biological warfare.

Iraq had procured more than 800 Scud missiles from Soviet bloc countries before 1991 and had manufactured about 80 itself (most of which proved faulty). The Scud had a range of 300 kilometers and could carry a high explosive payload of up to one metric ton. Some Scuds, renamed Al Husseins, were redesigned and rebuilt to double their range—although the trade-off was diminished payload capacity. In 1990, the Muthanna State Establishment received a special shipment of 100 Al Husseins. Of these, twenty-five were fitted with biological warheads: thirteen with botulinum toxin, ten with aflatoxin, and two with anthrax. All reportedly were deployed before Operation Desert Storm commenced: ten in a deep railway tunnel and fifteen in holes dug along the Tigris river.[5]

The warheads of an unknown number of SAKR-18 122 millimeter rockets were filled with botulinum toxin, aflatoxin, or the simulant *B. subtilis*, and field-tested. As far as is known, no biological rockets were actually deployed.

All Iraqi munitions that depended on explosion for agent dispersal were of similar design—a tube filled with an explosive charge (burster) was placed in the center of a chamber containing the biological agent. At the moment of impact, the burster would explode, rupturing the outer wall of the munition and expelling the payload over a limited area. Further dispersal of the expelled agents would depend on meteorological forces, especially wind.

The Iraqis possessed several hundred modern Italian-made pesticide dispersal systems that were fitted with sprayer nozzles capable of generating aerosols of the one to five micron size optimal for biological warfare.

5. Anthony H. Cordesman, *Weapons of Mass Destruction in Iraq: A Summary of Biological, Chemical, Nuclear and Delivery Efforts and Capabilities* (Washington, D.C.: Center for Strategic and International Studies, 1996).

Some sprayers and appropriate holding tanks were installed on aircraft and land vehicles. Most important, in 1990, the Iraqis modified a MiG-21 fighter plane to be a remotely piloted vehicle and equipped it with a 2,200 liter belly tank (taken from a Mirage-F1 fighter plane) and a spray mechanism. In a field test carried out in January 1991, the remotely piloted vehicle sprayed a solution laden with a biological simulant over a practice target range. The results of this test are not known.

Reportedly, soon after Iraq had accepted a cease-fire under United Nations Security Council Resolution 687 in April 1991,[6] biological warfare program personnel were ordered to destroy all biological warfare agents. A two-step process was used for this purpose. First, stores of biological warfare agents were treated with formaldehyde and potassium permanganate, both of which are powerful disinfectants. Second, the residuum was poured onto the bare ground of the desert near Al Hakam's perimeter. Five years later, UNSCOM was unable to recover either residuum or its breakdown products from the claimed dumpsites. What this means is not clear. Natural forces might have completely degraded the residuum over time, and the degradation products may have been dispersed by wind and rain; Iraqi authorities may be mistaken as to the location of dumps; or they may be lying about the purported destruction. Since UNSCOM cannot ascertain what took place, it is unable to verify independently the destruction of biological warfare agent stores.

The munitions that contained the biological warfare agents supposedly were destroyed at the same time as their contents. Bombs and missile warheads were opened and formaldehyde and potassium permanganate were added to the solution they contained. After allowing the disinfectants to do their work for some days, munitions were crushed by bulldozers and burned in pits. Finally, munition remains were concealed by detonating general-purpose bombs among them. Many test munitions were simply thrown into the Tigris river. While some whole and many fragmented R-400s have been recovered by UNSCOM, the agency cannot certify that all biological bombs have been destroyed, nor does it have solid evidence on the fate of missile warheads.

United Nations Security Council Resolution 687 (1991) specifies that facilities and equipment used in support of any of Iraq's weapons of mass destruction programs are to be destroyed to the satisfaction of UNSCOM or IAEA. Actually, a few days before the first UNSCOM biological inspection team arrived at Salman Pak on August 2, 1991, the Iraqis themselves blew up the main part of their biological warfare research facility and

---

6. United Nations Security Council Resolution 687 (1991), UN Document S/RES/687 (1991), April 3, 1991.

used bulldozers to cover the leveled site with a thick layer of dirt. In addition, some implicative equipment, such as aerosol test chambers, were removed, crushed, and discarded on scrap heaps. However, other biological warfare facilities at Al Hakam and Al Manal remained operational and the Iraqis tried to conceal their real purpose. Nevertheless, by the end of 1995 UNSCOM had discerned their actual function.[7] Accordingly, in May and June 1996, Iraqi workers, overseen by UNSCOM inspectors, obliterated the Al Hakam plant and the equipment at Al Manal that had produced biological warfare agents.

In view of the many strange and even bizarre claims that have been made about Iraq's prowess in the biological area, it is worth making note of what UNSCOM has not found. Although a few Iraqi scientists are capable of using genetic engineering, particularly at the University of Baghdad, there is no evidence that such advanced biotechnology techniques were used in the biological warfare program. Claims, for example, that mycoplasmas were genetically engineered by the Iraqis for purposes of biological warfare and that such creations were the cause of the Gulf War syndrome cannot be supported by any information possessed by UNSCOM.[8]

Assessing Iraq's Biological Weapons Capability

Although Iraqi scientists investigated the biological warfare potential of numerous agents and toxins, by the late 1980s the decision had been made to develop just three of them for weapons use: *B. anthracis*, botulinum toxin, and aflatoxin. The reason for that decision is not known.

B. ANTHRACIS

In the past, *B. anthracis* has been weaponized by Japan, the United Kingdom, the United States, and the Soviet Union, so this bacterial species's attributes as a biological warfare agent are well known.[9] *B. anthracis*

---

7. Raymond A. Zilinskas, "Detecting and Deterring Biological Weapons: Lessons from United Nations Special Commission (UNSCOM) Operations in Iraq," in James Brown, ed., *Arms Control in a Multi-Polar World* (Amsterdam: VU University Press, 1996), pp. 193–210.

8. Ed Offley, "Gulf War Illness Linked to Iraqi Germ Weapons," *Seattle Post-Intelligencer*, December 11, 1996, p. 1; and Ed Offley, "Pentagon Feuds With Scientist on Gulf War Illness," *Seattle Post-Intelligencer*, December 20, 1996, p. 1.

9. Union of Soviet Socialist Republics, *Materials on the Trial of Former Servicemen of the Japanese Army Charged with Manufacturing and Employing Bacteriological Weapons* (Moscow: Foreign Languages Publishing House, 1950); Peter Williams and David Wallace, *Unit 731: The Japanese Army's Secret of Secrets* (London: Hodder & Stoughton, 1989);

spores are extremely hardy, and they retain virulence during storage. *B. anthracis* cells and spores dispersed in aerosol can inflict heavy casualties on unprotected populations, and, if treatment with appropriate antibiotics is not begun soon after exposure, a morbidity rate of 65–80 percent will result.[10]

B. anthracis slated for weapons may be produced as slurry (a watery mixture resembling mud) or dry powder. *B. anthracis*–containing slurry, while easier to manufacture than powder, is less efficient for biological warfare purposes: cells suspended in slurry lose virulence relatively quickly, and, more importantly, slurry is technically troublesome to disperse as an aerosol with particles of optimal size.[11] Yet, although Iraq possessed dryers and grinders that could have been used to produce dry anthrax, all of its deployed biological warfare munitions were filled with *B. anthracis*–containing slurry. The reason why dry powder was not used as filling for munitions is not known. My guess is that the Iraqis were unable to overcome the technical difficulties inherent to powder production, including safety problems.

BOTULINUM TOXIN

Since botulinum toxin is the most toxic chemical known to science, biological warfare programs in other nations have investigated its military

G.B. Carter, *Biological Warfare and Biological Defence in the United Kingdom 1940–1979* (Porton Down, England: Chemical and Biological Establishment, 1992); John Bryden, *Deadly Allies: Canada's Secret War 1937–1947* (Toronto: Canadian Publishers, 1989); Ralph E. Lincoln and Morris A. Rhian, *Anthrax in the BW Program* (BWL Technical Memorandum 2–37) (Fort Detrick, Md.: Process Research Division, Aerobiological Division, 1959); U.S. Department of the Army, *U.S. Army Activity in the U.S. Biological Warfare Programs 1942–1977*, Vol. II, *Annexes* (Washington, D.C.: Department of the Army Publication DTIC B193427 L, 1977); Milton Leitenberg, "Anthrax in Sverdlovsk: New Pieces to the Puzzle," *Arms Control Today*, Vol. 22, No. 3 (April 1992), pp. 10–13; Matthew Meselson, Jeanne Guillemin, Martin Hugh-Jones, Alexander Langmuir, Ilona Popova, Alexis Shelokov, and Olga Yampolskaya, "The Sverdlovsk Anthrax Outbreak of 1979," in this volume; U.S. Army Medical Unit, *Bibliography on Anthrax* (Fort Detrick, Md.: U.S. Army Chemical Corps, 1960); and Stockholm International Peace Research Institute (SIPRI), *The Problem of Chemical and Biological Warfare*, Vol. II, *CB Weapons Today* (New York: Humanities Press, 1973).

10. Jack Keene, *Feasibility of a Proposed Weapons System Concept Using Agent N, and Variation of Casualties with Dose for Man* (BWL Technical Memorandum 2–8) (Camp Detrick, Md.: Plans and Evaluation Office, Director of Development, 1958); and David L. Huxsoll, Cheryl D. Parrott, and William C. Patrick III, "Medicine in Defense against Biological Warfare," *Journal of the American Medical Association (JAMA)*, Vol. 262, No. 5 (August 4, 1989), pp. 677–679.

11. Keene, *Feasibility of a Proposed Weapons System Concept Using Agent N;* and *Development of "N" for Offensive Use in Biological Warfare* (Special Report No. 9) (Camp Detrick, Md.: Chemical Warfare Service, 1945).

utility.[12] While most cases of botulinum intoxication are caused by ingested contaminated food, aerosolized toxin is believed to be deadly for humans.[13] Theoretically, eight kilograms of the concentrated botulinum toxin dispersed over an area of 100 square kilometers would deliver a median infective dose (ID_{50}) to the entire unprotected population located therein, assuming optimal meteorological conditions.[14] These properties may have proven attractive to the Iraqis who, as noted above, had produced large quantities of botulinum toxin–containing solution of unknown concentration. Even if the botulinum toxin–containing solution produced by the Iraqis had contained a low concentration of the toxin, it is reasonable to assume that this solution would have been lethal in a small dose if it had been delivered effectively to the target population given the extreme lethality of the agent.

AFLATOXIN

It is difficult to understand why the Iraqis developed aflatoxin for weapons use. Although well known to medical science as a powerful nephrotoxin and hepatotoxin,[15] aflatoxin has no known property useful for biological warfare. Possible explanations for Iraq's interest in aflatoxin are that Iraqi scientists may have discovered that aflatoxin possessed a previously unknown property useful for biological warfare applications; Iraqi planners may have intended to use aflatoxin's long-term carcinogenic properties as a means of terrorizing targeted civilian populations; or since aflatoxin is easier to manufacture than most other toxins, the Iraqi biological warfare program's staff might have chosen to produce it to meet production goals set by higher authorities, rather than for its perceived biological warfare value. The last-mentioned explanation is, in my opinion, the most likely. Whatever the case, Iraq's aflatoxin-based weapons most probably would have had little military utility.

---

12. Operations Research Group, *Military Utility of Agent X* (Edgewood Arsenal, Md.: Army Chemical Center, 1952); David R. Franz, *Defense Against Toxin Weapons* (Frederick, Md.: U.S. Army Medical Research and Materiel Command, 1994); and SIPRI, *The Problem of Chemical and Biological Warfare.*

13. Stanley L. Wiener and John Barrett, *Trauma Management for Civilian and Military Physicians* (Philadelphia: W.B. Saunders, 1986), pp. 529–536; and David L. Huxsoll, William C. Patrick, and Cheryl D. Parrott, "Veterinary Services in Biological Disasters," *Journal of the American Veterinary Medical Association,* Vol. 190, No. 6 (March 15, 1987), pp. 714–722.

14. Franz, *Defense Against Toxin Weapons.*

15. Wiener and Barrett, *Trauma Management for Civilian and Military Physicians;* and Robert C. Patten, "Aflatoxins and Disease," *American Journal of Tropical Medicine and Hygiene,* Vol. 30, No. 2 (February 1981), pp. 422–425.

The Tactical Threat

Though in possession of several hundred biological weapons, Iraq's tactical biological warfare capability during the Persian Gulf War actually was quite limited. As noted, Iraqi biological warfare munitions depended on impact detonation for primary dispersal of pathogenic and toxin agents. This method is exceedingly inefficient because an explosion inevitably renders harmless most of the payload; impact detonation drives a substantial part of the surviving payload into the ground; the small part of the payload actually aerosolized by explosion generally is not propelled beyond a few tens of meters; and the sizes of aerosolized particles vary widely, from large clumps to dust-like particles of smaller size than one micron. (Large particles settle quickly to the ground and are filtered out by protective structures within the nasopharyngeal tract; fine dust is quickly dispersed by wind and may whiff in and out of the lungs without settling.) For these reasons, had Iraq's biological warfare munitions actually been used against coalition forces, their effect would have been limited to contaminating a relatively small area of ground surrounding the point of impact and exposing only nearby individuals to aerosolized pathogens or toxins. In addition, the Al Hussein missiles were unstable in flight, and because they lacked an inertial guidance system, they were inaccurate.[16] Therefore, had the Iraqis launched biological-weapons-laden Al Husseins in support of tactical military missions, the missiles probably would either have disintegrated in flight or missed the target.

Biological agents delivered by aerosol would have presented a more credible threat to coalition forces, but such a system most probably had not reached the operational state by the time Operation Desert Storm took place.

The defensive capabilities of coalition forces must also be taken into account in my assessment. In this regard, three factors were most important. First, coalition forces had overwhelming air superiority and unsurpassed ability to detect and destroy airborne aircraft. The probability of an aircraft bearing biological-weapons-laden bombs surviving long enough to deliver its load therefore would have been low. Second, Iraq's meteorological stations and communications network had been destroyed by coalition bombings.[17] Without accurate weather forecasts, airborne biological agents delivered by bombs or missiles might have been dispersed by winds over empty desert or even blown onto friendly forces.

---

16. Rick Atkinson, *Crusade: The Untold Story of the Persian Gulf War* (Boston: Houghton Mifflin, 1993).

17. Ibid.

Third, coalition forces had been trained to expect chemical attacks by Iraq, and were well equipped to defend themselves against them. Fortuitously, the standard anti-chemical defense methods and equipment with which coalition forces were equipped would have provided adequate protection against all known Iraqi biological weapons.

However, protection against biological and chemical weapons comes at a cost. As a consequence of wearing gas masks and protective suits, soldiers have limited observational powers, are constrained in their ability to perform complex manual tasks, perspire more than normal, and tire more quickly. For these reasons, the military effectiveness of troops garbed in protective suits inevitably is significantly less than troops wearing normal clothing.[18] Therefore, just by making the coalition forces believe that a biological attack is imminent, the Iraqis would have forced soldiers to garb themselves, which would have impeded their mobility and ability to fight.

Investigations of Operation Desert Storm after the fact found substantial deficiencies with biological warfare defense preparedness of coalition forces, including shortfalls in defensive equipment, inadequate training, and shortages in medical support.[19] However, the primary weakness of the coalition forces in regard to biological warfare was that they did not have "stand-off" or "point" detection capabilities (i.e., they could not reliably detect agent-laden aerosol clouds or plumes created by explosion at a distance or on-site). Therefore, had the Iraqis against all odds been able to mount a surprise attack with biological weapons that depended on aerosol dispersal, the coalition forces would have faced a very serious situation. Assuming that wind conditions would have been such that the agent-laden aerosol was carried into positions held by coalition forces, the fact that an attack was under way probably would not have been detected. Thus, no warning would have been sounded for troops to protect themselves by garbing or seeking shelter.

From what is known about Iraq's biological warfare program, it is likely that such an attack would have involved aerosolized anthrax or botulinum toxin (or both). Comparatively few coalition forces were vaccinated against these agents. Out of the approximately 697,000 U.S. per-

18. Henry L. Taylor and Jesse Orlansky, *The Effects of Wearing Protective Chemical Warfare Combat Clothing on Human Performance* (Report P-2433) (Alexandria, Va.: Institute for Defense Analyses, 1991).

19. U.S. General Accounting Office (GAO), *Operation Desert Storm: DoD Met Need for Chemical Suits and Masks, but Longer Term Actions Needed* (Report GAO/NSIAD-92–116) (Washington, D.C.: GAO, 1993); and U.S. GAO, *Chemical and Biological Defense: U.S. Forces Are Not Adequately Equipped to Detect All Threats* (Report GAO/NSIAD-93–2) (Washington, D.C.: GAO, 1993).

sonnel who served in the Persian Gulf region as part of coalition forces, 8,000 had been vaccinated against botulinum toxin and 150,000 had received one vaccination of the six vaccinations regime required for maximum protection against anthrax.[20] A much smaller number of the latter group had received a second vaccination against anthrax. In view of only approximately 22 percent of U.S. personnel having partial protection against anthrax and 1.1 percent against botulinum toxin, it is likely that the first indication of a biological attack would have become apparent three to six days after it had taken place, when exposed soldiers began to present symptoms of pneumonic anthrax or intoxication.

Although *B. anthracis* is susceptible to commonly available antibiotics, treatment would have to begin almost immediately after symptoms appear for the affected patient to have a reasonable chance of survival. However, pulmonary anthrax is difficult to diagnose, since its symptoms are similar to several other more common pulmonary diseases. Further, fewer than one U.S. physician in one thousand has personally seen a case of anthrax. For these reasons, a definitive diagnosis under the conditions considered here probably would have taken a few days. At that time there would be an immediate need for large quantities of antibiotics. It is questionable whether large enough supplies of medicine would have been on hand to provide adequate treatment to a large number of exposed individuals. Taking into consideration all these factors, it is probable that the coalition forces would have suffered heavy casualties had a biological aerosol attack taken place.

If the main biological warfare agent had been aerosolized botulinum toxin instead of *B. anthracis* in the hypothetical attack, then there is more uncertainty about what its outcome would have been. In contradistinction to anthrax, with which there is a long experience in human medicine, there is very little experience with the effects of aerosolized botulinum on human beings.[21] Similar to anthrax, if treatment of exposed individuals is begun before symptoms appear, there is a very good chance that the exposed persons will survive. The treatment in this case consists of administering an active immunization of a toxoid vaccine. However, from animal studies it appears that once symptoms of botulinum intoxication have appeared, the level of protection afforded by the toxoid vaccine is

---

20. Institute of Medicine, Committee to Review the Health Consequences of Service During the Persian Gulf War, *Health Consequences of Service During the Persian Gulf War: Initial Findings and Recommendations* (Washington, D.C.: National Academy Press, 1996).

21. John L. Middlebrook and David R. Franz, "Botulinum Toxins," in Frederick R. Siddell, Ernest T. Takafuji, and David R. Franz, *Medical Aspects of Chemical and Biological Warfare* (Washington, D.C.: Office of the Surgeon General, 1997), pp. 643–654.

low. Since there is so little experience with aerosol botulinum intoxication, it is reasonable to assume that diagnosis of persons exposed to a biological attack in which botulinum toxin was used would have been delayed past the point where symptoms had appeared. If so, coalition forces would have suffered heavy casualties.

It is likely that the difficulties with diagnosis and treatment would have been compounded for the defenders if the theoretical attack had been done with botulinum toxin and *B. anthracis* in unison. Human medicine has no experience with such an event. Therefore, one cannot predict what the result would have been, but it probably would have been more horrendous than if only one agent had been used.

Had the Iraqis been able to attack the coalition forces' rear positions, such as airfields, ports, and troop assembly areas, with aerosolized biological or toxin agents, similar situations to those described above would have ensued. Heavy casualties among troops and civilian workers, compounded by panic, would have caused serious disruptions. The coalition forces' ability to operate would have been severely compromised as the flow of vital supplies decreased to a trickle, communications were hindered, and medical facilities were overwhelmed.

The Threat Posed to Civilian Populations

During the Iran-Iraq war of 1980–86, an episode called the War of the Cities demonstrated that the Iraqi leadership is capable of, and unconcerned about, ordering attacks on purely civilian targets. It began when Iraq launched missiles, including Scuds, against helpless Iranian cities of no obvious military value. The Iranians retaliated in kind.[22] After an exchange of several hundred missiles, the episode ended with apparently neither side having gained militarily from the exchange. Neither side has published the costs to civilians of the War of the Cities. From anecdotal evidence it appears as if many thousands of civilians were wounded, of whom many died. In addition, the missiles caused incalculable misery for hundreds of thousands of city dwellers.

Cities were also targeted during the Persian Gulf War, but on a much smaller scale. The Iraqis launched 39 Scud missiles against Israeli cities.[23] They caused 1,060 Israeli casualties, including 11 deaths; however, "only"

---

22. Anthony H. Cordesman and Abraham R. Wagner, *The Lessons of Modern War*, Vol. II, *The Iran-Iraq War* (Boulder, Colo.: Westview, 1990).

23. Eric Karsenty, Joshua Shemer, Itzhik Alshech, Bruno Cojocaru, Marian Moscovitz, Yair Shapiro, and Yehuda L. Danon, "Medical Aspects of the Iraqi Missile Attacks on Israel," *Israel Journal of Medical Sciences*, Vol. 27, Nos. 11–12 (Winter 1991), pp. 603–607.

234 injuries and 2 deaths resulted directly from explosion.[24] The many destructive effects of this bombardment on the Israeli population has been thoroughly described and analyzed.[25] Of pertinence to this chapter is that a much larger number of persons were wounded and killed by occurrences secondary to missile impacts than by the impacts themselves. In particular, panicky actions by civilians led to many casualties.

Although all missiles launched against Israel carried high explosive warheads, Iraq was capable of having launched Al Hussein missiles equipped with biological warheads. If that had occurred, what would the consequences have been?

Since cities occupy large areas, it is likely that some of the Al Husseins would have reached their targets. (Also, solitary bombers equipped with R-400 bombs might have evaded detection by hugging the ground.) As noted in my assessment of Iraqi bombs and missiles presented above, after impact each of these weapons would have contaminated a small area and created a plume of debris. If a wind was blowing, the material in the plume would have been dispersed downwind, exposing people in the area where the plume's contents settled. Since the explosive load on missiles laden with biological agents is low (to avoid destroying the living payload), we can assume that Israeli officials analyzing the effects of a missile impact would immediately determine that there was something unusual about it. Most likely they would at that time suspect that the missile payload consisted of biological or chemical agents. Having quickly excluded chemical agents from further consideration (modern chemical agent detectors work in real time), microbiologists and toxicologists would have been brought to the site of impact and set to work analyzing missile contents. Within a few hours, a tentative finding could be made whether the payload consisted of bacteria or toxin. In either case, all persons at or near the site of impact, as well as downwind, could start

24. Yehuda L. Danon and Joshua Shemer, "Israeli Medical Lessons from the Gulf War: An Overview," *Israel Journal of Medical Sciences*, Vol. 27, Nos. 11–12 (Winter 1991), pp. 601–602.

25. Ibid.; Avraham Bleich, Shmuel Kron, Chaim Margalit, Giora Inbar, Zeev Kaplan, Shimon Cooper, and Zhava Solomon, "Israeli Psychological Casualties of the Persian Gulf War: Characteristics, Therapy, and Selected Issues," *Israel Journal of Medical Sciences*, Vol. 27, Nos. 11–12 (Winter 1991), pp. 673–676; Abraham Carmeli, Nira Liberman, and Lilach Mevorach, "Anxiety-Related Somatic Reactions During Missile Attacks," *Israel Journal of Medical Sciences*, Vol. 27, Nos. 11–12 (Winter 1991), pp. 677–679; and Carol S. Fullerton, George T. Brandt, and Robert J. Ursano, "Chemical and Biological Weapons: Silent Agents of Terror," in Robert J. Ursano and Ann E. Norwood, eds., *Emotional Aftermath of the Gulf War: Veterans, Families, Communities, and Nations* (Washington, D.C.: American Psychiatric Press, 1996), pp. 111–142.

receiving treatment within 12–24 hours of exposure, before symptoms appear. Thus, the number of casualties caused directly by pathogens or toxins carried by the missile probably would have been low.

However, on the basis of Israel's experience with Scuds, it is reasonable to surmise that the exposed population's terrified reaction to missile impacts that draw unusual official reaction probably would have caused much more harm than the weapons themselves. Therefore, the combination of direct casualties brought about by disease or intoxication in combination with casualties caused by the resultant panic likely would have caused more injuries and death than were produced by high explosives. Further, the outrage felt by the Israeli population most likely would have compelled Israel to retaliate with its own weapons of mass destruction or by deploying ground troops to secure the areas from which the missiles were launched.

A Resurgent Iraqi Weapons of Mass Destruction Program

Had Operation Desert Storm not intervened, it is likely that Iraq would have possessed a formidable suite of weapons of mass destruction by 1997.[26] It could have deployed ballistic missiles with a range of about 2,000 kilometers capable of delivering up to a one-ton payload. Further, Iraqi commanders would have been able to select the type of warhead required for a particular mission. Thus, a nuclear or biological warhead might have been used to achieve a strategic objective—for example, to destroy the capital of a neighboring country or to threaten more distant nations that might wish to intervene on the side of Iraq's opponent in any conflict. If, on the other hand, a tactical strike was to be undertaken, for example, to destroy a smaller target such as a troop formation, a short-range missile fitted with a chemical warhead might have been appropriate. Thus, the ballistic missile component was the heart of Iraq's weapons of mass destruction program; each missile could have been fitted with a warhead appropriate for achieving the tactical or strategic objective set for it before launching.

A resurgent overt program by Iraq to develop weapons of mass destruction is, for now, deterred by the IAEA's and UNSCOM's ongoing

---

26. Cordesman, *Weapons of Mass Destruction in Iraq*; Michael Eisenstadt, "The Iraqi Problem Remains," *Jane's Intelligence Review Yearbook 1994/95* (Surrey, England: Jane's Information Group, Ltd., 1995), pp. 76–80; Ghalib Darwish, "Interview with Iraqi Nuclear Scientist Dr. Husayn al-Shahristani, 'Now Resident in Tehran'," *Al-Majallah* (London), January 28, 1996, pp. 22, 24; and Al J. Venter, "How Saddam Almost Built His Bomb," *Jane's Intelligence Review*, Vol. 9, No. 12 (December 1997), pp. 559–566.

monitoring and verification program and the imposition of import/export controls.[27] If these agencies were removed from Iraq, either by the United Nations Security Council deciding to terminate their missions or by the Iraqi government expelling them, Iraq might restart such a program. If so, it probably would be reconstructed along lines familiar to Iraqi planners, beginning with the acquisition of a powerful ballistic missile capability.

It appears that Iraq may already be on its way to realizing such a capability. The main missile research station was Sa'ad 16. Located at Al Kindi, which was demolished by bombs during the Persian Gulf War, it has been completely rebuilt.[28] Iraq possesses hundreds of ballistic missiles with the range of 150 kilometers or less that is allowed by the terms of the 1991 cease-fire. It may also possess HY-2, SS-N-2, and C-601 cruise missiles (although UNSCOM has seen no firm evidence of this).[29] UNSCOM has dismantled or otherwise accounted for the destruction of most of the Scuds that survived the Persian Gulf War, but the commission believes that some operational Scuds still remain hidden and, thus, undetected.[30] Iraqi rocket scientists are believed to be honing their skills while working for Libya's leader, Mu'ammar Qaddaffi.[31] For these reasons, and despite limitations imposed by United Nations Security Council Resolution 687 (1991), Iraq might already possess potent ballistic and, perhaps, cruise missile capabilities and the trained personnel to deploy and operate them.

The question then is what kind of warheads could be fitted to these missiles to meet Iraq's desire for weapons of mass destruction. Nuclear warheads cannot be acquired for at least five years because the IAEA has destroyed most if not all Iraqi nuclear weapons–related facilities.[32] Simi-

---

27. *Letter Dated 7 December 1995 from the Chairman of the Security Council Committee Established by Resolution 661 (1990) Concerning the Situation between Iraq and Kuwait Addressed to the President of the Security Council. Annex I. Provision for the Mechanism for Export/Import Monitoring under Paragraph 7 of Security Council Resolution 715 (1991) of 11 October 1991,* UN Document S/1995/1017, December 7, 1995; and *Sanctions Committee Agrees on Export/Import Mechanism for Iraq,* UN Document SC/6137; IK/184, December 6, 1995.

28. Brian Johnson-Thomas, "SA'AD 16—Saddam's Missile Research Station," *ASA Newsletter,* No. 56 (October 11, 1996), pp. 1, 6.

29. Cordesman, *Weapons of Mass Destruction in Iraq.*

30. David C. Isby, "The Residual Iraqi 'Scud' Force," *Jane's Intelligence Review,* Vol. 7, No. 3 (March 1995), pp. 115–117.

31. Khadim Anwar, "Saddam Hussein, the Unrepentant," *International Review,* Vol. 16, No. 40 (September 28, 1995), pp. 1–3.

32. Eisenstadt, "The Iraqi Problem Remains," *Letter Dated 5 April 1995 from the*

larly, UNSCOM has supervised the destruction of most, perhaps all, of Iraq's chemical warfare agents, as well as equipment and facilities used by the chemical warfare program.[33] Thus, no chemicals would be available immediately to arm ballistic missiles (unless hidden stores of chemical warfare agents remain).

The situation differs markedly in regard to biological warfare. To begin, of the four sectors that once constituted Iraq's weapons of mass destruction program, the least is known about Iraq's efforts to acquire biological weapons.[34] Thus, Iraq might be hiding something that would enable it to reacquire biological weapons quickly. But what we know is worrying enough. The work force of more than two hundred persons who staffed Iraq's biological warfare program is intact. Iraq's civilian biotechnological infrastructure, comprising more than eighty research, development, and production facilities, is whole and well equipped.[35] Since most biotechnological equipment is dual use, some of the presently operative facilities could be rapidly converted to biological warfare work. It is prudent to assume that the Iraqis retain hidden stores of freeze-dried organisms from its former biological warfare program. Because Iraq maintains these human, biological, and industrial resources, I believe it could reconstitute a biological warfare program rapidly and be able to manufacture militarily significant quantities of biological warfare agents within six months. (Less time would be required to manufacture these agents for purposes of sabotage or terrorism.) Further, the armorers who adapted chemical munitions to hold biological agents before the Persian

---

Director General of the International Atomic Energy Agency to the Secretary General, UN Document S/1995/287, April 11, 1995; Eighth Report of the Director General of the International Atomic Energy Agency on the Implementation of the Agency's Plan for Future Ongoing Monitoring and Verification of Iraq's Compliance with Paragraph 12 of Resolution 687 (1991), UN Document S/1995/844, October 6, 1995; and Attachment. Report on the Twenty-Eighth IAEA On-site Inspection in Iraq Under Security Council Resolution 687 (1991), UN Document S/1995/1003, December 1, 1995.

33. Report of the Secretary-General on the Status of the Implementation of the Special Commission's Plan; Tenth Report of the Executive Chairman of the Special Commission; Report of the Secretary-General on the Activities of the Special Commission, October 11, 1996; Report of the Secretary-General on the Activities of the Special Commission, April 11, 1997; and Report of the Secretary-General on the Activities of the Special Commission, October 6, 1997.

34. Report of the United Nations Special Commission's Team to the Technical Evaluation Meeting on the Proscribed Biological Warfare Programme (Vienna, 20–27 March 1998), April 1, 1998.

35. Raymond A. Zilinskas, "UNSCOM and the UNSCOM Experience in Iraq," Politics and the Life Sciences, Vol. 14, No. 2 (August 1995), pp. 230–235; and Raymond A. Zilinskas, "The Quickest Fix Would Be Too Costly," Chicago Tribune, February 15, 1998, pp. 1, 8.

Gulf War are still available. With their assistance, stockpiled conventional munitions could be modified within the six-month time frame and loaded with biological warfare agents.

Weapons produced immediately by a resurgent Iraqi biological warfare program, even if unimproved over the weapons developed before 1991, nevertheless could be deployed in support of aggressive moves. Except for the coalition partner countries and Israel, the armed forces of the region's nations are probably inadequately prepared to defeat a biological attack. (All have chemical warfare training and doctrines, but are desultory about implementation.) Further, all of the region's civilian populations are unprotected. Thus, if Iraq were able to maintain secrecy and deploy biological weapons to tactical sites, opponents would face a very difficult situation because most soldiers and all civilians would be vulnerable both to diseases brought about by biological warfare agents and to the panic that these weapons would induce among threatened or attacked populations. Clearly, by once again possessing these weapons, Iraq would be in a position to intimidate neighboring countries.

If the Iraqi leadership were patient, its biological weapons could be significantly improved in a short time. Thus, I estimate that within a year of commencing a resurgent program, it is probable that Iraqi scientists could perfect techniques for drying biological warfare agents, and engineers could install improved aerosol-forming and disseminating equipment on suitable aircraft. Thereafter, remotely piloted vehicles, long-range fighter-bombers, or cruise missiles equipped with tanks and sprayers and programmed to avoid detection by flying low and following ground contours could reach populations located within 1,000 kilometers of Iraq's borders and disperse agents under conditions favorable for carrying out a successful biological attack. With these added capabilities, Iraq would be able to mount a militarily significant biological threat to even the most powerful opponent in the region.

Conclusion

The Iraq of today is similar to Iraq before the Persian Gulf War. The man who before the Gulf War was depicted as "the world's most dangerous man"[36] still retains dictatorial powers over the nation. Iraq possesses a large and powerful army, and is able to deploy a large, well-trained civilian work force to reacquire weapons of mass destruction, should it

36. "The World's Most Dangerous Man," *U.S. News & World Report*, Vol. 108, No. 22 (June 4, 1990), pp. 38–51.

decide to do so.[37] Its oil reserves are the world's third largest and the infrastructure for oil exploitation has been rebuilt and is gearing up for full production. As to its geopolitical standing, the same uneasy, distrustful relations exist between Iraq and its neighbors as before; in fact, Iraq's leader may perceive himself as even more beleaguered and as having additional scores to settle. In consideration of this unsettled situation, it is wise to prepare for the possibility of Iraq once again trying to gain a dominant position in the Middle East.

It is reasonable to assume that, as before, Iraq will attempt to overcome the numerical superiority of regional opponents by resorting to the use of weapons of mass destruction. Iraq's former ballistic missile, cruise missile, and biological warfare components would be the easiest and quickest to reassemble. How can such disquieting developments be prevented?

The key barrier to Iraq reacquiring weapons of mass destruction undoubtedly is the collective international will that sustains the several United Nations Security Council resolutions designed to ensure a subdued Iraq. A further reflection of that will is the support the Security Council gives the IAEA and UNSCOM, especially with regard to biological warfare. Before the Persian Gulf War, Iraq placed high priority on developing a strong biotechnological capability. This effort will probably be continued and expanded once the United Nations lifts economic sanctions. Iraq's government may attempt to apply biotechnology for various legitimate enterprises, including enhancing the ability of crop plants to withstand abiotic and biotic stress; manufacturing biological fertilizers and pesticides; producing single cell protein; and developing diagnostic methods for animal and human diseases. Due to the dual-use character of biotechnology, however, much of the expertise, equipment, supplies, and facilities devoted to civilian biotechnological pursuits could be redirected to biological weapons research, development, testing, and production. UNSCOM's actions to monitor closely and continuously Iraq's biological and biotechnological research, development, production, and testing facilities are the best guarantee that these facilities are unable to take up such work. Further, UNSCOM's awareness of the locations of Iraq's bioscientists and chemical engineers who staffed the former biological warfare program makes it less likely that they could be employed by secret facilities to perform illicit research and development. As long as UNSCOM is able to continue fulfilling its monitoring responsibilities,

---

37. Sean Boyne, "How Saddam Rebuilt His Forces," *Jane's Intelligence Review*, Vol. 8, No. 11 (November 1996), pp. 506–509.

Iraq's leadership is likely to be deterred from biological warfare acquisition. Clearly, UNSCOM must remain fully operational until such time as a leadership is established in Iraq that poses no threat to its neighbors.

Possibly the most important lesson for international arms control that can be drawn from UNSCOM's (and the IAEA's) experiences relates to the need to apply broad, multidisciplinary expertise to arms control. The Iraqis took a "holistic" approach toward acquiring weapons of mass destruction (i.e., rather than seeking to acquire only one type of weapon, it sought to acquire a comprehensive arsenal with ballistic missile, biological, chemical, and nuclear components). The agencies charged with destroying Iraq's former weapons of mass destruction program and making certain that it is not resurrected, UNSCOM and IAEA, were able to address this multifaceted problem by fielding inspection teams that included biological, chemical, and ballistic missile experts. No international treaty compliance regime is so flexible.

As matters now stand, international arms control treaties are disciplinary (i.e., each treaty addresses one type of weapon system, be it nuclear, chemical, or biological). Further, each treaty that specifies the establishment of a compliance regime, such as the Chemical Weapons Convention, also contains provisions that limit that regime's detection and monitoring functions to the discipline under the treaty's purview. Since no international arms control treaty has an interdisciplinary reach, no compliance regime has the capability to operate in a multidisciplinary weapons of mass destruction environment. For example, a Chemical Weapons Convention inspection team probably would not be able to detect activities that contravene treaties bearing on biological or nuclear weapons, and if such activity were detected, the team would be reporting to a treaty secretariat that could not act on this information.

The international arms control community must reassess its disciplinary approach. An improved response would be to negotiate multidisciplinary arms control treaties that encompass several types of weapons of mass destruction. The primary drawback to this approach is that negotiations to achieve multidisciplinary arms control treaties would be even more complex and drawn out than the difficult and extended negotiations undertaken to achieve single discipline treaties. For example, it took almost twenty years to accomplish the Chemical Weapons Convention. Yet, even while recognizing the problems inherent in developing multidisciplinary arms control treaties, it seems worthwhile to consider such a response. Nations that belong to major disarmament treaties, including the Biological Weapons Convention, Chemical Weapons Convention, and the Nuclear Non-Proliferation Treaty, would be in a good position to initiate this effort.

A response that could be accomplished more easily and quickly would be to establish one facility where all the compliance regimes would be headquartered. The tendency now is to headquarter each compliance regime in a city that offers the best package of inducements to the respective treaty organization. For example, the Chemical Weapons Convention compliance regime is located in The Hague and the Nuclear Non-Proliferation Treaty compliance regime is in Vienna. Substantial benefits could be derived from taking this unifying step: it would make it easier to create an environment where experts from all disciplines could consult with one another; the international arms control community could set up a comprehensive, unified computerized data base containing information from all disciplines; and costs would be reduced by eliminating the need for separate facilities for each compliance regime. Most important, by gathering the various treaty compliance regimes under one roof and taking steps to ensure that they communicate continuously with one another, the international arms control community would ensure that a major lesson from the UNSCOM/IAEA experience in Iraq has been learned, namely, the need to take an interdisciplinary approach towards limiting the development and use of weapons of mass destruction.

To conclude this chapter, I believe the time has come to give thought to the scientific and technical work force that operated Iraq's illegal biological warfare program.[38] This is especially important since economic sanctions on Iraq inevitably will be lifted, probably sooner rather than later. Pertinent lessons may be drawn from the response of the international community to the former Soviet Union's biological warfare program, which has been in a state of disintegration since 1992.[39] In the main, international efforts have been directed at improving possibilities of the scientists and engineers who operated that program to redirect their efforts to civilian endeavors.[40] Once economic sanctions on Iraq are lifted, programs similar to the International Science and Technology Center, International Association for the Promotion of Cooperation with Scientists

38. Zilinskas, "The Quickest Fix Would Be Too Costly"; and Raymond A. Zilinskas, "Bioethics and Biological Weapons," *Science*, Vol. 279 (January 30, 1998), p. 635.

39. Raymond A. Zilinskas, "The Other Biological-Weapons Worry," *New York Times*, November 28, 1997, p. A39.

40. Richard Stone, "The Perils of Partnership," *Science*, Vol. 275 (January 24, 1997), pp. 468–471; and Michael Freemantle, "Russian Science on the Rack," *Chemical & Engineering News*, Vol. 75, No. 51 (December 22, 1997), pp. 25–34.

from the New Independent States of the Former Soviet Union and the Civilian R&D Foundation for the Independent States of the Former Soviet Union ought to be instituted to benefit Iraqi scientists and engineers. If these persons were provided with opportunities to perform peacefully directed research and development, and were adequately remunerated for their work, their motivation to participate in a program to reacquire biological weapons would be lessened.

Chapter 9

Investigating Iraq's Biological Weapons Program

Stephen Black

From 1991 to 1995, Iraq stated categorically that it had no offensive biological weapons program and that it had never engaged in anything more than laboratory-scale defensive research with biological warfare agents. On July 1, 1995, Iraq's admission that it had in fact produced biological warfare (BW) agents at an industrial scale brought the investigation of Iraq's BW program to a state similar to that of the chemical and ballistic missile investigations around 1992. The disclosure of these activities allowed the United Nations Special Commission (UNSCOM) to move forward with its investigation. While the information disclosed by Iraq in 1995 formed the nucleus of UNSCOM's knowledge about the program, most aspects of the Iraqi disclosures are now either viewed with skepticism or have been rejected outright.

The piecemeal release of information by Iraq and uncertainties about the accuracy of Iraqi statements make a reliable assessment of the Iraqi BW program almost impossible. It is, however, possible to explain the state of UNSCOM knowledge at a given point in the investigation. Raymond Zilinskas, for example, provides a view of the Iraqi biological program as it was disclosed by Iraq in 1995.[1]

The Iraqi disclosure provided a significant increase in UNSCOM's knowledge of the illicit program but was far from a comprehensive declaration. The continuing verification by UNSCOM of subsequent Iraqi declarations and investigation of as-yet-undeclared activities have provided further insight on the 1995 disclosures.[2] In particular, a meeting of

---

The views expressed here are the author's and are not necessarily shared by the United Nations Special Commission.

---

1. See the chapter by Raymond A. Zilinskas in this volume.

2. United Nations Security Council, "Note by the Secretary-General," S/1998/332, April 16, 1998.

eighteen experts from fifteen countries in March 1998 provided a highly critical assessment of Iraq's disclosures. Even after almost three years of investigation by UNSCOM and clarifications from Iraq, the story of the BW program remains incomplete and inadequate.

Detection of the Iraqi BW Program

On the first of July 1995, a small group of UN investigators and their Iraqi counterparts met in a conference room in Baghdad to discuss a topic that had been highly secret since its inception—the Iraqi biological weapons program.[3] Since 1991, Iraq had denied to UN investigators, and the rest of the world, the existence of an offensive BW program. This meeting, allegedly held in earnest, was the beginning of the disclosure of the full extent of the program, which is now outlawed by Security Council Resolution 687 (1991).

Significant effort by UNSCOM was put into the investigation of a possible Iraqi BW program in the four years prior to the 1995 Iraqi admission. But those efforts had been directed at establishing and then proving the existence of a program in the face of Iraqi denials, rather than verification of the extent of past activities.

At the outset of the UN investigations in 1991, the Iraqi ballistic missile and chemical weapons programs were known to the world, but its nuclear and biological weapons programs were not yet public knowledge. It took a surprise inspection of an Iraqi nuclear facility in 1991, sparked by information from a defector, to establish the existence of "Petrochemical-3," the cover name for Baghdad's nuclear weapons effort. Uncovering the biological weapons program required significantly more effort by the UN.

Because it had not had the benefit of seized documents or fruitful initial inspections, the biological investigation used circumstantial evidence, pieced together minutiae, and held marathon interviews of Iraqi personnel in an effort to uncover the hidden program. This multifaceted inquiry came to fruition in 1995.

Evidence in three main areas came to form the central proof for UNSCOM's case that Iraq had undertaken a BW program.[4] First, UNSCOM had collected a large amount of data on Iraq's procurement of biological materials and equipment. Notable among these purchases were

---

3. United Nations Security Council, "Note by the Secretary-General," S/1995/864, October 11, 1995.

4. United Nations Security Council, "Note by the Secretary-General," S/1995/284, April 10, 1995.

thirty-seven tons of complex growth media used for the production of microorganisms. The nature and scale of these purchases indicated that they were intended for large-scale biological production efforts. Under intense UNSCOM questioning, Iraq was unable to provide a credible account of the fate of seventeen tons of this material.

Second, in 1991, UNSCOM inspectors visited a facility in the desert southwest of Baghdad, the design of which was difficult to explain. While Iraq stated that the Al Hakam site was intended for production of single-cell proteins for animal feed, UNSCOM analysts found the remote location of the facility, the highly secured perimeter, numerous bunkers, and the well-dispersed production buildings impossible to reconcile with Iraq's story of civilian animal feed production.[5]

Finally, UNSCOM knew that Iraq had operated large inhalation chambers and had purchased specialized munitions-filling equipment, spray dryers, and highly toxic microbiological agents.[6] While Iraq had declared that all of these dual-use items were used for peaceful purposes, UNSCOM experts questioned the real reasons for these acquisitions.

At the July 1995 meeting, Iraq surprised UNSCOM investigators by admitting, without fanfare, that it had produced biological warfare agents in large quantities. Seven weeks later Iraq admitted filling these agents into munitions—both aerial bombs and ballistic missile warheads. While this was a dramatic change in both Iraqi attitude toward the BW investigation and in the level of disclosed information on proscribed activities, it was, in essence, only the beginning of the process. The admissions of 1995 were merely the first steps on a path of still unknown length and uncertain destination.

The 1998 View of the Iraqi BW Program

As UNSCOM entered the summer of 1998, the investigation revolved around an Iraqi description of its BW program which was by and large unsupported by physical evidence or original documents. In some cases, the physical evidence actually contradicted Iraq's declarations. Not only was the Iraqi description unsupported and contradicted by evidence, but also three times it was found not to be technically credible by international experts.[7]

In 1997 and 1998, three panels of international experts in biology, biotechnology, and biological weapons convened to examine Iraq's Full,

---

5. Ibid.

6. Ibid.

7. United Nations Security Council, "Note by the Secretary-General," S/1998/332.

Final, and Complete Disclosures (FFCD) of its biological weapons program. In all three cases, the panel found the FFCD to be lacking in substance and inaccurate.

The most recent BW FFCD of September 1997 was examined by an expert panel in September 1997 and by a Technical Evaluation Meeting (TEM) in March 1998. The TEM, held in Vienna, found that a wide range of Iraqi BW activities required still further disclosure and clarification before the UN could accept Iraq's description of its program.

The TEM found that the following issues were incompletely described, inaccurate in their presentation, or were missing entirely.[8]

- Documented information on the origins, purpose, and current status of the offensive BW program was absent from the FFCD.
- Iraq failed to provide the rationale, justification, and requirements for sites involved in the BW program, including those for weapons tests, research and development, production, storage, munitions filling, deployment, and destruction sites for weapons, documents, and agents.
- The organization of the program at all levels, including the role of the Ministry of Defense, the intelligence organizations, and other senior government bodies in the BW program, is not sufficiently or accurately presented.
- The FFCD does not fully describe acquisition of supplies, materials, munitions, and equipment. This includes the omission of substantial quantities of microbial growth media, which remain undeclared.
- Acquisition and attempts to acquire specific microbiological isolates, including mycotoxin standards, and viral and fungal strains are not accurately or sufficiently explained.
- The numerical accounting for growth media material balance is flawed and is based in large part on Iraqi estimates, many of which are themselves based on still other estimates. None of the estimated values are supported by documentary evidence.
- The specific rationale behind agent selection, toxicity, and dissemination research and the constant expansion of the BW program up to 1991 is not adequately described in the FFCD. This includes the rationale for Iraq's work on genetic engineering, ricin, mycotoxins, and its virus research.
- The toxicological justification for development of aflatoxin as a biological weapon is inadequate and not credible.

---

8. Ibid.

- The technical sophistication of Iraq's aerobiology research is not adequately explained.
- The quantities of BW agent produced are not credibly explained. Specifically, Iraq does not address the reasons for the large gap between what Iraq was capable of producing and what it declares it actually manufactured—a far smaller amount.
- Additionally, Iraq's description of its aflatoxin production, production technology and organization, and weaponization is implausible. The production quantity and quality declared by Iraq could not have been attained using the processes described.
- Iraq has not provided a complete disclosure on the numbers, types, markings, and detailed accounting of individual BW weapons systems.
- Declarations by Iraq on the alleged unilateral destruction of Al Hussein missile warheads filled with BW agents do not match the physical evidence available.
- Iraq's description of its aircraft drop-tank project (for the spray delivery of BW agent) is deficient in all areas, including planning, procurement, testing, and production.
- For the chemical warfare (CW) and BW R-400 and R-400A aerial bombs, it is not possible to determine how many munitions were filled with which agents, nor how many empty munitions were produced; therefore, no confident assessment can be made of the number of biological weapons–filled bombs.
- Despite the fact that the BW program was concealed from UNSCOM until 1995, there is no description of the rationale for this concealment, the actions taken to conceal the program, or the organizations involved.
- Iraq states that the BW program was "obliterated" in 1991, yet facilities, growth media, equipment, and core groups of experts at Al Hakam were retained. This has not yet been explained.
- Probably most critical, Iraq has not provided any official document that states that the BW program has in fact ended.

The Future

When the verification of the elimination of BW agent and munitions present in Iraq as of April 1991 concludes, UNSCOM's work will focus on ensuring that no new proscribed BW agent or munitions are produced. While there is the appearance that the UN program of ongoing monitoring and verification (OMV) is separate from the disarmament process—

OMV is in place and functioning while disarmament is not yet complete—they are in fact closely linked. As UNSCOM has long said, an effective OMV system is predicated on a full understanding of Iraq's capabilities, in terms of both technical expertise and hardware, in its biological and other programs.[9] Without this understanding, UNSCOM cannot be sure that it is monitoring the full extent of Iraq's dual-use industries, equipment, materials, and technical expertise.

In the future, the biological OMV system may provide a deterrent and detection capability against a resurgent Iraqi BW effort, but it is not an effective cachepot for all of the uncertainties remaining in the disarmament effort. The OMV system was never designed to address disarmament issues. Its verification and monitoring tools were selected and are structured to check dual-capable sites, equipment, and materials that are being put to legitimate and peaceful purposes. OMV hopes to detect diversions of these monitored items to proscribed activities. Detecting existing dual-use or proscribed items, which exist outside the monitoring regime, was always the purview of UNSCOM's disarmament activities. It was never expected to be the responsibility of OMV.

Conclusion

For four years UNSCOM experts worked to prove the existence of a hidden Iraqi biological weapons program. In a flurry of disclosures, Iraq admitted the existence of its BW program and provided what at first glance appeared to be a sizeable amount of data. But as detection gave way to verification, UNSCOM experts began to see large gaps in Iraq's description of its pre-war BW program. Not only has UNSCOM identified critical issues that are completely ignored, but it has found Iraqi statements inconsistent with physical evidence.[10] As in the other areas of UNSCOM activity, chemical weapons and ballistic missiles, UNSCOM's efforts to discover and verify the truth about Iraq's BW program continue.

---

9.   United Nations Security Council, "Report of the Secretary-General on the Status of the Implementation of the Special Commission's Plan for the Ongoing Monitoring and Verification of Iraq's Compliance with Relevant Parts of Section C of Security Council Resolution 687 (1991)," S/1994/1138, October 7, 1994.

10.   United Nations Security Council, "Note by the Secretary-General," S/1998/332.

Part V
Detection and Use of Biological Agents:
Case Studies

Chapter 10

A Large Community Outbreak of Salmonellosis Caused by Intentional Contamination of Restaurant Salad Bars

Thomas J. Török, Robert V. Tauxe, Robert P. Wise, John R. Livengood, Robert Sokolow, Steven Mauvais, Kristin A. Birkness, Michael R. Skeels, John M. Horan, and Laurence R. Foster

Outbreaks of foodborne infection are caused by foods that are intrinsically contaminated or that become contaminated during harvest, processing, or preparation. It is generally assumed that such contamination events occur inadvertently; intentional contamination with a biologic agent is rarely suspected or reported.[1]

This chapter was adapted from Thomas J. Török et al., "A Large Community Outbreak of Salmonellosis Caused by Intentional Contamination of Restaurant Salad Bars," *Journal of the American Medical Association (JAMA)*, Vol. 278, No. 5 (August 6, 1997), pp. 389–395.

This chapter is dedicated to the memory of Laurence R. Foster, M.D., MPH, in honor of his investigation of this outbreak and his inspirational leadership as Oregon State Epidemiologist.

We thank the many hard working people from the Wasco-Sherman Public Health Department, the Wasco County Planning Department, the City of The Dalles, the Hood River County Health Department, the Umatilla County Health Department, and the Oregon Departments of Human Resources and Agriculture who participated in the epidemiologic investigation. We thank the Department of Social and Health Services Division of the state of Washington for providing laboratory and epidemiologic data from Washington; the California Public Health Laboratory for providing laboratory support; the National Veterinary Services Laboratory, U.S. Department of Agriculture, for supplying nonhuman S. Typhimurium isolates; the Food and Drug Administration for providing information on food sources and distributors; the U.S. Department of Justice for providing information about the criminal investigations; and our colleagues at the Centers for Disease Control and Prevention who provided advice and laboratory support.

1. P.R. Joseph, James D. Millar, and D.A. Henderson, "An Outbreak of Hepatitis Due

On September 17, 1984, the Wasco-Sherman Public Health Department in Oregon began to receive reports of persons ill with gastroenteritis who had eaten at either of two restaurants in The Dalles, Oregon, several days before symptom onset. Local and state public health officials confirmed an outbreak of *Salmonella* Typhimurium associated with the two restaurants and then noted an abrupt increase in reports of gastroenteritis the following week among persons who had eaten or worked at other restaurants in The Dalles. Because many patients reported eating food from salad bars, the local health department closed all salad bars in the town on September 25, 1984, and the Oregon Health Division requested assistance from the Centers for Disease Control (CDC) for further evaluation and control of the outbreak.

The epidemiologic investigation identified the vehicles of transmission as foods on multiple self-service salad bars and probable times when contamination occurred. Common mechanisms by which salad bars could have become contaminated were excluded. A subsequent criminal investigation found that members of a nearby religious commune had intentionally contaminated the salad bars on multiple occasions.

Background

The Dalles, Oregon, had a population of 10,500 in the 1980 census. It is the county seat of Wasco County, a region of orchards and wheat ranches that has a population of 21,000. Located near the Columbia River on Interstate 84, The Dalles is a frequent stop for travelers. Two independent water systems serve The Dalles: a smaller system supplied by a well and a larger system that serves most restaurants and uses surface water augmented by well water during the summer. From 1980 through 1983, only sixteen isolates of salmonellae were reported by the local health department; eight isolates were S. Typhimurium. No case of salmonellosis was reported in the first eight months of 1984.

In 1981, followers of Bhagwan Shree Rajneesh purchased a large ranch in Wasco County to build a new international headquarters for the Indian guru.[2] Construction of the commune was controversial from its inception; cultural values and land-use issues were the major areas of

to Food Contamination," *New England Journal of Medicine*, Vol. 273, No. 4 (1965), pp. 188–194; and James A. Phills, A. John Harrold, Gabriel V. Whiteman, and Lewis Perelmutter, "Pulmonary Infiltrates, Asthma, and Eosinophilia Due to *Ascaris suum* Infection in Man," *New England Journal of Medicine*, Vol. 286, No. 18 (1972), pp. 965–970.

2. Scotta Callister, James Long, and Leslie L. Zaitz, "For Love and Money: The Rajneeshees from India to Oregon," *Oregonian*, June 30–July 19, 1985, Supplement, p. 36; Scotta Callister, James Long, and Leslie L. Zaitz, "On the Road Again," *Oregonian*,

conflict. Part of the ranch was incorporated as the city of Rajneeshpuram, but the charter was challenged in the courts, effectively limiting new construction. Commune members believed that the outcome of the November 6, 1984, elections for Wasco County commissioners would have an important impact on further land-use decisions.[3]

Methods

CASE DEFINITION

A case was defined as an illness with diarrhea and at least three of the following symptoms: fever, chills, headache, nausea, vomiting, abdominal pain, or bloody stools, or by a stool culture yielding S. Typhimurium. A patient was considered to have had an outbreak-associated case if onset of symptoms or collection of an S. Typhimurium–positive stool specimen occurred between September 9 and October 10, 1984, and the patient resided in or had visited The Dalles during that interval. A case in a person who ate at a restaurant in The Dalles within seven days before the onset of illness or who worked at a restaurant in The Dalles was considered to be a restaurant-associated case. A single restaurant exposure (SRE) denotes that only one restaurant exposure occurred during the seven days before onset of symptoms. A case was considered to be secondary if it occurred in an individual who had not eaten or worked at a restaurant in The Dalles in the seven days before onset of symptoms, but was exposed to a case patient during that interval.

The thirty-eight restaurants in The Dalles were divided into three groups based on the number of culture-confirmed case customers with an SRE. Group 1 restaurants were definitely affected and had at least three culture-confirmed case customers with an SRE. Group 2 restaurants were possibly affected and had at least one case customer with an SRE, but fewer than three culture-confirmed case customers with an SRE. Group 3 restaurants were not affected and had no case customers with an SRE.

OUTBREAK INVESTIGATION

Cases were identified through passive surveillance. Press releases encouraged reporting by case patients and health care professionals. We interviewed possible case patients about symptoms and risk factors and obtained comprehensive food histories for restaurant meals eaten during the three-day period before onset of symptoms. Case customers with an

---

December 30, 1985, pp. B1–B10; and Frances FitzGerald, *Cities on a Hill: A Journey Through Contemporary American Cultures* (New York: Simon and Schuster, 1986).

3. Ibid.

SRE were asked to identify all other persons with whom they had eaten at the restaurant. Histories were obtained from persons so identified, and those who were not ill and reported no other restaurant exposure served as controls for food-specific case-control analyses. Potentially exposed cohorts, such as banquet participants and take-out food patrons, were identified from restaurant records, and attempts were made to interview these persons.

Employees of Group 1 restaurants were interviewed twice. During the outbreak, investigators interviewed employees when restaurant involvement was first suspected. In October 1984, immediately following the outbreak, all employees were asked to complete a self-administered questionnaire. Work schedules were obtained from review of time cards, interviews with restaurant managers, and review of insurance claims for workers' compensation.

LABORATORY METHODS

Stool specimens were submitted to local and regional laboratories to be cultured for enteric pathogens. Employees from Group 1 restaurants were required to submit a stool sample to be cultured or be excluded from work. Ill employees with a single negative stool specimen were required to submit a second stool specimen for confirmation before returning to work. The Oregon Public Health Laboratory and the Washington Public Health Laboratory serotyped human *Salmonella* isolates and performed antibiotic-susceptibility testing on a sample of isolates. A representative sample of outbreak isolates, based on epidemiologic criteria, was submitted to CDC for further biochemical characterization and plasmid profile analysis with restriction endonuclease digestion, using *Hind*III.[4] The Oregon Public Health Laboratory also submitted *S.* Typhimurium isolates from other outbreaks and sporadically occurring cases, collected during 1984 and thought to be unrelated to the outbreak, to CDC for comparison with the outbreak strain by plasmid analysis. The Oregon Department of Agriculture and the Oregon Public Health Laboratory cultured suspected foods.

The Dalles outbreak strain was compared with human isolates included in two national surveys of salmonellae in 1979 and 1980 and in 1984 and 1985.[5] To identify a possible animal reservoir, CDC characterized

4. H.C. Birnboim and J. Doly, "A Rapid Alkaline Extraction Procedure for Screening Recombinant Plasmid DNA," *Nucleic Acids Research*, Vol. 7 (1979), pp. 1513–1523; and Tom Maniatis, Edward Fritsch, and Joseph Sambrook, *Molecular Cloning: A Laboratory Manual* (Cold Spring Harbor, N.Y.: Cold Spring Harbor Laboratory, 1982), pp. 150–162.

5. Lee W. Riley, Mitchell L. Cohen, Jerry E. Seals, et al., "Importance of Host Factors

all available veterinary isolates of *S.* Typhimurium identified between October 1, 1984, and September 30, 1985, by the U.S. Department of Agriculture National Veterinary Services Laboratory in Ames, Iowa.

ENVIRONMENTAL STUDIES

Local health department sanitarians and U.S. Food and Drug Administration representatives investigated the distributors and original suppliers of foods used in Group 1 restaurants. All Group 1 restaurants were inspected by sanitarians. Records of the city water system were reviewed for the month of September 1984. Tap water samples from restaurants were collected during the outbreak for analysis. Temperatures maintained by ice-chilled salad bars were evaluated.

STATISTICAL ANALYSIS

Food exposure data were analyzed separately by restaurant and by date of onset of illness at the two restaurants that had recurrent outbreaks. Univariate analyses were performed and odds ratios (ORs) with 95 percent confidence intervals (CIs) were calculated using the Epi Info computer program Version 6.03.[6] Foods found to be associated with illness in univariate analyses were analyzed using a stepwise logistic regression model. Univariate analyses of employee survey data were performed, and relative risks (RRs) with 95 percent CIs were calculated using Epi Info.

CRIMINAL INVESTIGATIONS

Managers of affected restaurants were interviewed about unusual incidents or disgruntled employees. Suspicious events were referred to the Oregon State Police and the Wasco County sheriff for investigation. The Federal Bureau of Investigation (FBI) reviewed local investigation efforts. Following the completion of the epidemiologic investigation and after the collapse of the Rajneeshee commune, the FBI, with technical assistance from the Oregon Public Health Laboratory, investigated clinic and laboratory facilities in Rajneeshpuram. A sample of *S.* Typhimurium seized from the Rajneesh Medical Center on October 2, 1985, was compared with the outbreak strain.

---

in Human Salmonellosis Caused by Multiresistant Strains of *Salmonella*," *Journal of Infectious Diseases*, Vol. 149, No. 6 (1984), pp. 878–883; and Kristine L. MacDonald, Mitchell L. Cohen, Nancy T. Hargrett-Bean, et al., "Changes in Antimicrobial Resistance of *Salmonella* Isolated from Humans in the United States," *Journal of the American Medical Association*, Vol. 258, No. 11 (September 18, 1987), pp. 1496–1499.

6. Andrew G. Dean, Jeffrey A. Dean, Denis Coulombier, et al., *Epi Info, Version 6: A Word Processing, Database, and Statistics Program for Public Health on IBM-Compatible Microcomputers* (Atlanta: Centers for Disease Control and Prevention, 1995).

Table 10.1. Outbreak-Associated Cases of *Salmonella* Gastroenteritis by Group and Exposure Location.

Group and Exposure Location	Number of Culture-Confirmed Cases (Percent of Total)	Number of Clinical Cases (Percent of Total)	Number of Total Cases (Percent of Total)
Case employees			
Group 1 restaurants (n=10)	74(9.9)	17(2.3)	91(12.1)
Group 2 restaurants (n=12)	4(0.5)	5(0.7)	9(1.2)
Group 3 restaurants (n=16)	1(0.1)	0(0.0)	1(0.1)
Case customers			
Group 1 restaurants (n=10)	227(30.2)	267(35.6)	494(65.8)
Group 2 restaurants (n=12)	6(0.8)	19(2.5)	25(3.3)
Group 3 restaurants (n=16)	0(0.0)	0(0.0)	0(0.0)
Multiple restaurant exposures*	32(4.3)	40(5.3)	72(9.6)
Secondary cases	4(0.5)	7(0.9)	11(1.5)
Cases with incomplete information	40(5.3)	8(1.1)	48(6.4)
Total	388(51.7)	363(48.3)	751(100.0)

NOTE: A total of 69 (95.8 percent) of 72 case customers with multiple restaurant exposures reported eating in one or more Group 1 restaurants.

Results

We identified 751 patients who met the case definition; 441 patients (59 percent) were female and 310 (41 percent) were male. Patients ranged in age from newborn to 87 years; the median was 33 years. At least 45 persons (6 percent) were hospitalized; no fatalities were reported. The epidemic curve was biphasic. (See Figure 10.1.) The first wave of illness, September 9 through 18, peaked on September 15, and the second wave, September 19 through October 10, peaked on September 24. Of 674 patients (90 percent) with known date of symptom onset, 88 (13 percent) became ill during the first wave and 586 (87 percent) became ill during the second wave. There were 692 restaurant-associated cases (92 percent), 11 secondary cases (1 percent), and 48 cases (6 percent) with incomplete information on restaurant exposure. (See Table 10.1.) Among persons with restaurant-associated cases, 101 (15 percent) were employees and 591 (85 percent) were customers. There were 519 SRE case customers and 72 case customers with multiple restaurant exposures.

Ten of the thirty-eight restaurants in The Dalles were definitely affected (Group 1). (See Table 10.1.) Two Group 1 restaurants had culture-confirmed SRE case customers in the early wave (restaurants A and B),

Figure 10.1. Reported Cases of *Salmonella* Typhimurium Gastroenteritis by Date of Symptom Onset for 674 Cases (89.8 percent) with Known Date of Onset in The Dalles, Oregon, in 1984.

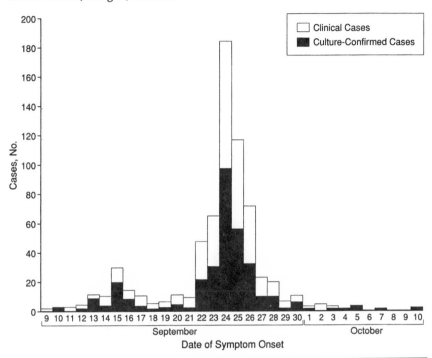

but all ten were affected in the late wave. (See Figure 10.2.) These ten restaurants were associated with 494 SRE case customers (95 percent), 69 case customers with multiple restaurant exposures (96 percent), and 91 case employees (90 percent). Twelve restaurants were possibly affected (Group 2), accounting for 25 SRE case customers (5 percent). Three case customers with multiple restaurant exposures (4 percent) had reported eating at a Group 2 restaurant but not at a Group 1 restaurant. Sixteen restaurants were not affected (Group 3). There was no geographic clustering of affected restaurants, but dates of exposure for culture-confirmed cases were clustered. (See Figure 10.2.) Restaurant involvement in the outbreak was associated with operating a salad bar. Eight (80 percent) of ten Group 1 restaurants compared with only three (11 percent) of the twenty-eight other restaurants in The Dalles operated salad bars (RR, 7.5; 95 percent CI, 2.4–22.7; $P < 0.001$).

INVESTIGATION OF ILLNESS AMONG CUSTOMERS
The four Group 1 restaurants where food-specific exposure rates were determined accounted for 283 (55 percent) of all 494 SRE case customers.

Figure 10.2. Dates of Exposure at Group 1 Restaurants Reported by 494 Case Customers with Single Restaurant Exposure.

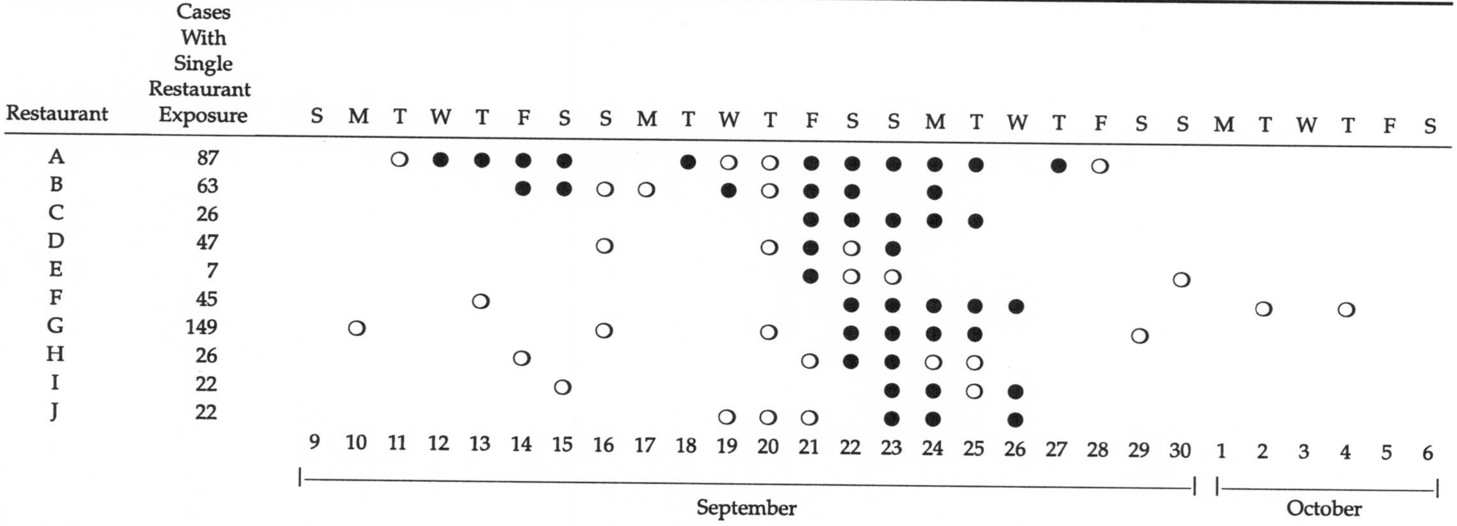

NOTE: Circles indicate days reported by case customers; filled circles indicate days when one or more customers had culture-confirmed *Salmonella* Typhimurium infection.

Customer illness in all four restaurants was associated with eating from the salad bar. Restaurant A was affected during both waves of the outbreak, but different items on the salad bar were implicated for each wave. During the first wave, eating either macaroni, potato, four-bean, or pea salads was associated with illness (OR, 35.8; 95 percent CI, 4.2–1563.4; P = 0.01), and during the second wave, blue cheese dressing was associated with illness (OR and 95 percent CI undefined because none of the non-case customers ate the blue cheese dressing; P = 0.03). Restaurants D and H were affected only during the second wave of the outbreak. By univariate analysis, lettuce (restaurant D: OR, 188.1; 95 percent CI, 37.0–1157; P < 0.001; restaurant H: OR, 31.2; 95 percent CI, 3.0–1417.3; P < 0.001) and many other salad bar ingredients were associated with illness at both restaurants. No independent risk for items other than lettuce was identified by multivariate analysis because most food items were eaten together as part of a lettuce salad. Restaurant G was affected only during the second wave of the outbreak. Potato salad had the greatest association with illness (OR, 4.0; 95 percent CI, 1.5–11.2; P = 0.005), but could account for only half of the cases. Eating a lettuce salad was independently associated with illness (OR, 2.5; 95 percent CI, 1.0–6.2; P = 0.04). Eating take-out food from restaurant G, which did not usually include salad, was not associated with illness.

Although case-control studies of food exposures were not conducted at the other six Group 1 restaurants, four had salad bars, with reported salad bar exposure rates for their SRE case customers ranging from 83 percent to 90 percent. The two restaurants without salad bars (restaurants E and J) accounted for the smallest number of case customers of all Group 1 restaurants, 29 total (4 percent).

Two of the Group 1 restaurants (restaurants A and B) had banquet facilities. No cases were identified among attendees of twenty banquets during the outbreak period, after customers with other restaurant exposures were excluded. Banquet salad bar items were made up in the same kitchen as the public salad bar items, but the banquet salad bars had a more restricted choice of foods and were in operation for only one to one and one-half hours per day. The sources of foods placed on the public salad bars were the same as those for banquets.

INVESTIGATION OF ILLNESS AMONG RESTAURANT EMPLOYEES

During September 1984, 254 employees worked at Group 1 restaurants; 242 (95 percent) were interviewed. Of these, 56 (23 percent) met the clinical case definition, 41 (17 percent) had at least one symptom but did not meet the case definition, and 145 (60 percent) were asymptomatic. At least one stool specimen was submitted by 231 employees (91 percent).

Specimens from 74 (32 percent) were culture-positive, including those from 39 employees whose symptoms met the case definition, 16 employees with at least one symptom but who would not have met the case definition except for their positive culture, and 19 asymptomatic employees. Of the 19 asymptomatic culture-positive employees, only 3 had possible exposures to another Group 1 restaurant or to ill friends or family members.

Onset of symptoms in employees did not, in general, precede exposure among restaurant customers. Five case employees (two culture-confirmed) at four Group 1 restaurants (restaurants C, D, F, and G) reported onset of illness before September 19, during the first wave of the outbreak. They had not worked at either restaurant (restaurants A and B) involved in that early wave, nor had they eaten at those restaurants on a date when any case customer was exposed in the early wave. There was no known social contact between the five case employees and any employee of restaurants A or B.

Detailed information on work schedules was available for employees of eight of the ten Group 1 restaurants (all but restaurants I and F), including data on 66 symptomatic case employees. Assuming an average symptom duration of three days, 40 case employees (61 percent) worked while symptomatic. When the work schedules of three case employees with early-onset illness were compared with dates reported for case customer exposure to their restaurant, one case employee's work schedule closely coincided with customer exposure. This employee had onset of symptoms on September 10, worked at restaurant G, and had primary responsibility for preparing the salads that were consumed by customers, including the potato salad that was most strongly associated with illness at this restaurant. This employee ate regularly from the salad bar at work, but had not eaten at either of the two restaurants with early involvement in the outbreak and reported having no social contacts with other ill employees of any other restaurant.

A total of 307 persons completed the second employee survey, including 227 (89 percent) of 254 employees of Group 1 restaurants. The attack rate (54 percent) for those employees who ate at their own salad bars was significantly greater than the attack rate (30 percent) for those who did not (RR, 1.8; 95 percent CI, 1.2–2.7; $P < 0.01$). This was true for case employees who were ill in the first wave and for those who were ill in the second wave, compared separately with control employees. Excluding employees who became ill in the first wave, the attack rate (53 percent) for those employees who ate at another Group 1 restaurant salad bar also was greater than the attack rate (28 percent) for those who did not (RR,

1.9; 95 percent CI, 1.2–2.9; P = 0.01). There was no association between illness and female gender (after controlling for eating from the salad bar), type or frequency of work performed, number of restaurant meals per week, amount of water consumed at work, raw egg consumption, raw milk consumption, antacid use, or travel.

LABORATORY INVESTIGATIONS

Salmonella Typhimurium was isolated from stool specimens of 388 patients (52 percent). The outbreak strain did not ferment dulcitol, which is an unusual biochemical characteristic found in only about 2 percent of nontyphoidal salmonellae.[7] The outbreak strain was sensitive to ampicillin, cephalothin sodium, chloramphenicol, gentamicin sulfate, kanamycin sulfate, nalidixic acid, sulfisoxazole, and trimethoprim-sulfamethoxazole. Intermediate sensitivity was noted to tetracycline and streptomycin sulfate. Plasmid profiles were determined[8] for fifty-two outbreak-associated isolates, including an isolate from at least one case employee and one case customer from each Group 1 restaurant. All outbreak isolates had the same plasmid profile, with a single plasmid of approximately 60 Md.

Salmonella Typhimurium was isolated from blue cheese salad dressing collected from restaurant B during the second wave of the outbreak, but was not isolated from dry mix used to prepare the dressing. *Salmonella* Typhimurium was not isolated from cultures of lettuce from restaurants D and G, which came from the same lettuce shipments used during the outbreak.

None of six *S.* Typhimurium isolates collected in Oregon from sporadically occurring cases between July and December 1984 resembled the outbreak strain from The Dalles. Two isolates of *S.* Typhimurium from two other outbreaks that occurred in Oregon during that time did resemble the outbreak strain by dulcitol metabolism, antibiogram, plasmid profile, and restriction endonuclease digests of plasmid DNA.

The two outbreaks included an outbreak in August 1984 affecting twenty-six persons who became ill after eating at a hospital cafeteria in the central Willamette Valley of Oregon. Illness was associated with eating

7. W.J. Martin and J.A. Washington II, "Enterobacteriacea," in Edwin H. Lennette, Albert Balows, William J. Hausler, Jr., and Joseph P. Truant, eds., *Manual of Clinical Microbiology*, 3rd ed. (Washington, D.C.: American Society for Microbiology, 1980), p. 207.

8. Birnboim and Doly, "A Rapid Alkaline Extraction Procedure"; and Maniatis, Fritsch, and Sambrook, "Molecular Cloning."

ranch dressing at the salad bar. The other outbreak of *S.* Typhimurium occurred after a banquet at a hotel in Portland, Oregon, in December 1984, affecting at least thirty-six persons; illness was associated with eating rare roast beef. Previously, in November 1984, another outbreak of *S.* Typhimurium occurred after a banquet at the same Portland hotel and affected at least seventy-three persons; illness was also associated with eating rare roast beef. That outbreak strain had a single plasmid similar to the strain in The Dalles, but no further laboratory comparisons were made. No links were identified between these outbreaks and the outbreak in The Dalles.

The 1979 to 1980 national survey included 233 strains of *S.* Typhimurium (excluding variant copenhagen); none had antibiograms similar to the outbreak strain in The Dalles.[9] The 1984 through 1985 national survey included 175 strains of *S.* Typhimurium (excluding variant copenhagen); 35 strains had antibiograms similar to the strain from The Dalles, and six of these did not ferment dulcitol.[10] One of the six strains was epidemiologically linked to the outbreak in The Dalles, but the other five isolates had no known link with the outbreak.

Among thirty-four animal *S.* Typhimurium isolates from the National Veterinary Services Laboratory collected from June 1984 through November 1984, one isolate that did not ferment dulcitol, collected from a turkey in June 1984, matched the outbreak strain by plasmid restriction endonuclease analysis.

ENVIRONMENTAL STUDIES

Review of records at the municipal water department showed no evidence of water treatment failure in September 1984. Tap water samples from ten restaurants were negative for bacteria and had acceptable turbidity readings, and nine had chlorine residuals of at least 1.0 mg/L.

Detailed information on distributors and suppliers was collected for eight of the Group 1 restaurants. Of forty food items served at four or more of the eight restaurants, no supplier or distributor provided a single food for more than four restaurants. There was no common supplier or distributor for any of the foods served by the two restaurants involved in the first wave of illness. Many of the distributors served large areas in Oregon and Washington.

Sanitary inspections revealed minor violations of hygienic food-handling practices in some restaurants. Employees commonly put out fresh,

---

9. Riley, Cohen, Seals, et al., "Importance of Host Factors in Human Salmonellosis."

10. MacDonald, Cohen, Hargrett-Bean, et al., "Changes in Antimicrobial Resistance of *Salmonella.*"

full containers of a food item on the salad bar, but then placed the remainder from the old container on top of the fresh items. All salad bars were ice chilled. An evaluation of temperatures maintained on a typical ice-chilled salad bar showed that the surface of a bowl of potato salad was likely to reach 13°C to 16°C (55°F–60°F), which exceeds the maximal temperature of 7°C (45°F) recommended by the Food and Drug Administration. In one restaurant, no soap dispenser or towels were available in the employee rest room.

CRIMINAL INVESTIGATION

During the criminal investigation, testimony by commune members indicated that the outbreak in The Dalles was the result of deliberate *S.* Typhimurium contamination of salad bars in multiple restaurants by residents of Rajneeshpuram.[11] Clandestine laboratories in Rajneeshpuram were used to prepare cultures of *S.* Typhimurium that were poured on food items on salad bars and, in some restaurants, into coffee creamers. Commune members said they were testing a plan to incapacitate voters in preparation for an upcoming election. They intended to make citizens of The Dalles sick on election day to prevent them from voting and thus influence the outcome of the election. The information obtained from informant testimony was incomplete or insufficiently precise to allow direct comparison of dates of contamination with dates of exposure for case customers and case employees on a restaurant-by-restaurant basis. It is likely that some salad bars were contaminated more than once. Informant testimony did indicate that other restaurants, in addition to the ten identified as Group 1 restaurants, might have been targets and that other foods were deliberately contaminated. In addition, produce in at least one supermarket was contaminated with *S.* Typhimurium, and plans were made to contaminate city water.[12]

Oregon State and FBI investigators confiscated an open vial containing a standard strain of *S.* Typhimurium (American Type Culture Collection 14028) from the clinic laboratory in Rajneeshpuram. Clinic records indicated that the laboratory had obtained this vial from a commercial supplier of biologic products before the outbreak. The *S.* Typhimurium strain was indistinguishable from the outbreak strain by antibiogram, biochemical markers, plasmid profiles, and restriction endonuclease digestion of plasmid DNA.

On March 19, 1986, two commune members were indicted for con-

11.   U.S. v. Sheela et al., CR 86-53, Indictment (D Ore 1986), based on 18 USC 1365(a) and 1365(e).

12.   Ibid.

spiring to tamper with consumer products by poisoning food in violation of the federal antitampering act.[13] In April 1986, the defendants pleaded guilty to the charges, and in July 1986, they were sentenced to four and one-half years in prison, to serve concurrently with other sentences.[14]

Conclusion

This outbreak of salmonellosis, affecting at least 751 persons, was caused by intentional contamination of restaurant salad bars by members of a religious commune. It was the largest outbreak of foodborne disease reported to the CDC in the United States in 1984. Despite extensive investigation, the source of S. Typhimurium initially went unrecognized. It was not until more than a year after the outbreak that sufficient evidence had accumulated to link the religious commune with the outbreak. Essential evidence was collected during the course of criminal investigations independent from the epidemiologic field investigation.

There was no evidence to suggest that the S. Typhimurium was waterborne. Employee illness was not associated with water consumption, and affected restaurants were served by two different water systems. Unaffected restaurants shared the same water supply with affected restaurants. Water testing detected no evidence of contamination during the epidemic period.

The outbreak was clearly associated with food consumption at restaurants. Almost all case patients either worked at a restaurant in The Dalles or reported eating at one or more restaurants located in the town during the week before onset of illness. Many culture-confirmed cases occurred in nonresidents who had a single restaurant meal as their sole exposure. Self-service salad bars were implicated in transmission of S. Typhimurium. Affected restaurants in The Dalles were much more likely to have a self-service salad bar than were unaffected restaurants, and eating food from self-service salad bars was highly associated with disease. Culture of salad dressing in one restaurant yielded the outbreak strain. The incidence of cases declined abruptly after all salad bars were closed, and this intervention may have terminated the outbreak. However, these findings were difficult to reconcile with the observations that sanitary practices in implicated restaurants were not grossly deficient, private banquets with salad bars were not affected, and no food sources

---

13. Joan Laatz, "Sheela Indicted in The Dalles Poisoning Plot," *Oregonian*, March 20, 1986, pp. A1, E6; and U.S. v. Sheela et al.

14. Joan Laatz, "Sheela Sentenced to Prison: $400,000 Fine Added to Term Behind Bars," *Oregonian*, July 23, 1986, pp. A1, B2.

were common to the majority of affected restaurants. Therefore, other possible modes of transmission were considered.

Transmission of nontyphoidal salmonellae from infected food handlers has been documented uncommonly in epidemiologic investigations.[15] In the outbreak in The Dalles, infected food handlers may have contributed to the spread of infection by inadvertent contamination of foods at restaurants where they worked. Some ill employees continued to work until they were excluded by the health department. Direct contamination of foods by ill employees may have occurred at one restaurant without a salad bar because of the lack of soap and hand towels in the employee lavatory. In one affected restaurant with a salad bar, a case employee was identified who prepared the salad bar food items, including the implicated potato salad, and whose work schedule coincided with the dates of exposure reported by case customers. Nonetheless, other findings suggested that contamination by employees was not the most important factor in transmission. Eating at restaurant salad bars was a risk factor for employees, not just customers. Exclusion of symptomatic and asymptomatic case employees occurred several days after the abrupt decline in new cases had begun, suggesting that exclusion of infected employees did not play a large role in terminating the outbreak.

Laboratory analyses were conducted to compare the outbreak strain with available human and animal isolates from national surveys. The characteristic antibiotic-sensitivity pattern, biochemical testing results, and plasmid analysis conclusively demonstrated a single outbreak strain and excluded the remote possibility of independent, simultaneous outbreaks. The outbreak strain was not common before the outbreak. None of the human isolates from the two national surveys, excluding several isolates obtained after the outbreak, matched the strain in The Dalles. The one animal isolate that matched the outbreak strain had no identifiable epidemiologic link to the outbreak in The Dalles. Isolates from three other 1984 Oregon outbreaks matched the outbreak strain, including a salad

15. J.V.S. Pether and R.J.D. Scott, "*Salmonella* Carriers: Are They Dangerous? A Study to Identify Finger Contamination with *Salmonellae* by Convalescent Carriers," *Journal of Infection*, Vol. 5 (1982), pp. 81–88; D. Roberts, "Factors Contributing to Outbreaks of Food Poisoning in England and Wales, 1970–1979," *Journal of Hygiene*, Vol. 89, No. 3 (1982), pp. 491–498; Dedra S. Buchwald and Martin J. Blaser, "A Review of Human Salmonellosis, II: Duration of Excretion Following Infection with Nontyphoidal *Salmonella*," *Reviews of Infectious Diseases*, Vol. 6, No. 3 (1984), pp. 345–356; A. Daniel Rubenstein and Robert A. MacCready, "Epidemic *Salmonella newport* Infection in a Metropolitan Area," *New England Journal of Medicine*, Vol. 248, No. 13 (1953), pp. 527–530; and Martin J. Blaser, Earle M. Rafuse, Joy G. Wells, Robert A. Pollard, and Roger A. Feldman, "An Outbreak of Salmonellosis Involving Multiple Vehicles," *American Journal of Epidemiology*, Vol. 114, No. 5 (1981), pp. 663–670.

bar–associated outbreak that preceded the outbreak in The Dalles. However, no connection between these outbreaks and the outbreak in The Dalles was ever established.

The source of the outbreak strain of S. Typhimurium was finally identified in October 1985. During a search by law enforcement agents, an Oregon Public Health Laboratory official found an open vial of commercial stock culture disks containing S. Typhimurium in a clinical laboratory operated by the religious commune. Records showed that it was purchased before the outbreak, and laboratory testing during the following months demonstrated that the isolate matched the outbreak strain.[16] Informant testimony provided additional information about the motives for the conspiracy and details of its implementation.[17] Testimony indicated that several attacks were directed at some restaurants. In some restaurants, liquid coffee creamer was also contaminated, produce was contaminated in a grocery store, and plans were made to contaminate municipal water supplies.[18] The epidemiologic investigation did not identify these other exposures as risk factors. The source of infection for employees who became ill before customer exposure was documented remains unknown. These illnesses may have been the result of an abortive early attempt at contamination. The informants indicated that the saboteurs were frustrated when their initial attempts did not cause widespread illness, and they may have used higher inocula in later attacks.[19]

In retrospect, intentional contamination is consistent with the epidemiologic findings. When S. Typhimurium was introduced into food on the ice-chilled salad bars, the holding temperatures may have permitted propagation; reuse of foods and addition of old products on top of new ones allowed S. Typhimurium to persist for several days, and other foods on the salad bar may have been cross-contaminated. Intentional contamination explains why different foods were contaminated in different restaurants and the nearly simultaneous involvement of many restaurants despite the lack of common food sources. It also explains why persons attending private banquets at two affected restaurants did not become ill even though salad bars were set up for these events. Most importantly, intentional contamination explains the observations without relying on multiple complex modes of transmission.

---

16. U.S. v. Sheela et al.

17. FitzGerald, *Cities on a Hill*; Laatz, "Sheela Indicted in The Dalles Poisoning Plot"; U.S. v. Sheela et al.; and Laatz, "Sheela Sentenced to Prison."

18. Ibid.

19. U.S. v. Sheela et al.

The possibility that intentional contamination caused the outbreak was specifically considered early in the investigation, but this hypothesis was initially rejected for several reasons: (1) No motive was apparent. Despite concern in The Dalles about the potential for election fraud, the outbreak of illness in September and October was not obviously related with elections occurring in November. We had not considered that this incident had merely been a trial run for further attacks at the time of the election. (2) No one claimed responsibility for the incident, and no demands or ultimata were issued. We assumed that if the motive was either extortion or terrorism, a public statement would have been issued to intimidate or create widespread fear. In fact, the incident was planned as a covert tactical strike. (3) Law enforcement officers investigated the few questionable activities reported among restaurant patrons and did not establish a recognizable pattern of unusual behavior. (4) No disgruntled employee was identified who might seek revenge on his or her employer. The criminal investigation confirmed that restaurant employees did not participate in the contamination efforts. (5) The epidemic exposure curves indicated that salad bars were contaminated multiple times during a several-week period, suggesting that a sustained source of S. Typhimurium was necessary. It seemed more likely to us that a saboteur would have acted on one occasion, rather than risk repeated attacks and exposure. (6) A few employees had onset of illness before the recognized patron exposures in their restaurants. (7) To our knowledge, such an event had never happened. We were aware of only two reports of foodborne illness caused by intentional contamination with biologic agents, and neither incident appeared to be politically motivated.[20] (8) On the basis of our experience in other investigations, we believed that other hypotheses, although more complicated, appeared more likely, because individually each of the components had been well documented in other outbreaks. (9) Finally, even in thoroughly investigated outbreaks, the source sometimes remains occult, and, of all the reasons considered for failing to identify a source, this would be the most common.

There was a risk that publicity about this outbreak may have had the unfortunate side effect of inciting other events, similar to the copycat poisonings following the Tylenol-cyanide poisonings in 1982. When the cause of the outbreak was identified, it was reported by the regional news media; however, we know of no additional outbreaks motivated by these reports. A report of the findings of the CDC investigation was distributed

---

20. Joseph, Millar, and Henderson, "An Outbreak of Hepatitis Due to Food Contamination"; and Phills, Harrold, Whiteman, and Perelmutter, "Pulmonary Infiltrates, Asthma, and Eosinophilia."

to state and territorial public health officials, but not submitted for publication. The recent discovery of the stockpiling and use of biological agents by the Japanese cult Aum Shinrikyo serves to remind us of a continuing threat that biological weapons might be used by other terrorist groups in the future.[21] It is hoped that wider dissemination today of the epidemiologic findings from the outbreak in The Dalles will lead to greater awareness of the possibility of other incidents and earlier recognition, when or if a similar incident occurs. This potential benefit should outweigh the risk of a copycat incident. It may be that with a higher index of suspicion in The Dalles, the source of *S.* Typhimurium would have been identified sooner. However, the epidemiologic method is inherently limited; it determines risk and association and can indicate how contamination probably occurred. It cannot establish motive.

Can another outbreak like the one that occurred in The Dalles be prevented? It seems unlikely that any regulation of commercially available pathogens could have prevented this outbreak. It would not be necessary to purchase them because this type of culture could be easily obtained from clinical isolates or from raw foods of animal origin available in grocery stores. Production of large quantities of bacteria is inexpensive and involves simple equipment and skills. Standard practices for maintaining salad bars may be inadequate to prevent similar outbreaks in the future with salmonellae or other pathogens. As in many areas of our open society, current practices are inadequate to prevent deliberate contamination of food items by customers.

With this in mind, the public is best protected when health care professionals and laboratories cooperate with local and state health departments to report notifiable diseases and unusual disease clusters. Routine reporting is essential in disease surveillance at both the local and national level, and efforts to improve surveillance will assist in the detection of future outbreaks in general. The epidemiologic approach to an outbreak need not be changed. The methods of determining the pathogen, vehicle, and route of contamination and relating them to time, place, and person remain the same. On the basis of our experiences in The Dalles, we also suggest that if investigation of a large and cryptic outbreak implicates a mechanism of contamination that does not resemble established patterns, then the possibility of intentional contamination should be considered, and law enforcement agencies should be asked to consider undertaking an independent investigation.

---

21. David E. Kaplan and Andrew Marshall, *The Cult at the End of the World* (New York: Crown, 1996).

Chapter 11

An Outbreak of *Shigella dysenteriae* Type 2 Among Laboratory Workers Due to Intentional Food Contamination

Shellie A. Kolavic, Akiko Kimura,
Shauna L. Simons, Laurence Slutsker,
Suzanne Barth, and Charles E. Haley

Shigella dysenteriae type 2, also known as Schmitz's bacillus, is a relatively rare organism that causes bacillary dysentery.[1] Although little historical information about this serotype is found in the medical literature, it was apparently first described by Karl Schmitz in 1917 after observing a winter epidemic of diarrhea in an eastern European prison camp during World War I.[2] Outbreaks from this serotype were not common in the general population, but outbreaks among patients in psychiatric hospitals in Wales were reported in 1938.[3]

Sporadic cases and outbreaks of *S. dysenteriae* type 2 infection are now uncommon in developed countries.[4] During the late 1980s, a small outbreak occurred among family members in Sicily, where *S. dysenteriae* type

This chapter was adapted from Shellie A. Kolavic et al., "An Outbreak of *Shigella dysenteriae* Type 2 Among Laboratory Workers Due to Intentional Food Contamination," *Journal of the American Medical Association (JAMA)*, Vol. 278, No. 5 (August 6, 1997), pp. 396–398.

1.   M.T. Parker, "Bacillary Dysentery," in Graham Wilson, Ashley Miles, and M.T. Parker, eds., *Topley and Wilson's Principles of Bacteriology, Virology and Immunity*, Vol. 3, 7th ed. (Baltimore: Williams & Wilkins, 1983), pp. 434–445.

2.   Karl E.F. Schmitz, "Eine neuer Typus aus der Gruppe der Ruhrbazillen als Erreger einer grosser Epidemie," *Z Hyg InfektKr*, Vol. 84 (1917), pp. 449–516.

3.   Ann C. Evans, "Dysentery Due to Bacterium Dysenteriae (Schmitz)," *Lancet*, Vol. 2 (1938), pp. 187–190.

4.   Martin J. Blaser, Robert A. Pollard, and Roger A. Feldman, "*Shigella* Infections in the United States, 1974–1980," *Journal of Infectious Diseases*, Vol. 147, No. 4 (1983), pp. 771–775.

2 had not been reported since 1953.[5] Surveillance data from 1985–95 from the U.S. Centers for Disease Control and Prevention indicate that an average of about twenty individual cases of *S. dysenteriae* type 2 are reported annually in the United States. The last reported outbreak in the United States occurred in 1983 among cafeteria workers in a Maryland medical center.[6]

Illness caused by *S. dysenteriae* type 2 is not well described. Although it may cause significant morbidity, *S. dysenteriae* type 2 appears to cause a milder illness compared with *S. dysenteriae* type 1.[7] Unlike *S. dysenteriae* type 1, which is associated with hemolytic uremic syndrome and toxic megacolon, *S. dysenteriae* type 2 does not produce Shiga toxin.[8]

Background

From October 29 through November 1, 1996, twelve laboratory workers at an urban medical center in Texas experienced a severe gastrointestinal illness after eating muffins and donuts anonymously left in their break room between the night and morning shifts of October 29. After stool cultures from these persons revealed *S. dysenteriae*, all local emergency departments and infectious disease physicians were alerted and urged to report any additional cases. This article describes the findings of our investigation to characterize the magnitude and source of this outbreak.

Methods

We defined a case-patient as a laboratory worker with a diarrheal illness beginning on or after October 29, 1996, with a positive stool culture for *S. dysenteriae* or an oral temperature greater than 37.8°C (100°F). A laboratory worker with diarrhea alone, with an oral temperature 38°C or less, or a negative stool culture was a probable case-patient. We interviewed

---

5. A. Nastasi, C. Mannina, M.R. Villafrate, G. Dicuonzo, E. Aiello, and G. Scaglione, "Re–emergence of *Shigella Dysenteriae* Type 2 in Sicily: An Epidemiological Evaluation," *Microbiologica*, Vol. 14 (1991), pp. 219–222.

6. Centers for Disease Control and Prevention, "Hospital Associated Outbreak *of Shigella dysenteriae* Type 2—Maryland," *Morbidity and Mortality Weekly Report*, Vol. 32 (1983), pp. 250–257.

7. Parker, "Bacillary Dysentery."

8. Abram S. Benenson, ed., *Control of Communicable Diseases Manual*, 16th ed. (Washington, D.C.: American Public Health Association, 1995); and Bernard Rowe, "*Shigella*," in Graham Wilson, Ashley Miles, and M.T. Parker, eds., *Topley and Wilson's Principles of Bacteriology, Virology and Immunity*, Vol. 2, 7th ed. (Baltimore: Williams & Wilkins, 1983), pp. 320–332.

laboratory personnel who worked during the morning and night shifts and assessed demographics, food histories, social activities, and signs and symptoms of illness. Stool was cultured on eosin methylene blue and xylose lysine desoxycholate agar media, then sent with a food specimen to the Bureau of Laboratories of the Texas Department of Health in Austin for further analysis and serotyping. The medical center's stock culture was also sent to the Texas Department of Health. Food was analyzed using established procedures from the Bacteriological Analytical Manual from the Food and Drug Administration.[9] In addition, pulsed-field gel electrophoresis (PFGE) was performed on the food and stool *S. dysenteriae* type 2 isolates and the hospital stock culture on *Xba I* and *Not I* New England BioLabs chromosomal DNA digests. The fragments were separated using a Chlamps Homogenous Electric Field (CHEF) Mapper, and the isolates were visually compared.

All epidemiologic data were collected onto standardized forms, entered into a computer, and analyzed using Epi-Info version 6 software.[10]

Results

We interviewed forty-five laboratory employees who worked during the first or third shifts. Six laboratory workers were unavailable for interview and one refused to participate; however, according to coworkers, six of these persons were not ill and did not eat pastries. One unavailable worker was reportedly ill, but attempts to confirm this were unsuccessful.

Laboratory employees recalled that during the night and morning shift change on October 29, an e-mail from a supervisor's computer appeared on laboratory computer screens with an invitation to eat pastries in the laboratory break room. The supervisor was temporarily away from the office at the time the message was sent. The break room is separate from the laboratory and cannot be accessed without entering a numerical security code. Two boxes of commercially prepared pastries containing blueberry muffins and assorted donuts were available in the break room.

Twelve workers who ate muffins or donuts reported diarrhea with

9. Association of Official Analytical Chemists, *Bacteriological Analytical Manual*, 7th ed. (Arlington, Va.: Association of Official Analytical Chemists, 1992).

10. Andrew G. Dean, Jeffrey A. Dean, Denis Coulombier, Karl A. Brendel, Donald C. Smith, Anthony H. Burton, et al., *Epi Info, Version 6: A Word Processing, Database, and Statistics Program for Epidemiology on Microcomputers* (Atlanta, Ga.: Centers for Disease Control and Prevention, 1994).

fever, headache, or vomiting. Eleven met the definition for case-patients and one was a probable case-patient. The mean age of the ill workers was 41 years (range: 33–52 years) and nine (75 percent) were women. Ill persons reported having eaten a pastry on October 29 between 7:15 AM and 1:30 PM. Additionally, one worker did not eat a muffin at work, but took it home and shared it with a family member around 7:00 PM. The onset of diarrhea among the laboratory workers occurred between 9:00 PM on October 29 and 4:00 AM November 1. (See Figure 11.1.) The mean incubation period until onset of diarrhea was 25 hours (median: 18 hours; range: 11–66 hours) and was preceded by nausea, abdominal discomfort, and bloating. Eleven patients were seen by a health care provider, while one consulted a physician by phone. Five workers were treated in emergency departments and released, whereas four others were hospitalized (mean: 4 days; range: 2–10 days). Eight patients received intravenous fluids. Stool cultures were obtained from eleven ill workers: eight cultures yielded *S. dysenteriae* type 2, and three were negative. The *S. dysenteriae* isolates were sensitive to all antibiotics tested for antimicrobial susceptibility. Eleven patients were treated with ciprofloxacin and one received a homeopathic medication. No deaths occurred among the ill workers.

The attack rate was 100 percent. All twelve persons who ate pastries became ill, versus none of the thirty-three persons who did not eat pastries, resulting in an undefined relative risk for shigellosis among those who ate pastries. There was no increased risk from eating food from the break room refrigerator or drinking any beverage, including coffee, tap water, or other drinks. Similarly, eating in the hospital cafeteria or attending social gatherings during the week of October 25 through 31 was not associated with a higher risk for disease.

Although no secondary transmission of the illness was observed, a family member of one worker became ill after eating a muffin that was brought home from the laboratory's break room. The worker reported ingesting some crumbs and also became ill. Stool cultures from the worker and family member yielded *S. dysenteriae* type 2.

Our investigation of the storage freezer in the laboratory suggested that the reference culture of *S. dysenteriae* type 2 had been disturbed. The laboratory stores various reference cultures, including *S. dysenteriae* type 2 in Microbank vials, a low-temperature storage system for microorganisms. Each vial contains twenty-five porous, donut-shaped beads that can be impregnated with microorganisms. The *S. dysenteriae* type 2 culture, which had been stored by the laboratory for several years, had been transferred to Microbank vials during the 1980s. During the outbreak investigation, the *S. dysenteriae* type 2 vial was discovered to have only nineteen beads, although it had reportedly never been used.

Figure 11.1. Cases of Shigellosis by Onset of Diarrhea among Laboratory Workers.

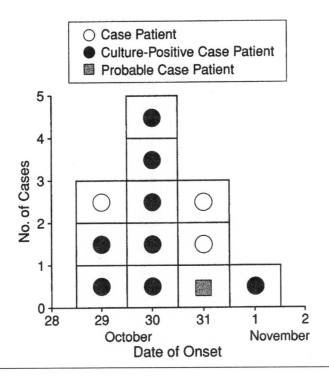

S. dysenteriae type 2 was isolated in virtually pure culture from *Shigella* broth enrichment cultures of the muffin specimen. *S. dysenteriae* type 2 was also isolated from the stools of eight patients. Additionally, *S. dysenteriae* type 2 was confirmed in the medical center's reference culture. Pulsed-field gel electrophoresis revealed that the reference culture isolates were indistinguishable from those of the muffin and the stool cultures but differed from two non-outbreak isolates of *S. dysenteriae* type 2 from other Texas counties in 1995 and 1996. (See Figure 11.2.) The outbreak strains differed from the non-outbreak strains by more than five bands. Useful information was not obtained on the dose of *S. dysenteriae* type 2 in the food sample.

Conclusion

The source of the organism was most likely the medical center's own stock culture of *S. dysenteriae* type 2. There is a strong epidemiological link between the ill persons, the uneaten food, and the laboratory's stock culture of this rare pathogen. All persons who developed shigellosis

literature. During the mid-1960s, several outbreaks of typhoid fever and dysentery in Japanese hospitals were traced to food contaminated by a research bacteriologist who later infected family members and neighbors.[13] In 1970, four Canadian university students became ill with pulmonary infiltrates, asthma, and eosinophilia after eating food maliciously contaminated with embryonated *Ascaris suum* ova, a large ringworm infecting pigs.[14] Later, in 1984, multiple *Salmonella* outbreaks in Oregon were suspected to be caused by intentional contamination of restaurant salad bars.[15]

The results of this investigation underscore the biological threat that accompanies malicious use of pathogenic microbiological agents. Although no system can provide absolute security, measures to reduce the risk of such occurrences might include controls similar to those implemented by the medical center described in this article. These include controlled access to laboratory areas where these materials are stored, locked freezers that can be opened only by designated personnel, and maintenance of a written record of persons entering these areas and handling these materials. Guidelines should be established for secure storage and close surveillance of laboratory stock cultures.

---

13. "Deliberate Spreading of Typhoid in Japan," *Science Journal*, Vol. 2 (1966), pp. 11–12.

14. James A. Phills, A. John Harrold, Gabriel V. Whiteman, and Lewis Perelmutter, "Pulmonary Infiltrates, Asthma and Eosinophilia Due to *Ascaris suum* Infestation in Man," *New England Journal of Medicine*, Vol. 286, No. 18 (1972), pp. 965–970.

15. Oregon Health Division, "Salmonellosis in The Dalles," *Communicable Disease Summary*, Vol. 33, No. 20 (1984), p. 1; "Baghwan's Top Aide Released, Deported," *United Press International* (Domestic News), December 14, 1988; and the chapter by Thomas J. Török et al. in this volume.

Chapter 12

The Sverdlovsk Anthrax Outbreak of 1979

Matthew Meselson, Jeanne Guillemin,
Martin Hugh-Jones, Alexander Langmuir,
Ilona Popova, Alexis Shelokov, and
Olga Yampolskaya

In April and May 1979, an unusual anthrax epidemic occurred in Sverdlovsk, Union of Soviet Socialist Republics. Soviet officials attributed it to consumption of contaminated meat. U.S. agencies attributed it to inhalation of spores accidentally released at a military microbiology facility in the city. Epidemiological data show that most victims worked or lived in a narrow zone extending from the military facility to the southern city limit. Farther south, livestock died of anthrax along the zone's extended axis. The zone paralleled the northerly wind that prevailed shortly before the outbreak. It is concluded that the escape of an aerosol of anthrax pathogen at the military facility caused the outbreak.

Anthrax is an acute disease that primarily affects domesticated and wild herbivores and is caused by the spore-forming bacterium *Bacillus anthracis*. Human anthrax results from cutaneous infection or, more rarely,

Reprinted with permission from *Science*, Vol. 266 (November 18, 1994), pp. 1202–1208. © 1994 American Association for the Advancement of Science.

We thank A.V. Yablokov, Counsellor to the President of Russia for Ecology and Health, for letters of introduction; Ural State University and its then rector, P.E. Suetin, for inviting us to Ekaterinburg; S.F. Borisov, V.A. Shchepetkin, and A.P. Tiutiunnik for assistance and advice; members of the Ekaterinburg medical community and the Sverdlovskaya Oblast Sanitary Epidemiological Service for discussions, notes, and documents; interview respondents for their cooperation; P.N. Burgasov, USSR Deputy Minister of Health at the time of the outbreak, for documents regarding livestock deaths; and People's Deputy L.P. Mishustina for the administrative list of those who died. I.V. Belaeva assisted with interviews. We also thank B. Ring, W.H. Bossert, P.J.M. Cannone, M.T. Collins, S.R. Hanna, J.V. Jemski, D. Joseph, H.F. Judson, M.M. Kaplan, J. Medema, C.R. Replogle, R. Stafford, J.H. Steele, and E.D. Sverdlov. This work was supported by grants to Matthew Meselson from the John D. and Catherine T. MacArthur Foundation and the Carnegie Corporation of New York. This chapter is dedicated to Alexander Langmuir.

from ingestion or inhalation of the pathogen from contaminated animal products.[1] Anthrax has also caused concern as a possible agent of biological warfare.[2]

Early in 1980, reports appeared in the Western press of an anthrax epidemic in Sverdlovsk, a city of 1.2 million people 1,400 kilometers east of Moscow.[3] Later that year, articles in Soviet medical, veterinary, and legal journals reported an anthrax outbreak among livestock south of the city in the spring of 1979 and stated that people developed gastrointestinal anthrax after eating contaminated meat and cutaneous anthrax after contact with diseased animals.[4] The epidemic has occasioned intense international debate and speculation as to whether it was natural or accidental and, if accidental, whether it resulted from activities prohibited by the Biological Weapons Convention of 1972.[5]

In 1986, Matthew Meselson renewed previously unsuccessful requests to Soviet officials to bring independent scientists to Sverdlovsk to investigate. This resulted in an invitation to come to Moscow for discussions with four physicians who had gone to Sverdlovsk to deal with the outbreak, including another of the authors, Olga Yampolskaya, who was a clinician in the intensive care unit set aside to treat the victims. In 1988, two of these Soviet physicians visited the United States, where they gave formal presentations and participated in discussions with private and government specialists. According to their account, contaminated animals and meat from an epizootic south of the city starting in late March 1979 caused ninety-six cases of human anthrax with onsets from April 4 to May 18. Of these cases, seventy-nine were said to be gastrointestinal and

---

1. Philip S. Brachman, "Anthrax," in Alfred S. Evans and Philip S. Brachman, eds., *Bacterial Infections of Humans: Epidemiology and Control,* 2nd ed. (New York: Plenum, 1991), pp. 75–86.

2. World Health Organization (WHO), *Health Aspects of Chemical and Biological Weapons* (Geneva: WHO, 1970).

3. *Posev (Frankfurt),* Vol. 1 (1980), p. 7; and Bernard Gwertzman, "Soviet Mishap Tied to Germ-War Plant," *New York Times,* March 19, 1980, p. A1.

4. I.S. Bezdenezhnykh and V.N. Nikiforov, "Epidemiologic Analysis of Anthrax in Sverdlovsk," *Zh. Mikrobiol. Epidemiol. Immunobiol.,* No. 5 (May 1980), p. 111; *Veterinariya,* No. 10 (1980), p. 3; and *Chelovek i Zakon,* Vol. 117, No. 9 (1980), p. 70.

5. Defense Intelligence Agency, *Soviet Biological Warfare Threat* (Washington, D.C.: U.S. Department of Defense, 1986), DST-1610F-057–86; Leslie H. Gelb, "Keeping an Eye on Russia," *New York Times Magazine,* November 29, 1981, p. 31; and J.P. Perry Robinson, "Discussion of 'The Soviet Union and the Biological Weapons Convention,' and a Guide to Sources on the Sverdlovsk Incident," *Arms Control,* Vol. 3, No. 3 (December 1982), p. 41.

seventeen cutaneous, with sixty-four deaths among the former and none among the latter.[6]

The impression left on those of us who took part in the U.S. meetings (Guillemin, Langmuir, Meselson, and Shelokov) was that a plausible case had been made but that additional epidemiological and pathoanatomical evidence was needed. Further requests by Meselson for an invitation led to an on-site study in Sverdlovsk, initiated there in June 1992, and a return visit in August 1993.

Starting in 1990, several articles about the epidemic appeared in the Russian press.[7] These included interviews with Sverdlovsk physicians who questioned the food-borne explanation of the epidemic and with officials at the military microbiology facility. These officials said that in 1979 they had been developing an improved vaccine against anthrax but knew of no escape of anthrax pathogen. Late in 1991, Russian President Boris Yeltsin, who in 1979 was the chief Communist Party official of the Sverdlovsk region, directed his Counsellor for Ecology and Health to determine the origin of the epidemic.[8] In May 1992, Yeltsin was quoted as saying that "the KGB admitted that our military developments were the cause."[9] No further information was provided. Subsequently, the chairman of the committee created by Yeltsin to oversee biological and chemical disarmament expressed doubt that the infection originated at the military facility and stated that his committee would conduct its own investigation.[10] The results of that investigation have not yet appeared.

Pathoanatomical evidence that the fatal cases were inhalatory, recently published by Russian pathologists who performed autopsies dur-

---

6. R. Jeffrey Smith and Philip J. Hilts, "Soviets Deny Lab Caused Anthrax Cases: Tainted Meat Blamed for 1979 Deaths," *Washington Post*, April 13, 1988, p. 1; Matthew S. Meselson, "The Biological Weapons Convention and the Sverdlovsk Anthrax Outbreak of 1979," *Federation of American Scientists Public Interest Report*, Vol. 41, No. 7 (September 1988), p. 1; and I.S. Bezdenezhnykh, P.N. Burgasov, and V.N. Nikiforov, "An Epidemiological Analysis of an Outbreak of Anthrax in Sverdlovsk" (U.S. Department of State Language Service, translation 126894, September 1988, unpublished manuscript).

7. N. Zhenova, *Literaturnaya Gazeta* (Moscow), August 22, 1990, p. 12; ibid., October 2, 1991, p. 6; S. Parfenov, *Rodina* (Moscow), May 1990, p. 21; Pashkov, *Isvestiya* (Moscow), November 11, 1991, p. 8; and V. Chelikov, *Komnsomolskaya Pravda* (Moscow), November 20, 1991, p.4.

8. N. Zhenova, *Literaturnaya Gazeta* (Moscow), November 13, 1991, p. 2.

9. D. Muratov, Yu. Sorokin, and V. Fronin, *Komnsomolskaya Pravda* (Moscow), May 27, 1992, p. 2.

10. L. Chernenko, *Rossiyskiye Vesti* (Moscow), November 13, 1991, p. 2.

ing the epidemic,[11] is summarized in an earlier report from the present study.[12] Here we report epidemiological findings that confirm that the pathogen was airborne, and we identify the location and date of its escape into the atmosphere.

Sources of Information

Local medical officials told us that hospital and public health records of the epidemic had been confiscated by the KGB. We nevertheless were able to assemble detailed information on many patients from a variety of sources: first, an administrative list giving names, birth years, and residence addresses of sixty-eight people who died, compiled from KGB records and used by the Russian government to compensate families of the deceased.[13] Comparison with other sources of information, including those listed below, indicates that the administrative list may include most or all of those who died of anthrax. Second, we conducted household interviews with relatives and friends of forty-three people on the administrative list and with nine survivors or their relatives (or both). The interviews (directed by Guillemin) were designed to identify the workplaces and other whereabouts of patients before their illness. Third, we found grave markers, giving names and dates of birth and death, which we inspected in the cemetery sector set aside for the anthrax victims. These included sixty-one markers with names that are also on the administrative list and five with illegible or missing name plates. Fourth, we read pathologists' notes regarding forty-two autopsies that resulted in a diagnosis of anthrax.[14] All but one of the forty-two, an unidentified man, are on the administrative list. The notes include name, age, and dates of onset, admission, death, and autopsy. Fifth, we looked at various hospital lists, with names, residence addresses, and, in some cases, workplaces or diagnoses (or both) of approximately 110 patients who were apparently screened for anthrax, 48 of whom are indicated to have died. Of the latter, forty-six are on the administrative list. Sixth, we examined full clinical case histories of five survivors hospitalized in May 1979.

Current street and regional maps were purchased in Sverdlovsk,

---

11. A.A. Abramova and L.M. Grinberg, *Ark. Patol.*, Vol. 55, No. 1 (1993), p. 12, 18, 23.

12. F.A. Abramova, L.N. Grinberg, O.V. Yampolskaya, and D.H. Walker, *Proc. Natl. Acad. Sci. U.S.A.*, Vol. 90 (1993), p. 2291.

13. Russian Federation, Statute 2667–1 (April 4, 1992).

14. A.A. Abramova and L.M. Grinberg, *Ark. Patol.*, Vol. 55, No. 1 (1993), p. 12, 18, 23; and F.A. Abramova, L.N. Grinberg, O.V. Yampolskaya, and D.H. Walker, *Proc. Natl. Acad. Sci. U.S.A.*, Vol. 90 (1993), p. 2291.

which is known again by its prerevolutionary name of Ekaterinburg. The city is the seat of an administrative region, or *oblast,* named Sverd-lovskaya. The city itself is divided among a number of districts, or *rayon,* the most southerly being Chkalovskiy *rayon.* A satellite photograph of the city taken on August 31, 1988, was purchased from SPOT Image Corpo-ration in Reston, Virginia. Archived meteorological data from the city's Koltsovo airport were obtained from the National Center for Atmospheric Research (Boulder, Colorado).

Case Data

Table 12.1 presents information on sixty-six patients who died and eleven who survived. The fatalities include the unidentified man and all people named on the administrative list, except for three patients for whom recent reexamination of preserved autopsy specimens does not support a diagnosis of anthrax.[15] For survivors, diagnoses of anthrax are supported by clinical case histories or hospital lists or both and by household interviews.

Overall, fifty-five of the seventy-seven tabulated patients are men, whose mean age was forty-two. The mean age for women was fifty-five. No man was younger than twenty-four, and only two women, aged twenty-four and thirty-two, were under forty. Recorded onsets span a period of nearly six weeks, April 4 to May 15, with a mean time between onset and death of three days. (See Table 12.1 and Figure 12.1.)

Approximately 60 percent of the thirty-three men for whom we have relevant information were described as moderate or heavy smokers and nearly half as moderate or heavy drinkers. None of the women was said to have smoked or to have consumed alcohol more than occasionally. Few patients were reported to have had serious preexisting medical condi-tions. Among the thirty-five men whose occupation in 1979 we could determine, the most common was welder, accounting for seven.

In descending order of frequency, symptoms reported in household interviews included fever, dyspnea, cough, headache, vomiting, chills, weakness, abdominal pain, and chest pain. Two of the survivors inter-viewed reported having had cutaneous anthrax, one on the back of the neck, the other on the shoulder. Hospitalized patients were treated with penicillin, cephalosporin, chloramphenicol, anti-anthrax globulin, corti-costeroids, osmoregulatory solutions, and artificial respiration. The aver-age hospital stay was one to two days for fatal cases and approximately

---

15. Personal communication with L. Grinberg.

those who died were placed in coffins with chlorinated lime and buried in a single sector of a city cemetery. Medical and sanitation teams recruited from local hospitals and factories visited homes of suspected and confirmed cases throughout the city, where they conducted medical interviews, dispensed prophylactic tetracycline to patients' households, disinfected kitchens and sick rooms, and took meat and environmental samples for bacteriological testing. Human anthrax is not considered contagious, nor was there any evidence of person-to-person transmission. In the part of Chkalovskiy *rayon* where most patients resided, building exteriors and trees were washed by local fire brigades, stray dogs were shot by police, and several previously unpaved streets were asphalted. Newspaper articles and posters warned of the risk of anthrax from consumption of uninspected meat and contact with sick animals. Uninspected meat in vehicles entering the city from the south was confiscated and burned at highway checkpoints.

Starting in mid-April, a voluntary immunization program using a live nonencapsulated spore vaccine (designated STI) was carried out for healthy persons eighteen to fifty-five years old served by clinics in Chkalovskiy *rayon*. Posters urged citizens to obtain "prophylactic immunization against anthrax" at designated times and places. Of the 59,000 people considered eligible, about 80 percent were vaccinated at least once.

Geographical Distribution of Human Cases

Most of the seventy-seven tabulated patients lived and worked in the southern area of the city shown in Figure 12.2. Of the sixty-six patients for whom we have both residence and workplace locations, nine lived and regularly worked outside of this area. Interviews with relatives and friends revealed that five of these nine had attended military reserve classes during the first week of April 1979 at Compound 32, an army base in the affected area. Respondents stated and, in one case, showed diary notes establishing that the first day of attendance was Monday, April 2, that classes began at 0830, and that participants returned home each evening. Assuming that the reservists were exposed while at or near Compound 32, this must have occurred during the daytime in the week of April 2.

In order to locate the high-risk area more precisely, we prepared a map showing probable daytime locations of the sixty-six patients during the week of April 2. Those with residence or work addresses in military compounds or attending reserve classes were placed in the appropriate military compound; night workers, pensioners, unemployed people, and vacationers were placed at their homes; and all other workers were placed

Figure 12.2. Probable Locations of Patients When Exposed.

NOTES: The part of the city shown in the photograph is enclosed by a rectangle in the inset. Case numbers, in black, correspond to those in Table 1 and indicate probable daytime locations of patients during the period April 2–6, 1979. Of the sixty-six patients mapped as explained in the text, sixty-two mapped in the area shown. This distribution may be somewhat biased against residence locations, because daytime workers not on vacation who both resided and worked in the high-risk zone are mapped at their workplaces. Proceeding from north to south, Compound 19, Compound 32, and the ceramics factory are outlined in gray. The five patients residing in Compound 32 are mapped at their apartments. Within the compound, the placement of an additional, part-time resident and of the five reservists is arbitrary, as is that of the five residents and a nonresident employee in Compound 19. Patients known to have worked in the ceramics pipe shop are mapped in the eastern part of the factory area, where the pipe shop is located. Calculated contours of constant dosage are shown in black. Approximately 7,000 people lived in the area bounded by the outermost contour of constant dosage, Compound 32, and the ceramics factory. The terrain slopes gently downward by about 40 meters from Compound 19 to the ceramics factory.

at their workplaces. This mapped fifty-seven patients in a narrow zone approximately 4 kilometers long, extending from the military microbiology facility to the southern city limit. The remaining nine worked outside this zone, but three of them resided within it. Placing the latter at their residences gives the distribution shown in Figure 12.2, with sixty of the sixty-six mapped cases in the high-risk zone, two cases east of it, and four cases north or east of the area of the figure. Of these six patients who both worked and lived outside the high-risk zone, three had occupations (truck driver, pipe layer, and telephone worker) that might have taken them there, one was temporarily working in Chkalovskiy *rayon*, one was on vacation, and inadequate information was available for another.

At the northern end of the high-risk zone is the military microbiology facility, Compound 19, followed to the south by Compound 32. Both compounds include numerous buildings, with four- and five-story apartment houses for about 5,000 people at the former and 10,000 at the latter. The administrative list includes five people who lived in Compound 19 and five who lived in Compound 32. All of the latter resided in four adjacent apartment buildings in the eastern part of the compound. Interviews in Compound 32 indicated that all of its residents who died of anthrax are on the administrative list. Interviews were not conducted in Compound 19.

Adjacent to Compound 32 and extending south-southeast for about 1.5 kilometers is a residential neighborhood with a 1979 population density of approximately 10,000 per square kilometer, composed of small single-story private houses and few apartment houses, shops, and schools. Just south of this is a ceramics factory that had about 1,500 daytime employees. Of the eighteen tabulated patients who were employees there, ten worked in a large unpartitioned building where ceramic pipe was made and which had a daytime work force of about 450. The attack rate at the ceramics factory therefore appears to be 1 to 2 percent. Still farther south are several smaller factories, apartment buildings, private houses, schools, and shops, beyond which begins open countryside with patches of woodland.

Animal Anthrax

Anthrax has been enzootic in Sverdlovskaya *oblast* since before the 1917 revolution.[17] Local officials recalled an outbreak of anthrax among sheep and cattle south of the city in early spring 1979. A detailed report of a

---

17.   V.M. Popugaylo, R.P. Sukhanova, and M.I. Kukhto, in *Current Problems of Anthrax Prophylaxis in the USSR* (Moscow, 1974), p. 50.

commission of veterinarians and local officials describes the epizootic in Abramovo, a village of approximately 100 houses 50 kilometers south-southeast of Compound 19. The report, dated April 25, 1979, records the deaths or forced slaughter of seven sheep and a cow with anthrax that was confirmed by veterinary examination. The first such losses were of two sheep on April 5, followed by two more on each of the next two days, another on April 8, and a cow on April 10, all belonging to different private owners. These losses were substantiated by interviews we conducted with owners of six of the sheep that died. Respondents said there had been no human anthrax in the village. During a livestock immunization program started on April 10, 298 sheep were given anti-anthrax serum or vaccine or both. The attack rate among sheep at Abramovo therefore appears to have been approximately 2 percent.

In addition, we obtained veterinary reports of bacteriological tests positive for anthrax in samples from three sheep from three farms in the village of Kashino, one sheep from Pervomaisky, and a cow from Rudniy, the earliest samples being received for testing on April 6. Although other documents cite the forced slaughter of a sheep in Rudniy on March 28 and the death of another in Abramovo on April 3, the earliest livestock losses for which we have documentation of a diagnosis of anthrax are those in Abramovo on April 5.

Altogether, Soviet publications[18] and the documents we obtained cite outbreaks of anthrax among livestock in six villages: Rudniy, Bolshoye Sedelnikovo, Maloye Sedelnikovo, Pervomaiskiy, Kashino, and Abramovo. All six villages lie along the extended axis of the high-risk zone of human anthrax. (See Figure 12.3.) The centerline of human and livestock cases has a compass bearing of 330° ± 10°.

Meteorology

Surface (10 meters) observations reported at three-hour intervals from Koltsovo airport, 10 kilometers east of the ceramics factory, were examined in order to identify times when the wind direction was parallel to the centerline of human and animal cases. During the time that the reservists who contracted anthrax were at Compound 32, but before the first recorded human onsets, this occurred only on Monday, April 2, when northerly winds from the sector 320° to 350° were reported throughout the period 0400 to 1900 local time. (See Figure 12.4.)

During the rest of April, winds from this sector seldom occurred, accounting for fewer than 2 percent of reports. During the period of

18. *Veterinariya*, No. 10 (1980), p. 3; and *Chelovek i Zakon*, Vol. 117, No. 9 (1980), p. 70.

Figure 12.3. Villages With Animal Anthrax.

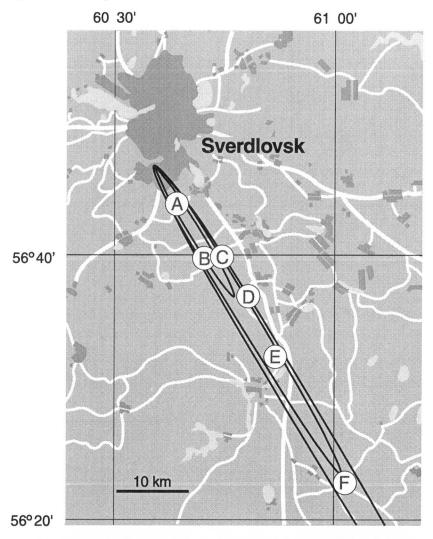

NOTES: Six villages where livestock died of anthrax in April 1979 are A, Rudniy; B, Bolshoye Sedelnikovo; C, Maloye Sedelnikovo; D, Pervomaiskiy; E, Kashino; and F, Abramovo. Settled areas are shown in dark gray, roads in white, lakes in light gray, and calculated contours of constant dosage in black.

Figure 12.4. Wind Directions and Speeds Reported from Koltsovo Airport for the Period April 2–4, 1979.

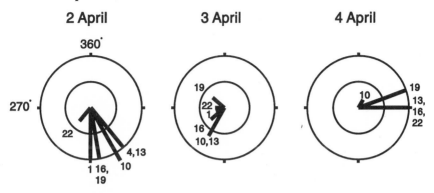

NOTES: Numbers at the downwind end of each line are local standard times. Inner and outer concentric circles designate wind speeds of 2.5 and 5.0 m s⁻¹, respectively. Zero wind speed was reported for 0400 on April 3 and for 0100 and 0400 on April 4. No data were reported for 0700.

northerly wind on April 2, which followed the passage of a cold front, the wind speed was 4 to 6 meters s⁻¹, the temperature –10° to –3°C, the relative humidity 50 to 66 percent, the sky cloudless, and the midday sun 39° above the horizon. These conditions of insolation and wind speed indicate that the atmosphere near the surface was of neutral stability.[19] As is consistent with this, temperature measures at 500 to 1000 meters indicated a slightly stable atmosphere at 0400 and 1000 hours, becoming neutral by 1600.

Discussion

We have presented evidence that most people who contracted anthrax worked, lived, or attended daytime military reserve classes during the first week of April 1979 in a narrow zone, with its northern end in a military microbiology facility in the city and its other end near the city limit 4 kilometers to the south; livestock died of anthrax in villages located along the extended axis of this same zone, out to a distance of 50 kilometers; a northerly wind parallel to the high-risk zone prevailed during most of the day on Monday, April 2, the first day that the military reservists who contracted anthrax were within the zone; and the first cases of animal anthrax appeared two to three days thereafter.

19. S.R. Hanna, G.A. Briggs, and R.P. Hosker, *Handbook of Atmospheric Diffusion* (Washington, D.C.: U.S. Department of Energy Report No. DOE/TIC-11223, 1982).

We conclude that the outbreak resulted from the windborne spread of an aerosol of anthrax pathogen, that the source was at the military microbiology facility, and that the escape of the pathogen occurred during the day on Monday, April 2. The epidemic is the largest documented outbreak of human inhalation anthrax.

The narrowness of the zone of human and animal anthrax and the infrequency of northerly winds parallel to the zone after April 2 suggest that most or all infections resulted from the escape of anthrax pathogen on that day. Owing to the inefficiency of aerosol deposition and resuspension,[20] few if any inhalatory infections are likely to have resulted from secondary aerosols on subsequent days. A single date of inhalatory infection is also consistent with the steady decline of fatal cases in successive weeks of the epidemic.

Accepting April 2 as the only date of inhalatory exposure, the longest incubation period for fatal cases was forty-three days and the modal incubation period was nine to ten days. This is longer than the incubation period of two to six days that has been estimated from very limited data for humans.[21] Experiments with nonhuman primates have shown, however, that anthrax spores can remain viable in the lungs for many weeks and that the average incubation period depends inversely on dose, with individual incubation periods ranging between two and approximately ninety days.[22]

The absence of inhalation anthrax patients younger than twenty-four remains unexplained. Although nothing suggests a lack of children or young adults in Chkalovskiy *rayon* in 1979, they may have been underrepresented in the aerosol plume. Alternatively, older people may have been more susceptible, which may also explain the lack of young people

---

20. D.E. Davids and A.R. Lejeune, *Secondary Aerosol Hazard in the Field* (Ralston, Canada: Defence Research Establishment Suffield Report No. 321, 1981); and A. Birenzvige, *Inhalation Hazard from Reaerosolized Biological Agents: A Review* (Aberdeen, Md.: U.S. Army Chemical Research, Development and Engineering Center Report No. TR-413, 1992).

21. Philip S. Brachman, Stanley A. Plotkin, Forrest H. Bumford, and Mary M. Atchison, "An Epidemic of Inhalation Anthrax: The First in the Twentieth Century. II: Epidemiology," *American Journal of Hygiene*, Vol. 72 (1960), p. 6.

22. D.W. Henderson, S. Peacock, and F.C. Belton, "Observations on the Prophylaxis of Experimental Pulmonary Anthrax in the Monkey," *Journal of Hygiene*, Vol. 54 (1956), p. 28; C.A. Gleiser, C.C. Berdjis, H.A. Hartman, and W.S. Gochenour, "Pathology of Experimental Respiratory Anthrax in Macaca Mulatta," *British Journal of Experimental Pathology*, Vol. 44 (1963), p. 416; and Harold N. Glassman, "Industrial Inhalation Anthrax—Discussion," *Bacteriol. Review*, Vol. 30 (1966), p. 657.

in epidemics of inhalation anthrax early in this century in Russian rural communities.[23]

It may be asked if the geographical distribution of cases is consistent with the distribution expected for an aerosol of anthrax spores released at Compound 19 under the daytime atmospheric conditions of April 2, 1979. Contours of constant dosage were calculated from a Gaussian plume model of atmospheric dispersion, with standard deviation given by Briggs for neutral atmospheric stability in an open country,[24] a wind speed of 5 meters min^{-1}, a nominal release height of 10 meters, and no limit to vertical mixing. (See Figures 12.2 and 12.3.) The aerosol is assumed to consist of particles of diameter < 5 μm, as can be produced, for example, by a laboratory aerosol generator,[25] and to have a negligible infectivity decay rate (<0.001 min^{-1})[26] and a deposition velocity <0.5 cm s^{-1}, which is insufficient to cause appreciable reduction of dosage at downwind distances less than 50 kilometers.[27] Dosage contours are not shown closer than 300 meters to the putative source, as the dosage at shorter distances depends sensitively on the effective release height of the aerosol and the configuration of nearby buildings.

People indoors will be exposed to the same total dosage as those outside if filtration, deposition, and infectivity decay of the aerosol are negligible. The negligibility of these factors is supported by the absence of significant dosage reduction in field studies of protection afforded by tightly constructed buildings against an outside spore aerosol.[28]

The calculated contours of constant dosage, like the zone of high human and animal risk, are long and narrow. Contours are shown at 10, 5, and 1×10^{-8} Q spore minutes per cubic meter (Figure 12.2) and at 0.5,

23. A.V. El'Kina, *Zh. Mikrobiol. Epidemiol. Immunobiol.*, No. 9 (1971), p. 112.

24. Hanna, Briggs, and Hosker, *Handbook of Atmospheric Diffusion.*

25. Joseph V. Jemski and G. Briggs Phillips, "Aerosol Challenge of Animals," in William I. Gay, ed., *Methods of Animal Experimentation*, Vol. I (New York: Academic Press, 1965), pp. 273–341.

26. WHO, *Health Aspects of Chemical and Biological Weapons.*

27. A.C. Chamberlain, *Proc. R. Soc. London A*, Vol. 296 (1967), p. 45; Thomas W. Horst, "A Review of Gaussian Diffusion-Deposition Models," in David S. Shriner, Chester R. Richmond, and Steven E. Lindberg, eds., *Atmospheric Sulfur Deposition* (Ann Arbor: Ann Arbor Science, 1980), pp. 275–283; and Å. Bovallius and P. Ånäs, in A.W. Frankland, E. Stix, and H. Ziegler, eds., *Proceedings of the 1st International Conference on Aerobiology*, International Association for Aerobiology, Munich, West Germany, August 13–15, 1978 (Berlin: Erich Schmidt, 1980), pp. 227–231.

28. G.A. Cristy and C.V. Chester, *Emergency Protection Against Aerosols*, Report No. ORNL-5519 (Oak Ridge, Tenn.: Oak Ridge National Laboratory, July 1981).

0.2, and 0.1×10^{-8} Q spore minutes per cubic meter (Figure 12.3), where Q is the number of spores released as aerosol at the source. The number of spores inhaled is the dosage multiplied by the breathing rate. On the innermost contour of Figure 12.2, for example, a person breathing 0.03 m^3 min^{-1}, as for a man engaged in light work,[29] would inhale 3×10^{-9} Q spores.

The calculated dosage at Abramovo is more than an order of magnitude lower than at the ceramics factory. This suggests that sheep, reported to be more susceptible to inhalation anthrax than are monkeys,[30] are also more susceptible than humans.

It has been suggested that if Compound 19 were the source, there would have been many more cases in its close vicinity than farther downwind.[31] This expectation may be misleading, for as a cloud moves downwind it also widens. The total crosswind-integrated dosage will therefore decrease more slowly with distance than does the dosage along the centerline. In the present case, whereas the calculated centerline dosage decreases by a factor of 40 between 0.3 and 3 kilometers downwind, the crosswind-integrated dosage decreases by a factor of only 4. Depending on the dose-response relation, the crosswind-integrated attack rate may decrease even more slowly than this. Considering, in addition, the lack of information regarding the exact locations of people in Compounds 19 and 32 at the time of exposure, the distribution of cases is not inconsistent with a source at Compound 19.

More detailed comparison of the geographical distribution of cases with the calculated distribution of dosage would require knowledge of the precise locations of individuals in relation to the plume, the number of spores released as aerosol, and the relation between dosage and response for the particular spore preparation, aerosol, and population at risk.

By far the largest reported study of the dose-response relation for inhalation anthrax in primates used 1,236 cynomolgus monkeys exposed to an aerosol of the Vollum 1B strain of *B. anthracis*.[32] This provided data that, when fitted to a log-normal distribution of susceptibility to infection, gave a median lethal dose (LD$_{50}$) of 4,100 spores and a slope of 0.7 probits

29. Dorothy S. Ditmer and Rudolph M. Grebe, eds., *Handbook of Respiration* (Philadelphia: W.B. Saunders, 1958).

30. George A. Young, M.R. Zelle, and Ralph E. Lincoln, "Respiratory Pathogenicity of Spores," *Journal of Infectious Diseases*, Vol. 79 (1946), p. 233.

31. L. Chernenko, *Rossiyskiye Vesti* (Moscow), November 13, 1991, p. 2.

32. Glassman, "Industrial Inhalation Anthrax—Discussion," p. 657; and personal communication with J.V. Jemski.

per log dose.[33] This LD_{50} may be compared with an LD_{50} of 2,500 spores obtained in an experiment done under identical conditions with rhesus monkeys[34] and with a U.S. Defense Department estimate that the LD_{50} for humans is between 8,000 and 10,000 spores.[35] For a log-normal distribution with LD_{50} = 8,000 and slope = 0.7, the dose causing 2 percent fatalities, as recorded at the ceramics pipe shop, approximately 2.8 kilometers downwind of the source, is nine spores. According to the Gaussian plume model we have used, this dose would be inhaled by individuals breathing 0.03 m^3 min^{-1} at the pipe shop if the aerosol released at the source contained 4×10^9 spores. In contrast, a release 150 times larger is estimated if the calculation is based on an LD_{50} of 4.5×10^4 spores, which has been obtained for rhesus monkeys by other investigators,[36] and if it is assumed that spores act independently in pathogenesis and that all individuals are equally susceptible.[37] This estimate would be lowered if allowance were made for nonuniform susceptibility. If these divergent estimates bracket the actual value, the weight[38] of spores released as aerosol could have been as little as a few milligrams or as much as nearly a gram.

In sum, the narrow zone of human and animal anthrax cases extending downwind from Compound 19 shows that the outbreak resulted from an aerosol that originated there. It remains to be learned what activities were being conducted at the compound and what caused the release of the pathogen.

---

33. Glassman, "Industrial Inhalation Anthrax—Discussion," p. 657; and C.I. Bliss, *Ann. Appl. Biol.*, Vol. 22 (1935), p. 134.

34. Personal communication with J.V. Jemski.

35. Defense Intelligence Agency, *Soviet Biological Warfare Threat*; Gelb, "Keeping an Eye on Russia," p. 31; and Robinson, "Discussion of 'The Soviet Union and the Biological Weapons Convention'," p. 41.

36. H.A. Druett, D.W. Henderson, L. Packman, and S.J. Peacock, "Studies on Respiratory Infection. I. The Influence of Particle Size on Respiratory Infection with Anthrax Spores," *Journal of Hygiene*, Vol. 51 (1953), p. 359.

37. H.A. Druett, "Bacterial Invasion," *Nature*, Vol. 170 (1952), p. 288.

38. René Scherrer and Vivion E. Shull, "Microincineration and Elemental X-ray Microanalysis of Single *Bacillus cereus* T Spores," *Canadian Journal of Microbiology*, Vol. 33 (1987), p. 304.

Chapter 13

Unlawful Acquisition and Use of Biological Agents

W. Seth Carus

Until relatively recently, only a handful of scholars devoted attention to the potential dangers posed by the unlawful use of biological agents. The result was a small literature focused primarily on the dangers of biological terrorism.[1] Until recently, however, little effort was made to study incidents in which it was alleged that terrorists or criminals used, or considered using, biological agents. All too often, the same reports are repeated by one source after another without any effort being made to ascertain the validity of the original story.

The lack of empirical data also has hampered our ability to develop policy responses to the potential threats posed by biological agents. Until recently, lack of awareness of the dangers posed by unlawful use of biological agents left public health, law enforcement, and national security officials ill-equipped to appreciate the problem.

To fill the gap in our empirical understanding of unlawful use of biological agents, I have undertaken a comprehensive survey of publicly reported instances in which a non-state actor used, attempted to use, acquired, or considered acquiring biological agents. This chapter summarizes some of the results of that research.

The views expressed here are those of the author and do not necessarily reflect the official policy or position of the Department of Defense or the U.S. government.

---

1. A relatively comprehensive review of past studies of biological terrorism is found in Ron Purver, *Chemical and Biological Terrorism: The Threat According to the Open Literature*, Canadian Security Intelligence Service, June 1995.

Methodology

In this section, I review the methodology used to identify and research incidents involving the illicit use of biological agents. Among the topics reviewed are the case definition, the techniques used to identify cases, the procedures for researching specific cases, and the topics selected for further analysis. Finally, some comments are made concerning the comprehensiveness of the survey.

CASE DEFINITION

This survey is based on a review of more than one hundred cases in which a non-state actor, either a terrorist or a criminal, allegedly used, threatened to use, acquired, attempted to acquire, or expressed an interest in biological agents.[2] Cases involving criminals have been included for reasons discussed in more detail below.

To merit inclusion, the following factors were required. First, a biological agent had to be involved. A biological agent is a pathogen or a toxin derived from a plant or animal. The toxin can be either natural or a synthesized version of a natural substance.[3] Second, the involvement of biological agents included use, threatened use, acquisition, attempted acquisition, or a serious expression of interest in biological agents. Third, the target of the biological agents could have been people, animals, crops, or processed foods. If animals or crops were targeted, the action or planned action must either violate the laws of the jurisdiction where the act was committed or otherwise involve a prohibited activity. Fourth, cases that involved poisonous animals, such as insects or snakes, were excluded, except when insects were used as a vector for a pathogen. Fifth, cases involving transmission of disease directly from an infected person

---

2. The overall study includes approximately 120 cases, including seventeen in which the perpetrators were employed by a state organization and approximately twenty-five that occurred or came to the attention of the author after the cut-off date for the analysis.

3. There is no one standard definition of a biological agent. The one used here is essentially the same one used in Frederick R. Sidell and David R. Franz, "Overview: Defense Against the Effects of Chemical and Biological Warfare Agents," pp. 4–5, in Frederick R. Sidell et al., eds., *Medical Aspects of Chemical and Biological Warfare* (Washington, D.C.: Office of the Surgeon General, Department of the Army, 1997): "Biological agents are either replicating agents (bacteria or viruses) or nonreplicating materials (toxins or physiologically active proteins or peptides) that can be produced by living organisms. Some of the nonreplicating biological agents can also be produced through either chemical synthesis, solid-phase protein synthesis, or recombinant expression methods."

were not included.[4] Finally, incidents involving only chemical agents were excluded. The events associated with the case must have occurred on or after January 1, 1900, but before March 1, 1998. The incidents could have occurred anywhere in the world.

The cases analyzed here are limited to those involving non-state actors: terrorists, who use biological agents to further political agendas, and criminals, who are motivated by considerations that are more personal.[5] In some instances, it is difficult to determine whether perpetrators were motivated by political or criminal motivations. Several perpetrators tried to extort money from governments, but also made political demands. Since such political demands could have been a cover for financial motivations, it is generally impossible to ascertain the true motivation for the threats if the perpetrators were never caught.

Excluded from the study are incidents in which health care providers poison patients using biological agents with common medicinal uses, such as digitalis or curare.[6] This is an admittedly arbitrary exclusion. Health care providers have opportunities for using certain toxins not available to other perpetrators. First, they have legitimate access to toxins, or can easily steal from facilities that have a legitimate need for the substances. Second, health care providers have routine access to victims that other perpetrators do not have. (There are few other settings in which people willingly allow strangers to stick them with needles.) Thus, the activities of health care providers give little insight into what a terrorist

---

4. This excludes instances in which people infected with transmissible diseases deliberately engage in risky behavior, such as HIV carriers engaging in unprotected sex.

5. For purposes of this study, terrorists include any individuals or groups motivated by political, religious, ecological, or other ideological objectives. In contrast, the official U.S. government definition of terrorism is more narrowly focused: "the unlawful use of force or violence against persons or property to intimidate or coerce a Government, the civilian population, or any segment thereof, in furtherance of political or social objectives." See Federal Bureau of Investigation, *Terrorism in the United States 1995*, as found at http://www.fbi.gov. This definition excludes groups with apocalyptic visions who are uninterested in influencing governments and seek instead to inflict mass casualties.

6. According to Eric W. Hickey, *Serial Murderers and Their Victims*, 2nd ed. (Belmont, Calif.: Wadsworth Publishing Company, 1997), pp. 219, 248–250, health care providers accused of poisoning patients commonly use potassium chloride, pavulon, succinyl-choline, and digoxin. Only one of these could be considered a biological agent, digoxin, which is one of the active ingredients of digitalis. See John Mann, *Murder, Magic, and Medicine* (New York: Oxford University Press, 1992), pp. 170–171. While the true incidence of murder by health care providers in medical settings is unknown, Hickey suggests that it is a substantial and growing problem.

might be able to accomplish. Finally, there appear to be a significant number of cases of this type; including them in the study would distort analysis of the data.

IDENTIFYING CASES FOR RESEARCH
This survey includes every identified case in the unclassified literature that meets the case definition. The starting point for locating cases was the open source literature on biological terrorism.[7] Approximately half of the cases examined were identified by using these earlier studies. Additional cases were found through a survey of press reports, books, and other published material. Much of this effort focused on regional newspapers, because the major national newspapers in the United States ignored most of the cases discussed here. Books discussing the criminal use of poisons also were consulted, primarily to identify old cases. Finally, a number of cases were brought to my attention by other researchers.

RESEARCHING THE CASES
Five main sources of information were used to describe the cases. First, the bulk of the information came from press reports. Most of the incidents received little coverage in major national newspapers. For this reason, it was necessary to rely on regional newspapers.[8] Second, some of the accounts rely on descriptions that came from books and articles discussing terrorist use of biological agents. In a few cases, it appears that these sources had access to intelligence or law enforcement information that was not available elsewhere. Third, a few of the cases have been described in detail in the medical literature, including specialized forensic medicine publications. Fourth, in some cases court records and other legal or law enforcement documents were used. Finally, I interviewed individuals associated with some of the cases, usually public health or law enforcement officials.

---

7. The primary source was Purver, *Chemical and Biological Terrorism,* supplemented by Joseph D. Douglass, Jr., and Neil C. Livingstone, *America the Vulnerable: The Threat of Chemical and Biological Warfare* (Lexington, Mass.: Lexington Books, D.C. Heath and Company, 1987), pp. 183–187. In addition, Bruce Hoffman of St. Andrews University shared data from the *RAND-St. Andrews Terrorism Chronology,* an electronic database of international terrorism incidents, by providing an extract of "All Chemical/Biological Incidents, 1968–1995."

8. A complete description of the sources used to research this chapter can be found in W. Seth Carus, *Bioterrorism and Biocrimes: The Illicit Use of Biological Agents in the 20th Century,* Working Paper, Center for Counterproliferation Research, National Defense University, August 1998.

Information about the activities of many of the alleged perpetrators is scanty. For this reason, each case was reviewed for the quality of the supporting material. Cases were included in the analysis only if verified by an authoritative source, such as a government official talking on the record, or if confirmed by at least two independent sources. Whenever there were serious questions concerning the accuracy of the allegations, the case was excluded from the analysis.

The difficulties entailed in identifying cases are exemplified by two specific cases. First, intensive investigations by highly skilled researchers sometimes cannot determine whether or not biological agents were deliberately misused. This is evident in the case of a Florida dentist, Dr. David Acer, who has been accused of deliberately infecting at least six of his patients with HIV in the late 1980s. Despite an extensive investigation, the Centers for Disease Control and Prevention has been unable either to exonerate Dr. Acer or to confirm his culpability.[9] For this reason, the Acer case is excluded from the analysis. Second, in other cases the available information is too scanty to permit a definitive determination of what happened. For example, individuals associated with the Polish resistance have claimed that they employed pathogens to kill hundreds of Germans using biological agents. While there is sufficient evidence to include the case in the survey, there is insufficient supporting evidence to confirm the alleged repercussions of the claimed use. Accordingly, the case was included, but unsubstantiated claims of casualties were excluded.[10]

HOW COMPLETE IS THE SURVEY?
Despite efforts to make the research as comprehensive as possible, the list of incidents is clearly not complete. The circumstances in which several of the cases came to light tend to reinforce the view that there are additional unidentified cases. Several of the incidents became known only because of information obtained by law enforcement agencies or other authoritative sources well after the event. It was a year after the salmonellosis outbreak in The Dalles, Oregon, before law enforcement officials obtained information linking the outbreak to use of biological agents by the Rajneeshees.[11] Similarly, Japanese authorities only learned of the ef-

---

9. Dennis L. Breo, "The Dental AIDS Cases—Murder or an Unsolvable Mystery," *Journal of the American Medical Association*, Vol. 270, No. 22 (December 8, 1993), p. 2732.

10. Robert Harris and Jeremy Paxman, *A Higher Form of Killing: The Secret Story of Chemical and Biological Warfare* (New York: Hill and Wang, 1982), p. 89; and Jan Nowak, *Courier from Warsaw* (Detroit: Wayne State University Press, 1982), pp. 62–63.

11. See the chapter by Thomas J. Török et al. in this volume.

forts by Aum Shinrikyo to employ biological agents after the cult collapsed and former members confessed to police.[12]

In addition, the sources used in researching the cases also necessarily limit the comprehensiveness of the study. Most of the sources consulted during the research originated in the United States, and almost all are in English. A thorough exploration of foreign language material probably would uncover further cases. In addition, the research relied heavily on searches of electronic databases. More cases almost certainly would emerge by searching through sources available only in print. Unfortunately, such research is totally impractical given the amount of material that would need to be covered. At present, publications in the United States are more readily available on-line than those published elsewhere, which leads to over-representation of incidents that occurred in the United States. Finally, some cases may not have been described in publicly available sources. Therefore, there is little doubt that additional cases could be identified and added to the list in the study. It is impossible to ascertain, however, how many cases are not included. For instance, there are cases not included in the analysis because they were identified after the cut-off date. Inclusion of the missing cases is, however, unlikely to change the analysis significantly. It is possible that any additional, unknown cases involved massive casualties, but it seems unlikely that incidents with massive consequences escaped detection. Accordingly, additional cases are likely to be similar in character to those already incorporated, and would serve only to illustrate the points derived by considering the cases included in the data set described below.

Results

Only forty-five cases were analyzed. This includes all the cases that met the case definition, were identified prior to March 1, 1998, and for which there was at least minimal corroborating information. A summary overview of these cases appears in Table 13.1. Drawing on these data, the following account characterizes the perpetrators associated with the illicit use of biological agents, the types of agents adopted or considered by those perpetrators, and the consequences of the use of biological agents.

CHARACTERIZING THE PERPETRATORS
The perpetrators are characterized by the type of perpetrator (whether terrorist, criminal, or unknown); by the objective of the perpetrators in

---

12. David E. Kaplan and Andrew Marshall, *The Cult at the End of the World* (New York: Crown Publishers, 1996).

Table 13.1. Cases of Illicit Use of Biological Agents.

Type	Terrorist	Criminal	Other/Uncertain	Total Cases
Acquire and Use	5	9	0	14
Acquire	3	5	2	10
Interest	3	4	0	7
Threat/Hoax	1	10	3	14
Total Cases	12	28	5	45

SOURCE: W. Seth Carus, *Bioterrorism and Biocrimes: The Illicit Use of Biological Agents in the 20th Century*, Working Paper, Center for Counterproliferation Research, National Defense University, August 1998.

considering biological agents; by the size of the perpetrating group; and by the level of scientific expertise.

PERPETRATOR TYPE. Both terrorists and criminals have been implicated in the illicit use of biological agents. Approximately thirty of the cases researched involved claims that a terrorist group used, acquired, threatened use, or took an interest in biological weapons. The accuracy of most of these cases cannot be verified using publicly available information. For this reason, only twelve cases involving alleged terrorist involvement with biological weapons are included in the analysis here.

The complete survey also includes forty-four criminal cases. Sixteen of these cases were dropped from the analysis for various reasons, including insufficient evidence to support the allegation or because the perpetrator was a health care provider using drugs available for legitimate purposes in a medical setting.

Finally, there were fourteen cases in which it proved impossible to determine the character of the perpetrators. Only five of those cases, however, were sufficiently documented to justify inclusion in this analysis. Thomas Lavy, a survivalist living in Arkansas, was arrested in 1995 on charges related to the possession of the toxin ricin. His motivations for acquiring the ricin were never clarified before he committed suicide.[13] Nor is it clear why Larry Wayne Harris purchased *Yersinia pestis*, the organism associated with the plague. Although he had links to white supremacist groups, including the Aryan Nations, Harris claimed that he needed the culture to develop medical treatments. Law enforce-

13. William C. Lhotka, "Suicide Leaves Questions in Poison Case," *St. Louis Post-Dispatch*, December 31, 1995, p. E1.

Table 13.2. Objectives for Using Biological Agents.

Type	Terrorist	Criminal	Other/Uncertain	Total Cases
Mass murder	2	0	0	2
Murder	3	11	0	14
Incapacitation	2	0	0	2
Revenge	0	1	0	1
Extortion	0	10	3	13
Political statement	1	0	0	1
Anti-animal	1	2	0	3
Terrorize	2	1	0	3
Unknown	2	3	2	7

NOTE: Because some perpetrators had multiple objectives, the totals in this table exceed the total number of cases.

ment agencies were unable to prove that he had a more nefarious objective.[14]

PERPETRATOR OBJECTIVES. At least six different objectives for using biological agents can be identified from the cases. These are summarized in Table 13.2.

In one case, the perpetrators used biological agents to make a political statement. This was the objective of Dark Harvest, an otherwise unknown group that spread anthrax-contaminated dirt taken from Gruinard Island as a protest against the continued contamination of that island from the anthrax experiments conducted by the British military in the 1940s.

Two cases involved groups intending to murder large numbers of people. Steven Pera and Allan Schwandner formed a group, which they called R.I.S.E., with the objective of using pathogens and toxins to murder the entire human population, except for a small group of appropriately immunized members of the group. Aum Shinrikyo also wanted to murder large numbers of people as part of their efforts to seize control of Japan.

Killing individuals is the most common motive for using biological agents. Use of biological agents results from a desire to employ an undetectable murder method, so that medical and law enforcement officials will assume that the victims died of natural causes. Nearly 30 percent of the cases were motivated by murder as an objective.

In at least two instances, the perpetrators wanted to incapacitate large numbers of people without necessarily killing anyone. According to press

14. Robert Ruth, "Bubonic Plague Case Trial Set," *Columbus Dispatch*, March 12, 1997, p. B1.

accounts, the Weatherman organization attempted to obtain biological agents to infect water supplies. They hoped the repressive reaction of the government to such an incident would radicalize the general population and create additional supporters for the Weatherman group. The Rajneeshees wanted to incapacitate the citizens of The Dalles, Oregon, so that the people of the community could not vote in an upcoming election.

At least one case, involving the Japanese physician Dr. Mitsuru Suzuki, appears to have been motivated by desire for revenge. It appears that Suzuki was angry about the treatment he was receiving as a resident in his medical training, and retaliated by infecting other health care providers and patients. Suzuki's motivations are complicated by suggestions that he may have been creating clinical cases to further his academic research on S. typhi.

In nearly 29 percent of the cases, the perpetrators attempted to extort money from companies or government entities by threatening use of biological agents. Generally, the target was a food or grocery company. In only one of these cases is the perpetrator known to have had the capability to undertake the threatened contamination.

In three cases, the perpetrators specifically targeted animals. Farmers in New Zealand allegedly smuggled a rabbit pathogen into that country, and released the disease in contravention of national law. One terrorist group, the Mau Mau, is alleged to have used a plant toxin to kill cattle, but the motivation is not known.

In at least three cases, the perpetrators employed biological agents, or employed what was claimed to be a biological agent, to terrorize a target population. Thus, a Polish resistance figure claims that envelopes infected with B. anthracis were mailed to the Gestapo in Poland during World War II to convince the Germans to stop reading anonymous denunciation letters.

Finally, the full list of cases includes several instances in which the perpetrators targeted crops, but lack of sufficient confirming evidence or the involvement of a government led to the exclusion of those cases from this analysis.

SIZE OF THE PERPETRATING GROUP. The perpetrating groups were characterized according to the number of people involved in the illicit use of biological agents. The categories are summarized in Table 13.3. Anyone who participated, whether in the planning, production, or distribution, was counted.

In twenty cases, a single individual was responsible for perpetrating the plot, including five involving actual use. There are eleven cases in which small groups of two to five people were involved. In most of these

Table 13.3. Size of Perpetrating Group.

Type	Terrorist	Criminal	Other/Uncertain	Total Cases
Lone	0	17	3	20
Small group (2–5)	3	8	0	11
Large group (6+)	3	0	0	3
Unknown	6	3	2	11
Total Cases	12	28	5	45

cases, it appears that only one of the participants had the essential skills for acquiring and using the biological agents.

There are only three cases in which more than five people were known to be involved in the efforts of a non-state-supported group to acquire and use biological agents. Approximately a dozen members of the Rajneeshee sect have been identified as participants in their efforts to acquire, use, and disseminate biological agents. At least as many people probably were involved in the Aum Shinrikyo efforts to acquire biological agents, but the available information is incomplete. In a third case, it can be assumed that more than five participated. It is unclear how many members of the Polish resistance were involved in its apparent efforts to employ biological agents, but the scope of its activity suggests that a considerable number of people must have participated.

Finally, in eleven cases, there is not enough information available to estimate the number of people involved. In most such cases, the perpetrating group was never fully identified.

SCIENTIFIC AND TECHNICAL EXPERTISE.   The perpetrators were also characterized by the level of scientific or medical expertise available to them. This information is summarized in Table 13.4.

In seventeen of the cases, the available evidence suggests that the perpetrators had no special scientific or medical expertise. In eighteen cases, the perpetrators had some scientific or medical expertise. The level of expertise varied considerably, from the equivalent of a laboratory technician through trained microbiologists. In at least eleven cases, a physician or a Ph.D.-level microbiologist was involved. In about one-quarter of the cases, the available evidence makes it impossible to assess the expertise of the perpetrators.

CHARACTERIZING THE AGENTS
In this section, I examine the types of agents used, acquired, or considered for adoption by the perpetrators, the dissemination techniques, and the mode of agent acquisition.

Table 13.4. Perpetrator Expertise.

Type	Terrorist	Criminal	Other/Uncertain	Total Cases
Medical or scientific expertise	4	12	2	18
No known expertise	3	13	1	17
Unknown	5	3	2	10
Total Cases	12	28	5	45

TYPES OF AGENT. Perpetrators have considered both pathogens and toxins. In a small number of cases, they considered both. Table 13.5 summarizes the data on agent selection.

In nearly 63 percent of the cases, the perpetrators considered pathogens. In two cases, the perpetrator considered two pathogens, and in one instance it is claimed that three pathogens were involved. A large number of different pathogens appear. *B. anthracis* appears in seven of the cases. HIV appears in five cases, invariably in extortion cases in which it is unclear whether HIV was present. *S. typhi* appears once, while *Yersinia pestis* and *Shigella dysenteriae* strains are mentioned in connection with two cases. Seven other pathogens are associated with only one case. Bacterial agents were involved in almost all the cases, but there were a few exceptions. In one case, the perpetrators employed a viral agent, rabbit hemorrhagic disease. Another perpetrator used a parasite, *Ascaris suum*, a worm that infects pigs and is not known to appear naturally in humans.

In 42 percent of the cases, a toxin was involved. Multiple toxins were considered in several cases. In one of these cases, the perpetrators acquired the toxins produced by *Corynebacterium diphtheria* and *Vibrio cholerae*. In another, the alleged perpetrator had acquired tetrodotoxin and evinced an interest in botulinum toxin. The most common toxin was ricin, which appeared in ten cases, followed by botulinum toxin, which appeared in six.

Table 13.5. Type of Agent Involved.

Type	Terrorist	Criminal	Other/Uncertain	Total Cases
Pathogen	7	18	4	29
Toxin	5	12	2	19
Unknown	1	0	0	1
Total Cases	13	30	6	49

NOTE: Because some perpetrators considered multiple agents, the totals in this table exceed the total number of cases.

Table 13.6. Dissemination Techniques.

Type	Terrorist	Criminal	Other/Uncertain	Total Cases
Aerosol dissemination	2	0	0	2
Direct injection/ Topical application	3	5	0	8
Contaminate food	1	15	0	16
Contaminate water	3	0	2	5
Insect/Natural vectors	0	1	1	2
None	2	0	0	2
Unknown	4	9	2	15

NOTE: Because some perpetrators considered multiple agents, the totals in this table exceed the total number of cases.

In four cases, the perpetrators considered use of both pathogens and toxins. In two of the cases, the perpetrators were interested in both *B. anthracis* and botulinum toxin. Finally, in one case, it was impossible to identify what kind of agent the perpetrators were interested in employing, probably because no actual agent was involved.

DISSEMINATION TECHNIQUES. A number of alternative techniques, summarized in Table 13.6, have been used to disseminate biological agents. Only two groups are known to have considered aerosol dissemination of biological agents: Aum Shinrikyo and R.I.S.E. In five instances, the perpetrators threatened or planned to contaminate water supplies. The Chicago group, R.I.S.E., wanted to put botulinum toxin into the Chicago water supply as part of a plan to kill large numbers of people. In contrast, it was alleged that the Weatherman organization conceived of biological agents as something that could be used to contaminate water supplies to make a great many people sick. At least sixteen cases involve perpetrators who considered contamination of food.

In at least eight cases the perpetrators planned to apply a biological agent directly, by either parenteral delivery (injection) or topical application. Injection has been used to deliver both toxins and pathogens. Dr. Suzuki injected *S. typhi*, as did the French murderer Henri Girard. Topical application generally involves use of toxins, although the Rajneeshees tried to spread *S. typhimurium* by contaminating objects, such as door knobs and urinal handles, hoping that the intended victims would transfer the organisms to their mouths. The Minnesota Patriots Council planned to use a mixture of ricin and DMSO, apparently expecting that the DMSO would transport the ricin. More plausibly, William Leahy mixed DMSO with pure nicotine hoping to achieve the same result.

Table 13.7. Mode of Biological Agent Acquisition.

Type	Terrorist	Criminal	Other/Uncertain	Total Cases
Legimate supplier	1	6	1	8
Theft	1	3	0	4
Self-manufactured	1	2	1	4
Natural source	2	0	0	2
Unknown	3	3	0	6
Total Instances	8	14	2	24

Finally, in at least two cases, the threatened dissemination technique involved insects. In one case, an individual sent letters containing ticks, threatening to spread infection in that way. There is no evidence, however, that the ticks carried any pathogens, and, in any case, the insects were dead on delivery.

MODE OF BIOLOGICAL AGENT ACQUISITION. In only twenty-four of the cases is there evidence that the perpetrators actually acquired a biological agent. The data on acquisition routes are summarized in Table 13.7.

In one-third of the cases involving actual acquisition, the perpetrators obtained biological agents or toxins from legitimate suppliers. The American Type Culture Collection (ATCC) was the source of the agent in at least two cases. Larry Wayne Harris obtained Y. pestis, while Kevin Birch and James Cahoon acquired Clostridium botulinum and Clostridium tetani. The Rajneeshees purchased their seed stock of Salmonella typhimurium from a medical supply company. Similarly, Benoyendra Chandra Pandey acquired the Y. pestis that he used to murder his brother from the stocks of a medical research institute, but only after several failed attempts to obtain it illicitly from the same source.

In nearly 17 percent of the cases, the perpetrators acquired their biological agents by stealing them from research or medical laboratories. Almost all of the thefts involved people who had legitimate access to the facilities where the biological agents were kept. J.A. Kranz, a graduate student in parasitology, took the Ascaris suum eggs that he used against his roommates from the collections in the university laboratory where he studied. It appears that a laboratory technician removed the Shigella dysenteriae 2 used to infect hospital laboratory technicians from the culture collection of the hospital where she worked. Similarly, Dr. Suzuki stole S. typhi cultures from the Japanese National Institute of Health, and reportedly used those cultures in preference to the ones he cultured himself from specimens taken from typhoid patients.

In only one of the reported incidents was an effort allegedly made to infiltrate a laboratory to steal a biological agent. It was alleged that the individuals associated with the Weatherman organization attempted to suborn an employee at the U.S. military research facility at Fort Detrick to obtain pathogens. There is no evidence that the alleged perpetrators ever acquired a biological agent.

In four cases, just under 17 percent, the perpetrators manufactured the agent themselves. This has been especially common with toxins. There have been numerous cases of people extracting ricin toxin from castor beans. Similarly, there were several instances in which people tried to culture *C. botulinum* to produce botulinum toxin. There is no case in which the toxin was successfully produced.

Finally, in two cases the perpetrators obtained biological agents from a natural reservoir and transmitted them without any processing.

CONSEQUENCES OF USE

The forty-five cases included only fourteen in which the perpetrators used or attempted to use biological agents. In nine of these cases there were human casualties, including deaths in four cases. In all, there were 980 human victims, including eight deaths. This information is summarized in Table 13.8. The incidents leading to death are listed in Table 13.9.

Insights About the Use of Biological Agents

The results provide a snapshot of my ongoing research into the illicit use of biological agents by non-state actors. While the results are preliminary, they provide some interesting insights about the use of biological agents.

PERPETRATORS

A review of the data provides several interesting insights into the perpetrators interested in biological agents. First, malefactors have shown an interest in using biological agents through much of the twentieth century. Indeed, the first known attempt to use a biological agent occurred before

Table 13.8. **Casualties from Use of Bioagents.**

	Total Casualties	Deaths
Bioterrorism	751	0
Biocrimes	229	8
Other/Uncertain	0	0
Total Cases	980	8

Table 13.9. Deaths from Biological Agents.

Perpetrator	Victims	Date/Location	Number of Deaths	Agent Employed
O'Brien de Lacy and Dr. Vladimir Pantchenko	Captain Vassilli Buturlin	Russia, 1910	1	Direct injection of diphtheria toxin
Henri Girard	M. Pernotte, Mme. Monin	France, 1909–18	2	Food contamination and direct injection using pathogen *Salmonella typhi* and unknown poisonous mushroom
Benoyendra Chandra Pandey	Amarendra Pandey	India, 1933	1	Direct injection of the pathogen *Yersinia pestis*
Dr. Mitsuru Suzuki	Hospital employees	Japan, 1964	4	Food contamination using the pathogen *Salmonella typhi*

1910. The number of cases has significance for explanations regarding the apparent lack of interest by terrorists in biological agents. There are sufficient indications of interest in biological agents; this suggests that the limited interest in biological terrorism should be ascribed to some factor other than disinterest. It is more likely that biological agents appear less useful than alternative weapons, such as explosives and small arms. This may reflect greater familiarity with the alternatives, or it may suggest that effective use of biological agents requires greater skill than more traditional weapons. It is also possible that the unique characteristics of biological agents tend to make them attractive only for niche objectives. Thus, a terrorist interested in incapacitating, but not killing, a relatively large number of people might find biological agents attractive. Similarly, a terrorist interested in killing very large numbers of people also might desire a biological warfare capability.

Second, contrary to an often-expressed view that use of biological agents requires limited skill, the available evidence suggests that some degree of scientific and medical expertise is necessary. Every known attempt to use biological agents involved perpetrators with a degree of scientific or medical training.

In several cases, individuals with medical training instigated use of biological agents. A nurse, Ma Anand Puja, created the Rajneeshee biological warfare capability. She relied on the expertise of a trained laboratory technician to culture the *Salmonella typhimurium* used to contaminate the salad bars in The Dalles, Oregon. Dr. Suzuki, a physician and bacteriologist with considerable laboratory experience, allegedly infected two hundred people, including four who died, with typhoid and dysentery.

In a few cases, the person who conceived the notion of using biological agents lacked the requisite skills, and enlisted the services of unscrupulous physicians. Benoyendra Chandra Pandey drew on the medical skills of Dr. Taranath Bhatacharya, who was responsible for culturing the *Y. pestis* that was used in the 1933 murder of Pandey's brother. Similarly, in 1910 Patrick O'Brien de Lacy's brother-in-law was murdered by an injection of diphtheria toxin given by a physician, Dr. Vladimir Pantchenko, who obtained the agent from a research laboratory in Russia.

While the survey uncovered seventeen cases with perpetrators appearing to lack scientific or medical training, in only six of those cases did those perpetrators acquire biological agents. In general, those cases involved ricin toxin extracted from castor beans. Seven of the remaining cases involving untrained perpetrators were extortion plots. Significantly, the perpetrator actually possessed a biological agent in only one extortion case, and that occurred in a case where the perpetrator also had considerable scientific expertise. Michael Just, who was convicted in 1996 for threatening to contaminate milk with *Yersinia enterocolitica,* had a Ph.D. in microbiology.

The perpetrators appear to have acquired their information from several types of sources. Many relied on widely available medical and scientific publications. In a considerable number of cases, perpetrators also have used "how-to" manuals, including *The Poisoner's Handbook* and *Silent Death.* No longer available is Maynard Campbell's *Catalogue of Silent Tools of Justice,* which was used by the Minnesota Patriot's Council to guide them in their ricin production.

AGENTS

First, in only twenty-four of the forty-five cases does evidence suggest that the perpetrators actually acquired a biological agent. Significantly, the earliest of these cases dates to before 1910, indicating that availability of pathogens is not a new phenomenon.

Second, in almost all instances, pathogens were acquired from culture collections, although many of the perpetrators possessed the skills to culture organisms acquired in nature. This may reflect the relative ease with which the cultures can be obtained. It also may result from the difficulties in processing a culture to prevent cross-contamination from other organisms and to ensure that the strain has the desired characteristics. In contrast, toxins were generally produced by the perpetrators, perhaps due to the availability of "how-to" manuals, although some exotic toxins also were acquired from medical supply firms.

Despite efforts to enhance controls on biological agents, it is unlikely that any determined perpetrator will be prevented by legal constraints. First, only a relatively small number of agents are subject to the most stringent controls. Second, many agents actually used in criminal or terrorist acts remain uncontrolled and extensively available. Third, it remains possible to steal the agent from a legitimate user. Finally, the supply of biological agents is global, and controls on them are unlikely to be enforced with equal vigor everywhere in the world.

These factors suggest that we should not assume that it will be easy to prevent illicit acquisition of biological agents. There are too many legitimate circumstances that would permit an individual access to a range of poisons and pathogens. Accordingly, while efforts to impede easy access to biological agents may be worthwhile, they do not solve the problem.

Third, the only perpetrator known to have explored aerosol dissemination is the Aum Shinrikyo. Most other perpetrators adopted techniques that were unlikely to result in mass death. The most dangerous dissemination method adopted appears to be injection. At least three deaths resulted from direct injection, two involving a pathogen and the other a toxin. It is unclear from the available accounts whether or not any of the fatalities caused by Dr. Suzuki resulted from injections, although he is known to have made some of his victims seriously ill in this way.

Fourth, terrorists and criminals may not use the same agents as those selected by military biological weapons programs. A comparison between the biological agents commonly considered suitable for military use and those actually adopted by the perpetrators of the cases studied here is shown in Table 13.10. Agents selected for military use are expected to meet criteria that may not be of interest to non-state actors. The differences are perhaps evident from a review of the criteria adopted by the U.S. offensive biological weapons program for the selection of biological agents. There were five requirements that an agent had to meet: consistent production of the desired effect; potential to be produced on a large scale; stability in storage; capability of efficient dissemination; and stability after dissemination.[15] Such characteristics may or may not be important to a terrorist or criminal. In particular, such perpetrators may be content with agents available only in relatively small quantities and may not care that the organism consistently produces the same effect.

Alternatively, terrorists and criminals may be attracted to organisms that produce disease through the oral route. Military programs emphasize, almost exclusively, aerosol dissemination. While terrorists may be interested in such dissemination capabilities, they also may attempt contamination of food and water. As a result, they may adopt agents considered totally unsuited to military use.

Finally, there are indications that barriers to the use of biological agents to inflict mass casualties are greater than often people recognize. The apparent failure of Aum Shinrikyo to develop a biological warfare capability is suggestive. The group drew on the skills of a relatively large cadre of trained people, and apparently devoted considerable resources to their biological warfare efforts. However, it appears that they failed to produce an effective biological weapon. Unfortunately, too little is known about their activities to determine why they failed.

CONSEQUENCES

There are several aspects of this review of past use of biological agents that merit some attention. Most obvious is the small number of cases that

---

15. U.S. Departments of the Army and Air Force, *Military Biology and Biological Agents*, Departments of Army and Air Force manual TM 3–216/AFM 355–56, March 12, 1964, as quoted in Stockholm International Peace Research Institute, *The Problem of Chemical and Biological Warfare*, Vol. II (New York: Humanities Press, 1971), p. 311.

Table 13.10. Biological Agents for Military Use and for Biocrime and Bioterrorist Use.

	Traditional Biological Warfare Agents	Agents Associated with Biocrimes and Bioterrorism
Pathogens	*Bacillus anthracis**	*Ascaris suum*
	Brucella suis	*Bacillus anthracis**
	Coxiella burnetii	*Giardia lamblia*
	Francisella tularensis	HIV
	Smallpox	*Rickettsia prowazekii* (typhus)
	Viral encephalitides	*Salmonella typhimurium*
	Viral hemorrhagic fevers	*Salmonella typhi*
	Yersinia pestis*	*Shigella* species
		Schistosoma species
		Vibrio cholerae
		Yellow fever virus
		Yersinia enterocolitica
		Yersinia pestis*
Toxins	Botulinum*	Botulinum*
	Ricin*	Cholera endotoxin
	Staphylococcal enterotoxin B	Diphtheria toxin
		Nicotine
		Ricin*
		Snake toxin
		Tetrodotoxin
Anti-crop agents	Rice blast	
	Rye stem rust	
	Wheat stem rust	

* These agents appear on both lists.
SOURCES: The list of biological warfare agents is drawn from the chapters by David R. Franz, et al. and George W. Christopher, et al. in this volume.

can be identified. Given the substantial number of terrorist incidents, and the even larger number of criminal homicides, the total number of cases involving biological agents is remarkably small. Even allowing for the certainty that the list of cases is incomplete, it is evident that biological agents are employed in only a small fraction of the terrorist and criminal incidents involving harm to people.[16]

Second, the consequences of the use of biological agents also have been remarkably limited. Nine of the fourteen cases involving use of biological agents resulted in one or more people becoming ill. While a substantial number of people became ill through use of biological agents, more than 97 percent of the illnesses resulted from only two of the cases: the Rajneeshees (751) and Dr. Suzuki (200). The deaths resulted from the activities of four different perpetrators, although Dr. Suzuki's activities accounted for half of the reported deaths. In the past, therefore, biological agents have rarely been associated with mass casualties, which is the source of greatest concern regarding future use of such agents.

To some extent, this conclusion was affected by the decision to exclude use of toxins by health care providers in medical settings. Accusations lodged against perpetrators suggest that they were responsible for harming large numbers of patients, and that hundreds of people may have died. In most such cases, however, the number of fatalities definitively proven to be the responsibility of the perpetrator is far smaller than the alleged total. In part, this reflects the difficulties in meeting standards of proof required for criminal proceedings against perpetrators using biological agents. Such cases merit additional study.

Conclusion

Researching incidents involving the illegal use of biological agents provides an opportunity to better understand the potential dangers posed by misuse of pathogens and toxins. The insights derived from studying such incidents are necessarily tentative. Additional research will broaden and extend this analysis, although it is unclear if the patterns identified will change appreciably as more cases are identified and as additional information is acquired about the existing cases.

There is one significant caveat about this research. None of the perpetrators had access to state-developed biological warfare capabilities. Experts involved in the U.S. biological weapons program and the similar

---

16. At least three additional cases involving likely use are currently under research. They would probably add a few additional casualties to the total, including some fatalities, should the evidence support the allegations.

activities conducted by the former Soviet Union believe that biological agents, effectively disseminated as aerosol clouds, can produce mass casualties. A terrorist incident that involved the wide area release of an aerosol cloud of a virulent strain of certain biological agents, such as anthrax, would produce results qualitatively and quantitatively different from those of any previous use of biological agents. Hence, the relative ineffectiveness of past use of biological agents provides little insight into the potential consequences of use involving technologies similar to those developed by military biological weapons programs.

Part VI
Policies for Responding to the Threat of
Biological Warfare

Chapter 14

Biological Terrorism: Preparing to Meet the Threat

Jeffrey D. Simon

The threat of terrorists using biological warfare (BW) agents has received increased attention in recent years. Congressional hearings,[1] research studies,[2] government warnings,[3] and commentaries[4] have all pointed to

This chapter was adapted from Jeffrey D. Simon, "Biological Terrorism: Preparing to Meet the Threat," *Journal of the American Medical Association (JAMA)*, Vol. 278, No. 5 (August 6, 1997), pp. 428–430. © 1997 American Medical Association.

I would like to thank Cornelius G. McWright, Douglas M. Snyder, Susan Snyder, Laura J. Broadie, Annette Flanagin, and the two anonymous reviewers for their helpful comments on this chapter.

1. *Global Proliferation of Weapons of Mass Destruction, Hearings before the Permanent Subcommittee on Investigations of the Committee on Governmental Affairs*, U.S. Senate, 104th Cong., 1st sess., Part 1, October 31 and November 1, 1995 (Washington, D.C.: U.S. Government Printing Office [U.S. GPO], 1996). (Hearings also held by the Subcommittee on March 20, 22, and 27, 1996.)

2. U.S. Congress, Office of Technology Assessment (OTA), *Proliferation of Weapons of Mass Destruction: Assessing the Risks*, OTA-ISC-559 (Washington, D.C.: U.S. GPO, August 1993); U.S. Congress, OTA, *Technologies Underlying Weapons of Mass Destruction*, OTA-BP-ISC-115 (Washington, D.C.: U.S. GPO, December 1993); Kathleen C. Bailey, *Doomsday Weapons in the Hands of Many: The Arms Control Challenge of the '90s* (Urbana: University of Illinois Press, 1991); and Robert H. Kupperman and David M. Smith, "Coping with Biological Terrorism," in Brad Roberts, ed., *Biological Weapons: Weapons of the Future?* (Washington, D.C.: Center for Strategic and International Studies, 1993), pp. 35–46.

3. G-7 (Group of Seven industrialized nations—United States, Japan, Germany, Britain, France, Italy, and Canada) Declaration on Terrorism, G-7 Economic Summit in Lyon, France, June 27, 1996.

4. Joan Stephenson, "Confronting a Biological Armageddon: Experts Tackle Prospect of Bioterrorism," *Journal of the American Medical Association (JAMA)*, Vol. 276, No. 5 (August 7, 1996), pp. 349–351; and Annette Flanagin and Joshua Lederberg, "The

a potentially more ominous future. Many factors account for this concern, including revelations that Iraq, a state sponsor of terrorism, stockpiled anthrax, botulinum toxin, and other BW agents during the Persian Gulf War; the discovery that Aum Shinrikyo, the Japanese religious cult that released the chemical agent sarin in the Tokyo subway system in 1995, had a research and development program for BW agents; the low cost and minimum scientific knowledge required for producing BW agents; and the tendency for terrorists to move into new areas of violence when current ones no longer achieve the same effect—publicity, reaction, chaos—of previous attacks.[5]

Despite this growing concern, however, we still know very little about the nature of BW terrorism. There has never been a major BW terrorist attack; therefore, there is no track record of incidents, groups, tactics, motives, and targets to analyze in order to determine the best strategies for combating this global threat. In this regard, today we are with respect to BW terrorism where we were thirty years ago with respect to "conventional" terrorism. A new international threat was emerging then, but it was unclear what direction it would take.

It took several years after the first major international hijacking in 1968 for the diverse nature of conventional terrorism to become clear and for governments to take action against the threat. Hijackings ultimately proved to be only one small part of terrorists' arsenal of tactics, which eventually included midair plane bombings, prolonged hostage crises, suicide truck bombings, car bombings, massacres, and other violent acts. Terrorist targets ranged from airliners and airports to crowded shopping centers, commercial buildings, and government and military facilities. Terrorist groups were not limited to Palestinian extremists, but included European and Latin American left-wing revolutionaries, U.S. anti-government right-wing and white supremacist groups, Islamic militants, and a variety of ethnic, nationalist, and religious extremist groups throughout the world. State sponsorship of terrorism also became an important aspect of the threat, with foreign governments providing training, safe haven, and financial and technical assistance to terrorist groups, and in some cases, actively planning and carrying out terrorist attacks.

As each new dimension of conventional terrorism emerged, governments took measures to try to thwart the threat. Airport security

---

Threat of Biological Weapons: Prophylaxis and Mitigation: Call for Papers," *JAMA*, Vol. 276, No. 5 (August 7, 1996), pp. 419–420.

5. Jeffrey D. Simon, *The Terrorist Trap: America's Experience With Terrorism* (Bloomington: Indiana University Press, 1994).

improved from the screening of passengers and carry-on luggage for weapons to the occasional screening of checked-in baggage for bombs. Physical security at embassies and other government buildings increased from the use of metal detectors to prevent terrorist incidents to the use of bomb-shatterproof glass to reduce casualties in the case of an explosion. The international community gradually adopted a variety of treaties and other agreements to deal with the problems that arose from terrorist violence. Combating conventional terrorism became a reactive strategy. Each new type of terrorist attack would lead to new counterterrorist measures.

Biological warfare terrorism, however, will not allow governments, publics, and the international community the luxury of time to watch this threat unfold and then determine the proper responses. Since BW terrorist attacks could have catastrophic effects in terms of lives lost and create a medical, political, and social crisis unparalleled in our history, it is important to prepare now for this new age of terrorism.

The first step is to accept the reality that we will not be able to prevent every act of BW terrorism. Governments have learned that painful lesson with respect to conventional terrorism. While preventive measures must continue to be pursued, the greatest payoff in fighting BW terrorism lies in improving the response to an incident. There will be more opportunity for saving lives in the emergency medical response to a BW terrorist attack than in the response to a conventional terrorist attack. Whereas most of the fatalities in a conventional terrorist bombing occur immediately or shortly after the explosion,[6] in BW terrorism the incubation period for the virus, bacterium, or toxin could be several days. Accurate diagnosis and speedy treatment could save many lives.

The medical and health communities will therefore play the most significant role in combating BW terrorism, and they will have to carry out their duties at a time of unprecedented crisis and fear throughout the country. To the extent that we can reduce the uncertainty about how BW terrorist incidents are likely to unfold, the better the medical and health professions will be prepared to deal with the aftermath of this most dangerous form of global terrorism.

---

6. The 1995 bombing of the Alfred P. Murrah Federal Building in Oklahoma City killed 168 people, including a nurse who died during the rescue effort. Of the 167 people who died directly from the blast, 162 died at the scene, 3 were dead on arrival at an emergency department, and 2 persons died two days after hospitalization. See Sue Mallonee, Sheryll Shariat, Gail Stennies, Rick Waxweiler, David Hogan, and Fred Jordan, "Physical Injuries and Fatalities Resulting from the Oklahoma City Bombing," *JAMA*, Vol. 276, No. 5 (August 7, 1996), pp. 382–390.

BW Terrorism: Likely Tactics and Targets

The most distinguishing feature separating BW terrorism from conventional terrorism is the extraordinarily larger number of casualties that could follow a major BW terrorist attack. Whereas bombings of airplanes or buildings with conventional explosives have occasionally resulted in a few hundred deaths each, BW terrorism could result in hundreds of thousands or even millions of casualties.[7] Adding to the death toll would be the fact that civilian populations are not immunized against most BW agents and do not have protective equipment, such as filtered respirators and gas masks, readily available.[8]

Some biological agents have been used in the past for selective, low-level attacks. For example, Bulgarian agents assassinated Georgi Markov, a Bulgarian émigré and writer for the British Broadcasting Corporation, by stabbing him in London with an umbrella-type weapon that contained ricin,[9] which is a potent protein toxin derived from the bean of the castor plant (*Ricinus communis*).[10] However, a terrorist group that uses BW agents will likely be attracted to the mass killing potential of these weapons. It makes little sense for terrorists to experiment with dangerous biological agents—they could be killed in handling and using them—if their goal is a limited attack that could have been achieved by using safer and more familiar conventional weapons.

Biological warfare terrorism will also encompass a narrower range of tactics than conventional terrorism. Although BW agents could be used during a hijacking or hostage situation, there would be little incentive for terrorists to do so. The projected death toll would be no higher than if conventional weapons were used. And while BW agents could be deliv-

---

7. U.S. Congress, OTA, *Proliferation of Weapons of Mass Destruction*.

8. *Global Proliferation of Weapons of Mass Destruction*. Although U.S. troops are being inoculated with vaccines for anthrax, it is likely to be too costly and impractical to attempt to do so for the entire civilian population and for all types of BW agents.

9. Christopher Andrew and Oleg Gordievsky, *KGB: The Inside Story* (New York: Harper Collins, 1990), pp. 644–645. Another Bulgarian émigré, Vladimir Kostov, was attacked in a similar fashion in Paris in 1978 but lived when doctors removed the pellet containing ricin from his body. More recently, four members of a small anti-government tax protest group known as the Patriot's Council manufactured ricin with the intent to use it in an assassination attempt. The men were convicted in Minnesota in 1995 for violating the Biological Weapons Anti-Terrorism Act of 1989. The group had planned to kill a deputy U.S. marshal and a sheriff who had previously served papers on a Patriot's Council associate.

10. U.S. Army Medical Research Institute of Infectious Diseases, *Medical Management of Biological Casualties Handbook* (Ft. Detrick, Md.: August 1993), p. 92.

ered against a target by means of a bomb or missile, the likelihood that the organisms will be destroyed in the explosion makes this an unattractive delivery method.[11]

Rather, the most likely BW terrorist tactic will be to release BW agents—anthrax spores, botulinum toxin, ricin, or other deadly agents—into the air as a biological aerosol, a stable cloud of suspended microscopic droplets of bacterial or virus particles.[12] Since BW agents are invisible, odorless, and tasteless, nobody would know that a terrorist attack is under way. The aerosol release of BW agents could be accomplished in several ways, including using low flying airplanes, crop dusters, or trucks equipped with spray tanks releasing the BW agent upwind of populated areas; leaving aerosol canisters filled with the BW agent and timing devices in subways, airports, air conditioning/heating systems in buildings or other crowded places; or directly contaminating bulk food supplies in restaurants, supermarkets, or other places with a BW agent. However, large water supplies such as a city water supply would not be an attractive target for contamination due to the large amount of BW agent required and the water purification procedures used by most cities in the United States.

Biological weapons could be readily obtained or manufactured by a determined terrorist. The precursors for biological agents are available, and the scientific and medical knowledge necessary to manufacture such weapons is not that difficult to acquire. Several biological warfare agents can be produced either at home or in a small laboratory without sophisticated scientific knowledge. There is also a wealth of publicly available information about manufacturing biological weapons, including information provided on the Internet. Terrorist groups that decide to use biological agents would also have little difficulty recruiting somebody with enough scientific expertise to produce certain agents.

Therefore, a terrorist group that wants to launch a BW attack will not face insurmountable obstacles. Most terrorist groups, however, will not be attracted to biological weapons, because their use could create a backlash among the groups' supporters. Ethnic, nationalist, and revolutionary terrorist groups, such as the Irish Republican Army, the Basque separatist group ETA (Basque Fatherland and Liberty), and others, depend upon the support—political, logistical, and financial—of significant segments of the population. While its "constituents" may not necessarily approve of the group's violent tactics, they nevertheless support the group's political objectives. However, that support could be eroded if such groups used

---

11. U.S. Congress, OTA, *Proliferation of Weapons of Mass Destruction.*

12. U.S. Congress, OTA, *Technologies Underlying Weapons of Mass Destruction.*

weapons of mass destruction. The much higher number of potential casualties and the moral implications of using BW weapons would inhibit terrorist groups that are concerned about public opinion. There is also the element of personal risk for terrorists that use biological weapons. Unless they are convinced that they can vaccinate themselves against the disease—and that the vaccine is effective—the fear of being infected by the BW agent will deter most terrorists from venturing into this dangerous arena.

The terrorist groups that are likely to use biological or chemical weapons will probably exhibit the following characteristics: a general, undefined constituency whose possible reaction to a BW attack does not concern the terrorist group; a perception that conventional terrorist attacks are no longer effective and that a higher form of violence or a new technique is needed; and a willingness to take risks by experimenting with and using unfamiliar weapons.[13]

Among the terrorist groups that could be described as meeting these criteria would be doomsday religious cults, global revolutionary groups, and neo-Nazis and white supremacist groups. These types of terrorist groups have amorphous constituencies for which concern about a public backlash would not likely deter the use of biological weapons. They are also apt to view conventional terrorist tactics as insufficient to gain the attention and reaction that they seek and would therefore be willing to experiment with unfamiliar weapons. For example, among the reasons cited for Aum Shinrikyo's sarin attack in the Tokyo subway was to set in motion a sequence of events that would eventually lead to Armageddon, a prediction that had been made by the cult's leader, Shoko Asahara.[14] Another reported reason for the attack was to create a crisis in Japan that would preoccupy or topple the Japanese government and thereby prevent an anticipated raid by Japanese authorities on the cult's headquarters. Conventional weapons were likely viewed by the cult as inadequate to bring about either of these objectives.

The case of Larry Wayne Harris, a former member of the white supremacist group Aryan Nations, is another example of how certain extremists can be attracted to weapons of mass destruction. Harris was arrested in 1995 in Ohio for illegally obtaining three vials of bubonic plague bacteria. He had lied about owning a laboratory when he ordered the cultures of *Yersinia pestis* bacteria, which causes bubonic plague. After pleading guilty to wire fraud and being sentenced to eighteen months

---

13. Jeffrey D. Simon, *Terrorists and the Potential Use of Biological Weapons: A Discussion of Possibilities*, R-3773-AFMIC (Santa Monica, Calif.: RAND, December 1989).

14. *Global Proliferation of Weapons of Mass Destruction.*

probation, he was again arrested in 1998 in Las Vegas along with another man for possession of a biological agent for use as a weapon. However, the biological agent that the men had in their possession turned out to be a nonlethal form of anthrax used as a veterinary vaccine. In an interview with a reporter in 1997, Harris warned that members of the Aryan Nations would strike at government officials and cities with biological weapons if necessary to achieve their goal of creating a separate nation for the white race.[15]

Religious extremists, state-sponsored terrorist groups, and individual criminals are also candidates for using BW agents. If a terrorist believes that acts of violence are not only politically but also morally justified, there is a powerful incentive for any type of terrorist attack. The belief that one is rewarded in the afterlife for violence perpetrated on earth encourages undertaking high-risk and high-casualty attacks. Groups that have the sponsorship of a foreign government would also be potential candidates for BW agents since they could easily be provided with the necessary training, resources, and weapons. The state sponsor would have to decide that a biological weapons attack by a terrorist group would accomplish the foreign government's objectives and not be traced back to the state sponsor. And individual criminals with scientific or medical knowledge who are obsessed with revenge or lured by the potential to extort large amounts of money from government or business targets would also be candidates for using or threatening to use BW agents.

Since there are currently no reliable detection systems at airports, subways, or other places in urban areas to warn that a terrorist is carrying a BW agent, terrorists will be able to strike any target they desire.[16]

---

15. David E. Kaplan, "Terrorism's Next Wave: Nerve Gas and Germs Are the New Weapons of Choice," *U.S. News Online*, November 17, 1997.

16. The U.S. military's Biological Integrated Detection System (BIDS) is designed to warn *after* a BW attack is under way. It is a vehicle-mounted system that currently can identify four BW agents by exposing suspected air samples to antibodies that react with a particular BW agent. These BW agents are *Bacillus anthracis*, which causes anthrax; *Yersinia pestis*, which causes bubonic plague; botulinum toxin, which is the poison released by botulism organisms; and staphylococcus enterotoxin B, which is released by certain staph bacteria. Since there are many more potential BW agents, BIDS cannot be relied upon to provide warning for all types of BW terrorist attacks. There is also the problem of where to place the detection systems if they become available for use in major cities in the United States. Since biological agents could be released virtually anywhere, including in shopping malls, subways, buses, and city streets, it may not be economically feasible to have early warning systems throughout the nation. See Leonard A. Cole, "The Specter of Biological Weapons," *Scientific American*, Vol. 275, No. 6 (December 1996), p. 63; and Cole, "Countering Chem-Bio Terrorism: Limited Possibilities," *Politics and the Life Sciences*, Vol. 15, No. 2 (September 1996), p. 197.

Whereas terrorists with conventional weapons have to be concerned about metal detectors, X-ray machines, and other physical security measures, terrorists with BW agents do not face that problem. With maximum casualties the likely goal, metropolitan areas are the most at risk. At the present time and in the future, major cities in the United States and around the world remain indefensible to a BW terrorist attack.

Responding to BW Terrorism: Unchartered Waters

The heightened concern regarding biological terrorism has led to studies of how well prepared the United States is to respond to a major incident. The findings are not encouraging. During hearings held in 1995 and 1996, the U.S. Senate Permanent Subcommittee on Investigations, for example, found that there was no plan that coordinated federal, state, and local agencies in managing the consequences of a terrorist attack with a weapon of mass destruction. The subcommittee also found that principal field officers with police, fire, and emergency service departments in major cities were inadequately trained and did not have basic equipment to deal with biological, chemical, or nuclear terrorism, including protective gear, breathing apparatus, decontaminants, and antidotes.[17] This was also the case in Japan, where rescue workers who treated victims of Aum Shinrikyo's first sarin attack in Matsumoto in June 1994 did so without wearing gas masks or using decontamination procedures because initially they did not know what the victims were suffering from. It was not until a week later that the exact cause of the disaster became known. Several rescue workers were found to have mild symptoms of sarin gas poisoning.[18]

Hospitals also need to have adequate supplies—or ways to quickly obtain supplies—of antibiotics and antitoxins that could be used to treat victims of BW agents. The Centers for Disease Control and Prevention estimated that the economic impact of a terrorist attack with anthrax would be $26.2 billion per 100,000 people exposed unless there is rapid implementation of a post-attack treatment program.[19] Medical personnel

---

17. *Global Proliferation of Weapons of Mass Destruction*; and Jeffrey D. Simon, "The New Age of Terrorism," *Boston Globe*, April 19, 1996, p. 19.

18. Hiroshi Okudera, Hiroshi Morita, Tomomi Iwashita, Tatsuhiko Shibata, Tetsutaro Otagiri, Shigeaki Kobayashi, and Nobuo Yanagisawa, "Unexpected Nerve Gas Exposure in the City of Matsumoto: Report of Rescue Activity in the First Sarin Gas Terrorism," *American Journal of Emergency Medicine*, Vol. 15, No. 5 (September 1997), pp. 527–528.

19. Arnold F. Kaufmann, Martin I. Meltzer, and George P. Schmid, "The Economic

should be trained to recognize the different symptoms of various BW agents so that victims can be treated quickly.

The lack of preparedness for biological terrorism in the United States and around the world is due to two factors. One is that since the casualties from a biological terrorist incident are so disturbing even to think about, many public officials cling to the hope that with the right mix of policies, security measures, and intelligence-gathering, BW terrorism can be prevented. Funding for emergency responses to BW terrorism therefore has not been given the high priority it deserves until very recently. The second factor is the difficult task of planning for an event that has never occurred before. Emergency response teams are therefore left only with alternative scenarios to guide them in their plans.

The Nunn-Lugar-Domenici amendment to the FY97 Defense Authorization Act addressed some of these issues by calling for better training, equipment, and coordination among emergency response personnel in the United States to deal with a terrorist incident involving a weapon of mass destruction.[20] The Domestic Preparedness Program in the Defense Against Weapons of Mass Destruction was established as a result of that amendment, with $42 million allocated for FY97 and $50 million for FY98. The program, which is managed by the Department of Defense in conjunction with the Department of Energy, the Environmental Protection Agency, the Federal Bureau of Investigation, the Federal Emergency Management Agency, and the Public Health Service, is aimed at enhancing the capabilities of local first-responders—firefighters, police officers, emergency medical personnel—in cities throughout the United States for dealing with a nuclear, chemical, or biological terrorist attack. During FY97, special Department of Defense–led teams visited 27 cities to provide such training. The program calls for 120 cities to receive the special training eventually. A Rapid Response Information System has been created by the Federal Emergency Management Agency to assist federal, state, and local emergency response professionals in dealing with a terrorist attack with a weapon of mass destruction, and the Public Health Service is forming Metropolitan Medical Strike Teams in cities across the United States. The Department of Defense also plans to create ten Rapid Assessment and Initial Detection teams consisting of specially trained National Guard units to assist in responding to terrorist incidents involving a weapon of mass destruction.

Impact of a Bioterrorist Attack: Are Prevention and Postattack Intervention Programs Justifiable?" *Emerging Infectious Diseases*, Vol. 3, No. 2 (April–June 1997), pp. 83–94.

20. John F. Sopko, "The Changing Proliferation Threat," *Foreign Policy*, No. 105 (Winter 1996/97), p. 18.

One important aspect of biological terrorism, however, has been virtually ignored by federal, state, and local agencies. This involves the psychological reactions among survivors, emergency workers, and the public in the aftermath of a BW terrorist incident. Terrorism is a form of psychological warfare, with terrorists oftentimes perpetrating their violence to cause fear among the public. In BW terrorism, that fear will understandably be great as people watch their fellow citizens fall ill and possibly die in large numbers due to anthrax, botulism, or other diseases. While the president and other top government officials will be attempting to calm the nation, it will be up to the medical profession to take the lead during the crisis and explain exactly what is unfolding and whether there is any further danger to public health. Contingency plans for dealing with public hysteria and disruption of health care delivery systems—including the possibility of health care professionals becoming ill from the BW attack or fleeing the affected area if they are not confident that they have adequate equipment to protect themselves—should be established in every large U.S. city.

The mental health of emergency workers and medical personnel will have to be monitored during a BW terrorism crisis. Research indicates that the most traumatic events for emergency nurses are the death of a child and the death of a co-worker.[21] A major BW incident will likely have many of these types of victims. Dealing with dead bodies can also cause emotional and psychological problems for disaster rescue and recovery workers.[22] During a BW terrorist incident, rescue workers will face the unique situation of dealing with large numbers of deaths in a setting that otherwise seems very normal. There will not be any collapsed or bombed-out buildings, fires, plane crashes, and so forth. The psychological impact of that situation upon first-responders needs to be addressed in contingency plans.

The Critical Incident Stress Debriefing (CISD) process could help in dealing with the psychological aspects of a BW terrorist attack. This process is part of a broad crisis intervention program known as Critical Incident Stress Management (CISM), which is designed to prevent or mitigate the development of adverse psychological reactions among emergency service and public safety personnel, nurses, physicians, and

21. Carolyn Burns and Nancy J. Harm, "Emergency Nurses' Perceptions of Critical Incidents and Stress Debriefing," *Journal of Emergency Nursing*, Vol. 19, No. 5 (1993), pp. 431–436.

22. Andrew A. Skolnick, "First Complex Disaster Symposium Features Dramatically Timely Topics," *JAMA*, Vol. 274, No. 1 (July 5, 1995), pp. 11–12.

disaster workers. The program has been used during earthquakes, plane crashes, terrorist bombings, and other tragic events. Through various psychological intervention techniques, a CISD team led by mental health professionals and including peer support personnel from the emergency services can help emergency workers and medical personnel recover as quickly as possible from the stress associated with the crisis.[23]

A potential problem, however, is that some CISD and CISM teams could become a hindrance to first-responders. They might interfere with the duties of emergency service personnel, or inadvertently aggravate the emotional trauma being experienced by making incorrect assessments of mental health needs. It is therefore crucial that CISD and CISM teams be properly trained for crisis intervention services.

The military will also play an important role in the aftermath of a BW terrorist attack. They will be called upon to assist federal and local authorities, just as they have helped local communities following domestic disasters such as hurricanes, floods, and earthquakes.[24] But since their BW training has focused on defending against biological warfare perpetrated by enemy troops in a battlefield setting, there will be a need to retrain them for responding to a BW terrorist attack in a civilian setting. The establishment of the Chemical/Biological Incident Response Force by the Marine Corps and the Technical Escort Unit by the Army are steps in the right direction. Much more needs to be done, however, to prepare soldiers both psychologically and militarily for a biological terrorist attack in a U.S. metropolitan area.

Future U.S. Policy Choices

The threat of terrorists using biological weapons is changing the nature of U.S. counterterrorism policy. It can no longer be assumed that what is effective in dealing with conventional terrorism will be effective in dealing with BW terrorism. As noted earlier, preventive measures such as metal detectors, X-ray machines, and concrete barriers, which were designed to stop terrorist attacks involving bombs and other conventional weapons, will be unable to stop the terrorist who is armed with anthrax, botulinum toxin, or other BW agents. Similarly, post-attack measures will

---

23. Jeffrey T. Mitchell and George S. Everly, Jr., *Critical Incident Stress Debriefing: An Operations Manual for the Prevention of Traumatic Stress Among Emergency Services and Disaster Workers*, 2nd ed. rev. (Ellicott City, Md.: Chevron Publishing, 1995, 1996).

24. Skolnick, "First Complex Disaster."

now have to take into account the risk that first-responders could fall victim themselves to the biological warfare agent.

U.S. counterterrorist forces will also face special problems in responding to a potential BW terrorist incident. During a "normal" counterterrorist mission, there is always the risk that terrorists may set off their explosives or fire their weapons before they are captured or killed. But there will be no room for error if the terrorists have biological weapons. The terrorists' release of a BW agent before the counterterrorist operation is over could expose nearby populated areas to great harm. Therefore, counterterrorist units will not be able to rely upon past strategies to guide them in responding to a BW terrorist threat situation.

The official U.S. policy of not granting concessions to terrorists will also be put to the test if terrorists possess biological weapons. The no-concessions policy is based upon the belief that denying terrorists their demands will discourage other terrorists from engaging in anti-U.S. attacks. But what should a president do if, instead of threatening the lives of a few hostages, terrorists are threatening the lives of hundreds of thousands of Americans by unleashing anthrax unless their demands are met? It will be difficult for any leader to categorically refuse to grant concessions to terrorists when the potential loss of life could be so high.

A wider range of policy options is available to deal with rogue states and potential state sponsors of BW terrorism than is available to deal with independent terrorist groups. The United States, for example, used a variety of countermeasures against Iraq in its attempt to force Iraqi President Saddam Hussein to allow United Nations inspection teams access to suspected chemical and biological weapons sites. These countermeasures included diplomatic and economic sanctions as well as the threat of military action. Independent terrorist groups would not be affected by such policies. International agreements and treaties, such as the 1972 Biological Weapons Convention (BWC), which prohibits the development, production, and stockpiling of biological warfare agents, can also be used to try to prevent governments from acquiring and using biological weapons or providing them to terrorist groups.

But even when the target of countermeasures is a visible government and not an elusive terrorist group, there are still many obstacles to implementing effective policies. The BWC, for example, has no verification provisions, a major weakness that BWC Review Conferences are attempting to address. Since BW agents can be easily hidden, and it only takes a small amount of some BW agents to inflict horrific damage, even on-site inspections cannot ensure that every biological weapon will be discovered and destroyed. Furthermore, much of the technology and equipment necessary for developing biological weapons is dual use, with legitimate commercial applications in the fermentation and biotechnology industries.[25] This makes it easier for countries to conceal BW weapons programs.

The large number of potential casualties from a BW terrorist attack will undoubtedly put pressure on U.S. policymakers to respond with extreme military measures if a foreign government is implicated in the incident. But exactly how much military force to use and against what targets within the culprit nation will be the dilemma. If, for example, tens of thousands of Americans are killed due to a state-sponsored BW terrorist attack, the United States will not be able to respond with just limited military action as it did in 1986 when it launched air strikes over Libya for that country's involvement in conventional terrorist attacks in Europe. There would probably be calls in Congress and other places for the United States to retaliate with devastating force, including the use of nuclear weapons. However, the global repercussions of that type of a response would likely make this an option that Washington would prefer not to use.[26]

The threat of biological terrorism will therefore present the United States with difficult policy issues both domestically and internationally. On the domestic front, the issues will range from how to increase public awareness about BW terrorism without causing unnecessary alarm, to how to prevent a bureaucratic nightmare from occurring as multiple federal, state, and local agencies become involved in BW terrorism planning and response. On the international front, the issues will range from how to use U.S. power and influence effectively to reduce the risk of foreign governments or other entities supplying terrorists with BW agents, to determining how to respond to a potential anti-U.S. BW terrorist attack without harming other U.S. foreign policy goals and interests.

Meeting the BW terrorist threat will require cooperation among the medical community, law enforcement, emergency services personnel, scientists, policymakers, the military, and the public. It will also require a serious effort by other countries to treat BW terrorism as the serious threat that it is.[27] The challenge for the United States and other governments will be to design and implement policies to deal with a type of terrorism that has never occurred before but is likely to occur in the near future.

---

25. U.S. Congress, OTA, *Technologies Underlying Weapons of Mass Destruction.*

26. Richard K. Betts, "The New Threat of Mass Destruction," *Foreign Affairs*, Vol. 77, No. 1 (January/February 1998), p. 31.

27. John D. Steinbruner, "Biological Weapons: A Plague Upon All Houses," *Foreign Policy*, No. 109 (Winter 1997/98), p. 94.

Conclusion

Following a failed attempt to assassinate Prime Minister Margaret Thatcher at the Conservative Party convention in Britain in 1984, the Irish Republican Army issued the following statement: "Today we were unlucky, but remember, we only have to be lucky once. You will have to be lucky always." That statement remains today the best description of the difficult task that governments face in the endless battle against terrorism. This is an age where small groups, and even criminals or mentally unstable individuals, can gain access to biological weapons. Whether they build the weapons themselves, whether they are supplied with the weapons by a foreign government, or whether they gain possession of the weapons by other means, the fact remains that a determined terrorist could wreak unimaginable suffering upon a country with a single attack.

Terrorists with BW agents pose a threat to this nation's—and all nations'—vital interests. In the 1960s, the physicist Herman Kahn wrote a book on fighting a nuclear war entitled *Thinking About the Unthinkable*.[28] Fortunately, this nation never had to experience that event, and the end of the Cold War hopefully means that it never will. But this nation faces a new threat at the dawn of the twenty-first century—one that must be both thought about and prepared for. By improving U.S. readiness to respond to a BW terrorist attack, many lives can be saved, and terrorists can be denied their goal of creating panic and crisis in this country.

---

28. Herman Kahn, *Thinking About the Unthinkable* (London: Weidenfeld and Nicolson, 1962).

Chapter 15

The Threat of Biological Weapons: Prophylaxis and Mitigation of Psychological and Social Consequences

Harry C. Holloway, Ann E. Norwood,
Carol S. Fullerton, Charles C. Engel, Jr.,
and Robert J. Ursano

Biological weapons have emerged as a significant threat in the 1990s.[1] The threat of biological attack by nations, terrorist groups, or a lone terrorist is credible. The likelihood of such an attack is uncertain. Specialists disagree on whether changes in terrorist organization, the end of the Cold War, and new technological opportunities will result in the use of new classes of weapons, such as biological weapons by terrorists. With the use of chemical weapons by the Iraqis and the Aum Shinrikyo cult, Robert Kupperman and Walter Laqueur suggest that the use of inexpensive weapons of mass destruction have become more probable.[2] They

---

This chapter was adapted from Harry C. Holloway et al., "The Threat of Biological Weapons: Prophylaxis and Mitigation of Psychological and Social Consequences," *Journal of the American Medical Association (JAMA)*, Vol. 278, No. 5 (August 6, 1997), pp. 425–427.

This work was done as part of our employment by the federal government and is, therefore, in the public domain. The opinions expressed in this chapter are those of the authors and do not necessarily reflect the views of the Department of Defense or the F. Edward Hebert School of Medicine, Uniformed Services University of the Health Sciences.

---

1. U.S. Congress, Office of Technology Assessment (OTA), *Technology Against Terrorism: The Federal Effort*, OTA-ISC-481 (Washington, D.C.: U.S. Government Printing Office [U.S. GPO], 1991); and Annette Flanagin and Joshua Lederberg, "The Threat of Biological Weapons—Prophylaxis and Mitigation," *Journal of the American Medical Association (JAMA)*, Vol. 276, No. 5 (1996), pp. 419–420.

2. Robert H. Kupperman, "A Dangerous Future: The Destructive Potential of Criminal Arsenals," *Harvard International Review*, Vol. 17, No. 3 (Summer 1995), pp. 46–48;

anticipate that weapons of mass destruction will become a part of the terrorist arsenal. They interpret attacks in Tokyo as predicting future use of biological warfare and chemical agents to carry out terrorist actions. Another prominent student of terrorism, Brian Jenkins, observes that terrorist groups have been using the same weapons—guns and explosives—for over a century and are likely to remain conservative in the weapons that they use.[3]

It is difficult to predict or to limit the extent of the consequences of biological weapons. Perhaps the examples of use of biological agents reported in this volume and the studies of natural outbreaks will help to clarify some of the consequences, but uncertainty remains. This uncertainty may make the use of these weapons particularly terrifying.

The very uncertainty associated with whether biological agents will be used influences the likely psychological impact of such weapons in both the political leadership and the general public. Ideological considerations and lack of experience with terrorist attacks using biological weapons may also influence recommendations for response plans to such attacks. Some recommend new methods of early detection, special protective gear, protective vaccines, and antibiotics. Such groups may involve national intelligence agencies, military, law enforcement, and civil disaster agencies. Many fear that programs purportedly developed for defensive purposes by the military and intelligence agencies will be used for creating new biological weapons. These experts favor control of the biological threat through international organizations and agreements and the management of national programs by civil rather than intelligence agencies and military medical groups.[4]

Uncertainty and a lack of consensus make planning and the commitment of resources to planning and training more difficult. As we will discuss below, good training and effective planning for the management of disasters are critical to reducing harmful psychological responses. The very existence of groups of experts that distrust each other assures suspicions that can make communication very difficult and encourage an atmosphere of paranoid assumptions.

---

and Walter Laqueur, "Postmodern Terrorism," *Foreign Affairs*, Vol. 75, No. 5 (1996), pp. 23–34.

3. Brian Jenkins, "The Limits of Terror: Constraints on the Escalation of Violence," *Harvard International Review*, Vol. 17, No. 3 (Summer 1995), pp. 44–46.

4. Robert Gould and Nancy D. Connell, "The Public Health Effects of the Use of Biological Weapons," in Barry S. Levy and Victor W. Sidel, eds., *War and Public Health* (New York: Oxford University Press, 1997), pp. 98–116.

The weapon user's motivation can determine the circumstances of the weapon's use. The user of weapons very frequently makes choices that are intended to produce terror and fright. It was appreciated by Fritz Haber, the inventor of gas warfare, that fear would tend to exaggerate the effects of poison gas.[5] In fact, the use of gas weapons in World War I was associated with the generation of psychiatric combat casualties. "Neurasthenia was likely to appear in any case of gas casualties," and "the borderland between gas poisoning, battle fatigue, and malingering were severely blurred."[6] Militaries developing biological weapons consider not only the capacity of such weapons to injure or kill but also their capacity to terrify. The doctrine for using weapons will consider how to produce the maximal unfavorable psychological impact on the enemy. Terrorists choosing weapons to produce terror must weigh a similar set of considerations.

Shifts in the motivation for terrorists may have consequences for changes in their tactics. During the Cold War, many terrorist groups were driven by secular, political ideology of the political right and left. Now there is a reemergence of religious terrorist groups. Approximately 20 percent of fifty international terrorist groups in 1993 had a "dominant religious component."[7] David Rapoport has pointed out that until the nineteenth century, religion was the most common justification for terrorist acts.[8] Such religious terrorists were motivated to satisfy their religious code, their god, or their supreme leader, but they did not require recognition or political approval from their fellow citizens to justify the destruction of evil unholy races, pagans, apostates, or heretics. The destruction of such unworthy people is frequently intended to give a message to believers and to demonstrate to unbelievers a concrete consequence of the error of their ways. With the decrease of support for political terrorists from the political left and right, there is a relative increase in religiously motivated, millennial, and apocalyptic groups. These groups may trace their roots to Christian, Muslim, Jewish, Buddhist, Sikh, Hindu, and other religious origins. Strongly held hatred and racist devaluation of their opponents' humanity motivate some of these terrorists. Suicidal sacrifice

5. Fritz F. Haber, *The Poisonous Cloud: Chemical Warfare in the First World War* (Oxford: Clarendon Press, 1986), p. 195.

6. Ibid., p. 195.

7. Bruce Hoffman, *Holy Terror: The Implications of Terrorism Motivated by a Religious Imperative*, Paper No. P-7834 (Santa Monica, Calif.: Public Good Reports, RAND, 1993).

8. David C. Rapoport, "Fear Trembling: Terrorism in the Three Religious Traditions," *American Political Science Review*, Vol. 78, No. 3 (1984), pp. 658–677.

may be acceptable to religiously motivated terrorists. Religious terrorists may be little interested in public opinion and therefore willing to employ weapons and attack targets that conventional terrorists consider unthinkable. The behavior of such groups may seem particularly irrational and terrifying to their victims.

This chapter discusses the complex psychosocial and physiological implications of biological agents particularly in the context of current terrorist threats. Recommendations for developing primary prevention and treatment are proposed.

Psychosocial Responses Following a Biological Attack

To most people, the microbial world is mysterious and threatening. The idea of infection caused by invisible agents is frightening. It touches a deep human concern about the risk of being destroyed by a powerful, evil, imperceptible force. These beliefs activate emotions that are extremely difficult to direct with the tools of reason. The response of specialists in medicine, epidemiology, infectious disease, molecular biology, nursing, and emergency medical services can bring some discipline and understanding to this situation. To be effective, the response must be very well organized, and communication must be made in terms that the public understands. Multiple organizations with conflicting and overlapping goals and responsibilities (e.g., health care, law enforcement, and social welfare) may increase the confusion and anxiety for the individual and the community. The novelty of biological weapons in combination with the activation of deeply rooted fears suggests that strong psychological and physiological responses will occur.

The immediate stressors associated with a biological terrorist attack are the threat and the consequences of infection or poisoning. The specific nature of these stressors will depend upon the organism or toxin used. Characteristics such as the incubation period, the virulence, and the toxicity will contribute to the psychological impact. The process of seeking and receiving immunization or treatment is potentially stressful. Examples of common psychosocial responses are noted in Table 15.1.

One can anticipate that there will be acute and chronic psychiatric casualties as in other disasters.[9] While the vast majority of people do not

9. Robert J. Ursano, Carol S. Fullerton, and Ann E. Norwood, "Psychiatric Dimensions of Disaster: Patient Care, Community Consultation, and Preventive Medicine," *Harvard Review of Psychiatry*, Vol. 3, No. 4 (November–December 1995), pp. 196–209; Robert J. Ursano and James R. Rundell, "Psychological Problems of Prisoners of War: The Trauma of a Toxic and Contained Environment," in Robert J. Ursano, ed., *Individual*

Table 15.1. Psychological Factors Associated with the Use of Biological Agents.

Horror
Anger
Panic
Magical thinking about microbes and viruses
Fear of invisible agents
Fear of contagion
Anger at terrorists/government
Attribution of arousal symptoms to infection
Scapegoating
Paranoia
Social isolation
Demoralization
Loss of faith in social institutions

develop long-term psychiatric disorders following disasters, certain groups are at higher risk, e.g., the previously traumatized, those without social supports, and first-responders (police, emergency medical personnel, etc.). Physical illness and injury secondary to the attack increase the risk of the development of Acute Stress Disorder and Post-Traumatic Stress Disorder (PTSD), as well as potential organic brain syndromes, depression, and bereavement in victims.[10] Certain conditions, including depression and anxiety disorders, increase the risk for development of PTSD. It is also important to remember that psychiatric disability is a likely chronic outcome of biological attack for some people. The incidence and prevalence of such problems must remain a matter of speculation, although past occurrences can be used to anticipate consequences. Expe-

Response to Disaster, DTIC: A203310 (Bethesda, Md.: Uniformed Services University of the Health Sciences, 1988), pp. 79–112; Robert J. Ursano, Carol S. Fullerton, and Brian G. McCaughey, "Trauma and Disaster," in Robert J. Ursano, Brian G. McCaughey, and Carol S. Fullerton, eds., *Individual and Community Responses to Trauma and Disaster: The Structure of Human Chaos* (Cambridge: Cambridge University Press, 1994), pp. 3–27; and Lars Weisaeth, "War-Related Psychopathology in Kuwait: An Assessment of War-Related Mental Health Problems," in Carol S. Fullerton and Robert J. Ursano, eds., *Posttraumatic Stress Disorder: Acute and Long-Term Responses to Trauma and Disaster* (Washington, D.C.: American Psychiatric Press, 1997), pp. 91–122.

10. American Psychiatric Association, *Diagnostic and Statistical Manual of Mental Disorders (DSM IV)*, 4th ed. (Washington, D.C.: American Psychiatric Association, 1994); and Arieh Y. Shalev, "Posttraumatic Stress Disorder Among Injured Survivors of a Terrorist Attack: Predictive Value of Early Intrusion and Avoidance Symptoms," *Journal of Nervous Mental Disorders*, Vol. 180, No. 8 (August 1992), pp. 505–509.

riences with chemical weapons used by terrorists have demonstrated that psychiatric casualties are likely.[11]

The psychiatric consequences will depend upon the nature of and the response to the assault. In contrast to explosive or chemical weapons, biological weapons may not produce instantaneously horrifying results. (An exception to this might be the use of a biological toxin that kills quickly and with frightening manifestations such as seizures or suffocation.)

As the attack is discovered and the media spread the news, exposed and unexposed individuals may experience acute autonomic arousal. Signs and symptoms of muscle tension, tachycardia, rapid breathing (perhaps hyperventilation), sweating, tremor, and a sense of foreboding are likely to generate health concerns. These signs and symptoms may be misattributed to infection or intoxication. The acutely stressed and symptomatic individuals will add complexity and additional patients for triage during the initial phase of the crisis. However, if initial triage and management are successful, the risk for the development of psychiatric problems can be minimized.

Forensic issues involved in the medical response influence psychological responses and treatment options. Preservation of evidence maximizes the possibility of the perpetrators being punished. The perception that justice is ultimately served can have a very positive psychological impact on victims and society. Some victims may be critical witnesses in future legal actions. This may have little consequence for immediate lifesaving care, but it might prompt the selection of psychotropic drugs that minimally interfere with recall or discourage the use of a technique like hypnosis that can potentially damage the future credibility of a witness report.

Acute Intervention Following a Biological Attack

Rapid, accurate triage and effective treatment or immunization will be the cornerstones of initial management. (See Table 15.2.) Distinguishing symptoms of hyperarousal from those of intoxication and infectious disease prodromes will be crucial. The type of exposure and any lack of complete information about the agent will increase uncertainty and the risk of psychiatric morbidity. The risk for secondary psychological trauma

---

11. Tetsu Okumura, Nobukatsu Takasu, Shinichi Ishimatsu, Shou Miyanoki, Akihiro Mitsuhashi, Keisuke Kumada, Kazutoyo Tanaka, and Shigeaki Hinohara, "Report on the 640 Victims of the Tokyo Subway Sarin Attack," *Annals of Emergency Medicine*, Vol. 28, No. 2 (August 1996), pp. 129–135.

Table 15.2. Acute Psychiatric Interventions Following a Biological Weapons Attack.

Prevention of group panic
Careful, rapid medical evaluation and treatment
Avoidance of emotion-based responses (e.g., "knee-jerk" quarantine)
Effective risk communication
Control of symptoms secondary to hyperarousal
  Reassurance
  Diazepam-like anxiolytics for acute relief, as indicated
Management of anger/fear
Management of misattribution of somatic symptoms
Provision of respite as required
Restoration of an effective, useful social role—perhaps as worker at triage site
Return to usual sources of social supports in the community

will increase if actions by leaders or helpers fail to provide a quick, accurate diagnosis, a sensitive process for communicating the nature of the risk, and a supportive environment for the victims and those exposed.

An attitude of expectation that those with hyperarousal or demoralization will soon return to normal activities should be conveyed. Patients should be moved out of the patient role as quickly as possible. Diazepam-like anxiolytics may be helpful in reducing anxiety for patients who do not respond to reassurance. The assignment of simple work tasks that facilitate the care of other patients can help restore function to the psychological casualties. The recovery environment should be constructed to create a sense of safety and to counteract the helplessness induced by the terrorist act.[12]

A well-organized, effective medical response contributes to the creation of a supportive environment and accurate data for the "at risk" population. Individuals can assess their risk and determine the actions that they can take to reduce that risk. Ideally, risk information should involve dialogue. Dialogue lets the "at risk" population define the information that they need, and it enables the community leaders to assess their effectiveness in communicating the right data. Failure to provide a forum for exchange may actually increase anxiety and health concerns, since individuals will have a tendency to appraise symptoms as indicating a dire problem rather than the effects of autonomic arousal. One consequence of appraisal error may be disabling somatic complaints

12. Beverly Raphael, John P. Wilson, Lenore Meldrum, and Alexander C. McFarlane, "Acute Preventive Interventions," in Bessel van der Kolk, Alexander C. McFarlane, and Lars Weisaeth, eds., *Traumatic Stress: The Effects of Overwhelming Experience on Mind, Body, and Society* (New York: Guilford Press, 1996), pp. 463–479.

offered in a setting where failure to find a medical or surgical disease is experienced as stigmatizing and sadistic by the patients. In this situation, the patient's life may become focused on an unending search for an "acceptable" diagnosis.[13] This process is likely to be influenced by professional conflicts about the diagnosis of symptomatic conditions of uncertain ideology, and by ongoing suspicion of the agencies responsible for managing the crisis and consequences of the biological attack.

Implications of Psychological Reactions for the Medical System

Physical injury, disruption of usual communal life, and increased use of public health facilities can create overwhelming demands upon the medical systems.[14] Feelings of helplessness and hopelessness will be increased if the rescue and post-disaster medical efforts appear to be failing.[15] Angry, intense competition for available but limited resources can generate even more societal disruption and casualties. The belief that treatment will be provided to some but not to others will contribute to the possibility of social disruptions, such as riot or panic. Panic will be a particular risk when biological agents are used to threaten or to attack a sizeable civilian population.[16] Demoralization can also be a response to the predicaments presented by a biological attack. Demoralized individuals often lose their sense of social and group responsibilities and roles. If major community institutions fail to provide protection, citizens can lose faith in the ideological metaphors that bind the community together. In this way, demoralization can increase isolation and feelings of hopelessness. In this complex setting, some are likely to demonstrate psychiatric symptoms. Given the stigma attached to psychiatric illness and the fact

13. Jerome P. Kassirer, "Our Stubborn Quest for Diagnostic Certainty," *New England Journal of Medicine*, Vol. 320, No. 22 (June 1989), pp. 1489–1491; Steven P. Schwartz, Paul E. White, and Robert G. Hughes, "Environmental Threats, Communities, and Hysteria," *Journal of Public Health Policy*, Vol. 6, No. 1 (March 1985), pp. 58–77; and Berry Blackwell and Nicholas P. DeMorgan, "The Primary Care of Patients Who Have Bodily Concerns," *Archives of Family Medicine*, Vol. 5, No. 8 (September 1996), pp. 457–463.

14. Institute of Medicine, "Committee on the Health Effects of Indoor Allergens Staff," in Constance M. Pechura and David P. Rall, eds., *Veterans at Risk: The Health Effects of Mustard Gas and Lewisite* (Washington, D.C.: National Research Council, March 1993), pp. 1–448.

15. Robert J. Ursano and Carol S. Fullerton, eds., *Performance and Operations in Toxic Environments*, DTIC: A203162 (Bethesda, Md.: Uniformed Services University of the Health Sciences, 1988).

16. Philip K. Russell, "Biologic Terrorism—Responding to the Threat," *Emerging Infectious Diseases*, Vol. 3, No. 2 (April–June 1997), pp. 203–204.

that the individuals who manifest them are more likely to have been injured and to have been exposed to multiple infectious, environmental, and toxicological risks, the diagnostic and therapeutic dilemmas will be quite difficult.[17]

Quarantine requires the development of a specialized environment that will limit exposure to secondary infections. The creation of such an environment may disrupt social supports that reduce the post-exposure risk of stress-induced disorders. It can create a situation characterized by separation from friends and family, isolation, and a sense of stigmatization. Prior planning can ensure that modern communication technology using telephone, television, and computer internet connections can be used to mitigate these untoward effects by providing ongoing contact with families and friends in the community outside of quarantine. The maintenance of contact between parents and children is particularly important for the children. This may result in putting unexposed adult caregivers in quarantine.

Additional stressors may arise from the mundane logistical demands associated with managing mass contamination and infection. One of the difficulties in the Japanese sarin attack was undressing patients and disposing of their clothing.[18] Obtaining the necessary shower facilities for so many people is problematic. The provision of privacy and assurance of conventional modesty may have to be sacrificed. It should not be forgotten that privacy and modesty are important to maintaining an individual's sense of control and autonomy. The imposition of special requirements, such as public bathing, should be accompanied by an explanation that attributes this undesirable demand to the terrorist attacker.

Disaster responders and medical personnel will also have to contend with their own psychological reactions. One of the terrorist's goals is to provoke intense emotions that interfere with the capacity of caregivers to react in a thoughtful, organized fashion. A biological attack using a highly infectious and virulent organism (e.g., anthrax), dispersed in a fine spray, poses special stressors. Medical responders may be required to work in protective clothing and masks ("moon suits"). This barrier protection will

17.   Robert J. Ursano and Carol S. Fullerton, eds., *Individual and Group Behavior in Toxic and Contained Environments*, DTIC: A203267 (Bethesda, Md.: Uniformed Services University of the Health Sciences, 1988); Carol S. Fullerton and Robert J. Ursano, "Behavioral and Psychological Responses to Toxic Exposure," in Ursano, *Individual Response to Disaster*, pp. 113–128.

18.   Okumura, Takasu, Ishimatsu, Miyanoki, Mitsuhashi, Kumada, Tanaka, and Hinohara, "Report on the 640 Victims."

make the care of patients more difficult and increase the risk of heat, fatigue, and isolation stress for medical personnel.[19] The fact that rescue and medical personnel wear protective gear, while potentially exposed others are not afforded such protection, may create problems. People unable to use protective suits may feel mistreated, and suited professional personnel may be ashamed that they are using special protection. Information programs should prepare victims and their families for encountering suited personnel at the attack site. These issues should be addressed in planning and training. The responders should anticipate the occurrence of protective mask and suit phobias in their personnel.[20] In choosing protective gear, it is important that first-responders be provided with gear that they train with and maintain. Some military gear such as MOPP (Mission-Oriented Protective Posture) suits may require logistical and training opportunities that the local communities cannot provide from their resources. Failure to choose equipment that will work properly when needed is likely to create exactly the sort of situation in which people feel hopeless and helpless. This situation is likely to produce behavioral dysfunction and panic. It will also be important to establish work/rest schedules and to limit exposure to the gruesome scenes.

Disaster plans for managing a biological attack must be developed, and realistic training provided in order to insure effective response to an actual terrorist event. These plans must assume that emotional and psychiatric problems will occur in the unexposed population as well as in the exposed population. The exercises should be carried out with sufficient realism, so that the process of disrobing and showering is practiced in real time. The medical responders will need to be trained to recognize the symptoms of anxiety, depression, and dissociation. It is critical that psychological responses be managed in ways that facilitate the triage, diagnosis, and treatment of those exposed or infected.[21] Such

---

19. Carol S. Fullerton and Robert J. Ursano, "Health Care Delivery in the High-Stress Environment of Chemical and Biological Warfare," *Military Medicine*, Vol. 159, No. 7 (July 1994), pp. 524–528; and Carol S. Fullerton, Robert J. Ursano, Tzu-Cheg Kao, and Vivek R. Bhartiya, "The Chemical and Biological Warfare Environment: Psychological Responses and Social Support in a High Stress Environment," *Journal of Applied Social Psychology*, Vol. 22, No. 20 (October 1992), pp. 1608–1623.

20. Elspeth C. Ritchie, "Psychological Problems Associated with Wearing Mission-Oriented Protective Posture Gear," in Frederick R. Sidell, Ernest T. Takafuji, and David R. Franz, eds., *Textbook of Military Medicine: Medical Aspects of Chemical and Biological Warfare* (Washington, D.C.: Borden Institute, 1997), pp. 393–396.

21. Carol S. Fullerton, George T. Brandt, and Robert J. Ursano, "Chemical and Biological Weapons: Silent Agents of Terror," in Robert J. Ursano and Ann E. Norwood, eds., *Emotional Aftermath of the Persian Gulf War: Veterans, Families, Communities, and Nations* (Washington, D.C.: American Psychiatric Press, 1996), pp. 111–142.

Table 15.3. Preparation for a Biological Weapons Attack to Mitigate
Psychiatric Casualties.

Summarize "lessons learned" from other types of terrorist attacks/terror-producing
agents
Educate the public about microbes and viruses
Coordinate responsible agencies prior to attack
Train emergency responders with biological warfare scenarios that include substantial
psychiatric casualties
Work with media to anticipate attack and the best way to communicate information

plans need to include strategies for prevention and mitigation of stress
for victims as well as for those responding to the crisis and its consequences. Debriefing, commonly used by emergency personnel following
trauma, has been used to mitigate the effects of severe stress and can be
helpful in identifying individuals who may need further assistance. Results from controlled studies of debriefing are only now beginning to
become available.[22] These will help to clarify the role of this intervention
in the alleviation of pain, prevention of disability, return to social involvement, and prevention of disease. Ironically, should a highly infectious
agent be used, bringing people together for a debriefing may be contra-
indicated. Perhaps "tele-debriefing" (analogous to telemedicine) is a technology that can be developed for such an occasion.

Psychological Considerations in Risk Communication

The communication of the risk to individuals following a bacteriologic
attack will be critical to how communities and individuals respond.[23] (See
Table 15.3.) The media coverage and behavior of public officials can
contribute to the stress and precipitate panic or demoralization, particu-

22. Justin A. Kenardy, Rosemary A. Webster, Terry J. Lewin, Vaughan J. Carr, Philip
L. Hazell, and Gregory L. Carter, "Stress Debriefing and Patterns of Recovery Following Natural Disaster," *Journal of Traumatic Stress*, Vol. 9, No. 1 (January 1996), pp. 37–49;
and Beverly Raphael, Lenore Meldrum, and Alexander C. McFarlane, "Does Debriefing After Psychological Trauma Work?" *British Medical Journal*, Vol. 310 (June
1995), pp. 1479–1480.

23. National Research Council, *Health Risks of Radon and Other Internally Deposited
Alpha-emitters (Beir IV)* (Washington, D.C.: National Academy Press, 1988); National
Research Council, *Improving Risk Communication* (Washington, D.C.: National Academy
Press, 1989); National Research Council, *Risk Assessment in the Federal Government:
Managing the Process* (Washington, D.C.: National Academy Press, 1983); National
Research Council, *Understanding Risk: Informing Decisions in a Democratic Society* (Wash-
ington, D.C.: National Academy Press, 1996); and *Presidential Advisory Committee on
Gulf War Veterans' Illness: Final Report* (Washington, D.C.: U.S. GPO, December 1996).

larly if inaccurate, confusing, or contradictory information is provided to the public. Rumors must be anticipated, monitored, and corrected with accurate information.[24] Any damage to public trust at the beginning of the crisis insures that distrust will continue throughout the crisis. There are psychological and physiological costs attendant to the loss of trust. Given the conflicts within the professional public health community concerning how one should prepare for biological attacks, it is important for that diverse community to maintain an ongoing dialogue. This dialogue should be carried out in an atmosphere of mutual respect even when disagreements and different points of view cannot be reconciled. Whatever their ideology or institutional affiliation, all responders should focus on the needs of the assaulted community and its members.

The handling of information by officials and the media during the Three Mile Island (TMI) nuclear accident became a major source of anxiety and stress for people living in the vicinity of the nuclear facility. At TMI, there were no casualties or severely injured individuals. The stress was fear and uncertainty about exposure to excess radioactivity, loss of faith in local authorities and those managing operations of the TMI reactor, and financial uncertainties.[25] Andrew Baum and colleagues followed individuals at the TMI site and at three control sites for ten years.[26] He found evidence of chronic arousal as indicated by elevated norepinephrine and epinephrine in some individuals, indicating that timely and appropriate communication of information should be a key consideration in managing a biological attack.

Conclusion

Governmental and private agencies should develop detailed strategies for responding to a biological terrorist attack that reflect consideration of the psychological and social impact of such agents. Inattention to the phenomenon of terror and its consequences for individuals, institutions, and society jeopardizes the efficacy of disaster mitigation efforts. Leaders, scientists, and the media should develop protocols covering a broad range of scenarios that communicate risk in ways that provide accurate information and diminish rumors. These primary prevention efforts will be critical in preventing panic and demoralization in the attacked community. The possible forensic responsibilities of first-responders should

---

24. Ursano and Fullerton, *Individual and Group Behavior.*

25. Andrew Baum, "Stress, Intrusive Imagery, and Chronic Distress," *Health Psychology*, Vol. 9, No. 6 (1990), pp. 653–675.

26. Ibid.

receive appropriate consideration in collecting data and preparing for future action that will determine responsibility for the attack.

Realistic training for biological attacks should include the probability of large numbers of psychological casualties. Training exercises should be designed to test cooperation and coordination between organizations as well as to test first-responders and hospital staff. Ideally, the media should also participate in order to try out the efficacy of risk communication. Hospital-accrediting bodies should encourage medical facilities to incorporate biological warfare scenarios into their annual training.

Planning and preparation for biological attacks and their attendant psychological consequences can diminish the terrorists' ability to achieve their overall goal—the induction of terror. Education of the public and institutional preparedness can mitigate the horror of terrorism. The media could play an active prevention role by realistically educating the public about the impact of terrorist attacks with biological weapons. Such preparation efforts should be given high priority.

Chapter 16

Potential Values of a Simple Biological Warfare Protective Mask

Karl Lowe, Graham S. Pearson, and Victor Utgoff

Proliferation of nuclear, biological, and chemical (NBC) weapons is a growing concern. Unless the spread of these weapons can somehow be halted, major changes will be required in allied defense strategy and capabilities. The risks and costs of defending vital interests will rise substantially. Correspondingly, the United States, the United Kingdom, and their allies will find defense of their important interests more difficult and painful, and other states will become far less willing to support such defense efforts. Recognizing this, the allies are aggressively searching for more effective political means to halt NBC proliferation, and, to the extent that it cannot be halted, for military and technical means to counter it.

Clearly these pursuits complement each other. Political measures can complicate, slow, and deter proliferation and strengthen the basis for international reaction when evidence of prohibited programs appears. Thus, they should reduce the number and scope of the NBC weapons programs to be countered, buy time to deploy countermeasures, and win domestic and international political support for difficult counterproliferation actions. At the same time, better means of countering NBC weapons should decrease demand for them by reducing their political and military utilities.

The authors greatly appreciate the helpful comments and assistance received during the development of this paper. Reviewers include Richard Aiken, John Bartlett, Lisa Bronson, Seth Carus, Marty Crumrine, Richard Danzig, Tom Dashiell, Paul Gebhard, Andy Hull, Chris Jehn, Barbara Johnson, Robert Kadlec, Edward Kerlin, Joshua Lederberg, William Patrick III, Brad Roberts, Douglas Schultz, Bernard Tucker, and Chris Walley. Jeff Preston and Craig Colton of the 3M Company and Michael Fuchs of UVEX were helpful in obtaining information and samples of potentially suitable BW masks. Johnathan Wallis was most helpful in researching key background information and performing repeated calculations. The authors note that the opinions expressed in this paper are their own and are not necessarily endorsed by the organizations with which they are or have been affiliated.

The purpose of this chapter is to provide a broad perspective on the value of simple biological warfare (BW) masks, particularly for civilians. We will argue that such masks are an essential ingredient of any strategy for countering BW proliferation; that history shows that populations are willing to take such unusual measures as wearing protective masks when a frightening disease threatens; and that masks may have the potential to prevent BW from becoming an even greater strategic threat than that posed by nuclear weapons.

Civilians are the primary focus for several reasons. NATO troops, at least if warned, have individual chemical warfare (CW) physical protection that guards against BW attacks as well. The United States, the United Kingdom, and their allies depend on civilians in overseas theaters to operate the ports, airbases, and infrastructure upon which intervention forces would depend. The vulnerability of civilian populations to BW attack, both at home and in overseas countries, could lead governments to hesitate in supporting interventions against a state assessed to have a BW capability. Nonetheless, we will discuss the more direct values of simple BW masks for military forces.

Comparing the Threats Posed by Nuclear, Chemical, and Biological Weapons

Nuclear, biological, and chemical weapons all have been described as "weapons of mass destruction." However, these three classes of weapons have very different potentials for causing mass destruction, and, in this respect, their proliferation should not be of equal concern. The most important measure of the difference in their potential to cause mass destruction is the residual threat they each pose after all practical countermeasures have been taken.

Nuclear weapons pose a high residual threat because the prospects of achieving a near-perfect defense against nuclear attack at reasonable cost seem poor, and the detonation of even a single nuclear weapon on an allied city or major military force would cause enormous numbers of casualties and great destruction.

Chemical weapons pose a substantially smaller residual threat. When used against concentrations of unprotected military or civilian personnel, they require considerably more weight on target to inflict the same numbers of casualties as would a single nuclear-armed missile. This implies that multiple delivery systems of substantial size must be used, providing opportunities for defenses to blunt a chemical attack, thus further raising the weight of attack needed to achieve nuclear-comparable results.

Additionally, a program of passive protection measures can substantially reduce the residual threat of chemical weapons. Given such a program, and assuming timely warning, civilians could remain in at least makeshift shelters, and, depending on the quality of the shelter, wear protective masks if needed. Causing large numbers of casualties among civilians thus protected would require far heavier quantities of agents in order to ensure that sufficient amounts of chemical agents to produce fatalities would penetrate through the protection of buildings and masks.

Military forces required to keep fighting also can be protected with masks, suits, CW detectors, antidotes, and decontamination. However, depending upon ambient temperature, training levels, required activities, and other factors, such protection can substantially reduce the efficiency of military personnel, thus requiring more time, personnel, or equipment to accomplish many military tasks. On balance, while the associated political, financial, and manpower costs would be substantial, the allies could configure their forces so that the casualties resulting from CW attacks by any regional enemy would be minimal, and the forces could achieve their military goals despite the burdens of chemical protection. Thus, the residual threat posed by CW is far smaller than that of nuclear weapons.

Biological weapons pose a particularly troubling threat. First, the weight of BW agent required for a devastating attack against an unprotected population is orders of magnitude less than that required for CW agents. Thus, BW attacks sufficient to destroy the populations of cities can be delivered by means that are extremely difficult to interdict. For example, a small drone could spray out as little as 6.5 kilograms of aerosolized anthrax in a crosswind line tens of kilometers upwind of a city. The resulting lethal cloud could drift over the city, causing hundreds of thousands of deaths within as little as 48 to 72 hours. Such an attack would most likely be done at night so as to avoid the ultraviolet light of the sun, which kills most biological agents in a matter of hours.[1]

---

1. A mathematical model widely employed by the U.S. Department of Defense was used to estimate the casualty-producing effects of chemical and biological weapons. Assuming favorable weather conditions, a night attack, and agent and dissemination technology equal to the best achieved by the United States, the model estimates that 0.65 kilograms of anthrax, dispersed as an aerosol along an upwind line, could cause 50 percent casualties over an area of 232 square kilometers. This coverage area was selected to facilitate the comparisons of the threats posed by NBC weapons that are presented later in the chapter.

An opponent could not confidently expect to bring such well-tuned agent and dissemination technologies and attack conditions together, however, and the likely conservatism of military planners suggests that somewhat heavier concentrations would be used to hedge against the possibility of less-than-expected effectiveness. Thus, we will assume that a practical estimate of the agent weight required for this

BW also is particularly troubling because, in a matter of a few weeks, easily acquired and innocent-looking facilities, equipment, and materials can allow the manufacture of sufficient quantities of biological agents to inflict massive casualties on unprotected populations. Thus, in the absence of comprehensive and intrusive monitoring arrangements, we have little chance of knowing whether a state is manufacturing a potentially devastating BW capability, of preventing its manufacture, or of destroying it by military means.

Taken together, these characteristics of biological weapons mean that it is extremely difficult to prevent a reasonably competent and determined opponent from delivering biological weapons against concentrations of personnel. Thus, *defense against a biological attack must emphasize protection of personnel jeopardized by agents arriving in their vicinities.* If this cannot be done well, biological weapons will pose a residual threat that is orders of magnitude greater than that posed by chemical or nuclear weapons. Worse yet, biological weapons using agents that are highly contagious, and for which the United States, the United Kingdom, and their allies have no ready counters, may pose a global threat greater than that posed by a large-scale nuclear war. The fundamental question is thus how well targets can be protected from BW agents delivered into their immediate vicinities.

Protecting Against BW Attacks at the Target

BW targets can be protected in three ways: by vaccines, post-exposure medication, or simple protective masks.

VACCINES
In concept, the most attractive defense against BW attack would be to develop inexpensive and effective oral vaccines to protect target populations. In fact, vaccines against some potential BW agents exist, and some of these vaccines have been stockpiled. Further, extensive research is being done to develop new vaccines against additional potential BW agents. Vaccines cannot be the complete answer, however, for a variety of reasons.

---

attack would be 6.5 kilograms. This is still considerably less than agent requirements estimated by Steve Fetter in similar calculations. (See "Ballistic Missiles and Weapons of Mass Destruction: What is the Threat? What Should be Done?" *International Security*, Vol. 16, No. 1 [Summer 1991]). It is also considerably less than the estimates one can create by scaling CW agent requirements for an equivalently lethal city attack by the ratio of anthrax to CW weights needed to create equivalently lethal volumes of air (1/1000 for anthrax wt./sarin wt.).

First, vaccines do not exist for a number of diseases that are considered usable for biological warfare. In addition, new strains of naturally occurring diseases can appear from time to time, either as natural mutations of the older variants of the disease, or as the result of efforts to create new BW agents. Available vaccines may be ineffective against these new strains.

Second, even where vaccines do exist against a disease, they may not be effective when victims are exposed to the disease in the unnatural ways that typify biological warfare. For example, some plague vaccines are generally ineffective when the disease is introduced into the body via inhalation of an aerosol rather than via flea bites. In addition, vaccines that are capable of countering agents introduced into the body in quantities typical of natural disease transmission can be overwhelmed by the far larger concentrations that may be delivered in BW attacks. Vaccines also have other limitations that can reduce their potential utility. They usually have to be administered well in advance of potential exposure, can require multiple boosters over a period of weeks to become fully effective, can cause adverse reactions in some recipients, can fail to be effective for others, and can be costly.

Third, it can be difficult to anticipate what diseases to vaccinate for. Vaccinating for several diseases to hedge against such uncertainties is more expensive, although polyvalent vaccines are being developed. In addition, the effects of multiple simultaneous vaccinations could cause health problems, especially for the very young or the old.

Despite these limitations, vaccines can play an important role in defending against BW at the target. They can save potential victims who have not received overwhelming doses of the agent that they protect against. They can undercut the effectiveness of an opponent's BW attack capabilities, perhaps dissuading BW use in wartime, or increasing the difficulty of creating an effective BW threat in peacetime. Vaccines can also help to maintain the confidence of those who might be at the greatest risk of being attacked.

In summary, though vaccines can play an important complementary role in defending against BW, they cannot be the complete answer. Thus, while development of improved vaccines should be pursued, other protective measures are clearly needed.

POST-EXPOSURE MEDICATION

Antibiotics, antidotes, and antitoxins are another important way to limit the effects of a BW attack, but they too leave significant gaps. Effective post-exposure medications have not yet been found for some known BW agents. In addition, some diseases for which otherwise suitable post-exposure medications exist cannot be treated effectively once they have progressed far enough to present physical symptoms.

Even when effective medications exist, and when the appearance of symptoms does not imply an already irreversible situation, proper and timely diagnosis may not be possible. Because some diseases have similar symptoms at onset, diagnosis can easily be confused until the disease worsens or blood tests can be completed. Simultaneous use of more than one agent can also confuse diagnosis. Confused diagnoses or the use of multiple agents can cause major problems when the drugs needed to treat one possible disease are incompatible with those needed to treat another.

As with vaccines, massive doses of BW agents can overwhelm treatment by otherwise effective medications. In addition, poorly controlled use of antibiotics can lead to the appearance of resistant disease strains. Finally, the vast numbers of people that could be simultaneously exposed to a BW attack, whether actually affected or not, could exceed the maximum practical capabilities of emergency medical treatment facilities, diagnostic laboratories, testing materials, and stocks of drugs. Clearly something more is needed to prevent these capabilities from becoming swamped.

SIMPLE PROTECTIVE MASKS

A particularly promising additional protective measure is a face mask, since the only practical way to cause mass casualties with BW is to use agents that attack through the respiratory system. Introducing BW agents via the digestive system is not practical, provided foods are reasonably carefully prepared, and the water supply is protected by a modern purification system or is sterilized by boiling or with chemicals. A few toxins are known to attack through the skin; an example is "T-2," one of the many varieties of tricothecene mycotoxins. Such materials are not attractive as weapons of mass destruction, however, as large amounts are required to produce lethal effects. In addition, simply washing the skin provides effective decontamination. Thus, the principal risks arising from BW attack are from agents that attack through the respiratory system.[2]

Masks that can protect against BW attacks through the human respiratory system can be far simpler, cheaper, and less burdensome than those

---

2. During the time that the United States maintained a program to develop BW weapons, it required lab and production personnel to wear only a simple rubber mask with a cloth filter that left the eyes and ears completely exposed. In addition, in thousands of U.S. tests with aerosols, none produced conjunctivitis in either lab animals or humans. This past practice and experience support our argument that attacks through the respiratory system are the significant problem.

required to protect against chemical agents. This is because filters that can remove biological warfare agent particles from the air are far easier to design and manufacture than the kinds of filters needed to remove CW agents.[3]

As the CW protection that is provided to many armed forces shields against BW attacks as well, a simple BW mask has two primary values: its potential to protect civilians from BW attacks and its potential for use by troops to avoid the larger burdens of wearing the CW mask, when chemical attack can be safely ruled out. Note that a given weight of biological weapons can cover far larger areas with lethal concentrations of agent, thus requiring much greater numbers of personnel to wear their CW masks and accept the associated burdens.

Clearly, if a cheap and sufficiently effective BW mask can be provided to civilians, it should be possible to reduce the residual threat posed by BW attacks well below that posed by nuclear weapons. The question is whether it is practical to equip large numbers of civilians with such masks, and whether such protection can be expected to have the desired effects.

Availability of Simple BW Protective Masks

Masks that can provide the necessary high levels of protection against BW attack are already available commercially. These masks are commonly used to protect workers in dusty environments containing radioactive or otherwise harmful particles. They are also sold in hardware stores for household use, and are effective in protecting hospital staff from diseases spread by sneezes.

In fact, during preparations for Operation Desert Storm, the Chemical and Biological Defence Establishment of the United Kingdom tested a simple dust mask available on the European market. This mask, which cost the government less than $4, allowed leakage of only 0.2 percent of the 1- to 5-micron-sized particles that would present a hazard in the event of BW attack. A mask of higher quality but approximately equal cost made for the U.S. market limited penetration to only 0.01 percent of the 0.8-micron-sized particles in the outside atmosphere, implying even

---

3. In order to be effective, BW aerosol particles must be in the 1- to 5-micron size range—small enough to be breathed in, but not so small as to be easily breathed out. Such particles can be removed by what are essentially fine dust filters. CW agents are normally gaseous materials that must be removed from breathing air by using activated charcoal to absorb the high boiling point vapors; they do not normally take the form of particles.

greater efficiency for larger particles in the 1- to 5-micron range.[4] In fact, a number of manufacturers and a variety of different masks are available to choose from.

The achievement of such limited penetration requires careful fitting of the mask, particularly around the nose. In the assessments provided below, we assume that any civilians to be protected would be provided at least with clear written instructions on how to adjust and test the fits of their masks. We also assume a leakage rate of 0.1 percent, which is slightly better than the rate for the poorer of the two masks mentioned above.

Gauging the Residual Threat Posed by BW When Masks are Available

To gauge the residual threat posed by biological weapons, one must first ask what it is about nuclear, biological, and chemical weapons that makes them weapons of mass destruction. As outlined in the arguments presented in the second section, we believe that a very good measure of the ability of these weapons to cause mass destruction is the reciprocal of the weight or volume of material that must be delivered in the vicinity of the target to cause devastating effects. The value of this measure can be illustrated by considering two extreme examples. If a pinch of some kind of dust thrown into the air inside a city would kill most of its inhabitants, the destruction of a city could be simply a matter of choice for an attacker. But, if destruction of the city were to require the equivalent of a super-tanker of some kind of fluid to be sprayed over it, defense of the city should be a tractable problem. Note that, in the former case, the reciprocal of the weight, our measure of mass destruction potential, is many orders of magnitude greater than in the latter.

To assess the effects of masks and other protective measures on the residual threat posed by BW, we must estimate how much more agent would have to be put into the environment in order to ensure that

---

4.   Prices and general technical data were provided by the 3M Corporation, especially Jeffrey Preston and Craig Colton. See "1992 POPS Catalog Reference Guide," 3M Part Number/National Stock Number, Federal Government Respiratory Protection Catalog for Department of Defense and Civilian Agencies, Worldwide Services. Information on UVEX masks was provided by Michael Fuchs.

The mask efficiency estimate was drawn from Shu-Kang Chen, Donald Vesley, Lisa Brosseau, and James Vincent, "Evaluation of Single-Use Masks and Respirators for Protection of Health Care Workers Against Microbacterial Aerosols," *American Journal of Infection Control*, Vol. 22, No. 2 (April 1994).

sufficient amounts would penetrate through the protection of buildings, masks, and any other protective "filters" to be deadly.

As a specific example, the second section stated that an unprotected city could be poisoned effectively with as little as 6.5 kilograms of aerosolized anthrax. If its population were equipped with masks with 0.1 percent leakage or less and could use them effectively, the density of agent in the surrounding atmosphere would have to be raised by a factor of at least 1,000 to make the atmosphere reaching the nose and mouth as deadly as without masks. To a first approximation, this would require attacking the city with at least 1,000 times as much agent, or, in this case, at least 6,500 kilograms of anthrax.

Similarly, if the population of the target city were to shelter itself in interior rooms whose doors were sealed with sticky tape, the amount of agent penetrating to potential victims would be reduced by at least another factor of 10.[5] In this case, the total weight of anthrax that would have to be launched at the target city to effectively destroy its population would become at least 65,000 kilograms.

Covert delivery of attacks of this weight is impractical. Instead, substantial numbers of readily detectable delivery vehicles would be required. The numbers of such delivery vehicles could be raised yet further by defenses deployed by the allies. If, for example, missiles had to be employed to deliver the 65,000-kilogram anthrax attack postulated above, and an anti-tactical ballistic missile (ATBM) system that could limit the number of missiles reaching the target city to 10 percent were present, then at least 650,000 kilograms of anthrax payload would have to be launched by the attacker. Launching this amount of payload at a target city would require the equivalent of more than 3,250 Scud missiles, an absurd proposition.[6]

5. Estimate based on information provided by Colonel William C. Patrick III, U.S. Army (ret.), President of BioThreats Assessment, formerly director of the U.S. Army's BW program.

6. Effective dissemination of BW agents delivered by ballistic missile requires the use of dispersible submunitions or devices for blowing aerosolized or finely ground dry agent overboard in the final moments before the missile impacts the ground. Either way, a modest fraction of the total payload weight of the missile becomes effectively disseminated agent. The BW dissemination system described in the following note delivers 6.5 kilograms of agent with a total weight of approximately 20 kilograms (37 percent of total weight is delivered agent). Suitably quick dissemination of larger amounts of agent would require a dissemination system somewhat less heavy than suggested by scaling the total weight up in proportion to the weight of agent to be delivered. Steve Fetter assumes that 30 kilograms of BW agent could be effectively delivered by a missile with a total payload weight of about 1,000 kilograms (3 percent

Finally, an opponent's preparations for attacks of even a small fraction of this magnitude would surely provide warning signs far easier to detect than those associated with BW attacks of the minute size needed when a target has not been protected. Such warning signs should enable more effective and timely political and military actions to blunt the impending BW attacks.

Implementing any of these defenses would take considerable preparatory effort. It would also require the deployment of detection systems and the adoption of well-understood means of warning target populations that BW attacks were imminent. Neither civilian populations nor military personnel can be expected to remain in shelters or to wear protective masks all the time.

In sum, protecting against BW at the target with simple masks and shelters can set up opportunities for other protective measures to become more effective. Warning, masks, and shelters force the BW attacker to deliver agent in amounts where detection would be likely, and active defenses and prelaunch attacks could be effective. Additionally, even where masks and shelters do not totally prevent exposure to BW agents, they can reduce exposure below the levels at which vaccines would be overwhelmed, to levels more typical of natural exposure to disease, and for which currently available vaccines have been designed.

Finally, while practical considerations are likely to limit achievable total protection factors to values below the total of 100,000 suggested in the above example, substantially smaller protection factors can go a long way toward reducing the residual threat posed by BW. The point is that the danger from BW attack can be massively undermined by relatively practical measures. In fact, the comparisons presented below indicate that the threat posed by BW is more responsive to simple protective measures than the threat posed by chemical weapons, and vastly more responsive to protection measures than the threat posed by nuclear weapons.

Comparing the Residual Threats Posed by NBC Weapons

We can estimate the relative magnitudes of the raw threats presented by nuclear, biological, and chemical weapons by calculating the reciprocal of the payload weights that would have to be launched against an unprotected city to cause as many deaths as would a single one-megaton-yield nuclear weapon. Our calculations of such estimates are explained in the

---

of total weight is delivered agent). Fetter, "Ballistic Missiles and Weapons of Mass Destruction." For purposes of our threat comparisons, we assume a Scud-like missile with an 800-kilogram payload could deliver approximately 200 kilograms of BW agent.

notes.[1,7,8] These raw threat estimates for each class of weapon are shown by the three bars on the left in Figure 16.1. The residual threats posed to a city protected by active defenses in all three cases, and by masks and shelters against CW and BW are shown on the right.

---

7.   A commonly used rule for estimating potential casualties from the detonation of a nuclear weapon over a modern city is to assume that all the population within the range at which the overpressure generated by the weapon would be six pounds per square inch or greater would be killed, and all beyond would survive. This rule implies that a nuclear weapon with a yield of one megaton would cause the equivalent of total destruction over an area of approximately 116 square kilometers.

For purposes of our calculations, we assume that a one-megaton-yield nuclear weapon would weigh 1,000 kilograms. Nuclear proliferators would probably start well below this yield-to-weight ratio, as reaching it requires a design employing thermo-nuclear fusion, rather than all fission. Alternately, exploitation of modern weapons simulation codes or the "reverse engineering" of a purloined Russian thermonuclear weapon might allow quick progress to light high-yield thermonuclear weapons. See Thomas B. Cochran, William M. Arkin, and Milton M. Hoenig, Natural Resources Defense Council, Inc., *U.S. Nuclear Weapons Data Handbook*, Vol. 1, *U.S. Nuclear Forces and Capabilities* (Cambridge, Mass.: Ballinger, 1984).

Our comparisons of the relative threats posed by nuclear and biological weapons are constructed as follows. Note 1 states that 6.5 kilograms of aerosolized anthrax can cause 50 percent destruction of the population of an area of 232 square kilometers. This is equivalent to the 100 percent destruction of an area of 116 square kilometers estimated for the 1,000 kilogram nuclear weapon. Dissemination of dry anthrax could be accomplished by a system of the kind designed by the United States when it had an offensive BW program. A system large enough to deliver 6.5 kilograms of dry anthrax can be built with a total weight of approximately 20 kilograms. This estimate is based on information provided by William C. Patrick III.

We take the relative weights of weapons of mass destruction sized to do equivalent damage as an appropriate measure of the relative magnitudes of the threats they each present. Taking the magnitude of the threat posed to an unprotected city by our example nuclear weapon as 1, the relative magnitude of the threat of a BW attack against an unprotected city would thus be 1,000 kilograms (the weight of the assumed nuclear weapon) divided by 20 kilograms (the weight of an equivalently destructive BW weapon) = 50.

To estimate the residual threat posed by nuclear weapons when an active defense system is present, we assume that such a defense system might be good enough to prevent significant damage by 90 percent of the nuclear delivery vehicles it sees. Faced with such a system, a nuclear attacker thus would have to launch an average of ten nuclear delivery systems toward a target in order to destroy it. If the threat posed by nuclear weapons against an unprotected city is taken as 1, the residual threat posed by such weapons would thus be one-tenth.

8.   The same mathematical model referred to in note 1 estimates that a 1,000-kilogram warhead delivering submunitions filled with the nerve agent sarin could lead to 50 percent casualties for an unprotected population over an area of 1.47 square kilometers, assuming favorable weather conditions. Thus, matching the effects assumed for a one-megaton nuclear weapon would require enough CW agent to destroy 50 percent of 232 square kilometers. This would come to $232/1.47 \times 1,000$ kilograms = 158,000

Figure 16.1. Estimated Relative Magnitude of Threats Posed to Civilians by Nuclear, Chemical, and Biological Weapons.

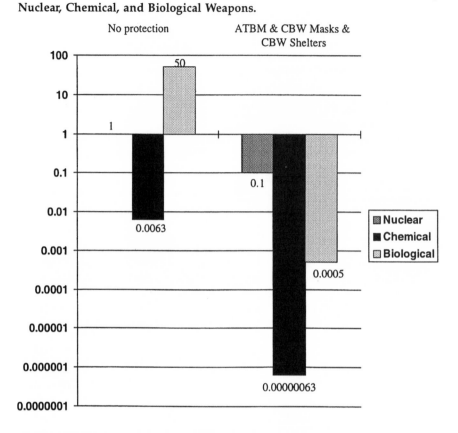

kilograms. The relative magnitude of the threat posed by CW attack is thus 1,000 kilograms (the weight of the example nuclear warhead)/158,000 kilograms = 0.0063.

Based on tests done by the Israeli Defense Force, we assume effective attack of populations that have well-fitted chemical protective masks and are well sheltered in buildings would require at least 1,000 times more chemical agent. If we also assume an ATBM with a 10 percent leakage rate, then achieving destruction equivalent to that done to an unprotected city by the example nuclear weapon requires 1,580,000,000 kilograms of CW payload to be launched against the target city. This means that the residual threat posed by chemical weapons against a city thus protected would be 1,000/1,580,000 = 0.00000063.

Similarly, based on the assumed effectiveness of the various BW defenses, the residual threat posed by BW would be 1/100,000th of that posed by BW against a completely unprotected city, or 0.00050.

The assumed protection factor of 1000, 100 for a CW mask, and 10 for a sealed shelter, is taken from "State Comptroller Faults Gas Mask Distribution," *Jerusalem Post* (English), April 15, 1991, p. 7, cited in Federal Broadcast Information Service Daily Report (FBIS)NES-91-075, April 18, 1991, p. 25.

It should be noted that these are point estimates only and are clearly subject to many uncertainties. Nevertheless, the differences in relative sizes of the raw and residual threats posed by the three types of weapons are of the right order of magnitude. It can be seen clearly that the combination of active defenses, simple protective masks, and shelters reduces the BW threat by five orders of magnitude, at least three of which come from the mask, one from sheltering within buildings, and one from the assumed missile defense. Thus, the threat of BW attack drops from approximately fifty times that posed by a nuclear weapon against an unprotected city to five ten-thousandths of the threat posed by a nuclear weapon against a protected city.

Alternately, one can compare the residual to the raw threats posed by BW and nuclear weapons respectively. In this example, the BW threat is at least four orders of magnitude more responsive to the defenses that can be deployed against it than the nuclear threat is to the single type of protection that can be deployed against it, active defenses. In other words, efforts to protect populations from BW attack will be rewarded far more readily than those made to protect them from nuclear attack.

Practical Questions

Two practical questions must be answered to assess the potential strategic benefits of a simple BW mask. First, are such masks affordable for states or regions that could be subject to BW attack? While the defense expenditures of some states and populations are very small, the general answer to this question has to be yes. For example, the entire urban populations of Saudi Arabia, Syria, and Israel (approximately twenty-four million people) could have been equipped with such masks during Operation Desert Shield for $90–100 million. This is roughly the price of three of the several thousand tactical aircraft involved in Operation Desert Storm.

If the citizens are to be spared the necessity of wearing their masks as continuously as possible during periods when the potential for BW attacks is high, sensors to provide warning of actual attacks would also have to be purchased. Several millions of dollars more might be required for each concentration of population to be provided with warning of a large-scale attack.

Producing and procuring large numbers of masks for stockpile could reduce their costs. Even guaranteeing that masks would be quickly available for sale would be useful. A manufacturer should be willing to maintain an extra inventory of in-production commercial masks for not much more than the cost of the capital thus tied up. At an interest rate of

10 percent, the cost of tying up $90–100 million in capital in the example inventory of 24 million masks mentioned above would come to less than $10 million per year.

The second practical question is: would target populations be willing to wear such masks? Populations at risk for BW attack would have to be given warning of the possibility of such attacks, and encouraged to wear masks as much as possible during periods of danger. The kinds of masks required to provide good protection against BW agents are not significantly burdensome to wear, and the potential dangers of not wearing a mask could be made known.

While the absence of large-scale chemical attacks in World War II eventually led to a relaxed attitude toward CW protection, urban populations in the United Kingdom and a few other countries were issued chemical protective masks; many carried them around during the early years of the war. Both Sweden and Switzerland have policies of providing total defense for their populations, which includes programs aimed at providing practical protective measures against nuclear, biological, and chemical weapons. In particular, Swiss homes have shelters provided with filtration systems, and the head of household is provided with a personal respirator in his capacity as a member of the Swiss Armed Forces.

Israel also has a well-developed program for protecting its citizens with masks. A variety of models are available to allow protection for all citizens including infants, small children, the aged and infirm, and special cases such as those who insist on retaining beards that prevent effective use of the simplest types of masks. Excellent manuals describing proper mask use are available to Israeli citizens.[9] New masks employing lightweight air pumps to provide breathing air under positive pressure are also being developed. These masks will essentially eliminate the risk of poor fits that allow agents to leak in. They will also eliminate the psychological burden felt when wearing current types of masks that require noticeable effort to draw in air. This Israeli program reflects widespread willingness of the citizens to make use of CW civil defense measures. Substantial numbers of urban Israelis wore relatively burdensome CW masks as a precaution against the possibility that Iraqi missiles fired at them during Operation Desert Storm were armed with CW warheads.

Today citizens in some countries already make a habit of wearing "courtesy masks" in crowds, masks that are generally similar to those referred to above. The wearing of such masks is becoming more common

---

9. Ilan Yeshua, "Chemical Warfare: A Family Defense Manual," *Jerusalem Post Edition* (Israel: Centre for Educational Technology, 1990).

and acceptable in areas that have high concentrations of smog, such as Japan and southern California. Further, masks of this type are commonly sold in hardware stores for use when working in dusty or chemically contaminated environments. Finally, Indian citizens frightened by the apparent breakout in 1994 of pneumonic plague in their country wore scarves over their faces, and Indian street vendors did substantial business selling a variety of commercial dust and surgical masks.[10]

Even if entire target populations could not be counted on to wear masks during a BW attack, their ready access to masks could help discourage a BW attack. Small initial attacks should have less than strategic effects, and would drive the surviving target populations to wear their masks, thus undercutting the effectiveness of later attacks. This could eliminate an aggressor's option to make graduated but politically effective use of BW to force the allies to give up their intervention plans and disengage. If an aggressor launched large-scale surprise BW attacks to cause massive casualties, the allies might be led to raise their war aims beyond the stakes that the aggressor intended to risk in order to win the issue at hand.

Achieving and maintaining a good fit is a requirement for obtaining the mask effectiveness projected above. One of the masks mentioned above comes in two sizes and has been determined to fit 95 percent of the population well enough to prevent them from smelling samples of a test aerosol. Additional sizes and instruction on how to achieve a good fit would be necessary. Beards will prevent a good fit, requiring that they be shaved off, or that a more complex protective hood be worn. (Such hoods are also already available commercially.) Because large-scale BW attacks are most likely to take place at night, the mask must remain well-fitted for use at night. This might require better positioning straps or other means for helping the mask to remain in place.

There are other practical problems to be solved. For example, masks are not a practical solution for infants, who require other protective measures such as confinement to a room provided with filtered air, or the use of crib covers fitted with filter material. In addition, means must be found for expeditiously distributing masks and other protective equipment when the potential for BW attacks arises. Recipients must also be instructed on their use. Further, political constraints may prevent distribution of masks and instruction in their use much in advance of need.[11]

---

10. *Washington Post*, October 2, 1994, p. A33.

11. Training to use masks effectively is required by the U.S. Occupational Safety and Health Administration (OSHA) regulations for hazardous working environments, and OSHA requires masks to be fit-tested to ensure their effectiveness. Masks are tested by

Potential Military and Other Values of a Simple BW Protective Mask

A simple BW mask also could be useful to military forces. Because BW agents are so much more toxic than CW agents, far larger areas can be made hazardous with a given amount of agent. Further, greater toxicity allows a wider variety of ways to expose forces to BW attack. This implies that an opponent would find it far easier to impose some burden of protection and risk on large numbers of forces with BW agents than with CW agents, thus increasing the value of equipping them with less burdensome BW masks. The British Army followed an analogous policy of providing simpler, less burdensome partial protection against CW for its troops. This took the form of a facelet that provided useful protection against CW agents. It was worn continuously, whenever there was a potential risk of CW agents being used, and provided protection until respirators could be donned for full protection.

Thus, even forces equipped with CW protection may find it useful to carry BW masks, which are relatively light and substantially less burdensome to use than the standard CW mask. Certainly sleeping in a simple BW mask would be far more restful than sleeping in the standard CW mask. The standard U.S. CW mask, for example, can be very hot because it covers most of the head with air-impermeable material.

A specialized BW mask also could reduce the penalties to allied forces of not yet having a BW detector with the broad capabilities currently sought. Low-burden BW masks could be donned whenever suspicious levels of dangerously sized particles were detected in the atmosphere. The delays currently needed to determine the exact nature of such particles would then be more tolerable.

Stocks of simple, readily transportable BW masks also could be maintained as a means of coping with a BW terrorist campaign. Masks may be particularly effective in this case, because the volumes and concentrations of BW agents employed may not be as high as those that a better equipped regular military opponent could deliver. Certainly, in the aftermath of the first attack, populations would be anxious to protect themselves.

Even more generally, BW masks can be a powerful tool for limiting the spread of contagious diseases, whether the product of human mischief

---

asking workers if they can detect a standardized sample of perfume sprayed into a covering test hood. A fully effective BW mask program would include peacetime instruction on the use of a mask. It would also test the fit of available sizes of masks on individuals to identify the minority posing special fit problems and requiring tailored masks or hoods.

or not. They can block what is far and away the most dangerous means of transmission—the breathing of air contaminated by the sneezes and coughs of the infected.

Finally, to the extent that a simple mask can prevent BW from emerging as a threat comparable to or even greater than that posed by nuclear weapons, it could render moot the question of whether the United States needs to consider nuclear retaliation as a deterrent to large-scale use of BW.

Additional Cautions

While a simple BW mask may play a very important role in reducing the threat of biological warfare, it is not a complete and final answer for a variety of reasons. For example, advances in biotechnology may open the possibility for practical BW agents that can attack through the skin, or present other challenges.

Further, even with a very well-implemented program to protect populations and forces from BW attack, a large-scale BW attack can cause great suffering to a state that experienced it. For example, a city of one million inhabitants that had adopted a BW defense strong enough to save 95 percent of its population nonetheless would sustain 50,000 casualties. Still, while a potential calamity of this magnitude would be a serious consideration in any leader's assessments, it is not nearly as disastrous as the potential death of most or all of a state's urban citizens.

Finally, the foregoing analysis shows that masks provide the most effective defense against BW by working synergistically with other protective measures, including warning systems, shelters, vaccines, and active defenses. Thus, a mask program should supplement, not replace, other measures to blunt the potential of BW attacks.

Conclusion

This short discussion indicates that a simple BW mask appears to have considerable promise as a tool for keeping the threat of biological warfare from rivaling or exceeding that posed by nuclear weapons. Consequently, an aggressive program to exploit its potential seems appropriate.

Where the primary responsibility should lie for pursuing this kind of BW "civil defense" capability is an important issue. Responsibility for civil defense of the United States has been managed by the Federal Emergency Management Agency. The U.S. Department of Health and Human Services and some of its subordinate agencies, such as the Centers for Disease Control, should have an interest in the potential of a mask program to supplement other measures for controlling the outbreaks of epidemics. Certainly, the U.S. Department of Defense (DoD) should be responsible for any program to supplement current CW defense for its personnel with a specialized BW mask, as well as for contingency programs to help protect future coalition partners from BW attack. In sum, a program to improve BW defense with a simple mask would cut across the responsibilities of many parts of the U.S. government.

Still, unless specific responsibilities for exploring the potential contribution of a simple BW mask are assigned to some specific agency, it is unlikely to get serious attention. Given the broader BW expertise of the Department of Defense, and the near-term potential for BW to have strategic effects on U.S. decisions to intervene with military forces overseas, there appears to be a good case for assigning to the DoD the lead responsibility for a program to aggressively develop and exploit the potential of a simple BW mask.

Finally, it may be useful to look from a longer historical perspective at the question of controlling disease epidemics.[12] Epidemics have cut wide swaths through humanity for thousands of years. They have come about as a result of contacts between animal and human populations that could tolerate such diseases and those that could not. Indeed, diseases that pose lethal threats to humans reside all around us. Advances in medicine, sanitation, common practices for personal hygiene, communications, and institutional preparations for rapid control of disease all are responsible for the absence of epidemics threatening substantial fractions of people in the last fifty years. Almost surely, this collection of tools has the capacity to blunt the effect of any purposeful effort to subject large populations to deadly disease.

The main difference between the disease control task posed by natural disease and that posed by biological warfare is that the former tends to first appear with discovery of a small number of cases in a few locations, while the latter could involve near-simultaneous infection of many thousands or more people in numerous geographically separated attacks. Such an enormous challenge will only be answered by means that have been planned in advance and that can be implemented by ordinary citizens, rather than trained specialists. Viewed in this light, simple masks and warning systems that provide effective protection against any BW agent that attacks through the respiratory system are clearly very powerful tools for disease control and BW counterproliferation, particularly in connection with other protective measures.

---

12. The historical information in this section is drawn from William H. McNeill, *Plagues and Peoples* (New York: Doubleday, 1977).

Contingent adoption of such a hygiene measure will be similar to relatively simple changes in behavior that humans have developed for many hundreds of years to prevent disease and its spread. By the twelfth century, the Chinese had learned the value of swabbing the noses of their children with cotton rubbed in the infections of smallpox victims. By the sixteenth century, Christian ports on the Mediterranean had all learned to quarantine arriving ships for forty days. Nomadic tribesmen of the Eurasian steppe region have long considered it bad luck to camp close to marmot colonies showing signs of sickness. Modern populations should be pleased to learn that a relatively straightforward behavioral change, based on a very simple piece of modern technology, can offer a good first step toward countering the threat of biological weapons.

Chapter 17

Bioterrorism: Threats and Responses

Jonathan B. Tucker

On March 20, 1995, Aum Shinrikyo, a bizarre Japanese cult, released sarin nerve gas on the Tokyo subway, inflicting twelve deaths and a few thousand injuries. A subsequent police investigation revealed that in addition to producing chemical weapons such as sarin and VX, the cult had built three biological laboratories in which it had cultivated dangerous biological agents such as anthrax, botulinum toxin, and Q-fever. On nine occasions between 1990 and 1993, cult members released anthrax or botulinum toxin in Tokyo in an attempt to inflict mass casualties, including an attack on the U.S. naval base at Yokosuka, the headquarters of the Seventh Fleet.[1] Fortunately, technical problems with the agent or the delivery system rendered all the attacks ineffective. After repeated failures at bioterrorism, Aum Shinrikyo switched to producing chemical nerve agents, which are easier to disseminate.

Other than Aum Shinrikyo, several terrorist groups or individuals over the past thirty years have taken steps to acquire biological or toxin agents, although nearly all failed or were arrested before they could carry out an attack. Some incidents that are widely cited in the terrorism literature may also be apocryphal.[2] Despite this checkered history, U.S. government officials are convinced that the risk of bioterrorism is increas-

This chapter was adapted from Jonathan B. Tucker, "National Health and Medical Services Response to Incidents of Chemical and Biological Terrorism," *Journal of the American Medical Association (JAMA)*, Vol. 278, No. 5 (August 6, 1997), pp. 362–368. © 1997 American Medical Association.

1.   David E. Kaplan and Andrew Marshall, *The Cult at the End of the World* (New York: Crown, 1996), pp. 93–98; and William J. Broad, "How Japan Germ Terror Alerted World," *New York Times*, May 26, 1998, pp. A1, A10.

2.   See the chapter in this volume by Seth Carus.

ing. According to Gordon Oehler, former director of the U.S. intelligence community's Nonproliferation Center, "Extremist groups worldwide are increasingly learning how to manufacture chemical and biological agents, and the potential for additional chemical and biological attacks by such groups continues to grow."[3]

A confluence of events in early 1998 brought the threat of bioterrorism to the attention of top policymakers, including U.S. President Bill Clinton. In February, the Federal Bureau of Investigation (FBI) arrested Larry Wayne Harris, a microbiologist with white-supremacist sympathies, after he boasted to an informant that he possessed vials containing enough military-grade anthrax to "wipe out" Las Vegas. This claim proved to be a hoax: the confiscated vials contained a harmless veterinary vaccine against anthrax.[4] Even so, the enormous publicity surrounding the incident demonstrated that the mere threat of a biological warfare (BW) attack can elicit considerable fear and disruption. The following month, a scare involving an alleged Iraqi plot to smuggle anthrax into the United Kingdom—purportedly in retaliation for planned U.S. and British air strikes against Baghdad that never materialized—called attention to the specter of biological weapons in the hands of international terrorists, possibly armed and equipped by state sponsors.[5]

Finally, despite the long history of sporadic terrorist interest in biological weapons, the FBI has recently reported a dramatic rise in the number of incidents.[6] In April 1998, FBI Director Louis J. Freeh testified at a congressional hearing that his agency had been alerted to 114 suspected cases involving preparations for chemical or biological attacks.[7] Although about 80 percent of these cases were hoaxes (such as threats involving *Bacillus thuringiensis*, a harmless bacterial insecticide that can be purchased off the shelf), some of the incidents reportedly involved

---

3. Robert Green, "Nuclear, Chemical Terror Threat is High, CIA Says," *Reuters News Service*, March 27, 1996.

4. Kevin Fagan, Susan Sward, and Bill Wallace, "Anthrax Scare—2 Held: Pair Charged with Possessing Deadly Bacteria," *San Francisco Chronicle*, February 20, 1998, pp. A1, A8; and Tamala M. Edwards, "Catching a 48-Hour Bug," *Time*, March 2, 1998, pp. 56–57.

5. Associated Press, "Britain On Alert For Anthrax Attack," March 23, 1998; Associated Press, "Panel Warns Senate on Biological Terrorism," March 5, 1998; and Paul Mann, "Warnings Raised About Iraqi Terrorism Threat," *Aviation Week & Space Technology*, Vol. 148, No. 5 (February 2, 1998), p. 22.

6. Richard Preston, "Taming the Biological Beast," *New York Times*, April 21, 1998, p. A25.

7. Tim Weiner, "Reno Says U.S. May Stockpile Medicine for Terrorist Attacks," *New York Times*, April 23, 1998, p. A12.

unsuccessful attempts to deliver dangerous pathogens or toxins.[8] Despite the significant technical hurdles involved in producing and disseminating biological agents, it may only be a matter of time before a successful attack occurs. Robert Blitzer, head of the FBI's Domestic Terrorism/Counterterrorism Planning Section, has warned that "it's not a matter of *if* it's going to happen, it's *when*."[9]

Until recently, governments hesitated to devote significant resources to preparing for bioterrorism because they assessed the risk as too low to justify the cost. Although the number of terrorist groups that have sought to acquire or employ biological agents is small, the case of Aum Shinrikyo suggests that there is little reason for complacency. Much like a nuclear reactor accident, bioterrorism is a "low-probability, high-consequence" contingency that poses difficult challenges for policymakers. Knowing how best to respond and how much money to invest requires a better understanding of the problem. What types of terrorist groups are most likely to resort to these weapons? How easy or difficult would it be for them to do so? How prepared are governments to deal with bioterrorism from the intelligence, law enforcement, and public health perspectives? And what are some practical policy options for dealing with this emerging threat?

Bioterrorism's Deadly Potential

Biological warfare involves the deliberate use of disease-causing microbes and naturally occurring poisons to cause illness or death in people, livestock, or crops. To infect a large number of people simultaneously, a microbial agent such as anthrax would have to be disseminated as a respirable aerosol—an invisible cloud of microscopic particles that can be inhaled deeply into the lungs. The microbes would then replicate in the victims' bodies and, following an incubation period lasting a few days, give rise to a systemic infection that is either incapacitating or fatal. A BW aerosol attack that exposed a large population would trigger an explosive outbreak of disease, similar to a natural epidemic but compressed in time.

BW agents developed for military purposes have generally been veterinary pathogens that rarely infect humans in nature, such as the bacteria that cause anthrax, tularemia, and brucellosis, and the virus that causes Venezuelan equine encephalitis (VEE). These agents give rise to an incapacitating or fatal illness in the population that is directly exposed,

8. Ibid.

9. David E. Kaplan, "Terrorism's Next Wave: Nerve Gas and Germs are the New Weapons of Choice," *U.S. News and World Report*, November 17, 1997, p. 28.

but they are not contagious in humans and hence do not spread from person to person. As a result, the outbreak caused by the deliberate release of a veterinary pathogen would be self-limiting and would not boomerang against the attacker's own troops or population.

Anthrax is considered the prototypical BW agent for several reasons. As a bacterium, it is much easier to cultivate than viruses or rickettsiae, which reproduce only inside living animal cells. Anthrax bacteria can also be induced to form microscopic spores that have a tough outer coat, rendering them resistant to environmental stresses such as heat, drying, and sunlight, and enabling them to survive for several hours when suspended in the air in aerosolized form. Since even spores can be killed by prolonged exposure to ultraviolet radiation, however, an anthrax attack would probably occur at night, dawn, or dusk, or on an overcast day.

Inhalation of only about 8,000 anthrax spores—a dose no larger than a speck of dust—is sufficient to infect a human being.[10] The spores lodge in the tiny air sacs of the lungs and then cross the epithelial lining and travel to the lymph nodes. There they germinate, multiply, and release potent toxins into the bloodstream, giving rise to systemic illness. Although the average delay between anthrax infection and the onset of illness is 72 hours, the incubation period can range from two to seven days as a function of the bacterial strain, the inhaled dose, and the immunological competence of the host. After an initial 24-hour period of nonspecific, flu-like symptoms, the acute phase sets in, including vomiting, choking cough, and labored breathing. Death from hemorrhagic pneumonia, respiratory failure, and toxic shock follows within a few days.

Since pathogenic microorganisms multiply within the host, a few kilograms of a highly infectious and virulent agent—if widely disseminated as a respirable aerosol—could potentially claim tens of thousands of victims. Weight-for-weight, microbial agents such as anthrax are thousands of times more potent than chemical nerve agents like sarin. Indeed, under optimal meterological conditions, inflicting 50 percent fatalities over a square-mile area would require about a metric ton of sarin but only about 10 grams of anthrax spores.[11]

---

10.   Barry J. Erlick, Testimony, U.S. Senate Committee on Governmental Affairs, Hearing, *Global Spread of Chemical and Biological Weapons: Assessing Challenges and Responses,* 101st Cong., 1st sess., February 9, 1989 (Washington, D.C.: U.S. Government Printing Office [GPO], 1990), p. 32.

11.   C.V. Chester and G.P. Zimmerman, "Civil Defense Implications of Biological Weapons," *Journal of Civil Defense,* Vol. 17, No. 6 (December 1984), pp. 6–12.

Unlike microbial agents, toxin agents are nonliving poisons synthesized by a variety of living organisms, including bacteria (e.g., botulinum toxin), fungi (mycotoxins), marine algae (saxitoxin), animals (cobra venom), and plants (ricin). More than 500 toxins have been characterized in nature. Ranging from small molecules to large proteins, they exert their effects with a latency period of from several minutes to a few days. Only a small subset of toxins have properties that would make them capable of inflicting mass casualties, such as high toxicity, ease of production, and stability during processing, storage, and dissemination. A theoretical analysis of 395 toxins revealed that only 17 are toxic enough for wide-area battlefield use, and that most of these are difficult to produce in quantity or are unstable in aerosol form.[12] Bacterial toxins such as botulinum also come in several different molecular forms, only a few of which are highly lethal. Despite these drawbacks, however, Iraq has produced large amounts of botulinum toxin, aflatoxin, and *Clostridium perfringens* ("gas gangrene") toxin, and experimented with ricin and fungal toxins known as trichothecene mycotoxins.[13]

Assessing the Threat

While it is clear that urban society is extremely vulnerable to bioterrorism, the nature of the threat is harder to assess. With more than one hundred terrorist organizations active around the world today, the challenge is to identify those groups or individuals most likely to resort to the use of biological weapons against civilians.[14] A priori, this category of terrorists is likely to lie at the intersection of three sets: those with the motivation and lack of moral constraints that would lead them to kill large numbers of people indiscriminately; those with the technical expertise to cultivate and deliver BW agents effectively; and those with a charismatic leader and organizational structure strong enough to plan and carry out an

12. David R. Franz, "International Biological Warfare Threat in CONUS," statement by Colonel David Franz, Deputy Commander, U.S. Army Medical Research and Materiel Command, before the Joint Committee on Judiciary and Intelligence, U.S. Senate, March 4, 1998, p. 5.

13. United Nations, *Report of the Secretary-General on the Status and Implementation of the Plan for the Ongoing Monitoring and Verification of Iraq's Compliance with Relevant Parts of Section C of Security Council Resolution 687 (1991)*, UN Security Council Document No. S/1995/864, October 11, 1995, pp. 6–7.

14. Jerrold Post and Ehud Sprinzak, "Searching for Answers: Why Haven't Terrorists Used Weapons of Mass Destruction?" *Armed Forces Journal International*, Vol. 135, No. 9 (April 1998), pp. 16–17.

Figure 17.1. Characteristics of Terrorists Most Likely to Employ Weapons of Mass Destruction (WMD).

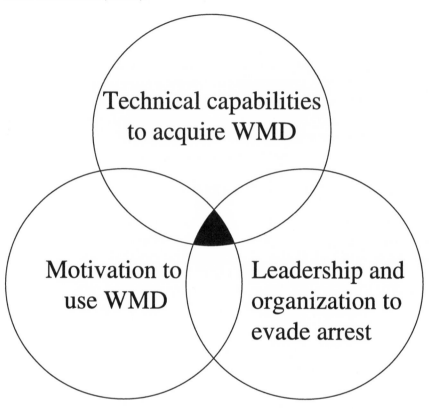

attack while evading detection and arrest by law enforcement authorities. (See Figure 17.1.)

Fortunately, this combination of traits appears to be quite rare. The capability to inflict mass casualties by disseminating a BW aerosol over a wide area would require a delivery system that outstrips the technical capabilities of all but the most sophisticated terrorists. And while sociopaths and mentally disturbed individuals may be motivated to acquire and use weapons of mass destruction, presumably only a small minority would have the technical expertise to produce and deliver a biological agent by themselves, or the ability to function in a cohesive group.

Still, the large and growing number of bioscientists has increased the probability that a few may be psychologically inclined to terrorism or susceptible to recruitment by terrorists.[15] U.S. industry currently employs about 60,000 biologists, and there are more than 1,300 biotechnology companies in the United States.[16] Although scientists are trained to be skeptical and hence may seem unlikely prospects for religious cults, Aum Shinrikyo's success at attracting highly educated chemists, physicists, and biologists from leading Japanese universities suggests that one should not place undue faith in scientific rationality. Indeed, if Unabomber Theodore Kaczynski had been a microbiologist rather than a mathematician, it is conceivable that he may have resorted to biological weapons.

The following sections explore the motivational and technical sides of the bioterrorist equation in greater depth.

OMINOUS TRENDS

Historically, terrorist groups who view themselves as fighters for a political cause have not sought to inflict mass casualties but have sought instead to elicit fear through the controlled, instrumental use of violence.[17] Political terrorists have employed hostage-taking, airplane hijacking, bombings, and assassinations as a form of "political theater" to attract media attention to their demands, to weaken public confidence in government by generating a pervasive sense of insecurity, to sabotage ongoing peace negotiations, to provoke an overreaction on the part of law enforcement, or to obtain bargaining leverage. In doing so, terrorists typically calibrate the level of violence they employ to that deemed sufficient to achieve their ends, while avoiding excessive or indiscriminate bloodshed that could alienate their supporters and bring down on their heads the full repressive power of the government or police.[18] The pervasive moral stigma attached to biological weapons has also deterred their use by political terrorists, who typically view themselves as relatively more ethical than the state or entity they are attacking.[19]

15. Richard Kelly Heft, "Looking for Mr. Nutbar," *Ottawa Citizen*, March 8, 1998, p. A13.

16. Robert Taylor, "Bioterrorism Special Report: All Fall Down," *New Scientist*, Vol. 150, No. 2029 (May 11, 1996), p. 32.

17. Spurgeon M. Keeney, Jr., "Tokyo Terror and Chemical Arms Control," *Arms Control Today*, Vol. 25 (April 1995), p. 2.

18. E. Hurwitz, "Terrorists and Chemical/Biological Weapons," *Naval War College Review*, Vol. 35 (May–June 1982), pp. 36–40.

19. Brad Roberts and Michael Moodie, *Combatting NBC Terrorism: An Agenda for Enhancing International Cooperation* (Alexandria, Va.: Chemical and Biological Arms Control Institute, 1998), p. 15.

In addition to the political drawbacks of biological weapons, they involve hazards, technical hurdles, and operational uncertainties much greater than those associated with firearms, explosives, or even chemical poisons. For open air dispersal, the dissemination of BW aerosols is strongly affected by the prevailing wind and weather conditions, making such releases difficult to control. Moreover, whereas chemical nerve agents such as sarin exert their lethal effects within minutes, microbial agents induce illness and death after an incubation period of a few days, so that the effectiveness of an attack cannot be assessed immediately. Because of this delay, an act of bioterrorism might not be recognized for weeks, potentially diluting its political impact.

In view of these liabilities, traditional terrorist organizations motivated by a political agenda and a sense of self-preservation have generally not sought to acquire or use biological weapons. Nevertheless, two ominous trends suggest that incidents of mass-casualty terrorism are becoming more likely.

INDISCRIMINATE ATTACKS. The first trend is that terrorists in recent years have shown a greater tendency to engage in acts of indiscriminate violence. Most terrorist incidents in the 1960s and 1970s involved the hijacking of aircraft, the taking of hostages, and occasional shootings that inflicted relatively few casualties. Since the late 1980s, however, incidents of international terrorism have become less frequent but more violent. The total number of international terrorist incidents peaked in 1987 at 665 and then gradually declined; in 1996, there were 296 such incidents, of which only 45 involved fatalities.[20] At the same time, however, the average number of casualties per incident rose as terrorists began to employ high explosives to kill and injure large numbers of innocent civilians indiscriminately. Examples of high-casualty terrorist incidents include the bombing of Pan Am Flight 103 over Lockerbie, Scotland, in December 1988, killing 259 passengers and 11 people on the ground; the bombing of the World Trade Center in New York in February 1993, killing 6 and injuring about 1,000; the bombing of the Alfred E. Murrah Federal Building in Oklahoma City in April 1995, killing 168 and injuring more than 500; and the bombings of the U.S. embassies in Kenya and Tanzania in August 1998, killing 224, and injuring about 5,400.

Terrorists may be perpetrating more sensational and indiscriminate attacks because they perceive that the public has become desensitized and

---

20. U.S. Department of State, *Patterns of Global Terrorism 1996*, Publication 10433 (Washington, D.C.: Department of State, April 1997), Appendix C: Statistical Review.

that traditional shootings and hijackings no longer attract sufficient media coverage or political leverage. At the same time, terrorists have been less likely to claim responsibility for mass-casualty attacks in an apparent bid to evade arrest and retribution.

CHANGING TERRORIST MOTIVATIONS. The second ominous trend is that the motivations for terrorism appear to be changing in a way that makes mass-casualty attacks more likely. In 1989, terrorism expert Jeffrey Simon published a hypothetical profile of a terrorist group most likely to resort to biological weapons. In his view, such a group would lack a defined constituency and thus be unconcerned about political backlash; would have a previous pattern of high-casualty-inflicting incidents; would demonstrate a certain degree of sophistication and innovation in weaponry or tactics; and would have shown a willingness to take risks.[21]

Simon's profile applies to an increasing number of terrorist organizations. Since the mid-1980s, the majority of groups resorting to political violence has undergone a dramatic shift from left-wing extremists and national separatist movements to religious fundamentalists, right-wing militants, and racial supremacists. This "new breed" of terrorists is no longer driven by a defined political agenda but rather by a broad religious, racial, or anti-government ideology.[22] Such groups are potentially more dangerous because they have fluid objectives, perceive fewer political or ethical constraints on the scope of their actions, are often interested in violence for its own sake, and are less easily deterred by threats of punishment. According to Joseph Nye and James Woolsey, the new type of terrorist is "less interested in promoting a political cause and more focused on retribution or eradication of what he defines as evil. . . . For such people, weapons of mass destruction, if available, are a more efficient means to their ends."[23]

Since BW agents are hazardous to handle, difficult to disseminate effectively, and unpredictable in their effects, terrorists would probably acquire and use these weapons only if they wished to achieve objectives not attainable with ordinary guns and explosives. As Walter Laqueur has

---

21. Jeffrey D. Simon, *Terrorists and the Potential Use of Biological Weapons: A Discussion of Possibilities* (Santa Monica, Calif.: RAND, December 1989, NTIS Document No. ADA220598), p. 17.

22. Jose Vegar, "Terrorism's New Breed," *Bulletin of the Atomic Scientists*, Vol. 54, No. 2 (March/April 1998), pp. 50–55.

23. Joseph S. Nye, Jr. and R. James Woolsey, "Heed the Nuclear, Biological and Chemical Terrorist Threat," *International Herald Tribune*, June 5, 1997, p. 8.

pointed out, "terrorists will not engage in overkill if their traditional weapons—the submachine gun and the conventional bomb—are sufficient to continue the struggle and achieve their aims."[24] Some possible motivations for terrorist escalation to biological warfare are summarized below.

First, terrorists may perceive that conventional tactics are no longer effective and that a more lethal and dramatic form of violence is needed to achieve their ends. Frustration or despair over the failure to achieve their goals by conventional means, or the prospect of imminent arrest or death at the hands of police, could lead to "a last desperate attempt to defeat the hated enemy by arms not tried before."[25] In addition, the shock value of a BW attack—or the mere threat of one—would capture the attention of the media and terrorize the population at risk. As John Steinbruner has pointed out, "the guaranteed public sensation of a biological agent attack is unquestionably an ominous temptation to extremists."[26] Even a hoax might cause serious disruption and casualties if large-scale panic ensued.

Second, terrorists might be motivated to acquire and use BW agents because of a desire to inflict mass casualties. Aum Shinrikyo's objective in releasing anthrax and botulinum toxin in central Tokyo was to kill hundreds of thousands of people and trigger social chaos as means of seizing control of the Japanese government and imposing a theocratic state. The cult had even established a "shadow government," including a full array of ministries, that was preparing to take power.[27]

Third, terrorists who sought to incapacitate rather than kill a large number of people might use a non-lethal biological agent.[28] In 1984, for example, the Rajneeshee cult in Oregon contaminated restaurant salad bars in the town of The Dalles with *Salmonella typhimurium* (food-poisoning) bacteria in a plot to sicken local residents and influence the outcome of a county election. A total of 751 people became ill, none fatally.[29]

---

24. Walter Laqueur, "Postmodern Terrorism," *Foreign Affairs*, Vol. 75, No. 5 (September/October 1996), p. 31.

25. Ibid.

26. John D. Steinbruner, "Biological Weapons: A Plague Upon All Houses," *Foreign Policy*, No. 109 (Winter 1997–98), pp. 85–96.

27. Eric Croddy, "Urban Terrorism—Chemical Warfare in Japan," *Jane's Intelligence Review*, Vol. 7, No. 11 (November 1995), pp. 520–523.

28. W. Seth Carus, "The Threat of Bioterrorism," *INNS Strategic Forum*, No. 127 (Washington, D.C.: National Defense University, Institute for National Strategic Studies [INNS], September 1997), p. 2.

29. See the chapter by Thomas J. Török et al. in this volume.

Fourth, terrorists wishing to avoid arrest and retribution might prefer to employ a biological rather than a chemical agent, since the effects of the former would be delayed and hence more difficult to trace.[30] A bioterrorist attack with a common pathogen might be mistaken for a natural outbreak of disease, making it "plausibly deniable." Indeed, the real cause of the Oregon *Salmonella* outbreak was not identified until more than a year later. The obvious drawback of a deliberate epidemic that appears natural is that it would have little utility as an instrument of terror or coercion. Bioterrorists employing an indigenous disease agent could therefore face the decision of whether to claim responsibility for the outbreak early on, allowing public health authorities to begin treatment and possibly mitigating the effects of the attack, or waiting and perhaps finding that their efforts were ignored.[31]

THE "NEW BREED" OF TERRORISTS
The "new breed" of terrorists who appear more prone to indiscriminate violence can be subdivided into four categories: fundamentalist and religious groups; racist and anti-government groups; millenarian cults; and "amateur" terrorists.[32] Groups or individuals in each of these categories vary with respect to the three parameters identified in Figure 17.1—technical capabilities, motivations and goals, and leadership and organization—making them more or less likely to resort to bioterrorism. Different types of terrorist entities also have characteristic motivations and targets. Whereas some groups seek to assassinate specific individuals such as judges, police, and tax collectors, others may wish to inflict indiscriminate casualties as a means of exacting revenge or eliminating hated minorities. Detailed descriptions of the four categories follow.

FUNDAMENTALIST AND RELIGIOUS GROUPS.   Dozens of militant religious groups exist in the world today, including Identity Christians, Islamic fundamentalists, ultranationalist Jews, radical Sikhs, and New Age cults, some of which espouse a dangerous mixture of political paranoia, messianic fervor, and obsession with apocalyptic prophecy. Whereas secular terrorists tend to view indiscriminate violence as immoral and counterproductive by alienating supporters and provoking severe retribution,

---

30. W. Seth Carus, "Testimony of W. Seth Carus Before a Joint Hearing of the Senate Select Committee on Intelligence and the Senate Judiciary Subcommittee on Technology, Terrorism and Government Information," March 4, 1998.

31. Charles Arthur, "Chemicals, Bugs and Deadly Toxins—The New DIY Terrorist's Arsenal," *Independent*, February 21, 1998, p. 12.

32. Vegar, "Terrorism's New Breed," pp. 50–55.

religious terrorists may see it not only as morally justified but as a necessary means for achieving their ends.[33] In 1968, none of the eleven international terrorist groups then active could be classified as religious in character or motivation. By 1995, however, 42 percent of the fifty-eight known terrorist groups were religious in nature. Moreover, although religious terrorists committed only 25 percent of the recorded incidents of international terrorism in 1995, they were responsible for 58 percent of the total number of fatalities.[34]

Terrorists inspired by religious fundamentalism, such as the Islamic groups Hezbollah and Hamas, are uncompromising in their goals and typically rationalize the use of violence as serving the will of God, while dehumanizing their victims. In the words of a Hezbollah terrorist, "We are not fighting so that the enemy recognizes us and offers us something. We are fighting to wipe out the enemy."[35] Although most fundamentalist groups have both religious and political objectives, the belief that their acts are divinely sanctioned makes them less susceptible to political or ethical constraints on the use of violence. Indeed, Hamas suicide-bombers voluntarily accept death in the belief that they will be rewarded in the next life. Children are recruited into the organization at an impressionable age and indoctrinated with fanatical hatred and the ideology of holy war.

Religious cults are also a phenomenon of growing concern. According to the American Family Foundation, more than 1,000 cults exist in the United States alone, and between five and ten million Americans have been at least transiently involved with cult groups.[36] To date, most of the violence expressed by cults has been focused inwards in the form of mass suicides. Examples include Jim Jones and the People's Temple, 913 of whom drank poison-laced Kool Aid in Guyana in November 1978; David Koresh and the Branch Davidians, 78 of whom died by setting fire to their own compound during a shoot-out with U.S. federal agents near Waco, Texas, in April 1993; Luc Jouret and the Order of the Solar Temple, some 60 of whom committed collective suicide at sites in Switzerland and Quebec in October 1994; and Marshall Applewhite and the Heaven's Gate cult, 39 of whom poisoned themselves near San Diego in March 1997.

---

33. Bruce Hoffman, "Holy Terror": The Implications of Terrorism Motivated by a Religious Imperative, Report No. P-7834 (Santa Monica, Calif.: RAND, 1993), p. 2.

34. Bruce Hoffman, "Terrorism and WMD: Some Preliminary Hypotheses," Nonproliferation Review, Vol. 4, No. 3 (Spring–Summer 1997), p. 48.

35. Charles L. Mercier, Jr., "Terrorists, WMD, and the U.S. Army Reserve," Parameters, No. 27 (Autumn 1997), pp. 98–118.

36. Michael D. Langone, "Cults: Questions and Answers," American Family Foundation web site (http://www.csj.org).

Nevertheless, some religious cults, such as Aum Shinrikyo, are capable of directing violence outward against perceived enemies. Cults may also have a fascination with poisons and disease agents because of their invisible and insidious effects, which give them quasi-mystical power.

A potential source of religious terrorism in the United States is the Christian Identity movement, which preaches that white "Aryans" are the true nation of Israel, that Jews are the offspring of Satan, and that African-Americans are soulless subhumans or "mud people." Identity adherents contend that God has ordered them to punish those who have strayed from Biblical laws; in many cases, the prescribed punishment is death.[37] According to James Coates, "because it is a religion with all the traditional trappings, preached by Bible-quoting pastors from pulpits in churches very much like those most Americans grow up in, Identity [Christianity] allows its born-again men and women to practice with suddenly clear consciences the bigotry, hatred and even criminal violence that they had been taught from childhood were sinful."[38]

During the 1980s, an Arkansas-based Identity group called the Covenant, the Sword, and the Arm of the Lord (CSA) plotted to assassinate federal officials, to poison municipal water supplies with potassium cyanide, and to bomb various sites, including the Oklahoma City federal building. These plans failed, and the CSA disbanded in 1985 after the FBI arrested its leaders.[39] Several other Christian Identity sects, however, continue to advocate violence against Jews and African-Americans.

RACIST AND ANTI-GOVERNMENT GROUPS. Tens of thousands of Americans today are active in the so-called "Patriot" movement, which encompasses a variety of far-right groups inspired by racism, nativism, Nazi ideology, survivalism, and bitter resentment of government taxation and affirmative action.[40] All of these groups are united in the belief that the

---

37. Joel Dyer, *Harvest of Rage: Why Oklahoma City is Only the Beginning* (Boulder, Colo.: Westview, 1997), p. 80.

38. James Coates, *Armed and Dangerous: The Rise of the Survivalist Right* (New York: Hill and Wang, 1987), p. 81.

39. Victoria Hicks, "About-Face from Hate: Book Traces Journey Out of Racist Group," *Dallas Morning News*, May 16, 1998, p. 1G.

40. Recent books on the right-wing Patriot/militia movement in the United States include: Dick J. Reavis, *The Ashes of Waco: An Investigation* (New York: Simon & Schuster, 1995); David H. Bennett, *The Party of Fear: The American Far Right Movement from Nativism to the Militia Movement* (New York: Vintage, 1995); Kenneth S. Stern, *The Force Upon the Plain: The American Militia Movement and the Politics of Hate* (New York: Simon & Schuster, 1996); and Morris Dees and James Corcoran, *Gathering Storm* (New York: Harper-Collins, 1996).

U.S. government has become increasingly tyrannical. Some Patriot organizations have established their own "common-law courts" in place of federal and state legal structures that they perceive as repressive and illegitimate. In addition, heavily armed "militias" conduct paramilitary drills in preparation for a future showdown with the U.S. government. In 1997, the Southern Poverty Law Center identified 523 Patriot organizations and 221 armed militias. Such groups are active in all fifty states, with the heaviest concentrations in the Midwest, Southwest, and along the Pacific coast.[41]

The shared stress, agitation, and sense of persecution experienced by many Patriot adherents make them psychologically vulnerable to far-fetched conspiracy theories, including sinister plots of world domination involving the United Nations and Jewish international bankers. According to psychologist Glen Wallace, "Once [people] enter the realm of the cult mentality, they can become convinced of anything. They can be convinced to do anything. It's very dangerous. The same community psychosis that pulls people into the anti-government movement in the first place can eventually lead to cult mentality."[42]

The most militant Patriot groups, such as the Montana Freemen, retreat to armed compounds where they reject the jurisdiction of the federal and state governments, refuse to pay taxes, and sometimes declare their independence as sovereign "townships" or "countries." Although standoffs with federal police authorities may lead to violence (as occurred at Ruby Ridge, Idaho in 1992 and Waco, Texas in 1993), only a small minority of Patriot groups routinely engage in criminal behavior. According to the FBI, hard-core, violence-prone extremists, such as neo-Nazi skinheads, number "in the hundreds" and are splintered into various sects and gangs.[43]

During the 1980s, the FBI successfully infiltrated leading far-right-wing organizations such as the Posse Comitatus, the American Nazi Party, and The Order. Today, however, law enforcement officials are concerned about a new strategy known as "leaderless resistance," in which anti-government militants operate in small, independent cells and receive their

41. Southern Poverty Law Center, Militia Task Force, "Patriot Movement Poses Continued Threat: Groups Are Growing in Number, Hardening in Attitude" [http://www.splcenter.org/klanwatch/kw-5.html]; and Cable News Network, "Southern Poverty Law Center Says Groups Plan for Race War," June 17, 1998.

42. Dyer, *Harvest of Rage*, pp. 212–213.

43. David E. Kaplan and Mike Tharp, "Terrorism Threats at Home," *U.S. News & World Report*, December 29, 1997/January 5, 1998, pp. 22–27.

marching orders from underground publications and Internet web sites.[44] This decentralized structure serves to immunize the movement's leaders from prosecution, while allowing each cell unlimited operational freedom. Since the cells are technically not part of larger groups, it is harder for federal and local law enforcement agencies to identify and track them.

How serious is the threat posed by right-wing extremists in the United States? After the devastation at Oklahoma City, the anti-government movement must be taken seriously, and the potential for further large-scale violence appears to exist.[45] Underground publications sold openly at gun shows and through mail-order houses provide detailed instructions on how to manufacture certain biological and toxin agents— particularly ricin, a toxin extracted from castor beans.[46] In four known cases, right-wing terrorists in the United States have sought to acquire BW agents but were arrested before they could use them:

• In 1992, four members of the Minnesota Patriots Council, a tax-resistance group based in Alexandria, Minnesota, extracted ricin (a potent toxin) from castor beans and conspired to assassinate federal and local law enforcement officials.[47]
• In May 1995, Larry Wayne Harris, an Arkansas lab technician with ties to the white-supremacist Aryan Nations, was arrested after misrepresenting himself when ordering three vials of bubonic plague bacteria from a Maryland microbial culture supply house.[48] Harris later threatened BW attacks against federal officials. "If they arrest a bunch of our guys, they get a test tube in the mail," he told a reporter.[49]

---

44. Lewis R. Beam, "Leaderless Resistance," reprinted in *Modern Militiaman: A Journal of the Modern Resistance Movement,* Issue No. 3, October 1996 [http://www.mo-net.com/~mlindste/mmmisu3.html#noleaders]. See also Kevin Whitelaw, "Terrorists on the Web: Electronic 'Safe Haven'," *U.S. News & World Report,* June 22, 1998, p. 46.

45. Dyer, *Harvest of Rage,* p. 214.

46. Brian Levin, "The Patriot Movement: Past, Present, and Future," in Harvey W. Kushner, ed., *The Future of Terrorism: Violence in the New Millennium* (Thousand Oaks, Calif.: SAGE Publications, 1998), p. 124.

47. Wayne Wangstad, "2 Minnesota Men First to be Convicted under Biological Weapons Act," *St. Paul Pioneer Press,* March 1, 1995, p. 3B.

48. Karl Vick, "Plea Bargain Rejected in Bubonic Plague Case," *Washington Post,* April 3, 1996, p. A8.

49. Kaplan, "Terrorism's Next Wave," p. 30.

- In December 1995, Thomas Lewis Lavy, an Arkansas man with survivalist connections, was charged with having tried to smuggle 130 grams of ricin from Alaska into Canada in 1993.[50] The day after his arrest, Lavy hung himself in his jail cell.
- In July 1998, three self-proclaimed members of the Republic of Texas, a right-wing secessionist group, were arrested in Brownsville, Texas. They had allegedly plotted to assassinate President Clinton and other senior federal officials by using a crude air-gun fashioned from a Bic lighter to fire cactus thorns coated with biological agents such as anthrax, botulism, or rabies.[51]

These cases suggest that it may be only a matter of time before far-right militants acquire enough technical expertise to engage in bioterrorism, either to assassinate perceived enemies or to avenge a previous incident in which federal agents have killed anti-government activists.

MILLENARIAN CULTS. As the year 2000 approaches, prophecies of the apocalypse are proliferating. According to one estimate, thousands of millenarian groups exist in the world today.[52] Comments Hal Mansfield, an expert on alternative religions, "We're in for a helluva ride with these millennial groups. Whatever technology is out there, they're going to use it."[53]

Militant Identity Christian groups, for example, interpret the New Testament's Book of Revelations to mean that the Final Judgement will come at the turn of the millennium, when the wicked will be destroyed and the "righteous remnant" will receive their reward. Identity adherents believe that they have been called upon by God to make war on the federal government, a war that will usher in the apocalypse and the millennial rule of Christ. In their view, "tribulation"—the violence-filled period leading up to the apocalypse—has already begun, and God has commanded them to start carrying out his judgments.[54] The prominent role of plagues (including anthrax) in the Bible suggests that millenarian

---

50. John Kifner, "Man Is Arrested in Case Involving Deadly Poison," *New York Times*, December 23, 1995, p. 7.

51. "3 men accused of plotting to kill Clinton, Reno, Freeh," *Deseret News* (Salt Lake City, Utah), July 16, 1998 (www.desnews.com).

52. David C. Rapoport, "The Celestial Connection: An Ancient Theme," *San Diego Union-Tribune*, April 4, 1997, pp. B5, B9, B11.

53. T. Post, "Doomsday Cults: 'Only the Beginning'," *Newsweek*, Vol. 125 (April 3, 1995), p. 40.

54. Dyer, *Harvest of Rage*, p. 81.

groups could potentially resort to biological weapons to help bring about Armageddon.

"AMATEUR" TERRORISTS. The diffusion of biotechnology equipment and scientific know-how has facilitated the rise of the "amateur" terrorist. In the past, terrorists tended to be professionals with specialized expertise, weaponry, and operational knowledge. Today, individuals can purchase small fermentation systems (such as beer-brewing kits) from commercial outlets and acquire "cookbook" manuals from mail-order publishers that provide detailed instructions for the manufacture of BW agents. Armed with such information, amateur terrorists can aspire to be as deadly as their professional counterparts.[55] Recent examples of lone terrorists with an interest in biological weapons include the following:

- On April 28, 1997, a Wisconsin man named Thomas Leahy, who was taking medication for schizophrenia, was arrested and charged with possessing ricin with the intent to use it as a weapon. Leahy pleaded guilty to the charge. His wife told police that he had many books and manuals on bacterial diseases and toxins and had threatened to poison family members.[56] A police search of Leahy's residence turned up biological growth media, petri dishes, several vaccines, castor beans, foxglove seeds, and pickle jars that may have been used in a failed attempt to produce botulinum toxin. An FBI informant said that Leahy plotted to use bacteria to kill his enemies through the U.S. mail.[57]
- In May 1997, the Internal Revenue Service arrested James Dalton Bell, a 38-year-old man living in his parents' house in Washington state, for allegedly harassing IRS personnel and using false social security numbers to evade income taxes. Federal agents later learned that Bell, who studied chemistry at MIT, had tried to manufacture botulinum toxin in the late 1980s.[58]

Some analysts contend that future terrorists will be solitary individuals like the Unabomber or small groups of extremists such as the perpetrators

---

55. Hoffman, "Terrorism and WMD," p. 50.

56. Kathleen Ostrander, "Man Faces Charge of Toxin Possession," *Milwaukee Journal Sentinel,* April 29, 1997, p. 5.

57. Kevin Murphy, "Judge Orders Man Held for Toxin," *Milwaukee Journal Sentinel,* May 2, 1997, p. 5.

58. John Painter, Jr., "IRS Says Suspect Discussed Sabotage," *Oregonian,* May 20, 1997, Metro Section, p. P-1.

of the Oklahoma City bombing. As Laqueur observes, "The ideologies such individuals and mini-groups espouse are likely to be even more aberrant than those of larger groups. And terrorists working alone or in very small groups will be more difficult to detect unless they make a major mistake or are discovered by accident."[59] Although sociopaths tend to be loners who avoid working in cohesive groups, the availability of Internet web sites promoting extremist ideas and conspiracy theories creates a "virtual community" of like-minded individuals, reinforcing their paranoid ideation and increasing the potential for violence.

In summary, the greatest threat of bioterrorism appears to lie with a small number of groups and individuals who have access to the necessary technology, materials, and know-how; are motivated by religious fanaticism, anti-government ideology, or racial hatred rather than a specific political agenda; and have sufficient leadership or organizational discipline to carry out an attack without being infiltrated and arrested in advance. For such groups, biological agents may be attractive because they are lethal in small quantities, relatively easy and cheap to produce, readily concealable, and suitable for delivery by a small number of people.[60]

Acquisition of Biological and Toxin Agents

A terrorist group's choice of which biological agents to acquire would be influenced by the objectives of the planned attack, as well as the availability of seed cultures, problems of manufacturing and storage, and the anticipated means of dissemination.[61] BW agents developed in the past for military purposes include anthrax, tularemia, Venezuelan equine encephalitis, and botulinum toxin.[62] Depending on their goals, however, terrorists might seek to acquire different agents than those stockpiled by countries. For example, a group aiming to sicken rather than kill a large number of people might employ a nonlethal agent such as food-poisoning bacteria. Conversely, terrorist groups bent on inflicting mass casualties

---

59. Laqueur, "Postmodern Terrorism," p. 34.

60. Marie Isabelle Chevrier, "Deliberate Disease: Biological Weapons, Threats, and Policy Responses," *Environment and Planning C: Government and Policy*, Vol. 11 (1993), pp. 395–417.

61. Harvey J. McGeorge II, "The Deadly Mixture: Bugs, Gas, and Terrorists," *Nuclear, Biological, and Chemical Defense & Technology International*, Vol. 11, No. 2 (May 1986), p. 59.

62. Bradley Graham, "Clinton Calls for Germ War Antidotes," *Washington Post*, May 21, 1998, p. 1.

and undermining social structures might deliberately produce and disseminate a contagious agent such as plague, with the aim of triggering an uncontrolled epidemic.

For would-be bioterrorists, acquiring seed stocks of highly infectious and virulent microbial agents would be a major hurdle. Although pathogenic or toxin-producing microorganisms can be collected from natural sources such as diseased animals or contaminated soil, only a few strains are deadly enough to make an effective weapon. Indeed, Aum Shinrikyo was foiled in its repeated attempts to use biological weapons by its inability to obtain sufficiently virulent forms of anthrax and botulism bacteria.[63]

Despite this obstacle, resourceful terrorists might obtain virulent strains by ordering them under false pretenses from a legitimate culture collection, stealing them from a university or industry laboratory, purchasing them from renegade weapons scientists, or culturing them from natural sources.[64] In 1992, for example, Aum Shinrikyo sent forty missionaries and a group of doctors and nurses to the former Zaire, ostensibly to assist in treating the victims of an Ebola virus outbreak. Their real mission was to obtain samples of the deadly virus to cultivate for BW purposes, although they failed to do so.[65] In the United States, militia groups have extracted the potent plant toxin ricin from castor beans purchased from plant nurseries.

Some analysts have expressed concern that terrorists might employ gene-splicing techniques to create pathogens that are more lethal, stable in the environment, or resistant to standard vaccines and antibiotics.[66] At present, this scenario appears unlikely. Although recombinant DNA methods are widely employed in science and industry, they require specialized know-how that is generally not available to terrorists. Moreover, because infectivity and virulence are complex traits controlled by multiple genes, simple genetic manipulations would probably have little effect. It is much more likely that terrorists would grow standard bacterial agents such as

63. Broad, "How Japan Germ Terror Alerted World," p. A10.

64. In 1986, Iraq purchased seed stocks of weapons-grade anthrax and botulism bacteria from microbial culture collections in the United States and France. See U.S. Senate, Committee on Banking, Housing, and Urban Affairs, Hearing, *United States Dual-Use Exports to Iraq and Their Impact on the Health of the Persian Gulf War Veterans,* 103rd Cong., 2nd Sess., May 25, 1994, S. Hrg. 103-900, pp. 264–275.

65. U.S. Senate, Committee on Governmental Affairs, Permanent Subcommittee on Investigations, "Staff Statement: Hearings on Global Proliferation of Weapons of Mass Destruction: A Case Study on the Aum Shinrikyo," October 31, 1995. See also Kaplan and Marshall, *The Cult at the End of the World,* p. 97.

66. Preston, "Taming the Biological Beast," p. A25.

anthrax, although they might employ classical selection techniques to develop antibiotic-resistant strains.

PRODUCTION AND DELIVERY

Techniques for cultivating harmful bacteria and their toxins do not differ substantially from the production of legitimate microbial products such as fermented beverages, vitamins, animal feed supplements, vaccines, and antibiotics. Indeed, efforts to control the spread of biological weapons confront a "dual-use dilemma": the fact that the same fermentation tanks used to produce essential products such as vaccines and pharmaceuticals can be diverted to nefarious activities. Basic techniques for growing bacteria are described in the scientific literature, and dual-capable fermentation equipment is marketed by scores of commercial companies—including simple kits for making wine and beer at home.[67]

Fortunately, although pathogenic bacteria are relatively easy to cultivate, employing them as a weapon is a more difficult task. Contamination of municipal water supplies would probably not be effective because large water-treatment systems include filtration and chlorination processes designed to kill harmful microorganisms. The enormous dilution factor would also necessitate the use of impractically large quantities of agent.[68] Thus, to serve as a mass-casualty weapon, BW agents would have to be delivered through the air as an aerosol that could infect a large number of people simultaneously through the lungs.

Although liquid slurries of bacteria or toxins are relatively easy to produce, they are hard to disseminate effectively as an infectious aerosol. Such wet agents must be stored under refrigeration until use and tend to lose viability and potency over time. In addition, since large amounts of energy are needed to aerosolize droplets in the appropriate size range for respiratory infection, more than 90 percent of the microorganisms in a liquid slurry would be killed during the aerosolization process, resulting in a limited downwind range.[69] Conversely, dry powders of microbial agent or toxin (having a consistency similar to talcum powder) are easier to store, handle, and disseminate than liquid slurries, yet are much harder to manufacture.[70] Drying and milling bacterial or toxin agents requires

67. Barbara Starr, "CW Detection Is Top of US Shortfall List," *Jane's Defence Weekly,* June 10, 1995, p. 26.

68. McGeorge, "The Deadly Mixture: Bugs, Gas, and Terrorists," p. 61.

69. Defense Intelligence Agency, *Soviet Biological Warfare Threat,* DST-1610F-057–86, 1986, p. 4.

70. William C. Patrick III, "Biological Terrorism and Aerosol Dissemination," *Politics and the Life Sciences,* Vol. 15, No. 2 (September 1996), pp. 208–210.

complex, costly equipment that is beyond the reach of most countries, let alone terrorist groups.

Moreover, most microbial and toxin agents (with the exception of spore-forming microorganisms such as anthrax) are highly sensitive to environmental stresses such as temperature, sunlight, and drying, and degrade rapidly in the atmosphere. In principle, the stability and persistence of non-spore-forming agents can be enhanced with a technique called "microencapsulation," which involves coating the microscopic particles or droplets containing pathogen or toxin with a thin coat of protective material.[71] In practice, however, microencapsulation is in the same category of technical difficulty as the production of dry agents, and is unlikely to be accessible to terrorists.[72] Finally, open air dissemination of microbial agents as a respirable aerosol would be influenced by complex environmental factors, including atmospheric conditions, wind, weather, and temperature, making the effects of a bioterrorist attack fairly difficult to control or predict.

Because of the significant technical hurdles that must be overcome to produce dry or microencapsulated agents, terrorists would probably be limited to the dissemination of wet slurries of pathogens or toxins in an enclosed space such as a building or a subway station, using simple equipment such as a garden pesticide fogger. Such a crude attack would not inflict mass casualties, but it could potentially sicken or kill tens to hundreds of people—a disaster on the scale of the Oklahoma City bombing—and elicit widespread fear and disruption.[73]

Sensational discussions of mass-casualty bioterrorist attacks in the press have tended to exaggerate the scale of the problem, often by conflating the capabilities of states with those of terrorist groups. Popular novels by Richard Preston and Tom Clancy have contributed to this misperception. However, according to David Franz, "Although it will always be possible to obtain virulent organisms from the environment, the technical hurdles between [a flask filled with microbes] and a cloud covering many square miles of one of our cities are significant."[74]

71. U.S. Congress, Office of Technology Assessment, *Technologies Underlying Weapons of Mass Destruction*, OTA-BP-ISC-115 (Washington, D.C.: U.S. GPO, December 1993), p. 94.

72. Telephone interview with William C. Patrick III, former U.S. bioweapons scientist, May 22, 1998.

73. Taylor, "Bioterrorism Special Report: All Fall Down," p. 32.

74. Franz, "International Biological Warfare Threat in CONUS," p. 6.

ASSISTANCE FROM BIOWEAPONS SCIENTISTS

The discussion above suggests that BW agent weaponization is technically demanding and that generating an aerosol cloud large enough to inflict mass casualties would outstrip the capabilities of most if not all terrorist groups. Indeed, despite its considerable technical and financial resources, Aum Shinrikyo failed in nine attempts to use anthrax and botulinum toxin against the population of Tokyo.

It is possible, however, that terrorists intent on acquiring sophisticated BW capabilities (such as production of dry agents, microencapsulation, and efficient aerosolization) could seek technical and financial assistance from a state with an advanced BW program or from unemployed bioweapons scientists. The former Soviet Union, for example, had the world's largest and most advanced BW program. In addition to five BW facilities operated by the Ministry of Defense, a complex of pharmaceutical institutes known as Biopreparat engaged in offensive BW activities under civilian cover. In the late 1980s, this huge organization employed up to 25,000 people and included nearly twenty research, development, and production facilities.[75]

Russian President Boris Yeltsin's April 1992 decree ordering the dismantling of the offensive BW program, which Russia had inherited from the Soviet Union, led to the firing or underemployment of a large number of bioweapons experts. Former CIA Director Robert Gates testified before Congress in 1992 that "a few thousand [former Soviet scientists] have the knowledge and marketable skills to develop and produce biological weapons." Gates added that the most serious threat of brain drain involves those individuals whose skills have no civilian counterpart, such as bioengineers specializing in the weaponization of BW agents.[76] According to Ken Alibek, a senior scientist in the Soviet BW program who defected to the United States in 1992, no one knows where most of the weapons scientists formerly employed by Biopreparat have ended up. Alibek fears that some of them may have smuggled seed cultures of military-grade pathogens to countries such as Iran and North Korea.[77]

Other proliferant states are known to have recruited foreign bio-

75. U.S. Department of Defense, *Nuclear/Biological/Chemical (NBC) Defense: Annual Report to Congress, February 1998* (Fort Belvoir, Va.: Defense Technical Information Center), p. xxii.

76. Former CIA Director Robert Gates, Testimony before the U.S. Senate, Governmental Affairs Committee, "Weapons Proliferation in the New World Order," January 15, 1992.

77. Tim Weiner, "Soviet Defector Warns of Biological Weapons," *New York Times*, February 25, 1998, pp. A1, A8; see also Richard Preston, "Annals of Warfare: The Bioweaponeers," *New Yorker*, March 9, 1998, pp. 52–65.

weapons scientists. In 1994, for example, U.S. intelligence agencies tracked Libyan agents attempting to lure South African BW experts to Tripoli to help Libya develop biological weapons.[78] Given this precedent, it is possible that sophisticated terrorist groups might attempt to recruit former bioweapons scientists for their deadly expertise.

Finally, some analysts have expressed concern that outlaw states such as Iraq might employ bioterrorism as a means of "asymmetric warfare" against the United States and other Western powers that enjoy a vast technological advantage in conventional military capabilities.[79] According to one report, the Japanese intelligence service discovered a 1989 arrangement between members of Aum Shinrikyo and the Iraqi secret service to trade information and know-how about biological and chemical warfare.[80] Nevertheless, no evidence in the public domain suggests that a leader like Saddam Hussein would be prepared to undertake the enormous risks associated with delegating the use of biological weapons to terrorist proxies. An obvious disincentive is that if evidence of state sponsorship of a bioterrorist attack were to come to light, the sponsoring government could expect severe retaliation.

Counterterrorism Strategy

Given the technical constraints discussed above, a small- to medium-scale attack is the most likely bioterrorist threat—the contingency against which federal, state, and local planning should primarily be directed. Although the vulnerability of urban centers to biological weapons is a frightening reality for which there are no easy technical fixes, policymakers can take some practical steps to contain the problem. An effective strategy would combine two complementary approaches: prevention of an attack if at all possible, and mitigation of the consequences if it occurs.

PREVENTION

Preventing bioterrorism presupposes the ability to detect such activities at an early stage and to place obstacles in the path of terrorists. Such a strategy would require an array of mutually reinforcing policies, such as improving the collection of intelligence on terrorist groups; strengthening

---

78. Lynne Duke, "Drug Bust Exposes S. African Arms Probes," *Washington Post*, February 1, 1997, p. A15.

79. Jonathan S. Landay, "Clinton's Antiterrorism Chief Marshals His Troops," *Christian Science Monitor*, July 1, 1998, p. 4.

80. "Terrorism: Links Between Aum and Baghdad," *Intelligence Newsletter*, No. 336 (June 4, 1998), p. 6.

the surveillance of unusual disease outbreaks; restricting access to dangerous pathogens and toxins; and controlling the publication of toxic "cookbooks."

IMPROVED INTELLIGENCE COLLECTION. Before the sarin attack on the Tokyo subway, the U.S. intelligence community knew almost nothing about Aum Shinrikyo despite the cult's worldwide efforts to acquire sensitive materials and production equipment for its weapons programs through a network of legitimate and front companies. During U.S. Senate hearings in November 1995, senior counterterrorism officials from the CIA, the FBI, and the Department of Defense admitted that they had focused their intelligence collection efforts on state-sponsored groups with a political agenda and thus had been unaware of the cult's activities.[81] To avoid such intelligence failures in the future, the U.S. government should allocate greater resources to monitoring "unconventional" fringe groups such as religious cults, survivalist militias, and racial supremacist organizations that appear capable of large-scale violence. This enhanced collection effort should involve the training of intelligence officers to monitor the new threats, the development of indicators suggestive of terrorist BW acquisition, and an increased emphasis on preemption and interdiction. The United States should also expand intelligence-sharing with friendly countries on international terrorist groups that might be contemplating mass-casualty attacks.

Since BW agent production equipment has legitimate commercial uses and is easily concealed, the acquisition of biological weapons is associated with few if any telltale "signatures" observable by reconnaissance aircraft or satellites. Thus, the ability to detect terrorist preparations for a biological attack relies heavily on human-source intelligence ("humint") provided by informants, defectors, and infiltrators. Unfortunately, humint is inherently unsystematic and fortuitous, and small terrorist cells may be difficult to identify and infiltrate.

Possible indicators of preparations for bioterrorism include: a history of illegal and violent behavior; statements of intent or ideology involving plagues, disease, or apocalyptic disaster; the recruitment of new members with bioscience backgrounds; efforts to purchase or steal microbial seed cultures, growth media, fermentors, laboratory glassware or brewing equipment, sterilizing agents, filter masks, or aerosolization devices; attempts to culture anthrax spores from the tissues of diseased animals or

---

81. R. Jeffrey Smith, "Senators Scold Spy Agencies Over Cult," *Washington Post,* November 2, 1995, p. A15.

contaminated soil; and suspicious inquiries by group members about infectious diseases. The development of a BW delivery system might entail field testing which, if detected, could provide an indication of nefarious intent. But terrorists could minimize the risk of detection by carrying out tests of live agents in an isolated, unpopulated area, or by using a simulant—a harmless bacterium whose aerosolization characteristics mimic those of a lethal agent such as anthrax.

In a democratic society like the United States, counterterrorism entails difficult trade-offs between civil liberties and public safety.[82] Whereas authoritarian states can crush terrorist groups on their territory through the massive use of surveillance and repression, democracies deliberately limit the power of the state to safeguard civil liberties and hence are less able to defend against mass-casualty weapons in the hands of extremists. Clearly, the desirable goal of preventing a bioterrorist attack before it occurs should never serve as a pretext to harass political or religious groups that espouse unpopular views but do not resort to violence. If, however, the FBI obtains compelling evidence—meeting the legal standard of "probable cause"—that an individual or group is seeking biological agents with an intent to use them for terrorist purposes, the FBI should obtain a warrant to engage in intensive surveillance. Such tactics, while intrusive, may be the only way to gain the strategic warning needed to prevent a deadly attack.

EPIDEMIOLOGICAL SURVEILLANCE. Another indicator of a clandestine BW program could be an unusual outbreak of infectious disease associated with an accident at a secret development, production, or testing facility. Such installations are vulnerable to accidents, particularly if they are operated with minimal safety standards by people with limited training. In order to pursue these leads, field epidemiologists should be trained to distinguish natural disease outbreaks from those resulting from a deliberate or accidental release of a BW agent.

The process of detecting and characterizing outbreaks of infectious disease is known as "epidemiological surveillance."[83] To establish a baseline of natural epidemics against which suspicious outbreaks can more easily be detected, it is important to improve the effectiveness of existing surveillance systems. Possible indicators of a suspicious disease outbreak

---

82. "Third Wave Terrorism" (interview with Alvin Toffler), *New Perspectives Quarterly*, Vol. 12 (June 22, 1995), pp. 4–6.

83. Arthur L. Reingold, "Outbreak Investigations—A Perspective," *Emerging Infectious Diseases*, Vol. 4, No. 1 (January–March 1998), pp. 21–27.

include the presence of a microbial strain that is nonindigenous, highly virulent, antibiotic-resistant, or genetically manipulated.[84] Another indicator of a non-natural outbreak is the rate of spread. Whereas a natural epidemic is characterized by a gradual rise in the number of sick individuals over a period of weeks caused by person-to-person transmission, a deliberate aerosol release of a BW agent that infected a large number of people simultaneously would result in an "explosive" outbreak of disease over a much shorter period of time.[85]

Because of the linkages between national and international disease outbreaks, disease surveillance mechanisms should be strengthened on a global basis.[86] Although the World Health Organization (WHO) established a new division in 1995 to enhance international disease surveillance, this unit currently monitors only plague, yellow fever, and cholera.[87] To improve the rapid detection of unusual outbreaks of disease, including those involving putative BW agents such as anthrax or tularemia, the U.S. Congress should appropriate funds to expand the epidemiological surveillance programs operated by the WHO and its collaborating centers around the world.

RESTRICTING ACCESS TO PATHOGENS. Although it is possible to culture anthrax bacteria and other pathogens from natural sources, the most virulent strains have been isolated or developed in laboratories over a period of many years and are most easily obtained from culture collections. Aum Shinrikyo's failure to obtain a sufficiently deadly strain of

---

84. Donald L. Noah, Annette L. Sobel, Stephen M. Ostroff, and John A. Kildew, "Biological Warfare Training: Infectious Disease Outbreak Differentiation Criteria," *Military Medicine*, Vol. 163, No. 4 (April 1998), pp. 198–201.

85. John P. Woodall, "WHO Health and Epidemic Information as a Basis for Verification Activities under the Biological Weapons Convention," in S.J. Lundin, ed., *Views on Possible Verification Measures for the Biological Weapons Convention*, Stockholm International Peace Research Institute (SIPRI) Chemical and Biological Warfare Series, No. 12 (Oxford: Oxford University Press, 1991), pp. 59–70.

86. Mark L. Wheelis, "The Role of Epidemiology in Strengthening the Biological Weapons Convention," in Erhard Geissler and Robert H. Haynes, eds., *Prevention of a Biological and Toxin Arms Race and the Responsibility of Scientists* (Berlin: Akademie Verlag, 1991), pp. 277–283; Peter Barss, "Epidemic Field Investigation as Applied to Allegations of Chemical, Biological, or Toxin Warfare," *Politics and the Life Sciences*, Vol. 11, No. 1 (February 1992), pp. 5–22; Stephen S. Morse, "Epidemiological Surveillance for Investigating Chemical or Biological Warfare and for Improving Human Health," *Politics and the Life Sciences*, Vol. 11, No. 1 (February 1992), pp. 28–29; and Mark L. Wheelis, "Strengthening Biological Weapons Control Through Global Epidemiological Surveillance," *Politics and the Life Sciences*, Vol. 11, No. 2 (August 1992), pp. 179–189.

87. Steinbruner, "Biological Weapons: A Plague Upon All Houses," p. 94.

anthrax from natural sources in Japan underlines this fact. The U.S. government, however, has only recently come to grips with the challenge of preventing terrorists from obtaining dangerous pathogens and toxins from legal sources.

This problem came to the fore in 1995, when American Type Culture Collection (ATCC), the leading U.S. supplier of microbial cultures to legitimate biomedical researchers, mailed three vials of seed culture for bubonic plague to Larry Wayne Harris, a reputed white supremacist.[88] Harris had placed the order under false pretenses by typing a request letter on fake letterhead bearing his home address, and using the identification number of the clinical laboratory where he worked as a technician. Although the order of plague bacteria was duly shipped, a staff member at ATCC became suspicious of Harris's repeated phone calls and notified the authorities. Because the purchase of hazardous microorganisms was not then illegal, Harris could only be prosecuted for mail fraud.

In response to this troubling incident, the U.S. Congress included in the Antiterrorism and Effective Death Penalty Act of 1996 a section mandating the Public Health Service to establish a licensing procedure for transfers of dangerous microorganisms and toxins. The new regulations, developed and enforced by the U.S. Centers for Disease Control and Prevention (CDC), seek to balance the legitimate need of research scientists for access to hazardous biological materials against the imperative to prevent them from falling into the wrong hands.[89] Commercial suppliers of twenty-four microbial pathogens and twelve toxins, and the government agencies, universities, research institutions, and private companies that work with these agents, must register with the CDC, pay an annual fee, keep detailed records, and undergo routine inspections. Both the shipping and receiving parties are required to file a special form whenever a listed agent is transferred.[90] According to the American Society for Microbiology, an estimated two hundred facilities in the United States are affected by the new regulations; medical diagnostic laboratories are exempt.[91] To ensure that the regulations are implemented effectively,

---

88. Rochelle Sharpe, "A Peek Inside a Giant Germ Warehouse," *Wall Street Journal*, March 10, 1998, pp. B1, B6.

89. Centers for Disease Control and Prevention, "Additional Requirements for Facilities Transferring or Receiving Select Agents; Final Rule," Code of Federal Regulations, 42 CFR Part 72 [http://www.cdc.gov/od/ohs/biosfty/42cfr72.html].

90. Kurt Kleiner, "US Bioterror Alert Prompts Tighter Rules," *New Scientist*, June 22, 1996, p. 8.

91. Ronald M. Atlas, University of Louisville, Kentucky, personal communication, June 19, 1998.

the CDC should receive more funding and personnel for this purpose. In addition, microbiologists who work with dangerous pathogens should be required to improve the physical security of their culture collections, which are often stored in unlocked freezers.

If the new CDC regulations on "germ commerce" are enforced, they could make a real difference in reducing the threat of domestic bioterrorism in the United States. Unfortunately, other countries have so far failed to follow the U.S. lead. More than 1,500 culture collections exist in countries around the world, including Iran and Pakistan. In August 1996, the World Federation of Culture Collections, which has some four hundred members in fifty countries, rejected a proposal to introduce international safeguards on transfers of dangerous pathogens.[92] This misguided decision should be reconsidered.

CONTROLLING TOXIC "COOKBOOKS." Over the past several years, books and videos providing step-by-step recipes for producing lethal agents such as ricin and botulinum toxin in a home laboratory have been distributed by groups on the extreme left and right of the political spectrum.[93] Today these deadly cookbooks are sold openly at gun shows and survivalist fairs, and from mail-order publishing companies.[94] A few recipes for toxin agents are also posted on the Internet, although the web sites change frequently and often require password access.

Controlling the publication of such potentially deadly information involves a delicate balance between protecting public safety and upholding the U.S. Constitution's protections on free speech.[95] A recent court case, however, has provided some useful precedent in this contentious area of the law. In 1993, James Edward Perry, a professional killer, was hired to murder his client's ex-wife, their brain-damaged son, and the child's nurse. In committing the crime, Perry closely followed the instructions in a book titled *Hit Man: A Technical Manual for Independent Contrac-*

92. Broad, "How Japan Germ Terror Alerted World," p. A10.

93. Jessica E. Stern, "Will Terrorists Turn to Poison?" *Orbis*, Vol. 37 (Summer 1993), pp. 393–410.

94. See Jim Hogshire, "Biochemical Warfare," *Icon Magazine*, March/April 1998, pp. 62–65, 159. Examples of poison cookbooks include *The Poor Man's James Bond* by Kurt Saxon, *The Poisoner's Handbook* by Maxwell Hutchkinson, *Assorted Nasties* by David Harber, and *Silent Death* by Steve Preisler (alias "Uncle Fester").

95. U.S. Senate, Committee on the Judiciary, Subcommittee on Terrorism, Technology, and Government Information, Hearing, *The Availability of Bomb-Making Information on the Internet*, 104th Cong., 1st sess., May 11, 1995, S. Hrg. 104–729 (Washington, D.C.: U.S. GPO, 1996).

tors, published by Paladin Press of Boulder, Colorado. A lawyer who believed that the publisher had "aided and abetted" the murderer sued Paladin Press on behalf of the dead wife's sisters.[96] During the trial in Federal District Court in Maryland, the publisher admitted that the book's intended audience included "criminals and would-be criminals" seeking information and instructions on how to commit crimes, yet the judge ruled that the book's publication and distribution were protected under the First Amendment. In November 1997, however, the Fourth Circuit Court of Appeals in Richmond, Virginia, overturned the district court's decision by finding that constitutional immunity does not apply to speech that amounts to "aiding and abetting of criminal conduct." The appeals court also held that a jury could reasonably conclude that the manual's "only genuine use is the unlawful one of facilitating such murders" and sent the case back to the district court for trial. On April 20, 1998, the U.S. Supreme Court refused to hear a pre-trial appeal by Paladin Press,[97] although it may review the case at a later date.

The precedent-setting appeals-court decision suggests that murder manuals do not constitute protected speech under the First Amendment. While banning such books outright would be impractical, future publication could be deterred through the threat of legal liability. To this end, Congress should pass legislation imposing treble damages on the author and publisher for injuries or death arising from the terrorist use of a poison cookbook, and enabling the federal government to recover costs associated with law enforcement.

Regulating the publication of deadly cookbooks on the Internet would be much harder, however. Since the World Wide Web transcends national borders, the United States would have to negotiate an international treaty covering content providers operating under other national jurisdictions. Skeptics also point out that since poison manuals are already fairly accessible—the first of the genre, *The Anarchist's Handbook*, was published in 1971—it may be too late to control their distribution. Nevertheless, since relatively few such manuals detail methods for producing biological (as opposed to chemical) agents, it would still be beneficial to constrain their further publication and distribution.

---

96. David G. Savage, "Did Hired Killer Go By the Book?" *Los Angeles Times*, May 7, 1997, p. A1.

97. Linda Greenhouse, "Supreme Court Roundup: Anti-Loitering Laws Will Be Revisited," *New York Times*, April 21, 1998, p. A19.

CONSEQUENCE MITIGATION

Given the difficulty of preventing terrorist attacks, responsible governments are preparing to mitigate the effects of potential bioterrorist incidents. The prospects for doing so are challenging but not hopeless because of important differences among the effects of nuclear, chemical, and biological weapons. Civil defense is largely useless in the case of a nuclear explosion because the destructive forces—shockwave, heat, and immediate radiation—are nearly instantaneous. In the case of an attack with a chemical nerve agent such as sarin, medical countermeasures are potentially more effective because the effects of the poison can be counteracted through the prompt administration of antidotes (atropine combined with an oxime and an anticonvulsant). A biological attack, if detected in time, is even more amenable to medical intervention because of the relatively long delay between infection and the emergence of life-threatening symptoms.

There are two possible types of emergency response to a bioterrorism incident: before the incident occurs, if the terrorists provide some advance warning; or after the hazardous agent has been released. In the former case, federal, state, or local government officials would receive a message threatening a biological attack unless some demand is met. Law enforcement authorities would then have a limited amount of time to track down the terrorists or the dissemination device before the agent was released. Even if the attack could not be prevented, emergency responders would be able to mobilize and prepare to intervene as rapidly as possible.

A no-warning biological attack, in contrast, would probably not be detected at the time it occurred because a BW aerosol is invisible, odorless, and tasteless. Moreover, whereas chemical nerve agents kill in minutes, the first indication of a covert BW agent release might not come until days after the release, when a large number of people suddenly and inexplicably fell ill and began showing up in doctors' offices and hospital emergency rooms. Tabletop exercises run by U.S. government agencies typically involve scenarios in which bioterrorists provide advance warning of an attack.[98] Based on the Aum Shinrikyo experience, however, a no-warning contingency may be more likely if the terrorists do not seek to promote a political agenda or extort money but merely to inflict heavy casualties.

The possibility of a covert, no-warning use of biological weapons has important implications for emergency response. Because the initial symptoms of inhalation anthrax resemble those of a cold or flu—fever, chills,

---

98. Jeff Stein, "We Are Not Ready," *Salon Magazine*, Newsreal section, December 10, 1997 [http://www.salonmagazine.com].

and muscle aches—the infection might easily be confused with far less serious conditions, particularly in the winter when common colds are rife. Lacking clear evidence of foul play, physicians would probably attribute the illness to natural causes. It might take public health officials several days to diagnose the infection and determine that it was the result of a deliberate attack, by which time the exposed population could have dispersed widely and the terrorists could have long since fled the area. Even more problematic, inhalation anthrax typically converts in 24 to 72 hours from mild flu-like symptoms into an acute illness involving severe respiratory distress, pneumonia, cyanosis, and shock, which is nearly always fatal. Thus, individuals exposed to a covert anthrax attack might be beyond medical help by the time the authorities finally made the correct diagnosis.

DETECTION OF A COVERT BW ATTACK. Because of the delayed and insidious effects of a covert BW attack, it would be necessary to rely on existing public health systems—including the astute observations of local hospital and private practice physicians—to identify the disease outbreak in time to initiate effective treatment. This task would include determining where and when the BW agent exposure had occurred and identifying the victims. Within a population exposed to a biological aerosol, individuals with a weak or compromised immune system would tend to develop acute symptoms of infection sooner than the general healthy population.

In the United States, epidemiological surveillance is the responsibility of local and state health departments, backed up by the CDC in Atlanta. Current capabilities for timely detection of unusual disease outbreaks— both from natural sources as well as terrorist incidents—vary greatly from city to city. To enhance the surveillance capabilities of local municipalities, the U.S. government should augment and strengthen existing surveillance systems by providing funds to state and city departments of public health to hire more field epidemiologists. The federal government should also upgrade disease-reporting mechanisms and computer networks so that epidemiological data collected by state and local public health departments can be sent rapidly to the CDC for analysis. Finally, the CDC should utilize the current system of public health alerts to highlight particular disease symptoms that physicians and nurse practitioners should be aware of.

TRIAGE AND TREATMENT. While improved epidemiological surveillance is the nation's first line of defense against bioterrorism, it must be backed up with the ability of the emergency medical system to execute a well-planned program of triage and treatment. Given the speed at which pathogens such as anthrax and plague can induce a life-threatening illness, rapid identification of the infectious agent and initiation of antibiotic therapy would be key to minimizing the effects of a BW attack on a civilian population. If left untreated, inhalation anthrax has a mortality rate of 95 percent or more, but early and intensive intervention can significantly reduce fatalities and improve victim recovery.[99] Treatment begun before the appearance of symptoms can bring mortality significantly below 70 percent.[100] Calculations by CDC experts also indicate that early detection and treatment could reduce the medical costs associated with a large-scale bioterrorist attack at least seven-fold.[101]

New York City has recently taken significant measures to improve its ability to respond to a biological attack.[102] Even so, most other metropolitan areas in the United States and elsewhere remain poorly trained and equipped to respond to the emerging threat of bioterrorism. Under the Defense Against Weapons of Mass Destruction Act of 1996, the U.S. domestic preparedness program has focused primarily on two activities: creating and deploying elite federal response teams to respond to incidents of chemical or biological terrorism; and training local "first-responders," or front-line law enforcement and emergency personnel who would arrive rapidly at the incident site. While both of these approaches are useful for managing the effects of chemical attacks, they are poorly suited to the threat of covert bioterrorism.

The Departments of Defense, Energy, and Health and Human Services have established elite units to respond to incidents of chemical or biological terrorism, such as the Marine Corps' Chemical and Biological

---

99. Although bacterial diseases such as plague and tularemia respond to intravenous antibiotics begun within 24 hours after infection, antibiotic therapy of anthrax is not curative but merely delays the disease process in individuals who have not previously been vaccinated. When the antibiotics are halted, the clinical disease may reappear. As a result, definitive cure of inhalation anthrax in an unvaccinated individual is only possible if the patient is vaccinated in conjunction with antibiotic treatment and is then capable of mounting a protective immune response. See David R. Franz, "Physical and Medical Countermeasures to Biological Weapons," in Kathleen C. Bailey, ed., *Director's Series on Proliferation*, Part 4, Report No. UCRL-LR-114070-4 (Livermore, Calif.: Lawrence Livermore National Laboratory, May 23, 1994), pp. 55–65.

100. Mercier, "Terrorists, WMD, and the U.S. Army Reserve."

101. Arnold F. Kaufman, Martin I. Meltzer, and George P. Schmid, "The Economic Impact of a Bioterrorist Attack: Are Prevention and Postattack Intervention Justifiable?" *Emerging Infectious Diseases*, Vol. 3, No. 2 (April/June 1997), pp. 1–12.

102. Judith Miller and William J. Broad, "New York Girds for Grim Fear: Germ Terrorism," *New York Times*, June 19, 1998, p. 1.

Incident Response Force (CBIRF).[103] Such teams are most effective when pre-deployed at high-profile public events to ensure maximum readiness in the event of a terrorist incident. For example, at the 1996 Summer Olympic Games in Atlanta, the January 1997 presidential inauguration in Washington, D.C., and the July 1997 G-7 Summit in Denver, the CBIRF and other federal counterterrorism units monitored the air and water for hazardous agents and planned for the treatment and evacuation of victims.[104] If terrorists launched a no-warning BW attack in a major U.S. city, however, no elite federal response teams would be in place, and the incident might not even be recognized for several days. As a result, the burden of detection and emergency response would fall on the shoulders of local public health and medical services, backed up with state resources such as the National Guard.[105]

The second major component of the federal domestic-preparedness program is a Pentagon-led effort to train local first-responders—police, firefighters, and emergency medical services personnel—in the nation's 120 largest cities. The curriculum includes information on how to approach the scene of an attack, how to identify toxic agents, and how to handle detectors, protective gear, and decontamination equipment.[106]

---

103. Paul Richter, "U.S. Germ War Defenses Porous, Officials Warn," *Los Angeles Times*, December 26, 1997, p. A1; and U.S. Department of Health and Human Services (DHHS), *Health and Medical Services Support Plan for the Federal Response to Acts of Chemical/Biological (C/B) Terrorism* (Washington, D.C.: DHHS, June 21, 1996), pp. 1–7, 14–17.

104. Bradley Graham, "U.S. Gearing Up Against Germ War Threat," *Washington Post*, December 14, 1997, p. 1.

105. Jonathan B. Tucker, "National Health and Medical Services Response to Incidents of Chemical and Biological Terrorism," *Journal of the American Medical Association*, Vol. 278, No. 5 (August 6, 1997), p. 366.

106. For a description of first-responder training programs around the United States, see the following articles: Richard A. Knox, "Biological Terror: Prepare for It, US Cities are Urged," *Boston Globe*, August 6, 1997, pp. A1, A12; Richard Parker, "Pentagon Prepares Cities to Fight Off a Chemical Hit," *Philadelphia Inquirer*, August 7, 1997, p. 3; Skip Thurman, "Cities Learn How to Handle Terrorists' Chemical Attacks," *Christian Science Monitor*, August 16, 1997, p. 3; Mark Peterka, "Taking a Gamble on a Sinister Threat," *Orlando Sentinel*, September 28, 1997, p. 1G; Ed Offley, "Preparing for Terror: Military Leads U.S. Agencies Training Cities in Chemical, Biological Defense," *Washington Times*, October 19, 1997, p. D8; V. Dion Hayes, "Cities Vulnerable to Germ Warfare," *Chicago Tribune*, November 16, 1997, p. 19; Bradley Graham, "Taking Steps Against an Emerging Threat: New Program Teaches Responses to Potential Germ, Chemical Attack," *Washington Post*, January 6, 1998, p. A1; Patrick O'Neill, "Emergency Workers Will Get Training for Terrorist Attack," *Oregonian*, February 21, 1998 (www.oregonlive.com); Sarah Gibbons, "US Congress Targets the Toxic Terrorists,"

Federal, state, and local agencies have also conducted several tabletop and field exercises focusing on bioterrorism scenarios.[107] Yet while first-responders would play a key role in responding to a chemical attack that inflicted immediate casualties (or the unlikely contingency of a BW attack with advance warning), they would have little or no role in responding to an outbreak of disease that developed days after a covert biological-agent release.

Managing the *delayed* consequences of a biological attack would place a greater burden on medical service providers at hospitals and walk-in clinics, who would treat the victims of a bioterrorist attack in the days and weeks after the event. Emergency room physicians, in particular, must be trained to recognize the symptoms of exotic diseases such as inhalation anthrax, which they would not normally encounter in their medical practice, and to report this information promptly to local public health authorities.

Other requirements associated with an effective medical response to bioterrorism include the following:

- *Rapid diagnosis.* Reporting mechanisms should be established so that when a large number of people show up at city medical clinics or emergency rooms with non-specific symptoms of infectious disease, public health departments will send out field epidemiologists to investigate. Procedures should also be established for the rapid collection of diagnostic specimens and the identification of the infectious agent at designated reference laboratories.

- *Medical response teams.* With federal assistance, major U.S. cities are developing Metropolitan Medical Strike Teams (MMSTs) to provide

International Police Review, No. 5 (January/February 1998), pp. 20–21; Jonathan D. Silver, "Pittsburgh Emergency Teams on Alert for Terrorism," *Post-Gazette*, August 16, 1998, p. A4; Jim Ritter, "City Drafts a Terrorist Attack Plan," *Chicago Sun-Times*, August 21, 1998, p. 4; and Ramona Smith, "Philly's First to be Ready: City to Drill for Terrorism," *The Philadelphia Inquirer*, August 22, 1998 (www.phillynews.com).

107. In 1993, the Federal Emergency Management Agency (FEMA) and other federal agencies participated in a major tabletop exercise called "CIVEX '93," in which the scenario involved the release of anthrax in the subway system of a fictional city called "Metropolis." In spring 1997, a field exercise named "Ill Wind" simulated a chemical and biological attack on the Washington, D.C. metropolitan area and assessed crisis- and consequence-management concepts, policies, plans, and procedures. Participants included federal agencies and metropolitan area governments (Washington, D.C., Virginia, and Maryland). New York City and other major U.S. cities have also conducted exercises involving the imagined terrorist release of anthrax. See William B. Wark, "Managing the Consequences of Nuclear, Biological, and Chemical (NBC) Terrorism," *Low Intensity Conflict & Law Enforcement*, Vol. 6, No. 2 (Autumn 1997), pp. 179–184.

emergency medical services in response to incidents of chemical or biological terrorism. To handle BW contingencies, such teams should include experts in infectious diseases, detection, and decontamination, as well as psychologists and public relations experts skilled at calming public panic and hysteria.

- *Triage.* Affected patients will have to be triaged according to the severity of the illness and matched with appropriate treatment facilities. A bioterrorist attack would trigger widespread anxiety, causing thousands of healthy but frightened people to flood hospitals seeking care. It will therefore be essential to differentiate between individuals who are truly sick and those experiencing psychosomatic symptoms. In the aftermath of the Tokyo sarin attack, for example, 80 percent of those who self-referred to hospitals were suffering from panic or hysteria but had no detectable chemical injury.[108]

- *Administration of antibiotics and vaccines.* On May 22, 1998, President Clinton announced the creation of a national stockpile of vaccines and antibiotics that will be distributed across the United States for use in the event of a bioterrorist incident.[109] To ensure that this measure is implemented effectively, federal, state, and local public health officials should develop and exercise plans for the rapid distribution of these medications to the site of an attack and their administration to large numbers of people. Stocks of medications must be rotated on a regular basis to ensure they are current, and arrangements made with pharmaceutical companies to increase production rapidly if the available stockpile has been exhausted. Without such careful logistical planning, stockpiling medications could be a waste of money.

- *Adequate hospital capacity.* Treating the victims of a large-scale bioterrorist attack could potentially require a large number of hospital beds. In the era of managed care, little surplus capacity exists in private medical centers, so patients may have to be evacuated to public,

---

108. After the March 1995 sarin attack on the Tokyo subway, 5,510 people were either transported to or self-referred at 278 hospitals and clinics. Casualties included 12 deaths, 17 critically injured (requiring intensive care), 37 severe (muscular twitching and gastrointestinal problems), and 984 moderate (pinpoint pupils). The remaining 4,000 casualties (80 percent) were suffering from panic or hysteria but had no detectable chemical injury. See Fred Sidell, M.D., "U.S. Medical Team Briefing," in U.S. Public Health Service, Office of Emergency Preparedness, *Proceedings of the Seminar on Responding to the Consequences of Chemical and Biological Terrorism, July 11–14, 1995* (Washington, D.C.: U.S. DHHS, 1995), pp. 2–32, 2–33.

109. William J. Clinton, "Remarks by the President at the United States Naval Academy Commencment," White House Press Release, May 22, 1998.

military, and Veterans Administration hospitals outside the affected area. Even more problematic is the potential need for isolation rooms to treat patients infected with a contagious agent, such as pneumonic plague, without putting the general patient population at risk.

• *Dissemination of information.* Procedures should be established to provide detailed advice to medical practitioners on the management of unusual infectious diseases such as plague and anthrax, and to inform the public about how to avoid exposure, recognize symptoms, and seek treatment. Public service announcements, prepared in advance of an attack and widely broadcast on radio and television during an incident, would help to calm panic and hysteria.

• *Decontamination procedures.* Nearly all BW agents cause infection through the lungs and do not penetrate intact skin; therefore, a gas mask offers effective individual protection.[110] Because a biological aerosol behaves like a gas flowing over surfaces, contamination of clothing is not significant, although particles of agent will tend to collect in hair. Decontamination of skin and clothing can be accomplished with a dilute solution of bleach or disinfectant, but buildings contaminated with persistent anthrax spores may require extensive cleaning with bleach and steam.

• *Research and development.* Congress should provide tax and other incentives for the pharmaceutical industry to develop new diagnostic kits, broad-spectrum anti-microbial drugs, and improved vaccines. Specific treatments are currently unavailable for most hemorrhagic viral infections and the great majority of toxin agents. Similarly, cheap, fast, and reliable detectors for BW agents do not yet exist, although some are under development.[111]

Conclusion

Sensational accounts in the media and depictions in popular fiction and film have exaggerated the threat of mass-casualty bioterrorism. Most misleading has been the tendency to conflate the capabilities of countries

---

110. Richard Danzig, "Biological Warfare: A Nation at Risk—A Time to Act," *INSS Strategic Forum*, No. 58 (Washington, D.C.: National Defense University, INSS, January 1996), pp. 3–4.

111. Clifford Beal, "An Invisible Enemy," *International Defense Review*, Vol. 28, No. 3 (1995), pp. 36–41. During the anthrax scare in Las Vegas in February 1998, it took authorities more than two days to determine that the confiscated vials did not pose a health threat. See Lee Dye, "Anthrax Scare Points Up Need for Early-Detection Technology," *Los Angeles Times*, March 23, 1998, p. D3.

such as the former Soviet Union and Iraq with those of small terrorist organizations. While states may be capable of staging large-scale BW attacks, they have thus far shown no inclination to transfer such weapons to terrorist proxies. Moreover, for a terrorist group to undertake a mass-casualty bioterrorist attack on its own initiative would require a rare combination of motivations, technical skills, and organizational capabilities.

On the motivational side, most extremist groups with political agendas have little incentive to seek mass-casualty weapons, the use of which would alienate their constituents and bring down on their heads the full repressive power of the authorities. Thus, the most likely suspects are religious or millenarian cults who believe that large-scale violence is the fulfillment of God's will, brutalized groups seeking revenge or hoping to exact a terrible price for their imminent demise, small terrorist cells or sociopathic individuals driven by paranoid ideologies, or combinations of the above.

From a technical standpoint, the hurdles involved in acquiring, producing, and weaponizing BW agents are significant. Unless terrorists were to acquire military-grade microbial strains and dissemination systems, either with the help of a state sponsor or former bioweapons scientists, it is extremely unlikely that they could produce and deliver enough of a BW agent to inflict tens to hundreds of thousands of casualties. Of greater concern is the possibility of small- to medium-scale attacks in enclosed spaces such as a federal building or a subway station, using a relatively simple dissemination system such as a garden pesticide fogger. If not detected in time, such an incident might kill tens to hundreds of people and could elicit significant disruption and terror.

From an organizational perspective, a terrorist group capable of carrying out a successful bioterrorist attack probably would require most or all of the following characteristics: a charismatic leader who inspires total devotion and obedience; a set of technically skilled individuals who subscribe to the groups' goals and ideology; a managerial structure for coordinating the acquisition and use of the weapon; a system of internal social controls that severely punish—and hence deter—deviation or defection; and an operational structure that is either largely invisible (e.g., "phantom cells") or that resists penetration by police or intelligence agencies.

In summary, the diffusion of technical know-how and production equipment and the recent shifts in terrorist motivations favoring a more indiscriminate use of violence appear to have made small- to medium-scale BW attacks more likely. These trends, combined with the potentially devastating impact of bioterrorism, warrant a significant investment in prevention and consequence mitigation, although not on the massive scale advocated by certain publicists and government officials.

The policy options outlined above offer some practical, low-cost steps for responding to the threat of bioterrorism. Given finite government resources, the prioritization of investments is essential. Primary emphasis should be on improving intelligence collection and interdiction in an effort to prevent such attacks from occurring. Reasonable preventive measures include developing early-warning indicators for the terrorist acquisition of BW agents, training intelligence and police officers in monitoring and interdiction techniques, and expanding intelligence-sharing arrangements with friendly countries. At the same time, a well-coordinated system for enhanced infectious-disease surveillance and emergency medical response will be essential in the event prevention fails.

To date, federal investments in consequence mitigation have been driven by vulnerability assessments, which are potentially unlimited and do not provide a realistic basis for policymaking. Without a solid assessment of the bioterrorist threat, including a detailed analysis of terrorist motivations, patterns of behavior, and likely targets, it will be impossible to develop tailored and cost-effective strategies for incident prevention and response. Drawing on a realistic threat assessment, civil defenses against bioterrorism should be based on "most-likely" rather than "worst-case" scenarios. Protective measures should also focus on the targets of highest risk, namely government buildings and enclosed public spaces such as airports, subways, and sports arenas.

Finally, government programs for responding to bioterrorism should be designed to be multipurpose rather than highly specialized, so that they are considered worthwhile regardless of how one assesses the threat. Strengthened epidemiological surveillance networks, for example, would benefit U.S. and international public health even if a biological attack never materializes. By devising policies that provide social benefits beyond their value in reducing the nation's vulnerability to bioterrorism, it will be easier to build political coalitions in support of these measures.

Chapter 18

Epilogue

Joshua Lederberg

As the chapters in this volume were being assembled, our policy perspectives were informed by new happenings, and by governmental actions and reactions. Saddam Hussein renewed his harassment of the UNSCOM inspectors seeking closure on Iraq's programs in biological weapons (BW) and other weapons of mass destruction. In December 1998, Iraq's obstruction of UNSCOM inspections led the United States and the United Kingdom to launch aerial attacks on Iraq. That escalation might be a deterrent and warning, or it might provoke unreasoned responses, including the use of BW if the regime inferred it had nothing more to lose. The dilemma persists on how to invoke punishment of deviant autocrats without injuring captive populations even more severely; so does the question of looking beyond violence to the causes of belligerency. At one level, we know the danger that violence will beget violence. At another, the history of nations has shown how the most violent exemplars, like Nazi Germany and Imperial Japan, could—at terrible cost to themselves and others—be pacified and become models of geopolitical restraint and economic success. Democracies which regard themselves as humane will be torn and sometimes self-deterred by such considerations, probably more than by threats of forceful retaliation. Saddam may not know this well enough to refrain from launching terrorist reactions; there is also always the cloak of fringe zealots acting on their own initiative.

This is the story line for the vicious bomb attacks on U. S. embassies in Kenya and Tanzania on August 8, 1998, which were attributed to Osama bin Laden. Bernard Lewis has retrieved bin Laden's formal declaration of war against the United States and its citizens from the Arabic press.[1] The aim is the expulsion of U.S. interests from the holy Arabian

---

1. Bernard Lewis, "License to Kill: Usama Bin Ladin's Declaration of Jihad," *Foreign Affairs*, Vol. 77, No. 6 (November/December 1998), pp. 14–19.

Peninsula. In the process, however, hundreds of native Africans have been injured or killed. This may go even beyond casual disregard of uninvolved bystanders—it conveys the message that diplomatic relations of any country with the United States entail a lethal liability.

This atmosphere has not triggered acute defensive precautionary mobilization beyond routine travel advisories. However, past months have witnessed a growing concern expressed in public pronouncements and official actions. U.S. Secretary of Defense William Cohen's foreword in this volume is reflected in President Clinton's Annapolis speech on May 22, 1998, which presents:

"three new initiatives—the first broadly directed at combatting terrorism; the other two addressing two potential threats from terrorists and hostile nations, attacks on our computer networks and other critical systems upon which our society depends, and attacks using biological weapons. . . . We will work to upgrade our public health systems for detection and warning, to aid our preparedness against terrorism, and to help us cope with infectious diseases that arise in nature. We will train and equip local authorities throughout the nation to deal with an emergency involving weapons of mass destruction, creating stockpiles of medicines and vaccines to protect our civilian population against the kind of biological agents our adversaries are most likely to obtain or develop. And we will pursue research and development to create the next generation of vaccines, medicines and diagnostic tools. The Human Genome Project will be very, very important in this regard. And again, it will aid us also in fighting infectious diseases. . . . To make these three initiatives work we must have the concerted efforts of a whole range of federal agencies—from the Armed Forces to law enforcement to intelligence to public health. I am appointing a National Coordinator for Security, Infrastructure Protection, and Counterterrorism, to bring the full force of all our resources to bear swiftly and effectively. "[2]

These decisions are reflected in Presidential Decision Directive 62 (PDD-62), and in the appointment of Richard Clarke of the National Security Council as the National Coordinator. Inter-agency discussions with regard to allocations of responsibility and budget are continuing. Significant announcements include the assignment of backup responsibilities to the National Guard.[3] The U.S. Atlantic Command (ACOM) already bears operational responsibility for "Homeland Defense," a theme much discussed in recent months, and it may be given further tasks in this arena. Not least of these is planning for the security of our ports of embarkation, the logistic chokepoints for maritime buildup and supply

---

2. Speech by President William Clinton, Annapolis, Maryland, May 22, 1998; text at www.whitehouse.gov. See also the foreword by William S. Cohen in this volume.

3. See the foreword by William S. Cohen in this volume.

of any U.S. force projection overseas. The Department of Justice will take over the training of local emergency responders to function safely and effectively in contaminated environments. Acting on its own, and impelled by past experiences like the attack on the World Trade Center in 1993, New York City has already mounted an extensive program that will be a model for other cities. [4] In addition, the FBI will establish a National Domestic Preparedness Office—a canonical shopping window for enquiries and appeals from local officials who are otherwise perplexed about where to turn for assistance from the complex federal establishment. These proposals go a long way toward meeting the criteria set out in a thoughtful paper by three recent members of the Clinton administration, Ashton Carter, John Deutch, and Philip Zelikow.[5] They remark, however, that "one should not place faith in czars. Real power still resides in the executive departments that have people, equipment, money, and the capacity to get things done."[6] These requirements have been elaborated in further detail by Richard Falkenrath and his colleagues.[7]

Efforts to engage Congress have been partly successful, but predictably face some resistance as "budget-busting" when incremental funding is sought. While there is substantial verbal endorsement of the priority that should be assigned to domestic bio-defense as an element of national security, it still fares poorly in competition with the long-established traditional military concerns, the end of the Cold War notwithstanding.

The R&D requirements for bio-defense are barely touched upon in the current volume. They range from the most far-reaching innovations that will be called upon to deal with exotic viral infections to banal items like inexpensive, citizen-adapted protective masks. Protocols for the management of infectious disease were neither designed nor validated for mass casualty settings, where, for example, available antibiotics are in short supply and rational schemes for extending those supplies will be desperately needed. Nor have our FDA and other regulatory and ethical regimes been confronted with emergent crises where thousands or millions of lives may be at stake, awaiting resolution of bureaucratic contradictions. Some of these matters have been given initial study by the

---

4. Judith Miller and William J. Broad, "New York Girding for Grim Fear: Deadly Germ Attack by Terrorists," *New York Times*, June 19, 1998.

5. Ashton Carter, John Deutch, and Philip Zelikow, "Catastrophic Terrorism: Tackling the New Danger," Foreign Affairs, Vol. 77, No. 6 (November/December 1998), pp. 80–94.

6. Ibid.

7. Richard A. Falkenrath, Robert D. Newman, and Bradley A. Thayer, *America's Achilles' Heel: Nuclear, Biological, and Chemical Terrorism and Covert Attack*, BCSIA Studies in International Security (Cambridge, Mass.: The MIT Press, 1998).

Institute of Medicine.[8] However, the delegation of responsibility to public authorities, and if so which ones, should be deliberated during times of peace, and informed consent conferred or denied; this cannot be achieved in the midst of crisis.

Among the triumphs of medical science and international cooperation in this century has been the global eradication of smallpox. Once among the major killers of humankind, smallpox has been eliminated from circulation by concerted programs of vaccination. The last authenticated case of naturally spread disease occurred in 1977, and the WHO officially declared eradication in 1979. Since then, abandonment of routine vaccination has been the accepted doctrine and general practice: the scourge had been lifted, and no further precautions were needed. Consequently we now have, globally, a whole generation of humans with no history of exposure either to smallpox virus or to the protective vaccine. This is unprecedented in human experience, though it may be likened to the condition of Western Hemisphere natives prior to the European exploration and conquest. With recent rumor and Russian defectors' reports of unabated experimentation with smallpox as a weapon in defiance of the BW treaty, anxieties about resulting U.S. vulnerability have been heightened.[9] Outbreaks have happened before, and they could probably be contained—but only if vaccine stocks, now all but depleted, are refreshed and pre-positioned.[10] This would not be very expensive; anti-viral medication would be equally valuable and an important complement if that could be materialized with renewed R&D.

My personal concern about the blight of biological weaponry, and the subversion of medical technology to the intentional spread of plagues, goes back many years. In 1970, I had occasion to address the United Nations Committee on Disarmament in Geneva, which focused on arms control as an important remedial device. The Biological Weapons Convention has been in force since 1975; it is now deeply embedded in the law of nations. The issue now is its enforcement, which depends on the institutionalized acknowledgment of and respect for that law. BW is a special weapon, with implications for civility of life that set it apart from many other kinds of violence. Most of the other arguments remain hardly

---

8. Institute of Medicine, "Improving Civilian Medical Responses to Chemical or Biological Terrorist Incidents," National Research Council, Washington, D.C., 1999.

9. Richard Preston, "The Bioweaponeers," *New Yorker*, March 9, 1998, pp. 52–65.

10. Joel G. Breman and D.A. Henderson, "Poxvirus Dilemmas—Monkeypox, Smallpox, and Biologic Terrorism," *New England Journal of Medicine*, Vol. 339 (1998), pp. 556–559.

altered, except for the burgeoning realization of what biotechnology could bring us, for good or for evil.

From the Author's Statement to the Conference of the UN Committee on Disarmament

Recent advances in molecular biology have important implications for human welfare. On the one hand, they help man to a deeper understanding of his own evolution and functioning as the most complex of life forms on earth. They support revolutionary advances in medicine in such fields as cancer, aging, congenital disease and virus infections. They will also play a vital role in agriculture and related industries.

On the other hand, molecular biology might be exploited for military purposes and result in a biological weapons race whose aim could well become the most efficient means for removing man from the planet. For example, Professor Gobind Khorana of the University of Wisconsin recently reported the synthetic assembly of a small gene through chemical operations on DNA components. It will be a major step to extend this technical capability to the synthesis of small viruses. But this surely could be accomplished within the next decade. This procedure will allow an unlimited range of experimental variations of the genetic structure of different viruses, a process that has many important potential applications for human health. It also offers us the prospect of engineering the design of viruses to exquisite detail, for vaccines or for weapons. Accomplishments like Khorana's have been possible in a small laboratory on an annual research budget that is minuscule compared to weapons hardware. A serious military investment in this area could be expected to outstrip this already breathtaking pace of advance by manyfold.

THREAT TO MAN

For many years biological warfare has been given only incidental attention as a subject of diplomatic discussion, for it seemed to have little bearing on the adjustments of power that were the main work of specialists in foreign affairs.

We now begin to realize that the intentional release of an infectious particle, be it a virus or bacterium, from the confines of the laboratory or of medical practice must be formally condemned as an irresponsible threat against the whole human community.

A large epidemic, involving millions of people spread over time and space, is an immensely complicated phenomenon about which it is very difficult to make accurate scientific predictions. This combination of very grave potential hazard with a high degree of unpredictability is a peculiar attribute of biological weaponry at its present stage of development. This has a great deal to do with the rational doctrine that so far has placed a relatively low value on its military utility.

IT COULD BE TOO LATE

The present situation thus might provide the most favorable opportunity for international action to regulate the further development and proliferation of biological warfare. I am convinced we know enough about it to have legitimate concern about its future prospects. Until now no nation appears to have staked its security to any significant degree on BW armaments. I would therefore hope this provides a basis for accord. If we wait until BW has been developed into a reliable armament for use under a range of military doctrine, we must all fear that it could then be too late to disengage important powers from their commitment to it.

The barriers that now give advanced countries a measure of protection against plague could be breached by further technical developments if a substantial effort were to be applied during the next decade to making the plague bacillus into a weapon.

Other infectious agents might be even more adaptable. Some of man's deadliest enemies are viruses which, like yellow fever, are transmitted by mosquitos or other arthropods. These have the advantage, from a military standpoint, that they should not start a potentially retroactive epidemic in areas where the vector insect does not normally abound. It is already evident that such insect-borne viruses could be applied in the first instance by direct aerial dissemination, with little or no further spread from the first wave of infected targets.

Recent reports of airborne or pneumonic rabies, a terrible disease, which is normally spread by the bite of an infected dog or animal, illustrate this possibility. There is then the danger that, if a large nucleus of people is attacked in this way, further evolution of the virus will occur to give rise to a new form of the disease that does spread from person to person, contrary to the calculations of the attacker. The Black Death itself underwent a similar evolution from the original bubonic flea-born plague to outbreaks of the far more contagious pneumonic variety.

We have learned in recent years that viruses undergo constant evolution in their own natural history, not only by mutations within a given strain, but also by the natural cross-hybridization of viruses that superficially appear to be only remotely related to one another. Furthermore, many of us already carry viruses in our body cells of which we are unaware for years, and which may be harmless—though they may eventually cause the formation of a tumor, or of brain degeneration or other diseases. At least in the laboratory, we can still cross-breed them with other viruses to give rise to many new forms.

My gravest concern is that similar scientific breakthroughs of a rather predictable kind will be made and their potential military significance exploited, so as to result in a transformation of current doctrine about "unreliable" biological weapons. We are all familiar with the process of mutual escalation in which the defensive efforts of one side inevitably contribute to further technical developments on the other and vice versa. The mere existence of such a contest produces a mutual stimulation of effort; moreover, there is no practical system of counterintelligence that will protect secret work for an indefinite period of time from becoming known to others. And the potential undoubtedly exists for the design and development of infective agents against which no credible defense is possible, through the genetic and chemical manipulation of these agents.

SUBVERSION OF SCIENCE

Permit me, now, to ask a rhetorical question: Can we establish a world order that will, in effect, protect "you," as representative of the global community, from the subversion of the scientific advances to which my own peers and myself have dedicated their careers?

I wish I could be sure that such a remark would always be received with an understanding of the ironic spirit with which it is uttered. I do not have to tell you of the worldwide attack on science, the flight from reason that has tempted so many young people and makes so many dilemmas for those of us in university life.

What the youth see as the perversion of knowledge is, I believe, an important aspect of their repudiation of us. Among the undergraduates at my own university, there is no prospect more disheartening than the idea that even health research is subject to exploitation in the most inhumane direction imaginable.

For many years I have advocated that the control of biological warfare be given a special place in international and national initiatives for reasons I have mentioned. I am deeply gratified that President Nixon's announcement last November 25, which disavowed offensive biological warfare development, has made it possible for me to address these issues in terms fully consistent with the policy of the government of my own country.

Even after agreement to eliminate biological weapons, we will still remain very vulnerable to a form of biological warfare that is beyond the reach of any covenant that we can make. This is the warfare practiced upon us by nature, the unremitting barrage of infection by old and by new agents that still constitute a very large part of the perils to normal and healthy life.

VEXING VIRUS INFECTIONS

We have all had vexing, perhaps even tragic, personal experiences with virus infections. You will all recall the global epidemic of influenza that was first identified in Hong Kong about three years ago. This was not a particularly severe form of the virus and its eventual mortality was probably only in the tens of thousands. It is wrong, however, to believe that there is any assurance that the next epidemic of this kind will be as mild; and we have still developed only the most feeble and precarious protection against this threat whose impact is shared by all the nations, but against which very little common defense has been erected.

You will also recall having read from time to time about small out-breaks of mysterious new diseases like "Lassa fever" and the "Marburg virus." These were both extremely dangerous threats; and while much credit must be given to the diligence of the medical people who dealt with the outbreaks, a large element of pure luck was involved in localiz-ing these incidents. We must expect that there are many additional viruses already indigenous to primate and human populations in primitive areas and to which the inhabitants of advanced countries are extremely vulner-able.

Yellow fever is a historically important disease that now belongs in the same category. It is now maintained on earth mainly through an animal reservoir of infection, in the monkeys in tropical jungles. Urban populations are now protected from yellow fever by campaigns to abolish the fever-carrying species of mosquitos in South America and by the availability of excellent vaccines in advanced countries. Mosquito species capable of transmitting yellow fever are, however, abundant in South Asia and the accidental introduction of yellow fever, for example, into India would be a human tragedy of catastrophic dimensions. Specialists in epidemiology are quite puzzled that this accident has not already hap-pened and we have no good explanation for this good fortune.

My purpose is not to suggest the vulnerability of the Asian continent to biological military attack but rather to point out immense gaps in the pattern of international cooperative defenses that should be mounted but which have a relatively feeble standing in the present day world.

THREAT TO CROPS

Countries that are undergoing a transition in the development of their agriculture are vulnerable to analogous threats in biological warfare di-rected against crops as distinguished from human targets. These crops are now newly vulnerable to destruction by plant pests of either natural or artificial origin. An outbreak of "coffee rust" is at this moment a serious threat to the agriculture and economy of Brazil; hoof-and-mouth disease made a costly incursion into British cattle a few years ago.

The promulgation of an international agreement to control biological warfare in a negative sense should, therefore, be accompanied by steps urgently needed to build positive efforts at international cooperation, a kind of defensive biological research against natural enemies of the human species.

One of the best assurances that any country might have that the microbiological research of its neighbors was directed toward human purposes would be constantly expanding participation in international health programs. Any country that publicly and avowedly subscribed to the total renunciation of secret BW research might conceivably be able to continue clandestine efforts without revealing their substantial content. It would, however, have great difficulty in maintaining such an effort, at any substantial level or quality of operation, while still keeping its very existence secret. Therefore, besides the obvious direct health benefits of expanded international cooperation we would also be rewarded by a higher level of mutual assurance that every party was indeed living up to the spirit of its obligations under a BW convention.

In conclusion, let me say that some of the speculations I have mentioned are ones that all of us must fervently hope will never materialize. But it would seem to me both foolish and arrogant to assume that our goodwill alone, without concrete arrangements, will serve to forestall the further development, proliferation and possible eventual recourse to what surely is one of the most ghastly methods of warfare imaginable.[11]

---

11. Joshua Lederberg, "Address to Conference of the Committee on Disarmament, August 5, 1970," Congressional Record, September 11, 1970, pp. E-8123–8124.

Contributors

Joshua Lederberg is a Nobel Laureate in Medicine, Sackler Foundation Scholar and President Emeritus of Rockefeller University, and Consulting Professor at the Center for International Security and Cooperation at Stanford University.

Suzanne Barth has been Chief of the Microbiological Investigation Section at the Texas Department of Health Bureau of Laboratories since 1983. The sectional focus has shifted in the last five years to encompass molecular epidemiology of community-acquired and nosocomial infectious diseases.

Pamela B. Berkowsky is Assistant Chief of Staff to the U.S. Secretary of Defense.

Kristin A. Birkness is at the National Center for Infectious Diseases and Epidemiology Program Office at the Centers for Disease Control and Prevention (CDC).

Stephen Black has served as Historian at the United Nations Special Commission (UNSCOM) since 1993.

W. Russell Byrne is Chief of the Bacteriology Division at the U.S. Army Medical Research Institute of Infectious Diseases (USAMRIID) at Fort Detrick, Maryland.

W. Seth Carus is a Visiting Fellow at the Center for Counterproliferation Research at National Defense University in Washington, D.C.

Marie Isabelle Chevrier is Associate Professor of Political Economy at the University of Texas at Dallas. She is the former Associate Director of the Harvard Sussex Program on Chemical and Biological Warfare Armament and Arms Limitation at the Belfer Center for Science and International Affairs

(BCSIA), Harvard University. She has written extensively on biological weapons and arms control.

George W. Christopher is an infectious disease physician in the U.S. Air Force Medical Corps. His interests include the formation of clinical practice guidelines for treating biological casualties.

Theodore J. Cieslak is a pediatric infectious disease physician in the U.S. Army Medical Corps. He has been active in a wide range of clinical, research, and educational activities, and is currently Chief of Field Operations at the Operational Medical Division of USAMRIID.

William S. Cohen is the U.S. Secretary of Defense. He represented the State of Maine in the U.S. House of Representatives from 1973 to 1978 and in the U.S. Senate from 1979 to 1996.

Richard Danzig is Secretary of the U.S. Navy. A Washington, D.C. lawyer, he served as Undersecretary of the Navy from November 1993 through May 1997.

Edward M. Eitzen, Jr. is Chief of the Operational Medicine Division of USAMRIID. He directs the division in multiple activities to enhance medical biological defense, including medical education, coordinating the basic scientific, medical, public health, and operational communities, and providing consultative expertise to military and other government agencies.

Charles C. Engel, Jr. is Assistant Professor at the F. Edward Hébert School of Medicine at the Uniformed Services University of the Health Sciences (USUHS) in Bethesda, Maryland. He is Chief of the Gulf War Health Center at Walter Reed Army Medical Center, where he runs the Department of Defense's multidisciplinary treatment program for individuals with persistent symptoms after Gulf War service. He has clinical and research experience in the behavioral aspects of caring for patients with unexplained physical symptoms, posttraumatic stress disorder, and mental health care in the primary care setting.

James R. Ferguson is affiliated with Northwestern University School of Law, Northwestern Medical School, and Sonnenschein Nath and Rosenthal.

Laurence R. Foster was at the Oregon Health Division, Portland, and is deceased.

David R. Franz is Vice President of the Chemical and Biological Defense Division of the Southern Research Institute.

Arthur M. Friedlander is a Senior Military Scientist at USAMRIID.

Carol S. Fullerton is a Research Associate Professor and Science Director at the Center for the Study of Traumatic Stress in the Department of Psychiatry at USUHS. Dr. Fullerton has published in the areas of posttraumatic stress response, the role of social support following trauma, and the stress on spouses of disaster workers. She is a Fellow of the American Orthopsychiatric Association and a member and journal reviewer for the American Psychological Association and the International Society for Traumatic Stress Studies.

Jeanne Guillemin is in the Department of Sociology at Boston College.

Charles E. Haley is a physician epidemiologist. He has served as an Epidemic Intelligence Services Officer with the CDC and as County Epidemiologist for Dallas County, Texas. He is the Associate Medicare Director of Blue Cross and Blue Shield of Texas.

Harry C. Holloway is at the F. Edward Hébert School of Medicine, where he serves as Professor of Psychiatry, Professor of Neuroscience, and Assistant Chairman for Research in the Department of Psychiatry. He served as the first Associate Administrator for the Office of Life and Microgravity Sciences and Applications at NASA from 1993 to 1996, and as Co-Director of the NASA Enterprise for the Human Exploration and Development of Space. Dr. Holloway is the author of over forty publications.

David L. Hoover is in the Department of Bacterial Diseases at the Walter Reed Army Institute of Research.

John M. Horan is at the National Center for Infectious Diseases and Epidemiology Program Office at the CDC.

Martin Hugh-Jones is in the School of Veterinary Medicine at Louisiana State University.

Peter B. Jahrling is Senior Research Scientist at USAMRIID.

Robert P. Kadlec is in the Office of the U.S. Secretary of Defense.

Akiko Kimura was an Epidemic Intelligence Service Officer with the CDC from 1996 to 1998. She is the medical director of the Los Angeles County Department of Health Services Immunization Program.

Shellie A. Kolavic was an Epidemic Intelligence Service Officer with the CDC from 1996 to 1998. She is now a medical epidemiologist with the Henry Jackson Foundation for the Advancement of Military Medicine and the U.S.

Army Center for Health Promotion and Preventive Medicine at the Directorate of Epidemiology and Disease Surveillance.

Alexander Langmuir was in the School of Hygiene and Public Health at Johns Hopkins University, and is deceased.

John R. Livengood is at the National Center for Infectious Diseases and Epidemiology Program Office at the CDC.

Karl Lowe is a retired colonel and has been a staff member at the Institute for Defense Analyses (IDA) since 1993. At IDA, he produced a series of studies on biological warfare threats and defense techniques for the U.S. Department of Defense. He also served on the Secretary of Defense's Bosnia assessment mission in 1995. He is a member of the Joint Advanced Warfare Program at IDA, which is developing strategy and joint operational concepts for 2010 and beyond.

Steven Mauvais is at the Oregon Health Division in Portland.

David J. McClain is a physician at Asheville Infectious Disease Consultants in Asheville, North Carolina.

Matthew Meselson is in the Department of Molecular and Cellular Biology at Harvard University.

Ann E. Norwood serves as Associate Professor of Clinical Psychiatry and Associate Chair for the Department of Psychiatry at the F. Edward Hébert School of Medicine at USUHS. She is a Lieutenant Colonel in the Army Medical Corps. Her major research interest is the area of psychiatric responses to trauma and disaster.

Julie A. Pavlin received her M.D. degree from Loyola University and her MPH from Harvard University. She specializes in preventive medicine and is working at the Walter Reed Army Institute of Research in the Department of Defense's Global Emerging Infections Surveillance and Response Team.

Graham S. Pearson is Honorary Visiting Professor in International Security in the Department of Peace Studies at the University of Bradford in the United Kingdom, where he is particularly active in the area of biological weapons arms control. Previously he was Director General and Chief Executive of the Chemical and Biological Defence Establishment at Porton Down from 1984 to 1995, when he retired from the British Ministry of Defence. He has participated in international negotiations related to both biological and chemical arms control.

Ilona Popova is in the Social and Political Sciences Division at Ural State University in Ekaterinburg, Russia.

Alexis Shelokov is in the Government Services Division of the Salk Institute in San Antonio, Texas.

Jeffrey D. Simon is President of Political Risk Assessment Company in Santa Monica, California. He is the author of *The Terrorist Trap: America's Experience with Terrorism* (Bloomington: Indiana University Press, 1994).

Shauna L. Simons is an Emerging Infectious Disease Laboratory Fellow with the Foodborne and Diarrheal Diseases Branch of the CDC.

Michael R. Skeels is at the Oregon Health Division in Portland.

Laurence Slutsker joined the CDC in 1987. Since 1994, he has been a medical epidemiologist with the CDC's Foodborne and Diarrheal Diseases Branch in the Division of Bacterial and Mycotic Diseases.

Robert Sokolow is at the Oregon Health Division in Portland.

Robert V. Tauxe is at the National Center for Infectious Diseases and Epidemiology Program Office at the CDC.

Thomas J. Török is at the National Center for Infectious Diseases and Epidemiology Program Office at the CDC.

Jonathan B. Tucker directs the Chemical and Biological Weapons Nonproliferation Project at the Center for Nonproliferation Studies of the Monterey Institute of International Studies in Monterey, California. From 1989 to 1996, Dr. Tucker served as an arms control fellow at the U.S. Department of State; an analyst at the Office of Technology Assessment; a foreign affairs specialist in chemical and biological arms control at the U.S. Arms Control and Disarmament Agency; and a senior policy analyst on the staff of the Presidential Advisory Committee of Gulf War Veterans' Illnesses. In 1993–1995, Dr. Tucker was a member of the U.S. delegation to the Chemical Weapons Convention Preparatory Commission in The Hague, and in February 1995 he served as a biological weapons inspector with UNSCOM in Baghdad, Iraq.

Robert J. Ursano is Professor of Psychiatry and Neuroscience and Chairman of the Department of Psychiatry at the F. Edward Hébert School of Medicine. He is a Fellow of the American Psychiatric Association (APA), Chair of the APA Committee on Psychiatric Dimensions of Disaster, and a member of the American College of Psychiatrists. Dr. Ursano has written more than one hundred publications on the effects of trauma, war, and disaster.

Victor Utgoff is Deputy Director of the Strategy, Forces, and Resources Division at IDA, where he has been since 1981. Prior to that, he was with the National Security Council staff, the Center for Naval Analyses, and several aerospace firms. His most recent work has focused on policy and technology for countering NBC weapons. He is a member of the Council on Foreign Relations, and is the author of several books and a variety of papers on national security issues.

Ann M. Vrtis is at the Department of Anesthesiology at the Malcolm Grow Medical Center at Andrews Air Force Base.

Robert P. Wise was at the National Center for Infectious Diseases and Epidemiology Program Office at the CDC, and is now at the U.S. Food and Drug Administration.

Olga Yampolskaya is with the Botkin Hospital in Moscow.

Allan P. Zelicoff is at Sandia National Laboratories in Albuquerque, New Mexico.

Raymond A. Zilinskas is Senior Scientist in Residence at the Center for Nonproliferation Studies, Monterey Institute of International Studies, Washington, D.C. His research focuses on biological arms control, the proliferation potential of the former Soviet Union's biological warfare program, and meeting the threat of bioterrorism.

Index

The Robert and Renée Belfer Center for Science and International Affairs

Graham T. Allison, Director
John F. Kennedy School of Government
Harvard University
79 JFK Street, Cambridge MA 02138
(617) 495-1400

The Belfer Center for Science and International Affairs (BCSIA) is the hub of research, teaching, and training in international security affairs, environmental and resource issues, and science and technology policy at Harvard's John F. Kennedy School of Government. The Center's mission is to provide leadership in advancing policy-relevant knowledge about the most important challenges of international security and other critical issues where science, technology and international affairs intersect.

BCSIA's leadership begins with the recognition of science and technology as driving forces transforming international affairs. The Center integrates insights of social scientists, natural scientists, technologists, and practitioners with experience in government, diplomacy, the military, and business to address these challenges. The Center pursues its mission in four complementary research programs:

- The International Security Program (ISP) addresses the most pressing threats to U.S. national interests and international security.

- The Environment and Natural Resources Program (ENRP) is the locus of Harvard's interdisciplinary research on resource and environmental problems and policy responses.

- The Science, Technology, and Public Policy (STPP) program analyzes ways in which science and technology policy influence international security, resources, environment, and development, and such cross-cutting issues as technological innovation and information infrastructure.

- The Strengthening Democratic Institutions (SDI) project catalyzes support for three great transformations in Russia, Ukraine, and the other republics of the former Soviet Union—to sustainable democracies, free market economies, and cooperative international relations.

The heart of the Center is its resident research community of more than one hundred scholars: Harvard faculty, analysts, practitioners, and each year a new, interdisciplinary group of research fellows. BCSIA sponsors frequent seminars, workshops and conferences, many open to the public; maintains a substantial specialized library; and publishes books, monographs, and discussion papers. The Center's International Security Program, directed by Steven E. Miller, publishes the BCSIA Studies in International Security, and sponsors and edits the quarterly journal *International Security*.

The Center is supported by an endowment established with funds from Robert and Renée Belfer, the Ford Foundation, and Harvard University, by foundation grants, by individual gifts, and by occasional government contracts.